W Juliet

Volume 9

Story & Art by Emura

W Juliet
Volume 9

Story and Art by Emura

Translation & English Adaptation/Naomi Kokubo & Jeff Carlson
Touch-up Art & Lettering/Krysta Lau, Imaginary Friends Studios
Graphic Design/Hidemi Sahara
Editor/Carrie Shepherd

Managing Editor/Annette Roman
Director of Production/Noboru Watanabe
Vice President of Publishing/Alvin Lu
Sr. Director of Acquisitions/Rika Inouye
Vice President of Sales & Marketing/Liza Coppola
Publisher/Hyoe Narita

Printed in the U.S.A.

Published by VIZ Media, LLC
P.O. Box 77010
San Francisco, CA 94107

10 9 8 7 6 5 4 3 2 1
First printing, March 2006

www.viz.com
store.viz.com

PARENTAL ADVISORY
W JULIET is rated T for Teen and is recommended for ages 13 and up. This volume contains mild sexual situations/humor and tobacco usage.

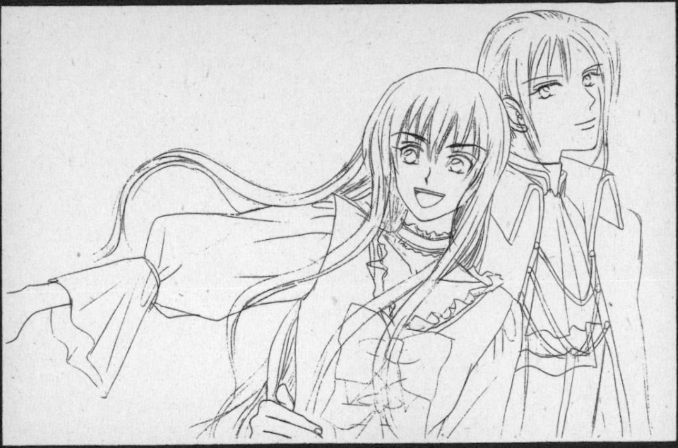

Swan Lake, front color splash-page (B4 size)

2001 Hana to Yume No. 17
cover art (B4 size)
Final draft

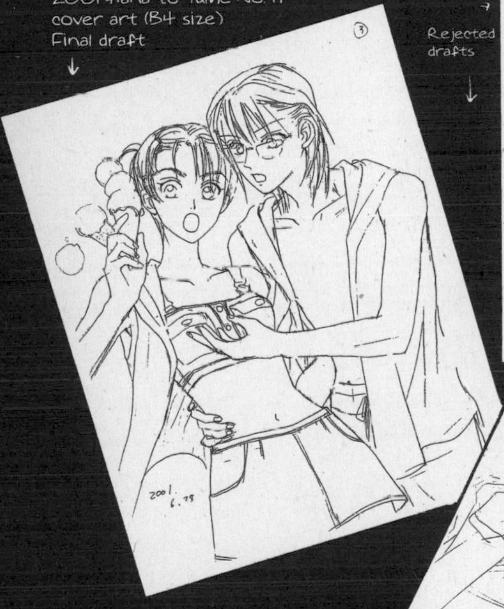

Rejected drafts

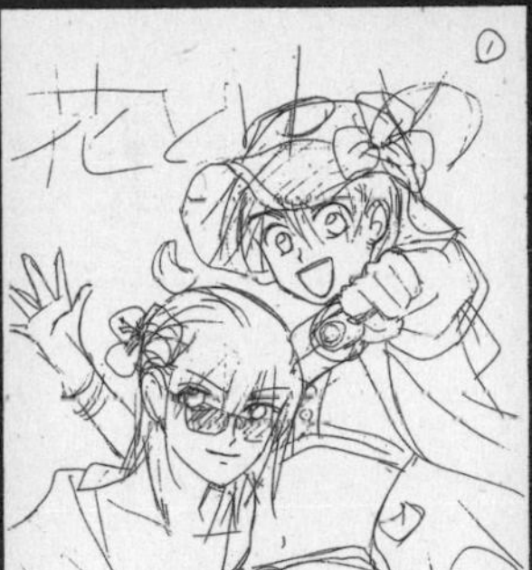

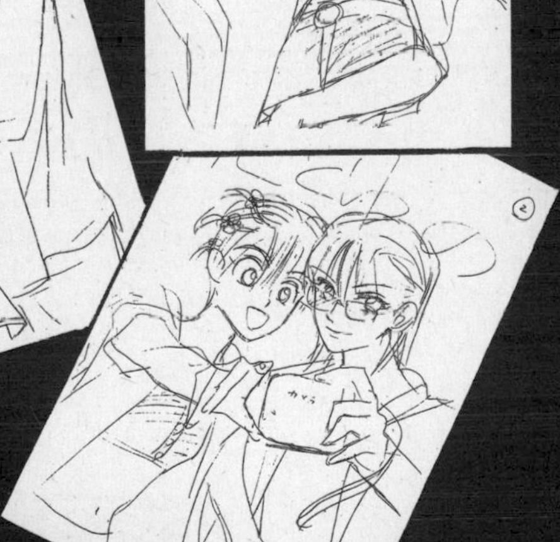

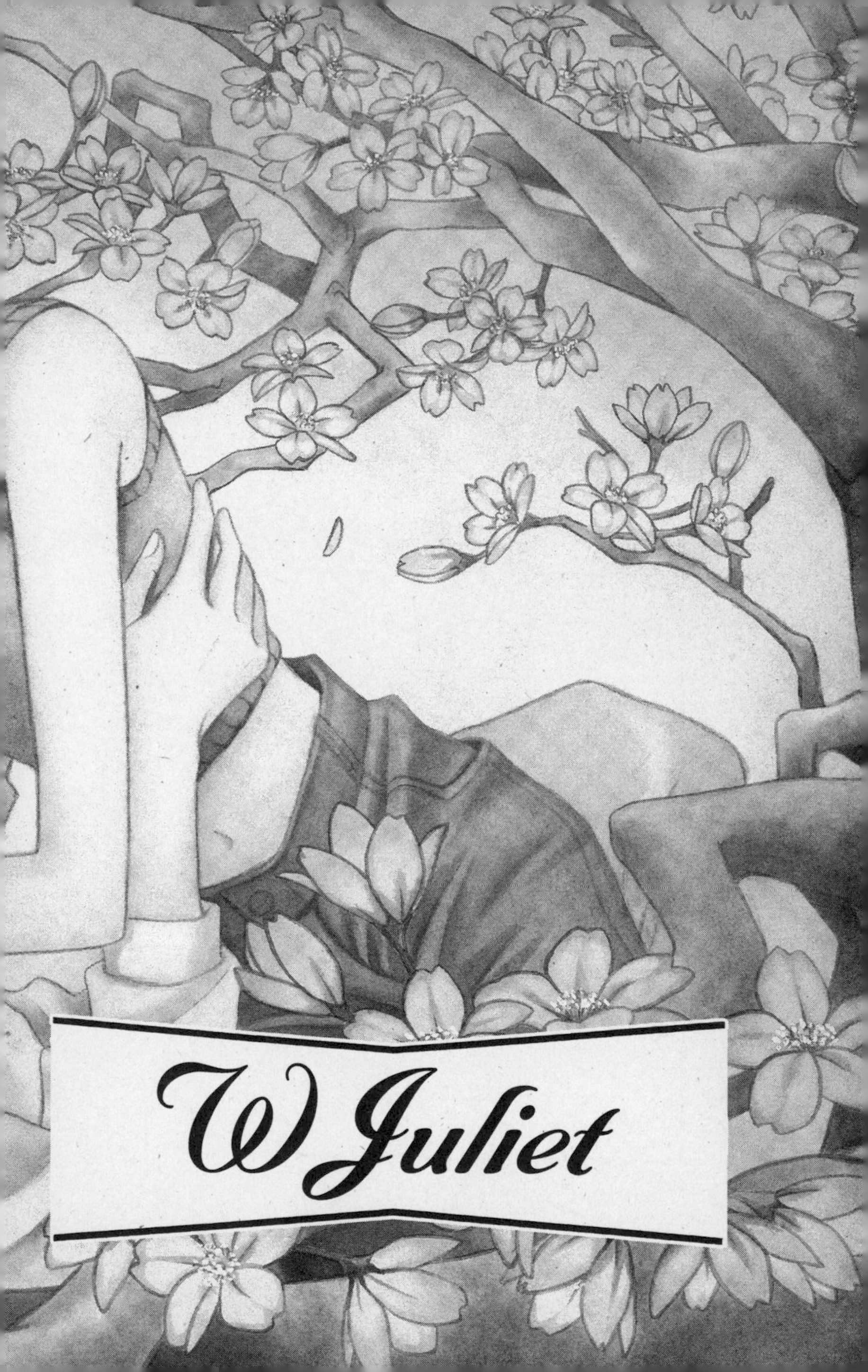
W Juliet

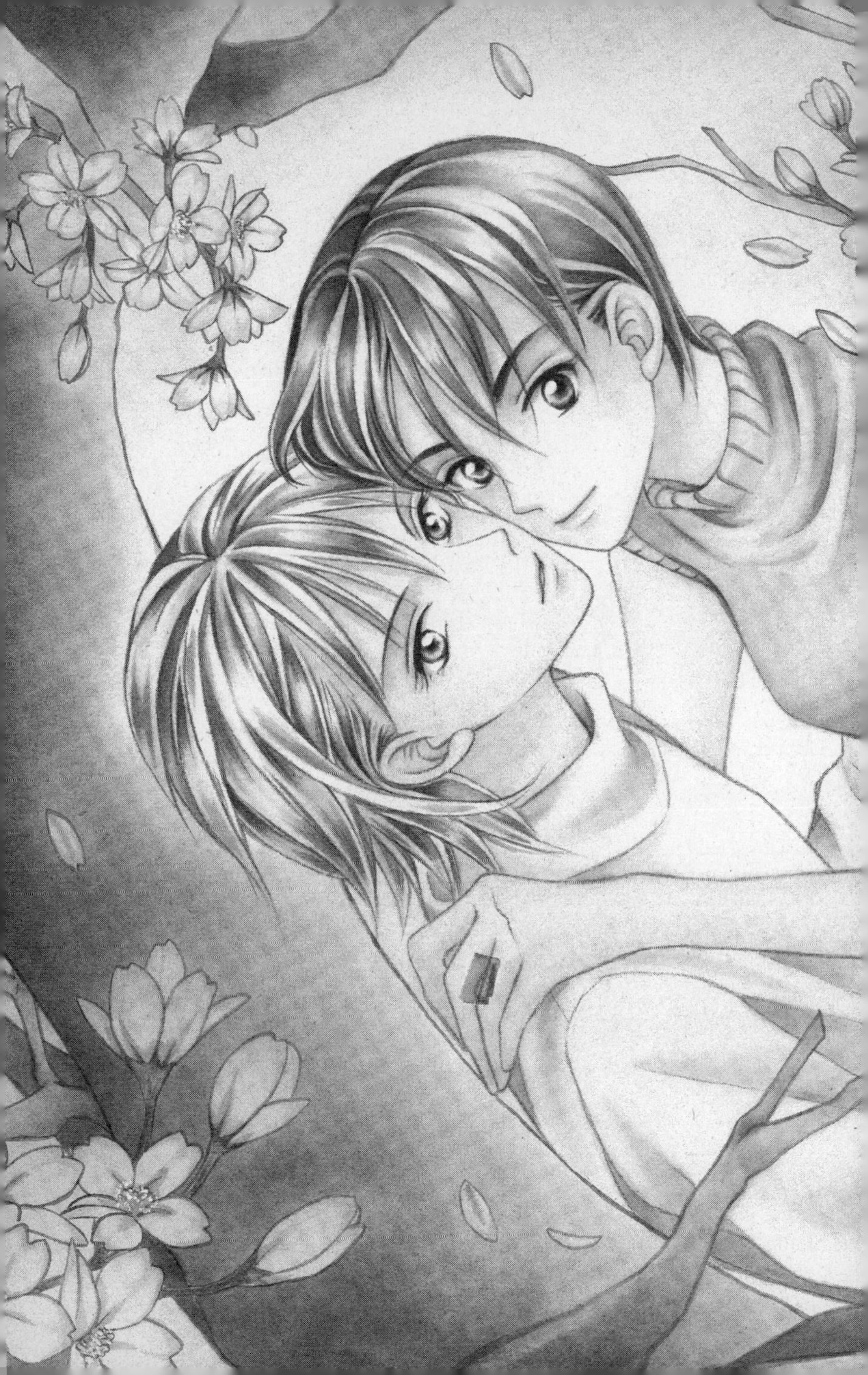

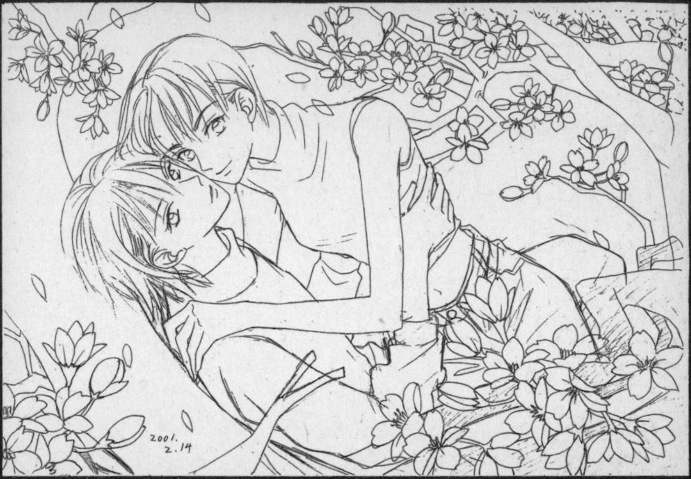
2001. 2.14

↑ 2001 Hana to Yume No. 8 front splash-page, draft (B5 size)

↓ Swan Lake preview art, draft (B4 size)

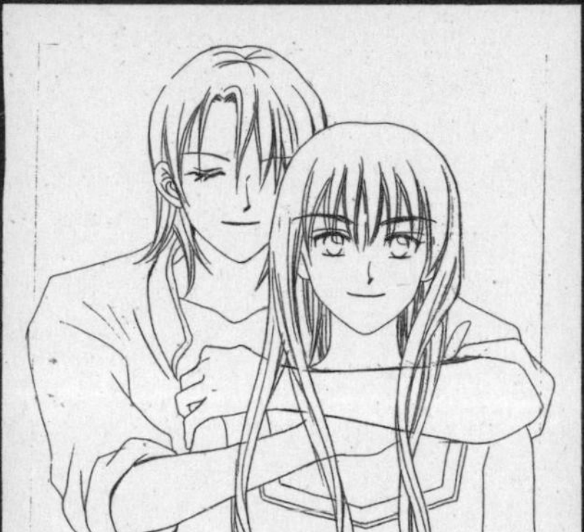

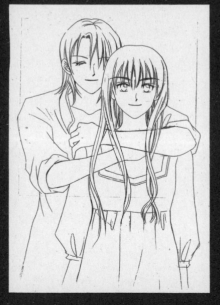

↓ 2001 Hana to Yume No. 12, opening page, draft (B4 size)

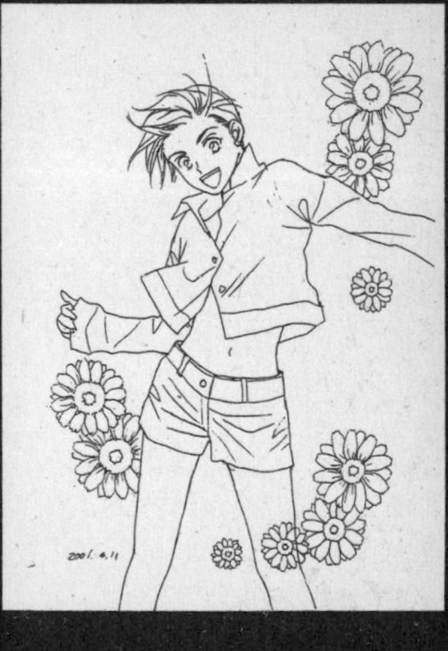
2001. 4.11

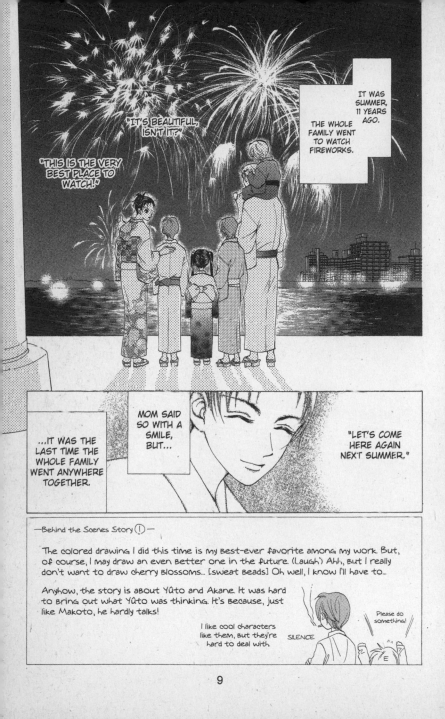

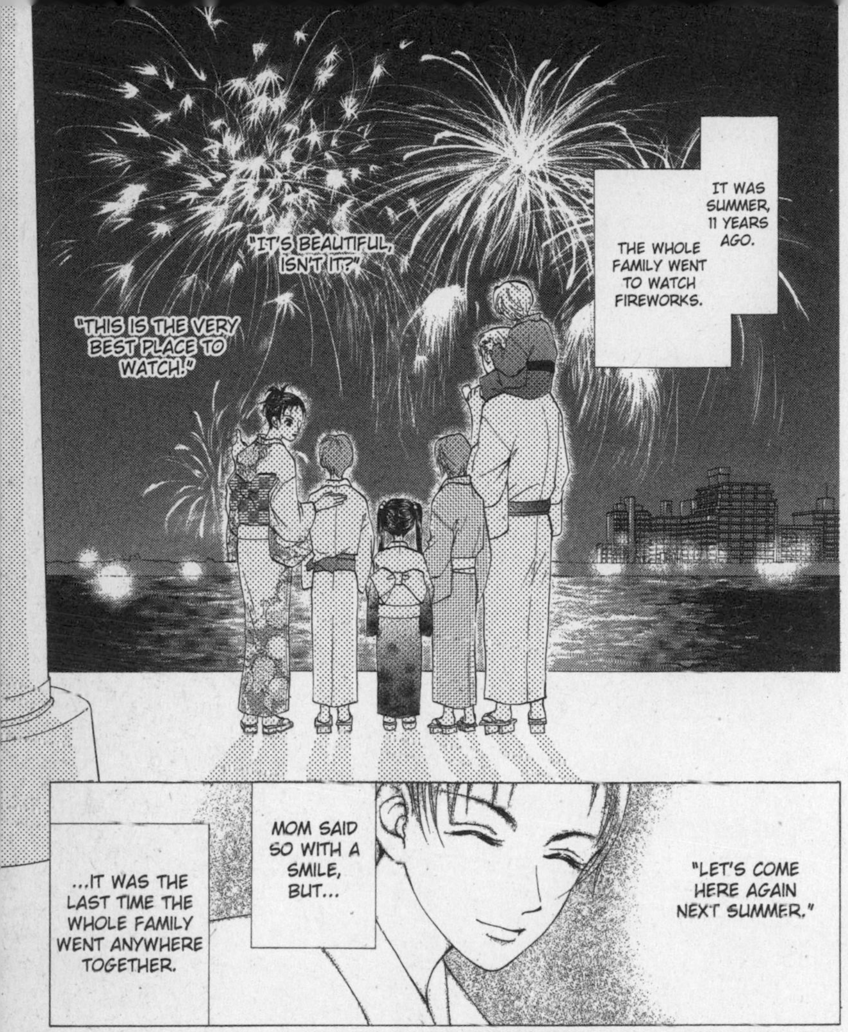
IT WAS SUMMER, 11 YEARS AGO.
THE WHOLE FAMILY WENT TO WATCH FIREWORKS.
"IT'S BEAUTIFUL, ISN'T IT?"
"THIS IS THE VERY BEST PLACE TO WATCH."
"LET'S COME HERE AGAIN NEXT SUMMER."
MOM SAID SO WITH A SMILE, BUT...
...IT WAS THE LAST TIME THE WHOLE FAMILY WENT ANYWHERE TOGETHER.

—Behind the Scenes Story ①—

The colored drawing I did this time is my best-ever favorite among my work. But, of course, I may draw an even better one in the future. (Laugh) Ahh, but I really don't want to draw cherry blossoms... [sweat beads] Oh well, I know I'll have to...

Anyhow, the story is about Yûto and Akane. It was hard to bring out what Yûto was thinking. It's because, just like Makoto, he hardly talks!

I like cool characters like them, but they're hard to deal with.

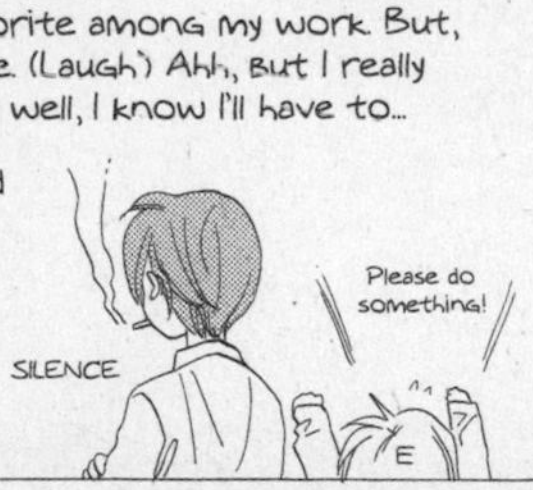
SILENCE
Please do something!

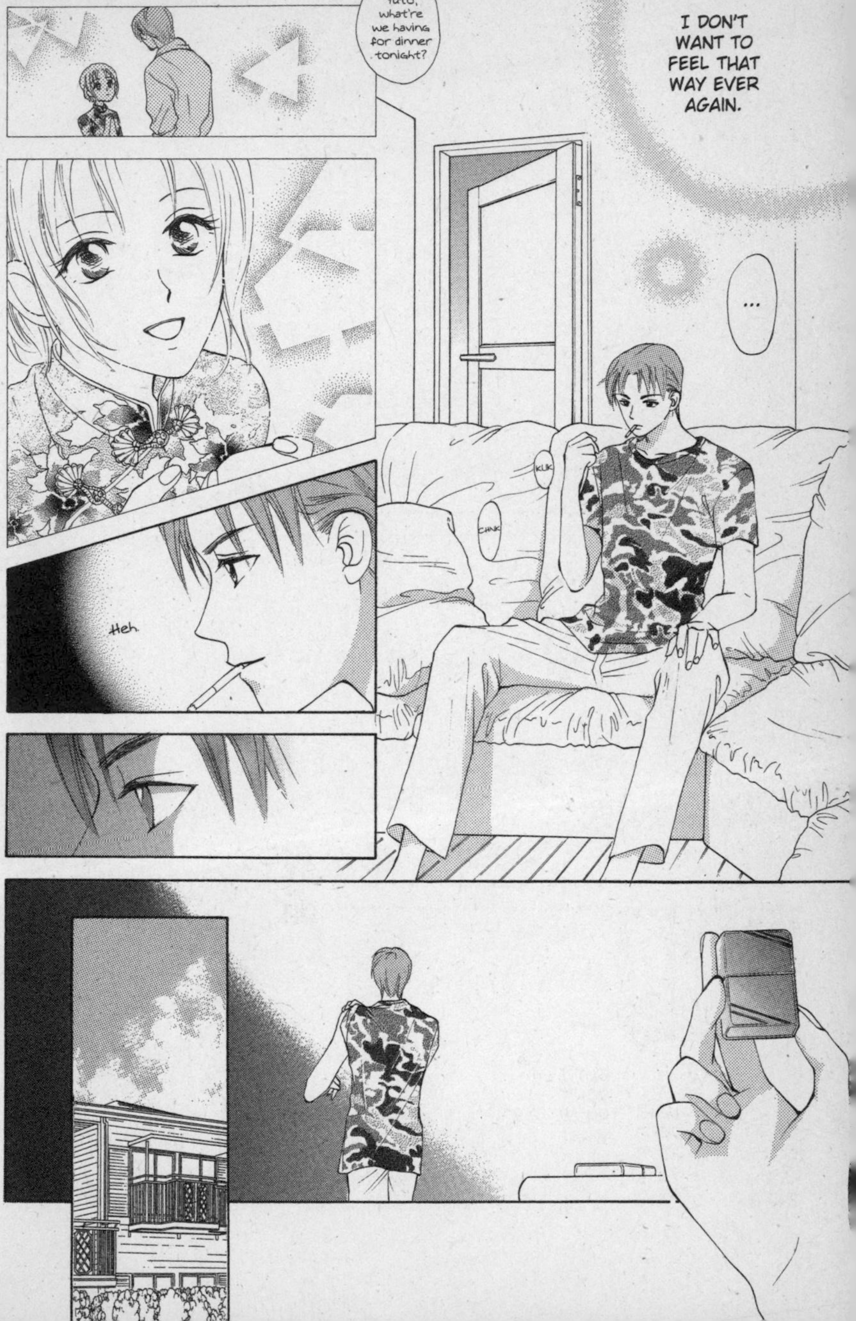
I DON'T WANT TO FEEL THAT WAY EVER AGAIN.
...
KUK
CHNK
Yûto, what're we having for dinner tonight?
Heh.

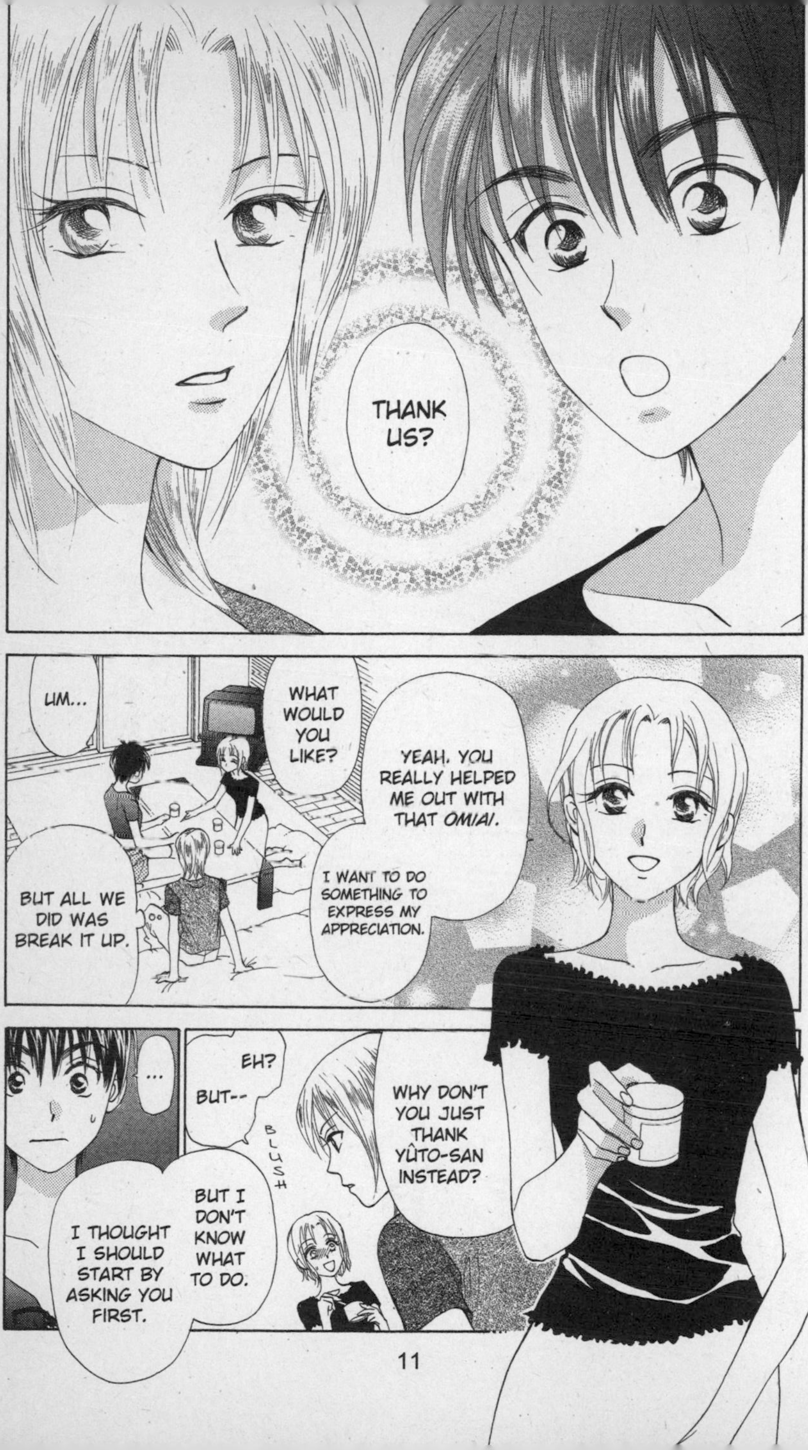
THANK US?
YEAH. YOU REALLY HELPED ME OUT WITH THAT *OMIAI*.
I WANT TO DO SOMETHING TO EXPRESS MY APPRECIATION.
WHAT WOULD YOU LIKE?
UM...
BUT ALL WE DID WAS BREAK IT UP.
WHY DON'T YOU JUST THANK YÛTO-SAN INSTEAD?
EH?
BUT--
BLUSH
BUT I DON'T KNOW WHAT TO DO.
I THOUGHT I SHOULD START BY ASKING YOU FIRST.
...

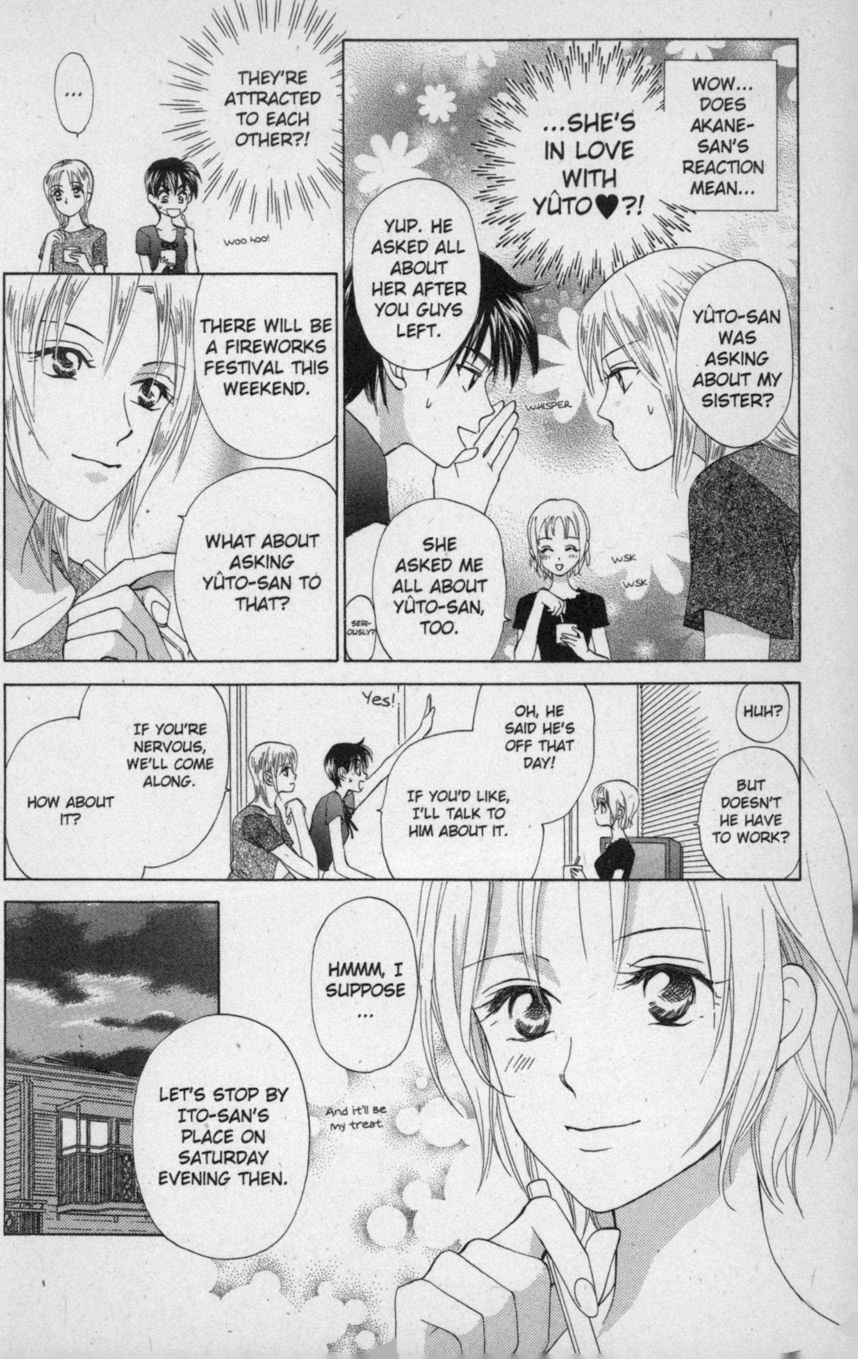
WOW... DOES AKANE-SAN'S REACTION MEAN...
...SHE'S IN LOVE WITH YÛTO♥?!
YÛTO-SAN WAS ASKING ABOUT MY SISTER?
YUP. HE ASKED ALL ABOUT HER AFTER YOU GUYS LEFT.
WHISPER
WSK
WSK
SHE ASKED ME ALL ABOUT YÛTO-SAN, TOO.
SERIOUSLY?
THEY'RE ATTRACTED TO EACH OTHER?!
...
Woo hoo!
THERE WILL BE A FIREWORKS FESTIVAL THIS WEEKEND.
WHAT ABOUT ASKING YÛTO-SAN TO THAT?
HUH?
BUT DOESN'T HE HAVE TO WORK?
OH, HE SAID HE'S OFF THAT DAY!
IF YOU'D LIKE, I'LL TALK TO HIM ABOUT IT.
Yes!
IF YOU'RE NERVOUS, WE'LL COME ALONG.
HOW ABOUT IT?
HMMM, I SUPPOSE...
LET'S STOP BY ITO-SAN'S PLACE ON SATURDAY EVENING THEN.
And it'll be my treat.

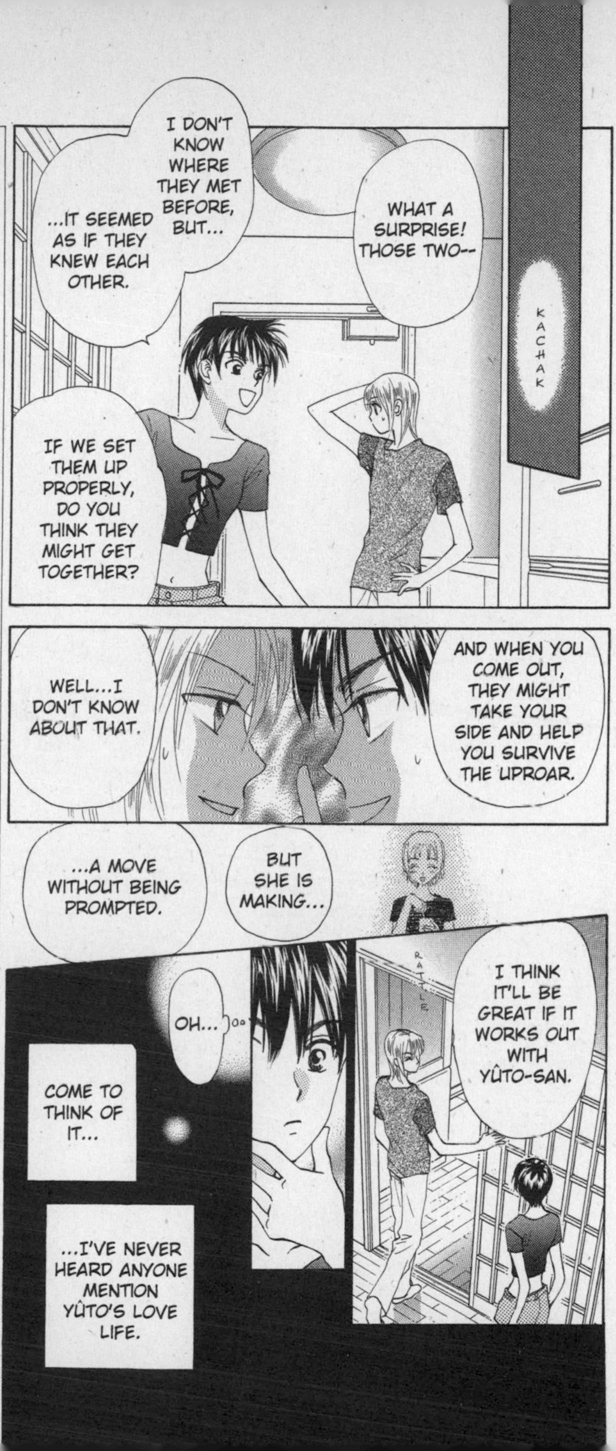
KACHAK
WHAT A SURPRISE! THOSE TWO--
I DON'T KNOW WHERE THEY MET BEFORE, BUT...
...IT SEEMED AS IF THEY KNEW EACH OTHER.
IF WE SET THEM UP PROPERLY, DO YOU THINK THEY MIGHT GET TOGETHER?
AND WHEN YOU COME OUT, THEY MIGHT TAKE YOUR SIDE AND HELP YOU SURVIVE THE UPROAR.
WELL...I DON'T KNOW ABOUT THAT.
BUT SHE IS MAKING...
...A MOVE WITHOUT BEING PROMPTED.
RATTLE
I THINK IT'LL BE GREAT IF IT WORKS OUT WITH YÛTO-SAN.
OH...
COME TO THINK OF IT...
...I'VE NEVER HEARD ANYONE MENTION YÛTO'S LOVE LIFE.

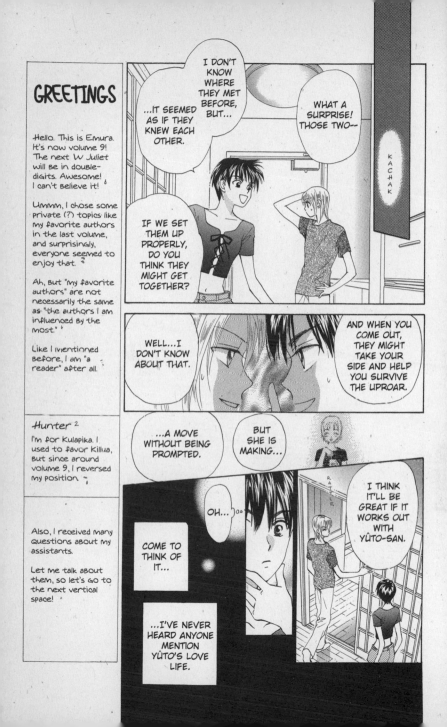

GREETINGS

Hello. This is Emura. It's now volume 9! The next W Juliet will be in double-digits. Awesome! I can't believe it!

Ummm, I chose some private (?) topics like my favorite authors in the last volume, and surprisingly, everyone seemed to enjoy that.

Ah, but "my favorite authors" are not necessarily the same as "the authors I am influenced by the most."

Like I mentioned before, I am "a reader" after all.

Hunter[2]

I'm for Kulapika. I used to favor Killua, but since around volume 9, I reversed my position.

Also, I received many questions about my assistants.

Let me talk about them, so let's go to the next vertical space!

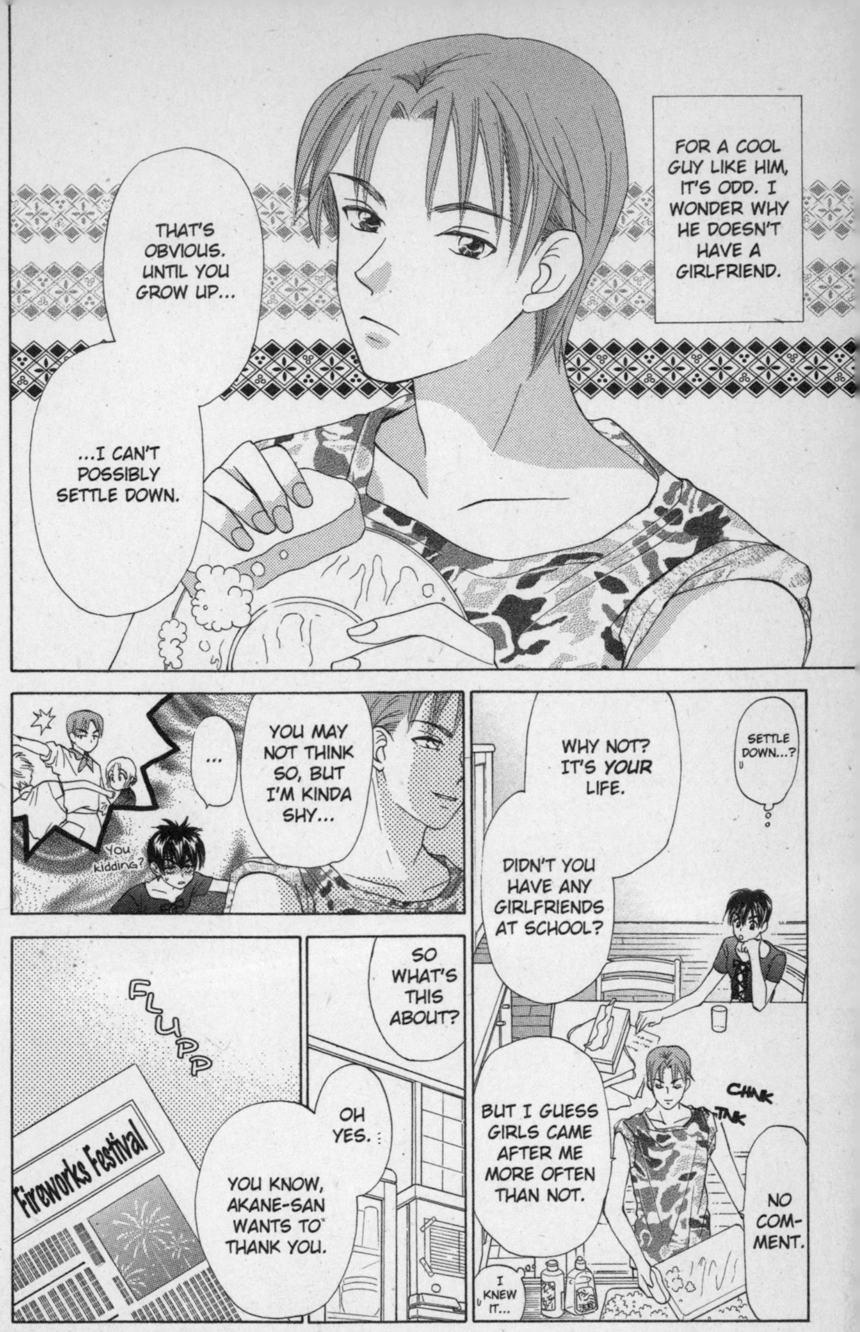

FOR A COOL GUY LIKE HIM, IT'S ODD. I WONDER WHY HE DOESN'T HAVE A GIRLFRIEND.
THAT'S OBVIOUS. UNTIL YOU GROW UP...
...I CAN'T POSSIBLY SETTLE DOWN.
SETTLE DOWN...?
WHY NOT? IT'S *YOUR* LIFE.
DIDN'T YOU HAVE ANY GIRLFRIENDS AT SCHOOL?
BUT I GUESS GIRLS CAME AFTER ME MORE OFTEN THAN NOT.
CHINK
TNK
NO COM-MENT.
I KNEW IT...
YOU MAY NOT THINK SO, BUT I'M KINDA SHY...
...
You kidding?
SO WHAT'S THIS ABOUT?
OH YES.
YOU KNOW, AKANE-SAN WANTS TO THANK YOU.
FLUPP
Fireworks Festival

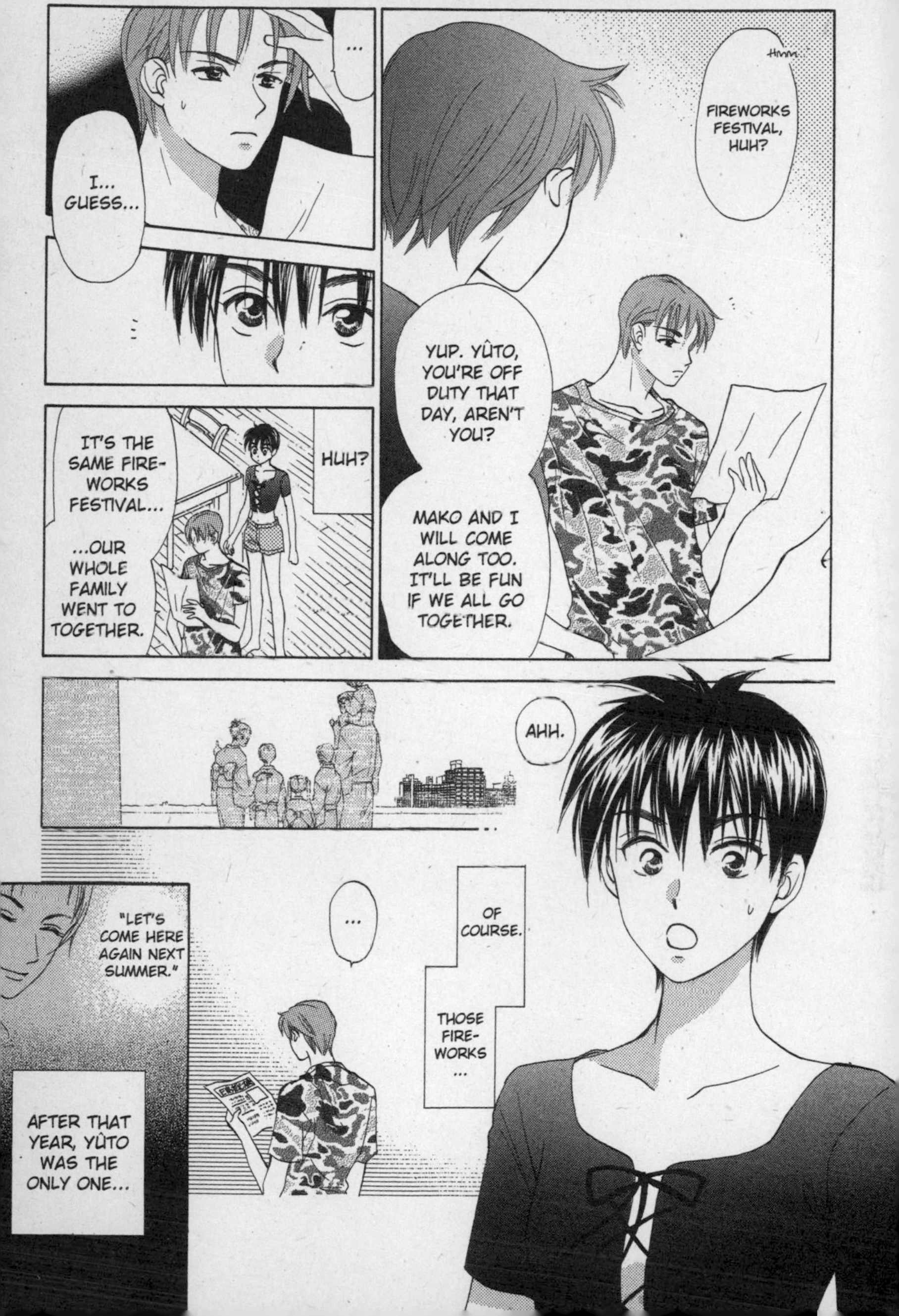
Hmm.
FIREWORKS FESTIVAL, HUH?
YUP. YÛTO, YOU'RE OFF DUTY THAT DAY, AREN'T YOU?
MAKO AND I WILL COME ALONG TOO. IT'LL BE FUN IF WE ALL GO TOGETHER.
...
I... GUESS...
HUH?
IT'S THE SAME FIRE-WORKS FESTIVAL...
...OUR WHOLE FAMILY WENT TO TOGETHER.
AHH.
OF COURSE.
THOSE FIRE-WORKS ...
...
"LET'S COME HERE AGAIN NEXT SUMMER."
AFTER THAT YEAR, YÛTO WAS THE ONLY ONE...

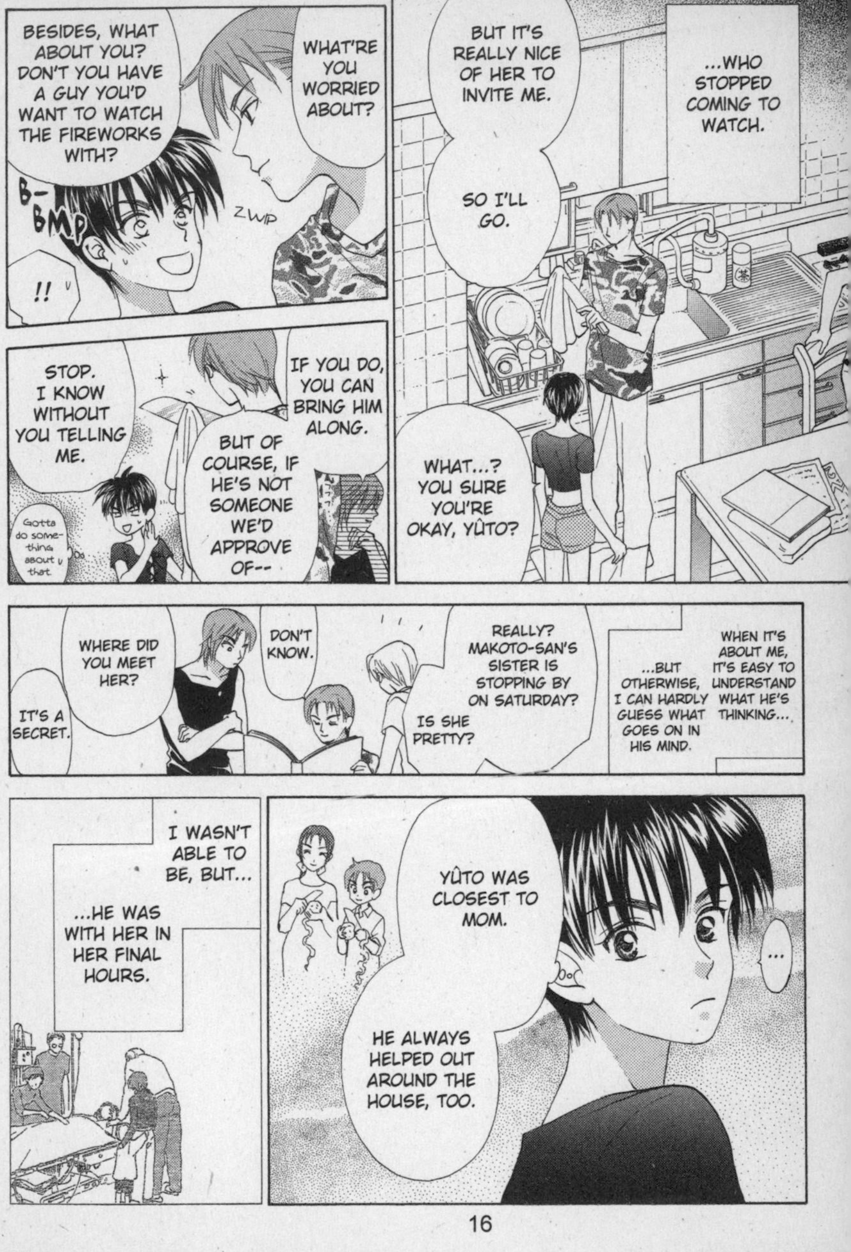
...WHO STOPPED COMING TO WATCH.
BUT IT'S REALLY NICE OF HER TO INVITE ME.
SO I'LL GO.
WHAT...? YOU SURE YOU'RE OKAY, YÛTO?
WHAT'RE YOU WORRIED ABOUT?
BESIDES, WHAT ABOUT YOU? DON'T YOU HAVE A GUY YOU'D WANT TO WATCH THE FIREWORKS WITH?
ZWIP
B-BMP
!!
IF YOU DO, YOU CAN BRING HIM ALONG.
BUT OF COURSE, IF HE'S NOT SOMEONE WE'D APPROVE OF--
STOP. I KNOW WITHOUT YOU TELLING ME.
Gotta do something about that.
WHEN IT'S ABOUT ME, IT'S EASY TO UNDERSTAND WHAT HE'S THINKING...
...BUT OTHERWISE, I CAN HARDLY GUESS WHAT GOES ON IN HIS MIND.
REALLY? MAKOTO-SAN'S SISTER IS STOPPING BY ON SATURDAY?
IS SHE PRETTY?
DON'T KNOW.
WHERE DID YOU MEET HER?
IT'S A SECRET.
...
YÛTO WAS CLOSEST TO MOM.
HE ALWAYS HELPED OUT AROUND THE HOUSE, TOO.
I WASN'T ABLE TO BE, BUT...
...HE WAS WITH HER IN HER FINAL HOURS.

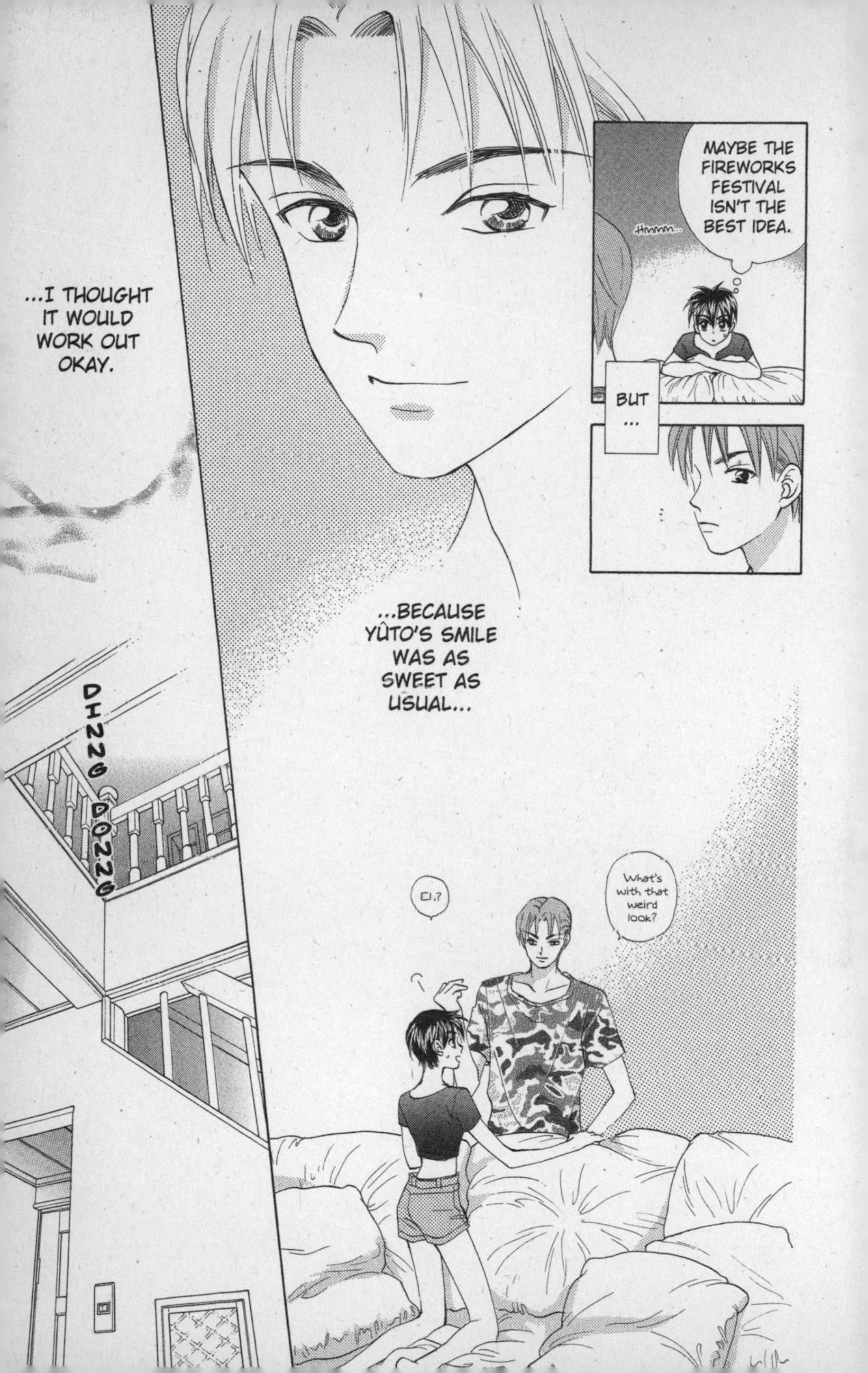
Hmmm...
MAYBE THE FIREWORKS FESTIVAL ISN'T THE BEST IDEA.
BUT ...
...I THOUGHT IT WOULD WORK OUT OKAY.
...BECAUSE YÛTO'S SMILE WAS AS SWEET AS USUAL...
What's with that weird look?
DINNG DONNG

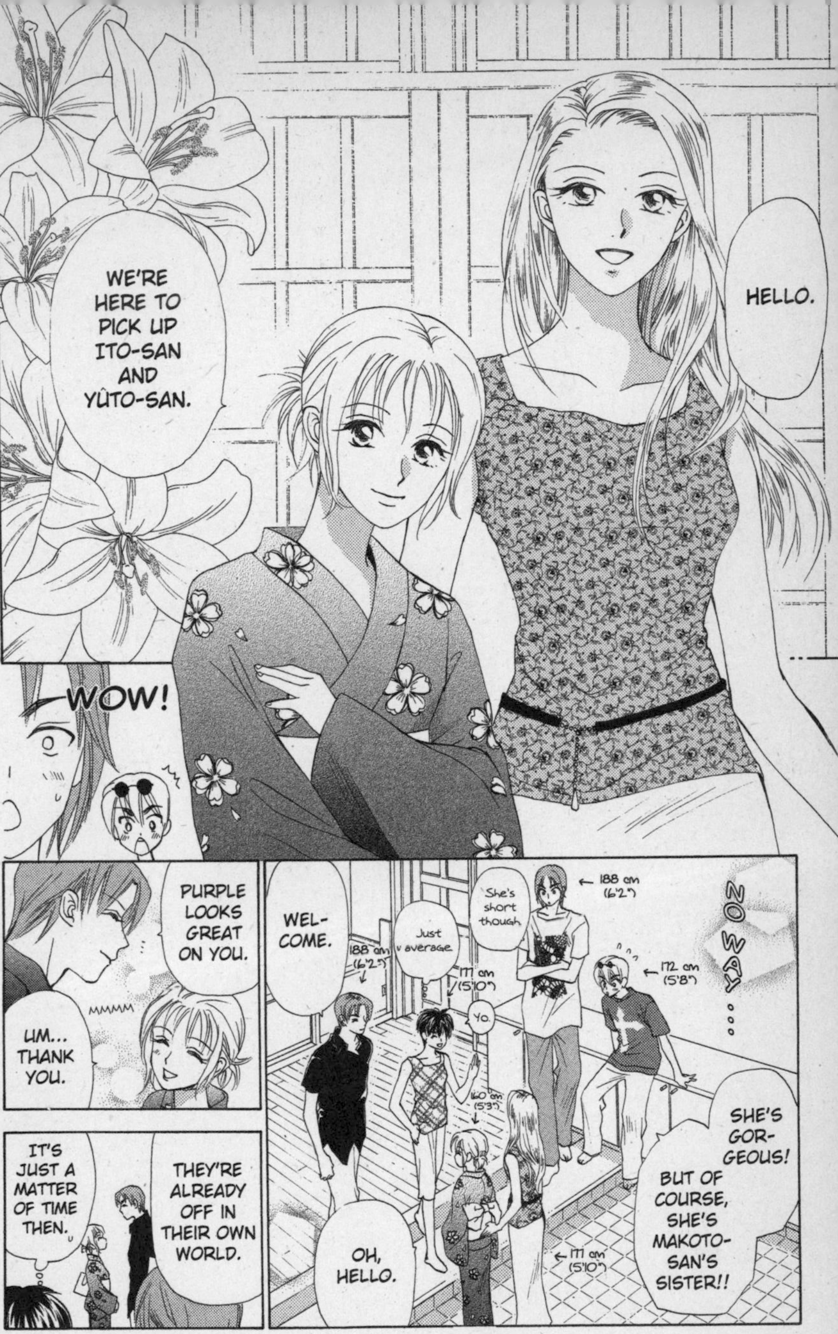
HELLO.
WE'RE HERE TO PICK UP ITO-SAN AND YÛTO-SAN.
WOW!
NO WAY...
← 188 cm (6'2")
She's short though
172 cm (5'8")
WEL-COME.
Just average
188 cm (6'2")
177 cm (5'10")
Yo.
160 cm (5'3")
SHE'S GOR-GEOUS!
BUT OF COURSE, SHE'S MAKOTO-SAN'S SISTER!!
← 177 cm (5'10")
OH, HELLO.
PURPLE LOOKS GREAT ON YOU.
MMMM
UM... THANK YOU.
THEY'RE ALREADY OFF IN THEIR OWN WORLD.
IT'S JUST A MATTER OF TIME THEN.

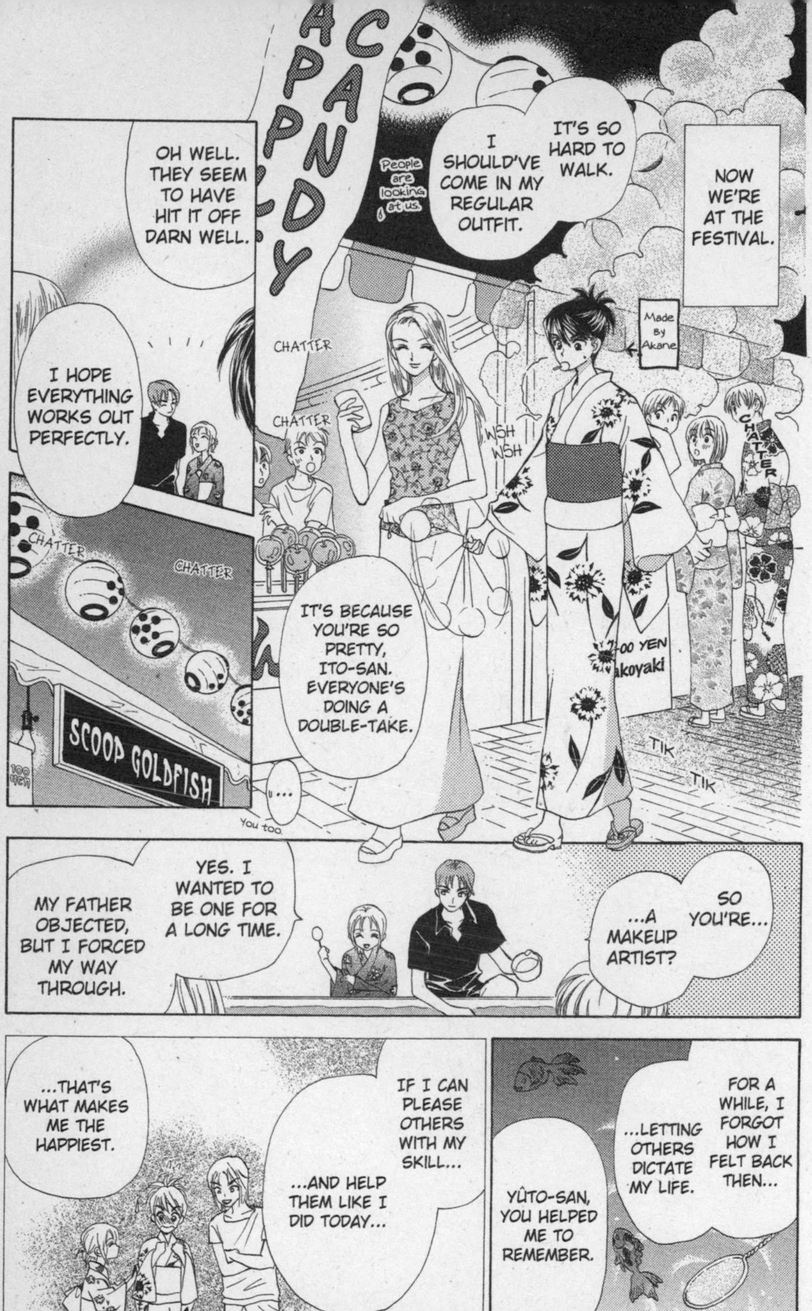
NOW WE'RE AT THE FESTIVAL.
CANDY
APPL
IT'S SO HARD TO WALK.
I SHOULD'VE COME IN MY REGULAR OUTFIT.
People are looking at us.
Made By Akane
CHATTER
CHATTER
CHATTER
WSH WSH
IT'S BECAUSE YOU'RE SO PRETTY, ITO-SAN. EVERYONE'S DOING A DOUBLE-TAKE.
...
You too.
TIK
TIK
OH WELL. THEY SEEM TO HAVE HIT IT OFF DARN WELL.
I HOPE EVERYTHING WORKS OUT PERFECTLY.
CHATTER
CHATTER
SCOOP GOLDFISH
100 yen
SO YOU'RE...
...A MAKEUP ARTIST?
YES. I WANTED TO BE ONE FOR A LONG TIME.
MY FATHER OBJECTED, BUT I FORCED MY WAY THROUGH.
FOR A WHILE, I FORGOT HOW I FELT BACK THEN...
...LETTING OTHERS DICTATE MY LIFE.
YÛTO-SAN, YOU HELPED ME TO REMEMBER.
IF I CAN PLEASE OTHERS WITH MY SKILL...
...AND HELP THEM LIKE I DID TODAY...
...THAT'S WHAT MAKES ME THE HAPPIEST.

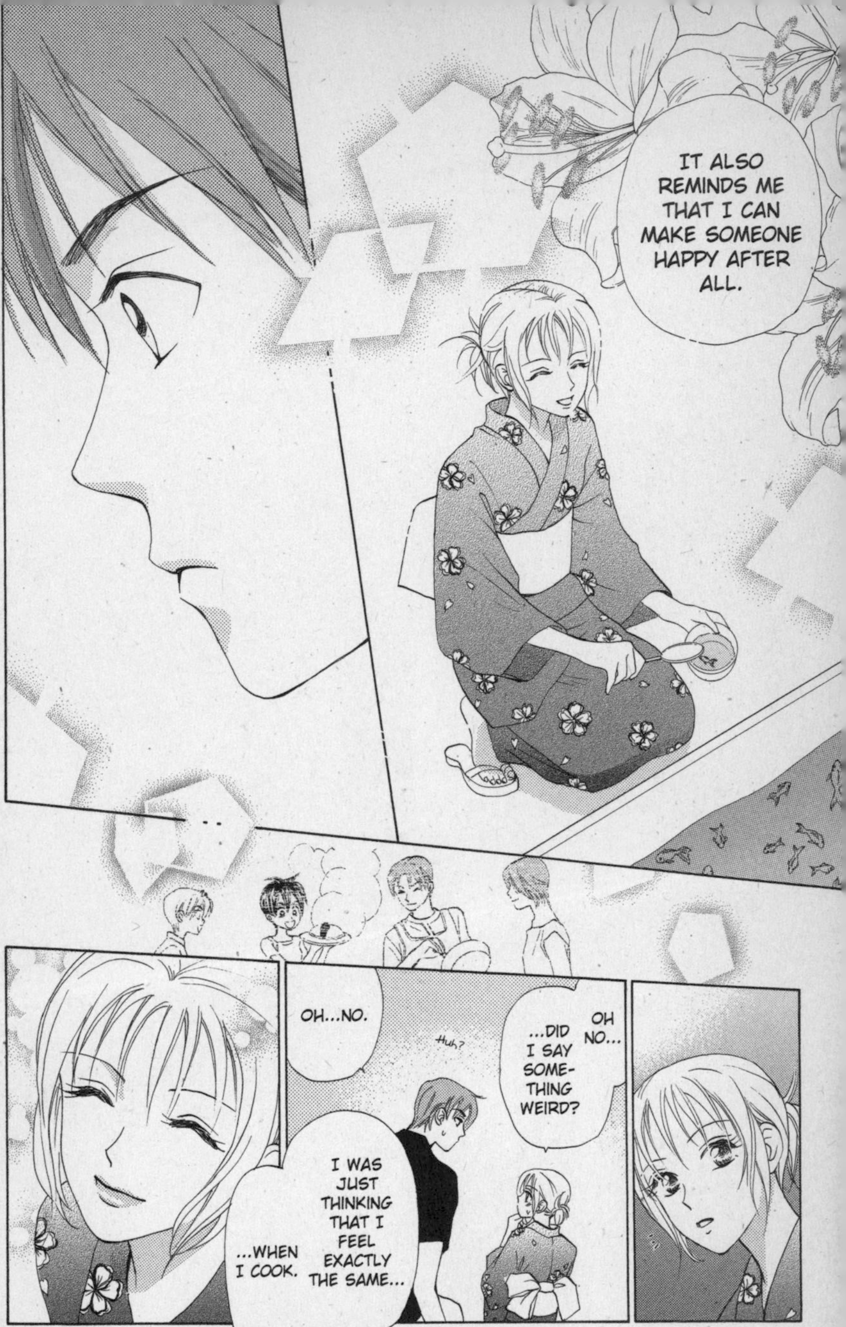
IT ALSO REMINDS ME THAT I CAN MAKE SOMEONE HAPPY AFTER ALL.
...
OH NO...
...DID I SAY SOME-THING WEIRD?
Huh?
OH...NO.
I WAS JUST THINKING THAT I FEEL EXACTLY THE SAME...
...WHEN I COOK.

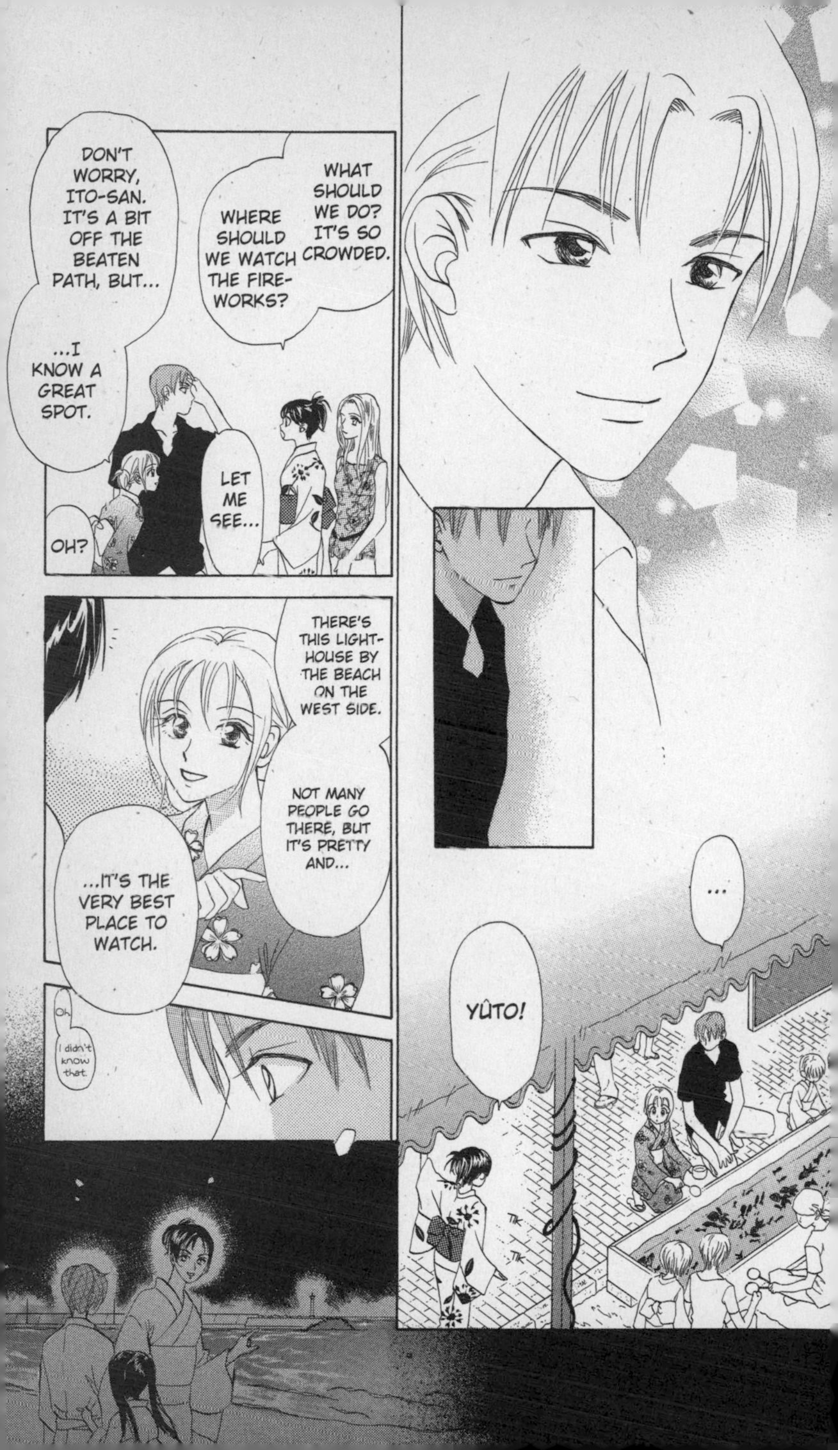
...
YÛTO!
WHAT SHOULD WE DO? IT'S SO CROWDED.
WHERE SHOULD WE WATCH THE FIRE-WORKS?
DON'T WORRY, ITO-SAN. IT'S A BIT OFF THE BEATEN PATH, BUT...
...I KNOW A GREAT SPOT.
LET ME SEE...
OH?
THERE'S THIS LIGHT-HOUSE BY THE BEACH ON THE WEST SIDE.
NOT MANY PEOPLE GO THERE, BUT IT'S PRETTY AND...
...IT'S THE VERY BEST PLACE TO WATCH.
Oh
I didn't know that.
TIK
TIK

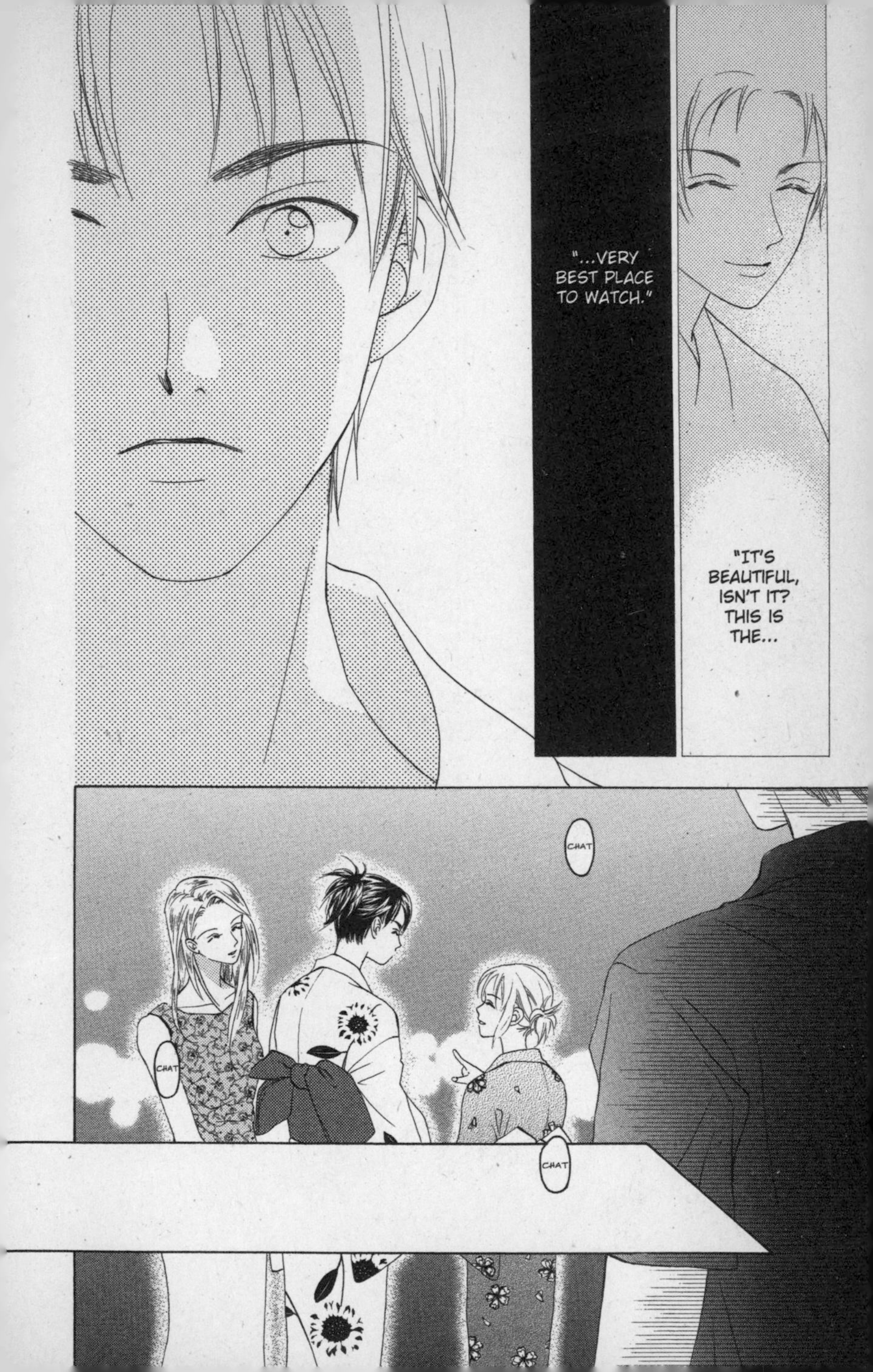
"IT'S BEAUTIFUL, ISN'T IT? THIS IS THE...
"...VERY BEST PLACE TO WATCH."
CHAT
CHAT
CHAT

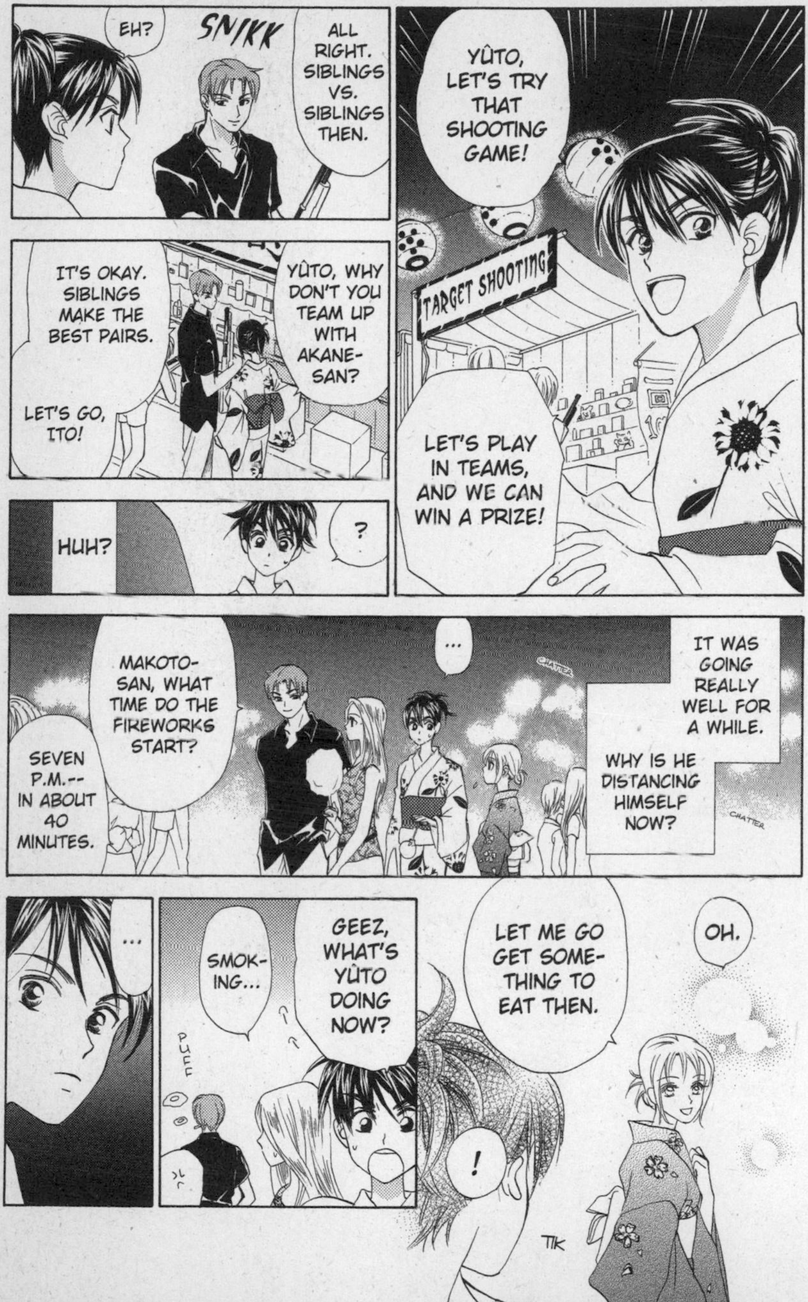
YÛTO, LET'S TRY THAT SHOOTING GAME!
TARGET SHOOTING
LET'S PLAY IN TEAMS, AND WE CAN WIN A PRIZE!
ALL RIGHT. SIBLINGS VS. SIBLINGS THEN.
SNIKK
EH?
YÛTO, WHY DON'T YOU TEAM UP WITH AKANE-SAN?
IT'S OKAY. SIBLINGS MAKE THE BEST PAIRS.
LET'S GO, ITO!
?
HUH?
IT WAS GOING REALLY WELL FOR A WHILE.
WHY IS HE DISTANCING HIMSELF NOW?
CHATTER
...
CHATTER
MAKOTO-SAN, WHAT TIME DO THE FIREWORKS START?
SEVEN P.M.-- IN ABOUT 40 MINUTES.
OH.
LET ME GO GET SOMETHING TO EAT THEN.
!
TIK
GEEZ, WHAT'S YÛTO DOING NOW?
SMOKING...
PUFF
...

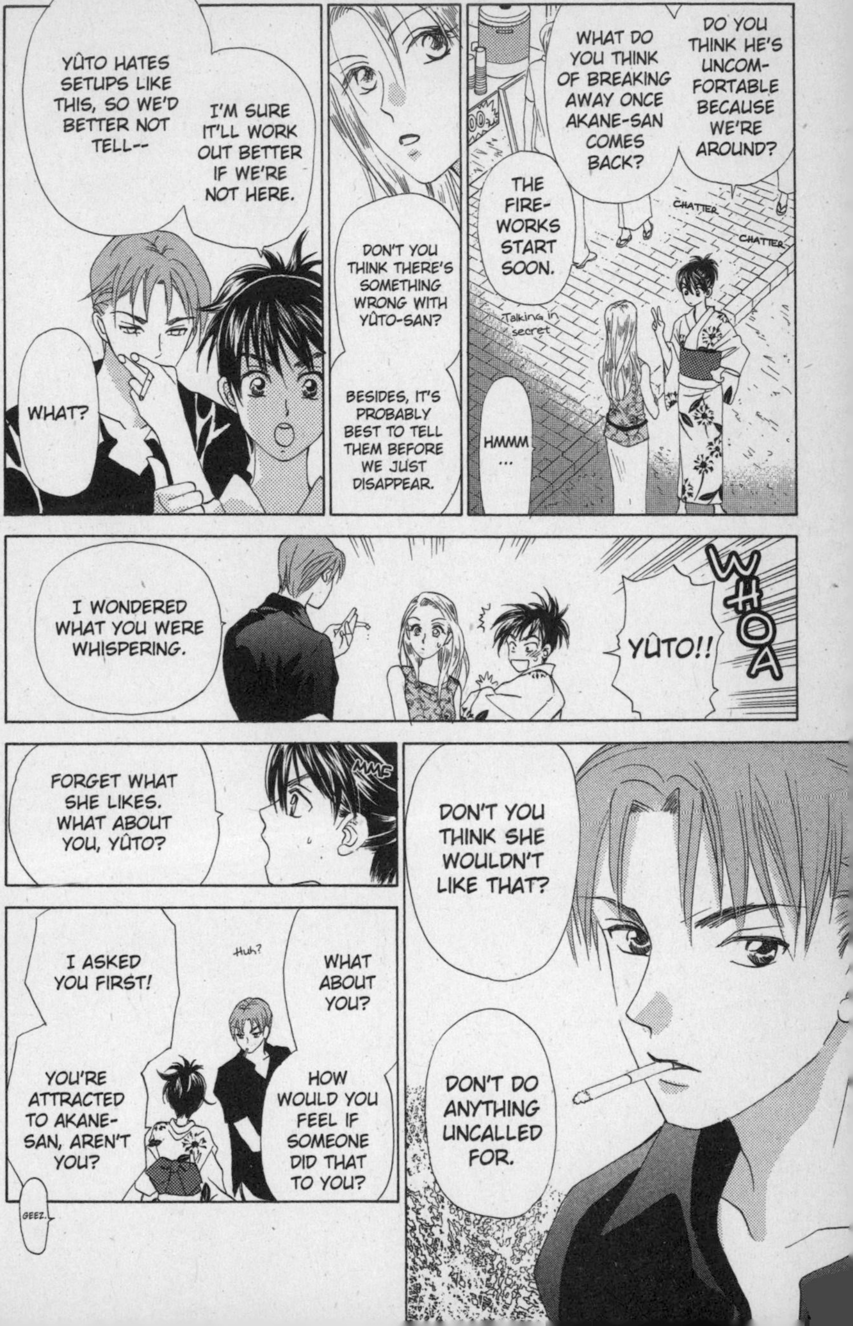
DO YOU THINK HE'S UNCOM-FORTABLE BECAUSE WE'RE AROUND?
WHAT DO YOU THINK OF BREAKING AWAY ONCE AKANE-SAN COMES BACK?
CHATTER
CHATTER
THE FIRE-WORKS START SOON.
Talking in secret
HMMM ...
DON'T YOU THINK THERE'S SOMETHING WRONG WITH YÛTO-SAN?
BESIDES, IT'S PROBABLY BEST TO TELL THEM BEFORE WE JUST DISAPPEAR.
I'M SURE IT'LL WORK OUT BETTER IF WE'RE NOT HERE.
YÛTO HATES SETUPS LIKE THIS, SO WE'D BETTER NOT TELL--
WHAT?
WHOA
YÛTO!!
I WONDERED WHAT YOU WERE WHISPERING.
DON'T YOU THINK SHE WOULDN'T LIKE THAT?
DON'T DO ANYTHING UNCALLED FOR.
MMF
FORGET WHAT SHE LIKES. WHAT ABOUT YOU, YÛTO?
WHAT ABOUT YOU?
Huh?
I ASKED YOU FIRST!
HOW WOULD YOU FEEL IF SOMEONE DID THAT TO YOU?
YOU'RE ATTRACTED TO AKANE-SAN, AREN'T YOU?
GEEZ.

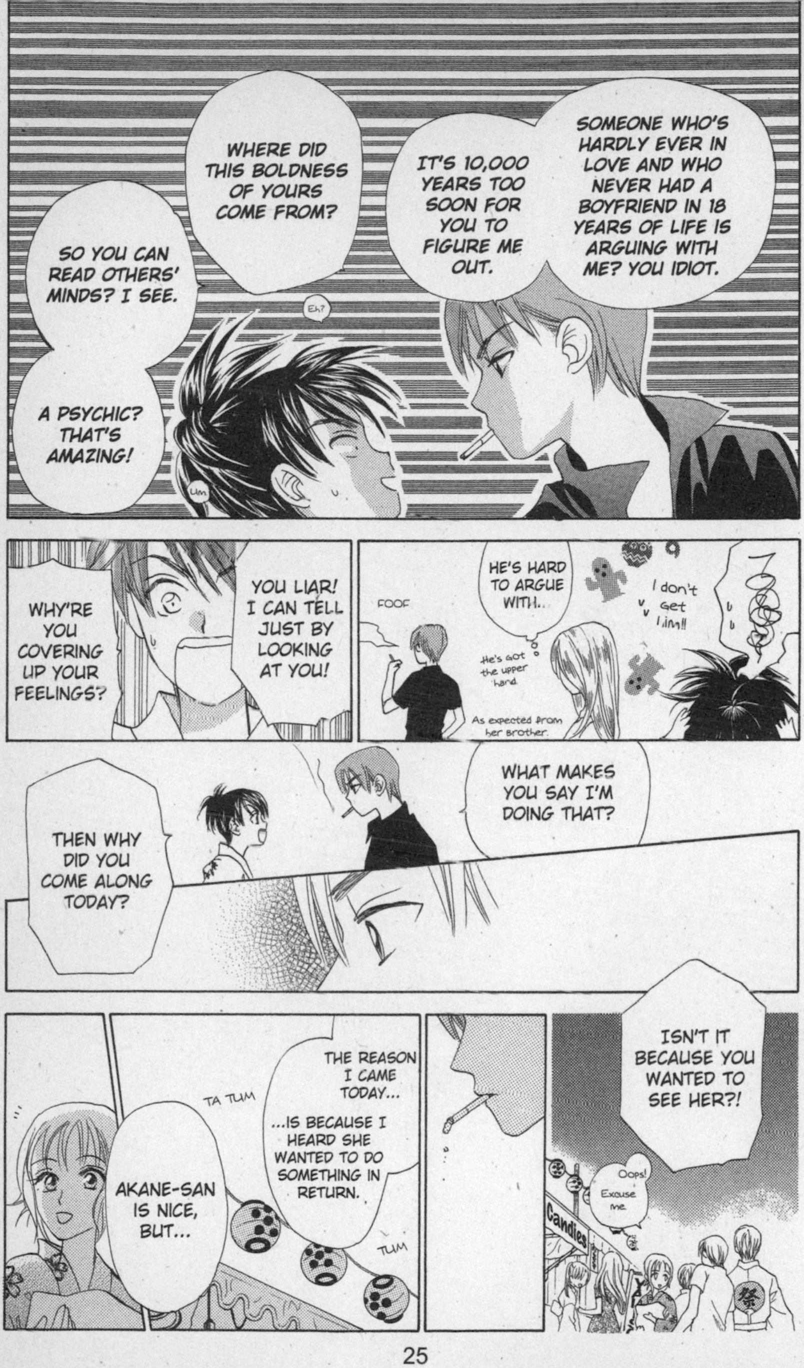
SOMEONE WHO'S HARDLY EVER IN LOVE AND WHO NEVER HAD A BOYFRIEND IN 18 YEARS OF LIFE IS ARGUING WITH ME? YOU IDIOT.
IT'S 10,000 YEARS TOO SOON FOR YOU TO FIGURE ME OUT.
WHERE DID THIS BOLDNESS OF YOURS COME FROM?
SO YOU CAN READ OTHERS' MINDS? I SEE.
Eh?
A PSYCHIC? THAT'S AMAZING!
Um.
I don't Get Him!!
HE'S HARD TO ARGUE WITH..
FOOF
He's got the upper hand.
As expected from her brother.
YOU LIAR! I CAN TELL JUST BY LOOKING AT YOU!
WHY'RE YOU COVERING UP YOUR FEELINGS?
WHAT MAKES YOU SAY I'M DOING THAT?
THEN WHY DID YOU COME ALONG TODAY?
ISN'T IT BECAUSE YOU WANTED TO SEE HER?!
Oops! Excuse me.
Candies
THE REASON I CAME TODAY...
...IS BECAUSE I HEARD SHE WANTED TO DO SOMETHING IN RETURN.
TA TUM
TUM
AKANE-SAN IS NICE, BUT...

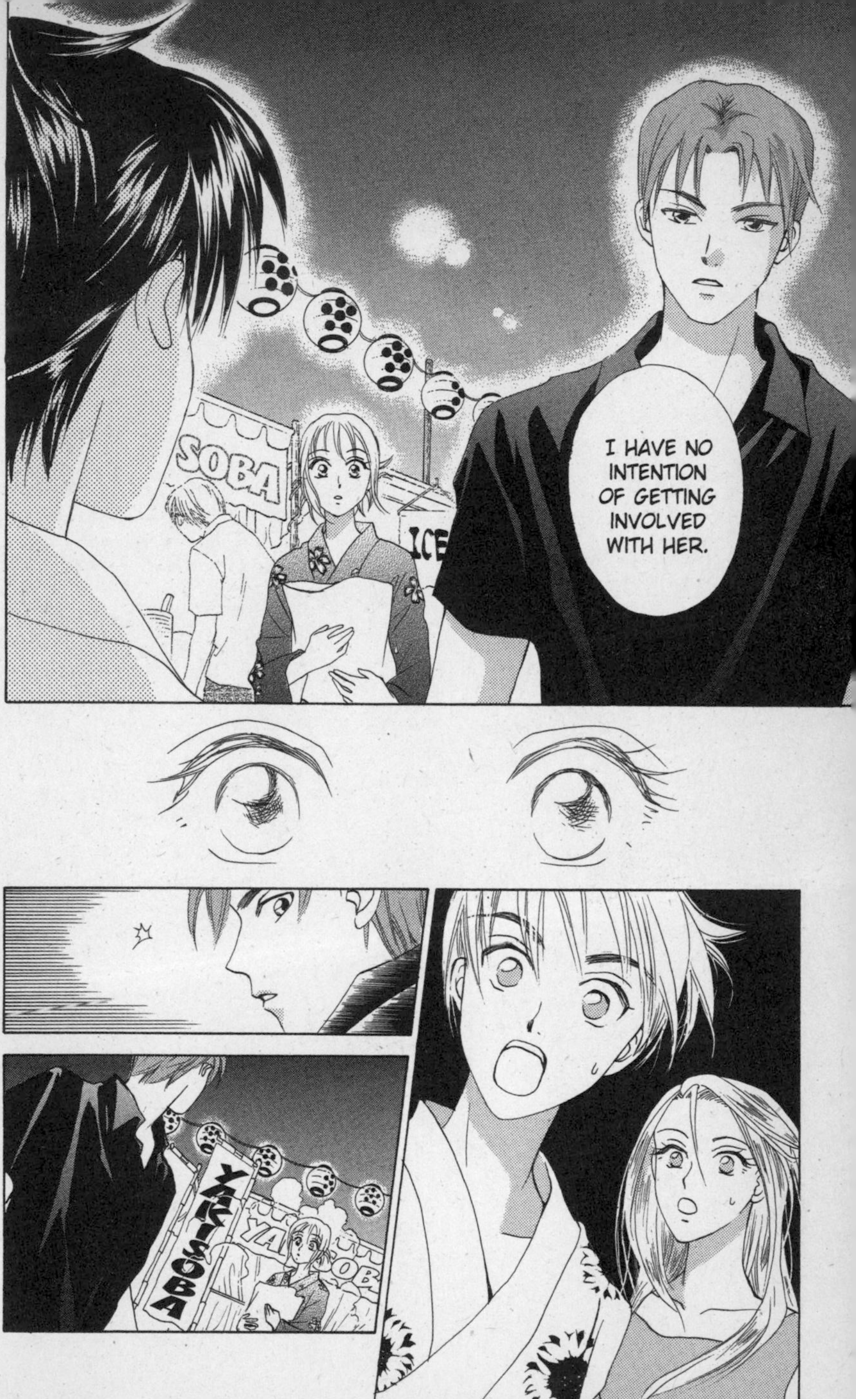
I HAVE NO INTENTION OF GETTING INVOLVED WITH HER.
SOBA
ICE
YAKISOBA
YA
OB

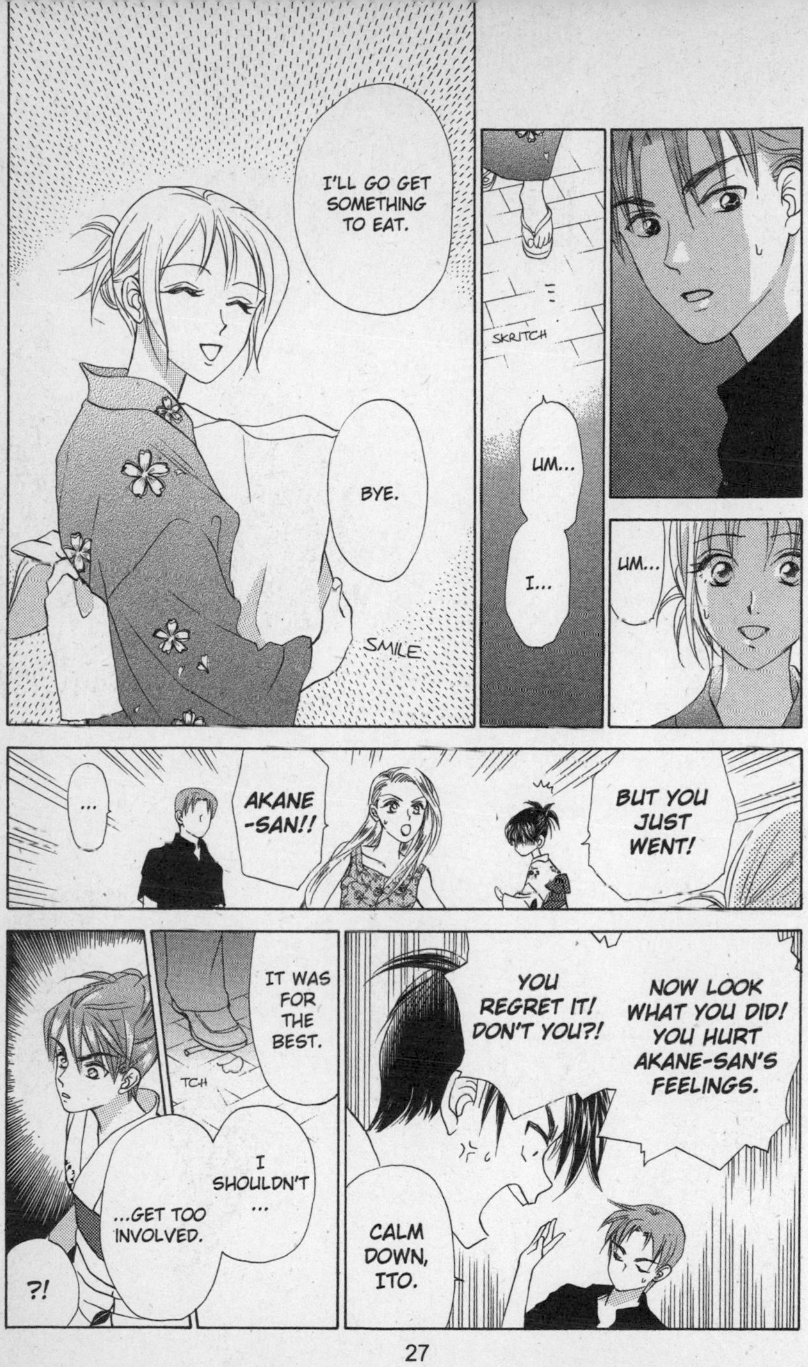
UM...
SKRITCH
UM...
I...
I'LL GO GET SOMETHING TO EAT.
BYE.
SMILE
BUT YOU JUST WENT!
AKANE -SAN!!
...
NOW LOOK WHAT YOU DID! YOU HURT AKANE-SAN'S FEELINGS.
YOU REGRET IT! DON'T YOU?!
CALM DOWN, ITO.
IT WAS FOR THE BEST.
TCH
I SHOULDN'T ...
...GET TOO INVOLVED.
?!

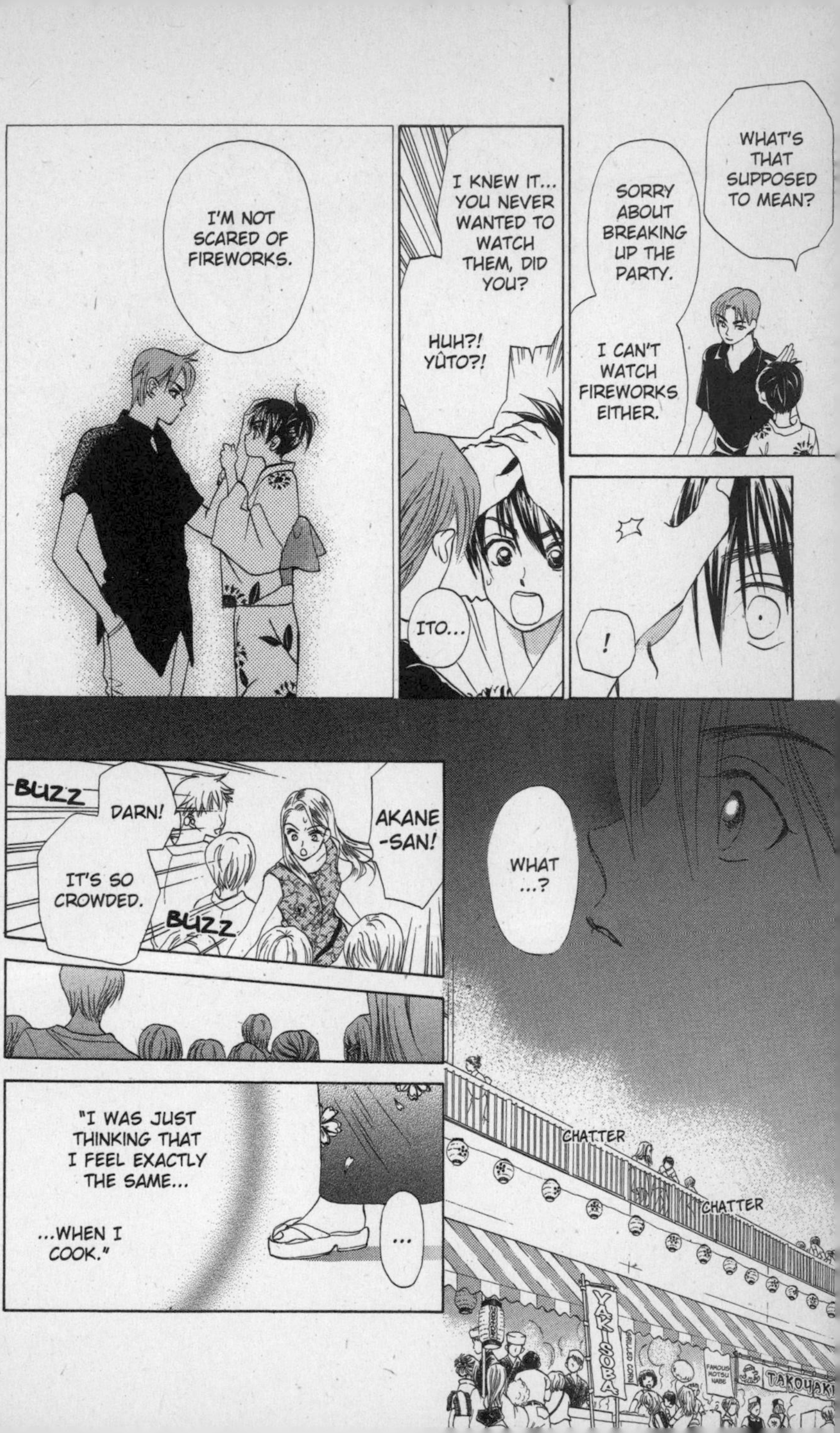
WHAT'S THAT SUPPOSED TO MEAN?
SORRY ABOUT BREAKING UP THE PARTY.
I CAN'T WATCH FIREWORKS EITHER.
!
I KNEW IT... YOU NEVER WANTED TO WATCH THEM, DID YOU?
HUH?! YÛTO?!
ITO...
I'M NOT SCARED OF FIREWORKS.
WHAT ...?
CHATTER
CHATTER
YAKISOBA
GRILLED CORN
FAMOUS MOTSU NABE
TAKOYAKI
AKANE -SAN!
BUZZ
DARN!
IT'S SO CROWDED.
BUZZ
"I WAS JUST THINKING THAT I FEEL EXACTLY THE SAME...
...WHEN I COOK."
...

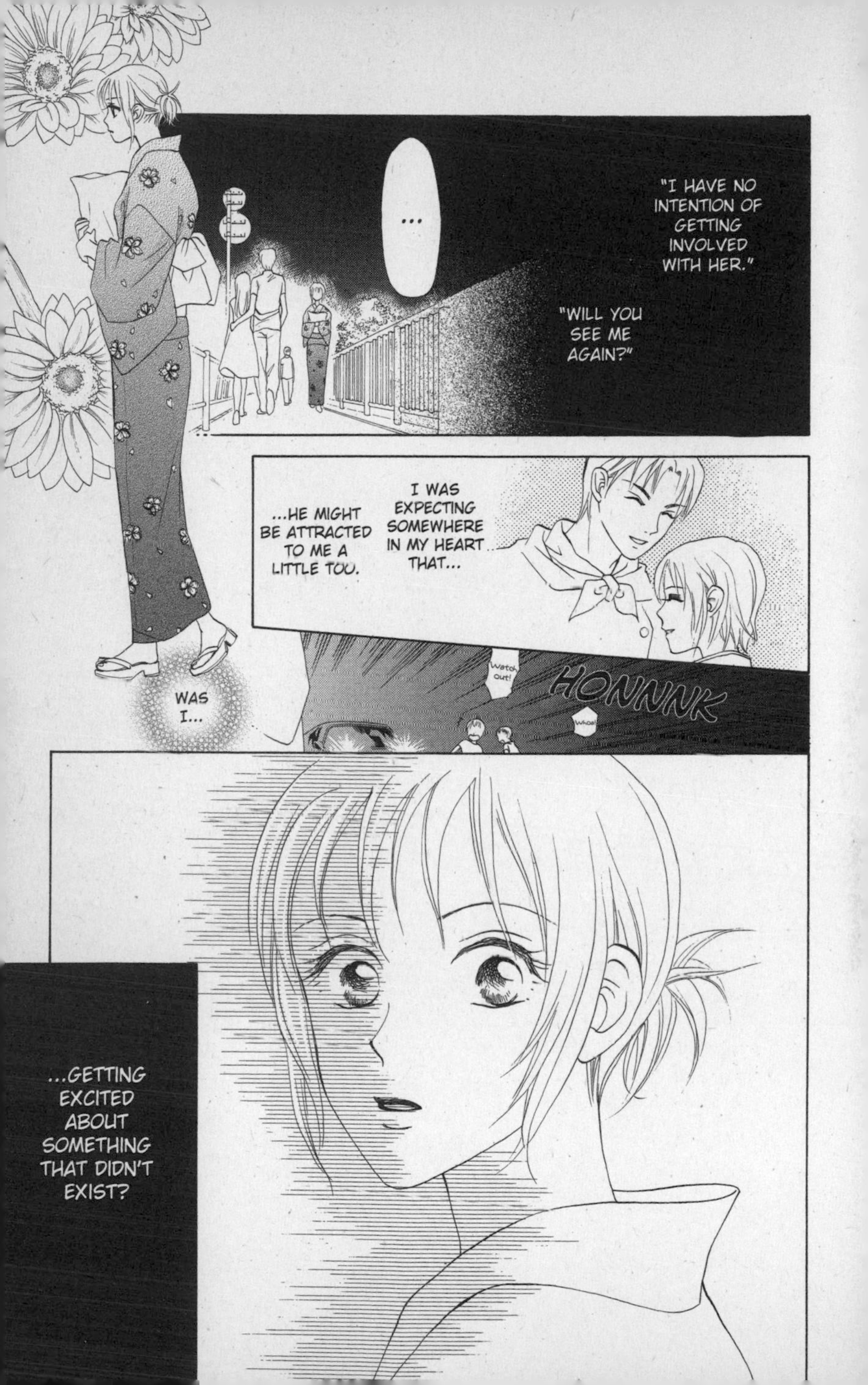
"I HAVE NO INTENTION OF GETTING INVOLVED WITH HER."
"WILL YOU SEE ME AGAIN?"
...
I WAS EXPECTING SOMEWHERE IN MY HEART THAT...
...HE MIGHT BE ATTRACTED TO ME A LITTLE TOO.
HONNNK
Watch out!
Whoa!
WAS I...
...GETTING EXCITED ABOUT SOMETHING THAT DIDN'T EXIST?

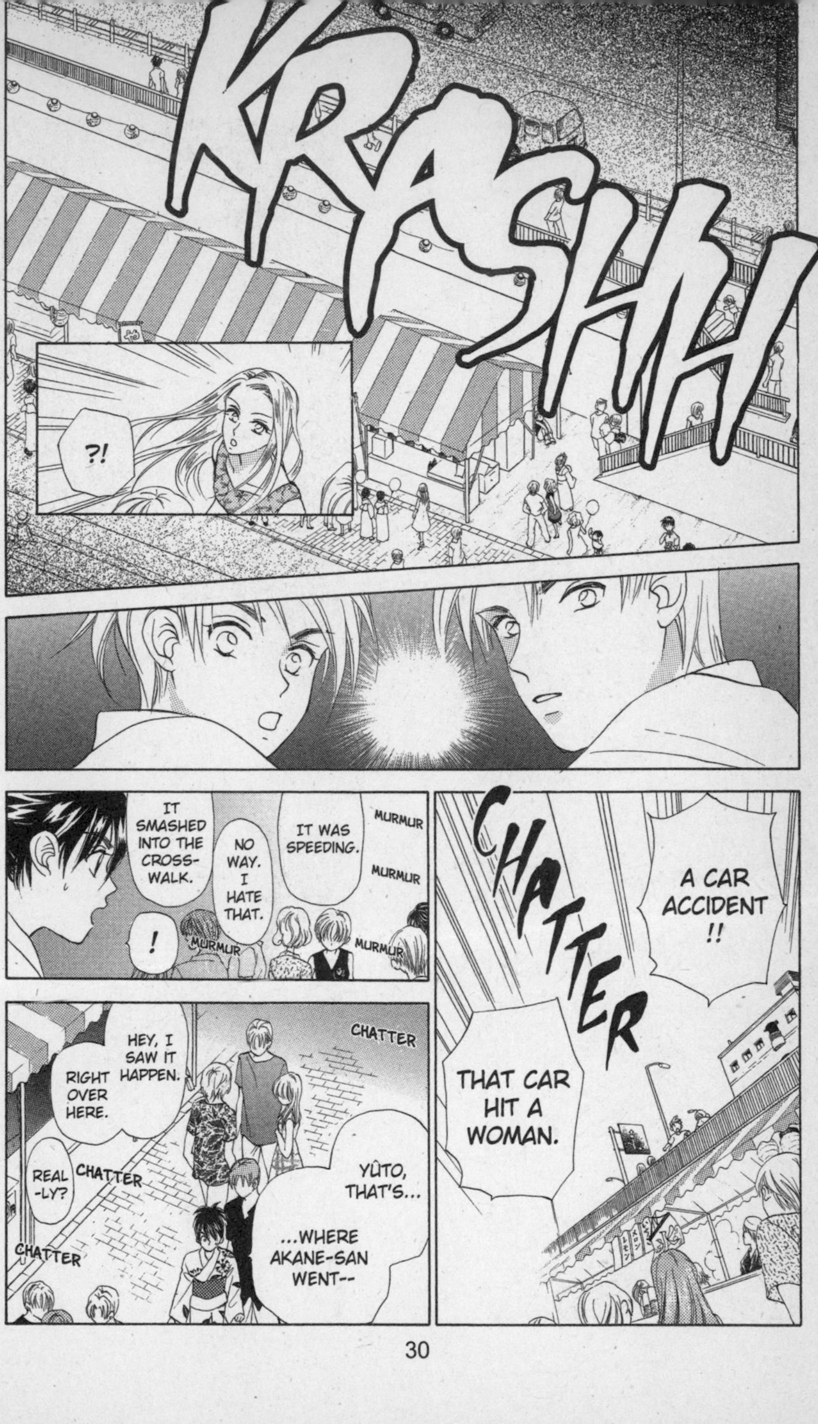
KRASHH
?!
CHATTER
A CAR ACCIDENT !!
THAT CAR HIT A WOMAN.
MURMUR
IT WAS SPEEDING.
MURMUR
NO WAY. I HATE THAT.
IT SMASHED INTO THE CROSS-WALK.
MURMUR
!
MURMUR
CHATTER
HEY, I SAW IT HAPPEN.
RIGHT OVER HERE.
YÛTO, THAT'S...
REAL-LY?
CHATTER
...WHERE AKANE-SAN WENT--
CHATTER

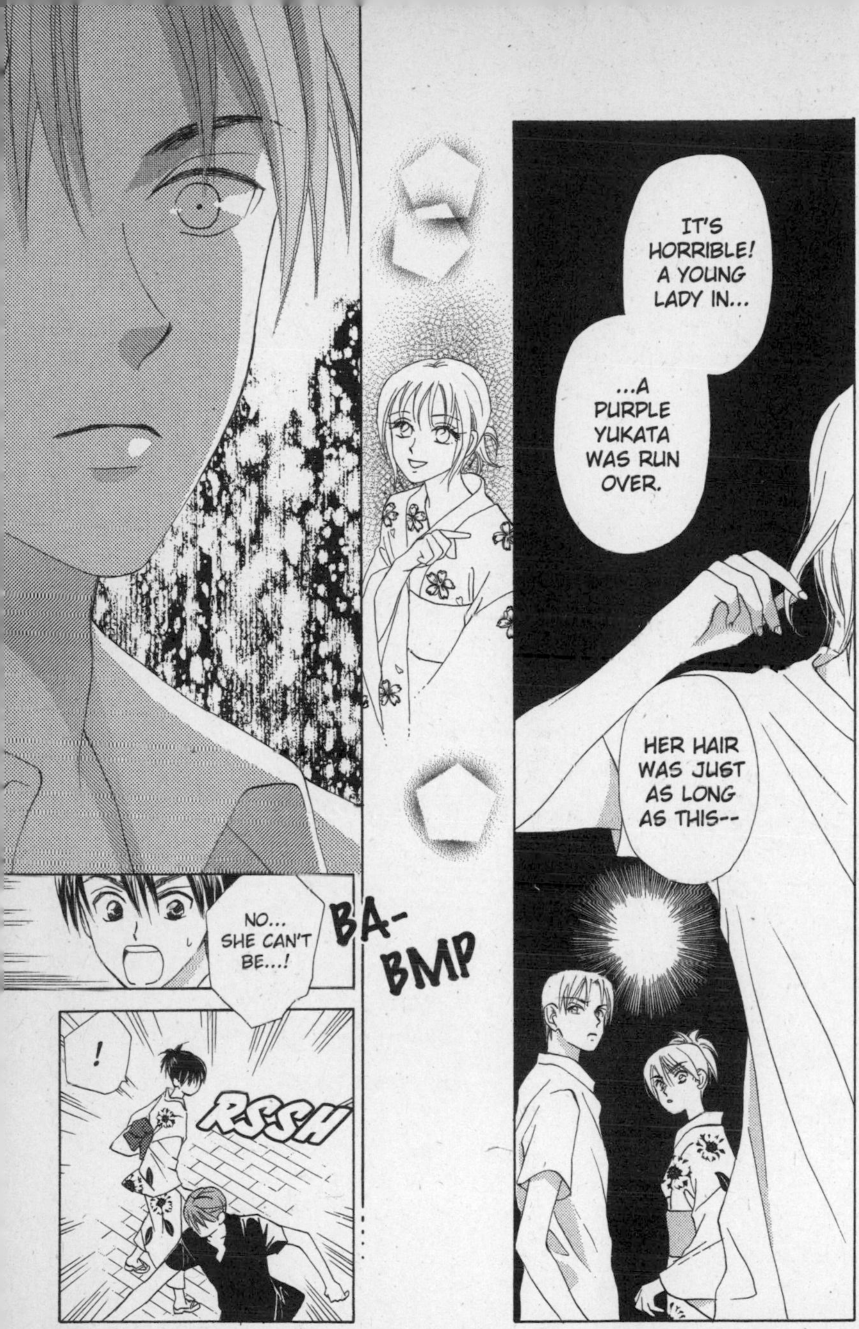
IT'S HORRIBLE! A YOUNG LADY IN...
...A PURPLE YUKATA WAS RUN OVER.
HER HAIR WAS JUST AS LONG AS THIS--
NO... SHE CAN'T BE...!
BA-BMP
!
RSSH

I CAN'T HELP IT. IF I DON'T DO THIS, I CAN'T RUN!

LOOK AT YOU!

CHATTER

CHATTER

YÛTO ...!

HE RAN OFF TO SEE THE ACCIDENT.

HE'S WORRIED IT MIGHT BE AKANE-SAN.

WHAT ABOUT YÛTO-SAN?

LOOK, WE DON'T KNOW YET.

NO WAY...!

BUT YÛTO IMMEDIATELY BOLTED.

THAT SHOWS HOW MUCH HE CARES!

ITO-SAN!

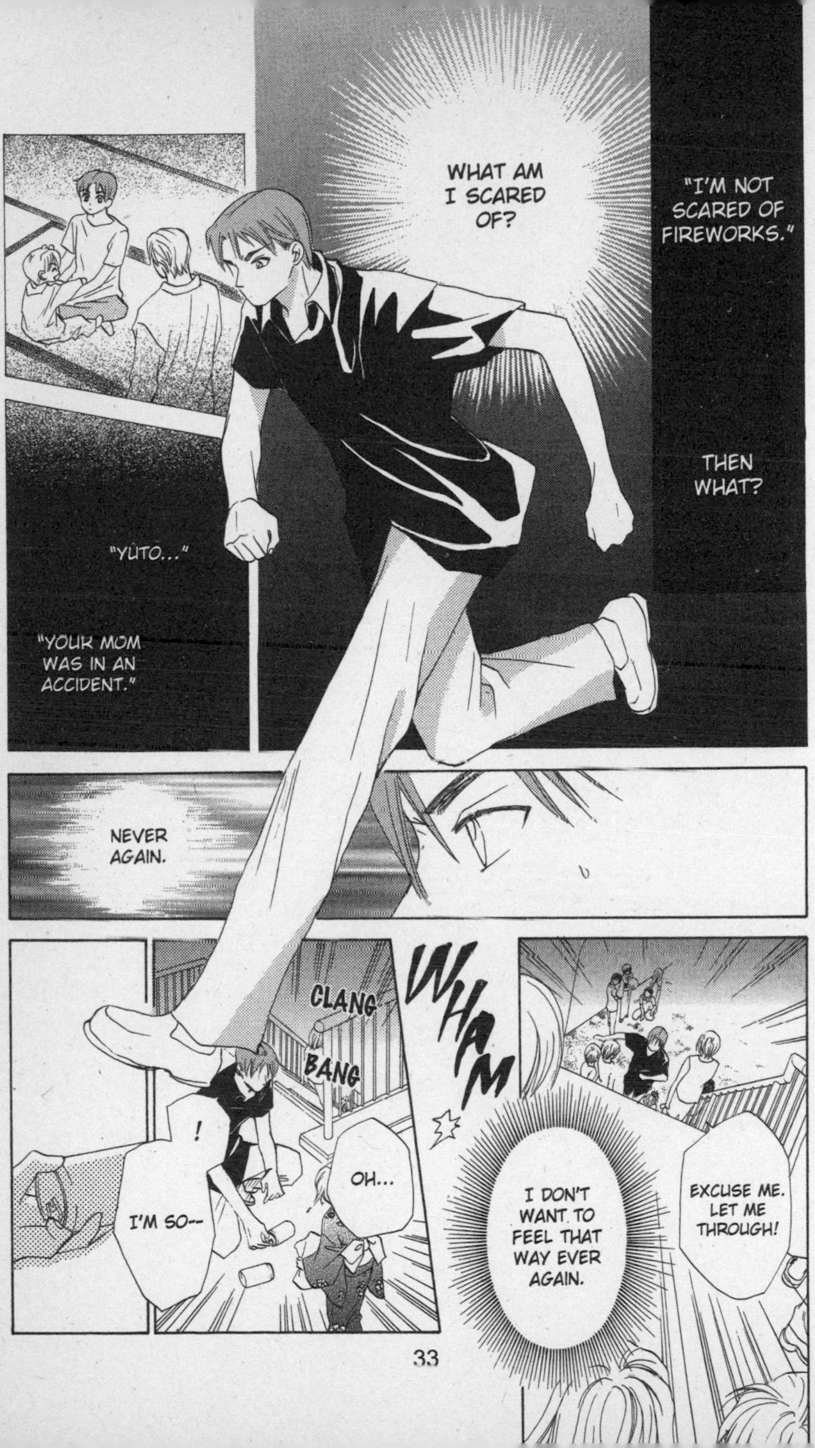
"I'M NOT SCARED OF FIREWORKS."
THEN WHAT?
WHAT AM I SCARED OF?
"YUTO..."
"YOUR MOM WAS IN AN ACCIDENT."
NEVER AGAIN.
EXCUSE ME. LET ME THROUGH!
I DON'T WANT TO FEEL THAT WAY EVER AGAIN.
WHAM
CLANG
BANG
OH...
!
I'M SO--

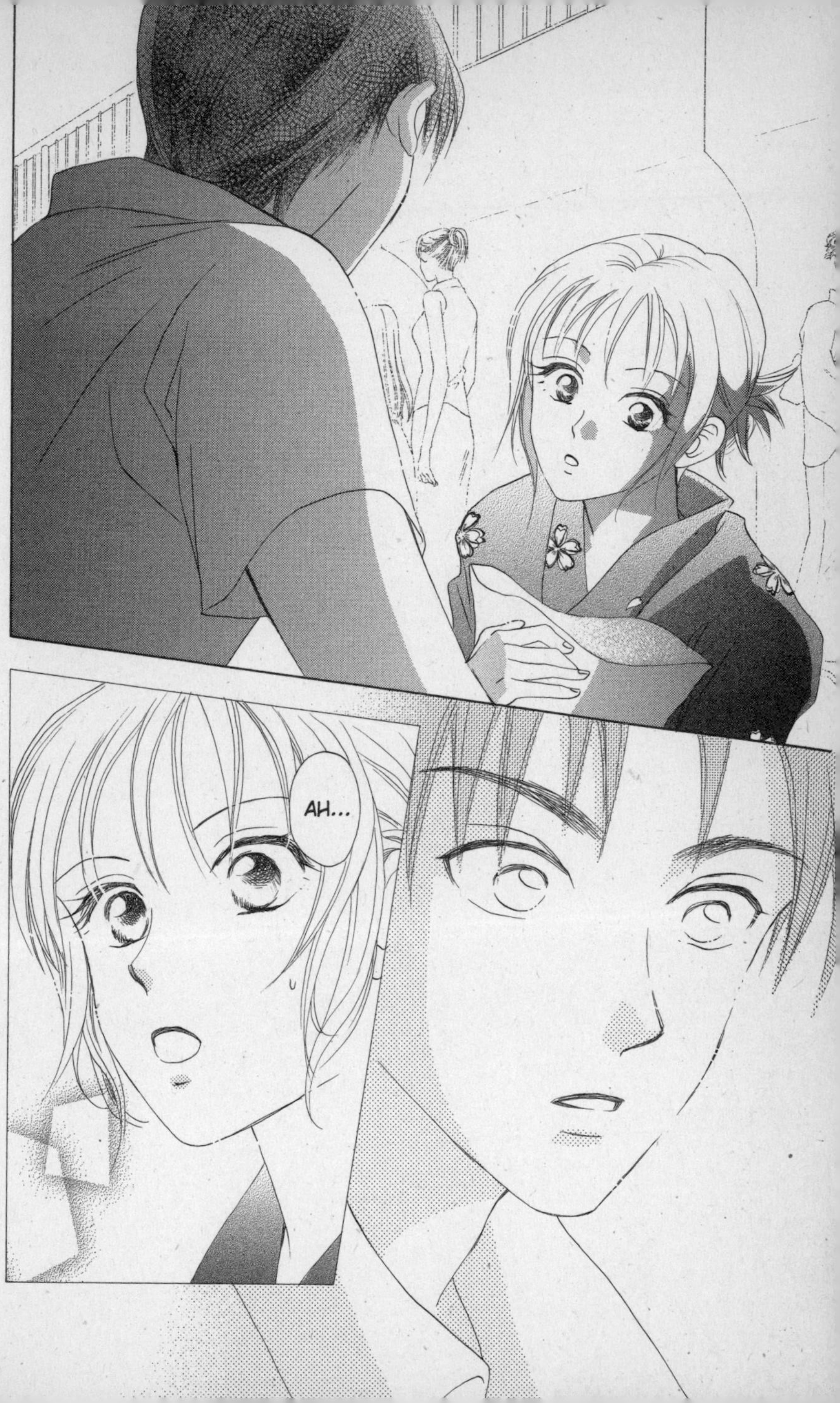
AH...

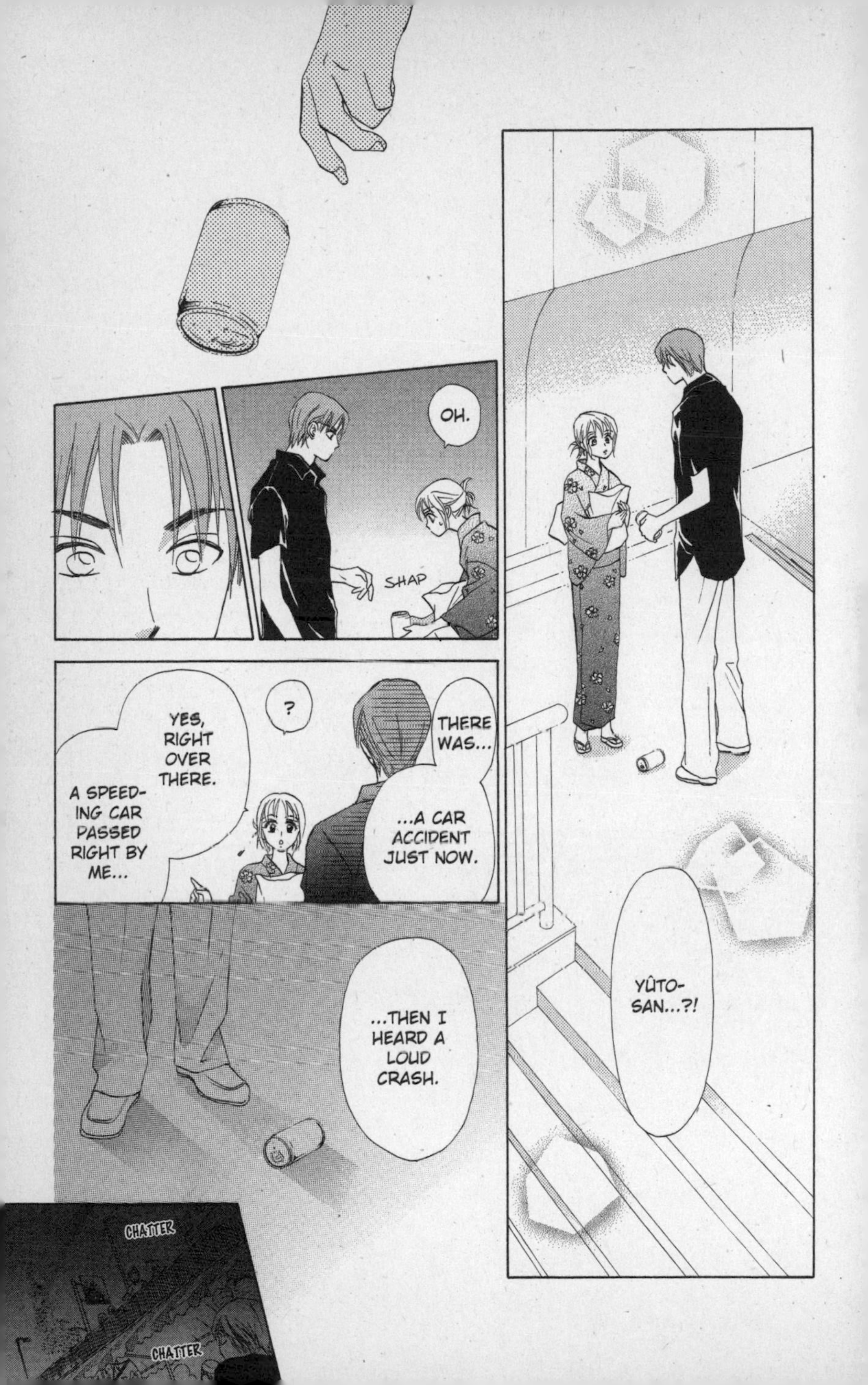
YÛTO-SAN...?!
OH.
SHAP
THERE WAS...
...A CAR ACCIDENT JUST NOW.
?
YES, RIGHT OVER THERE.
A SPEEDING CAR PASSED RIGHT BY ME...
...THEN I HEARD A LOUD CRASH.
CHATTER
CHATTER

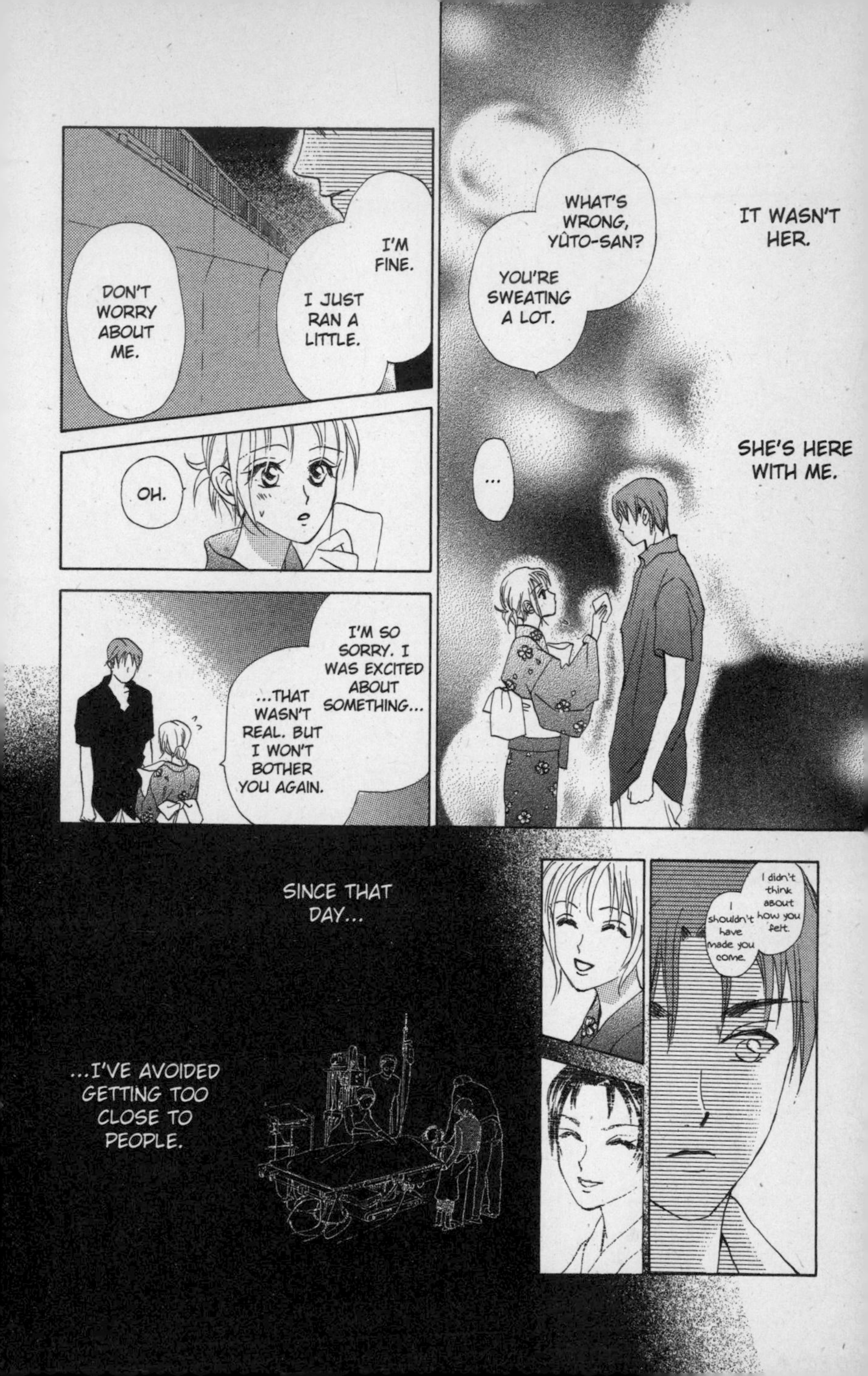
IT WASN'T HER.
WHAT'S WRONG, YÛTO-SAN?
YOU'RE SWEATING A LOT.
SHE'S HERE WITH ME.
...
I'M FINE.
I JUST RAN A LITTLE.
DON'T WORRY ABOUT ME.
OH.
I'M SO SORRY. I WAS EXCITED ABOUT SOMETHING...
...THAT WASN'T REAL. BUT I WON'T BOTHER YOU AGAIN.
I didn't think about how you felt.
I shouldn't have made you come.
SINCE THAT DAY...
...I'VE AVOIDED GETTING TOO CLOSE TO PEOPLE.

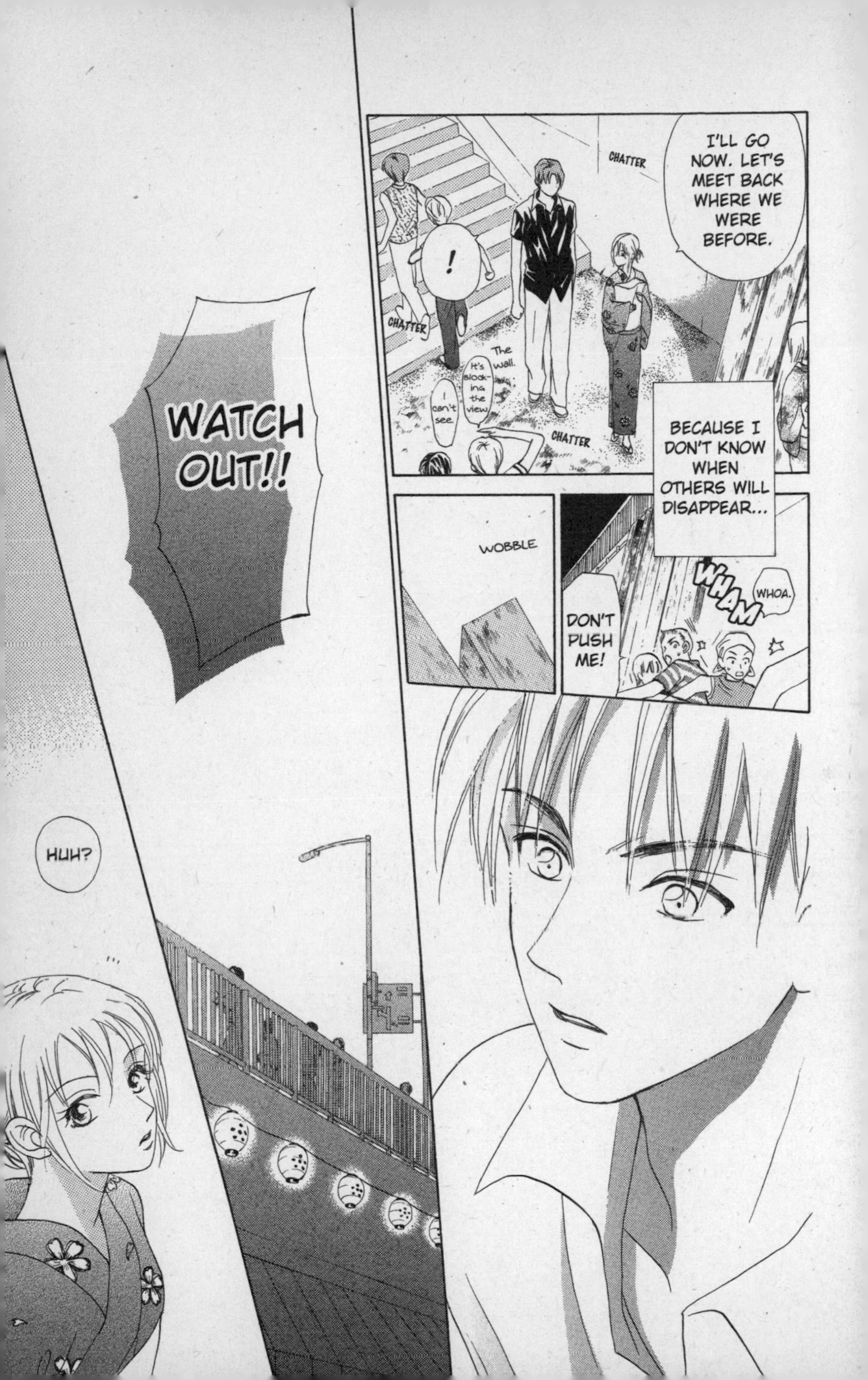
I'LL GO NOW. LET'S MEET BACK WHERE WE WERE BEFORE.
CHATTER
!
CHATTER
The wall.
It's blocking the view.
I can't see.
CHATTER
BECAUSE I DON'T KNOW WHEN OTHERS WILL DISAPPEAR...
WHAM
WHOA.
DON'T PUSH ME!
WOBBLE
WATCH OUT!!
HUH?
...

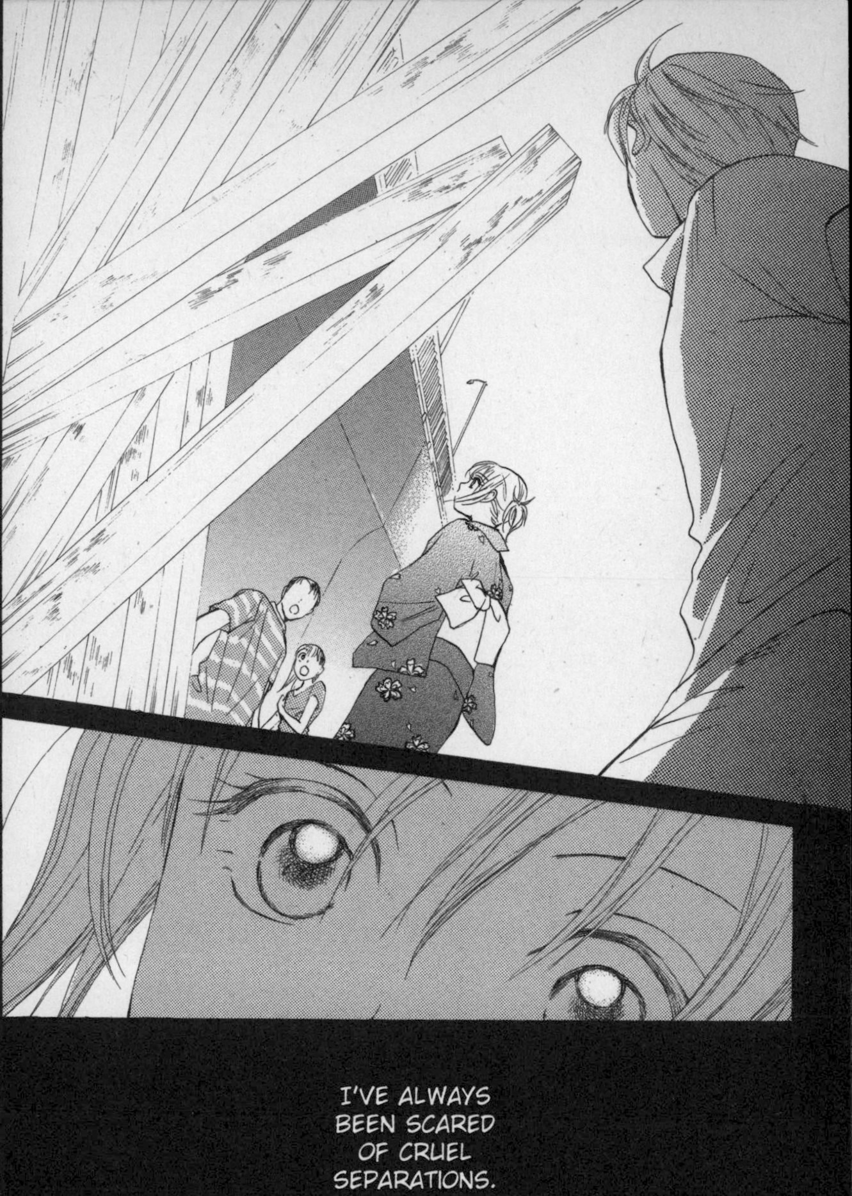
I'VE ALWAYS BEEN SCARED OF CRUEL SEPARATIONS.

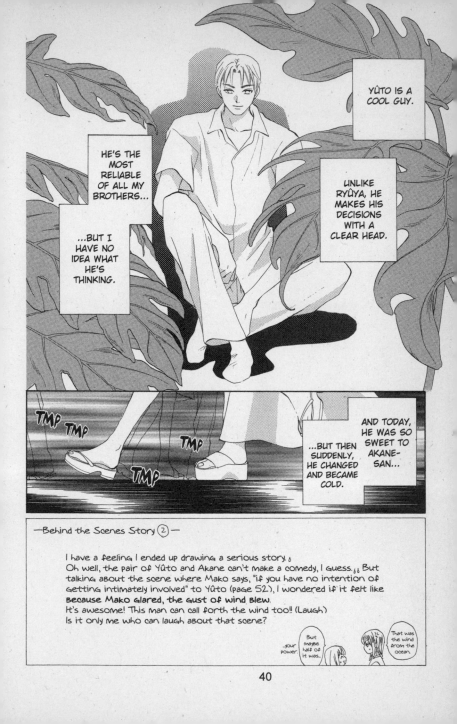

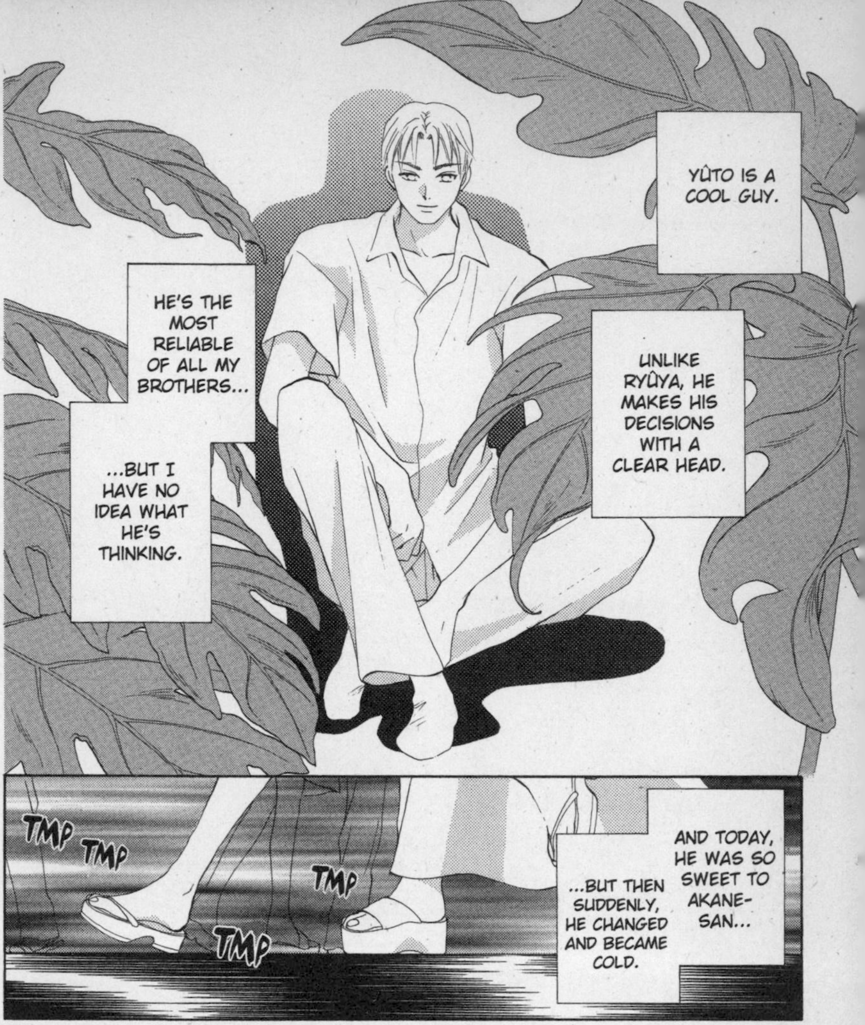
YÛTO IS A COOL GUY.
UNLIKE RYÛYA, HE MAKES HIS DECISIONS WITH A CLEAR HEAD.
HE'S THE MOST RELIABLE OF ALL MY BROTHERS...
...BUT I HAVE NO IDEA WHAT HE'S THINKING.
AND TODAY, HE WAS SO SWEET TO AKANE-SAN...
...BUT THEN SUDDENLY, HE CHANGED AND BECAME COLD.
TMP
TMP
TMP
TMP

—Behind the Scenes Story ②—

I have a feeling I ended up drawing a serious story.
Oh well, the pair of Yûto and Akane can't make a comedy, I guess. But talking about the scene where Mako says, "if you have no intention of getting intimately involved" to Yûto (page 52), I wondered if it felt like **because Mako glared, the gust of wind blew**.
It's awesome! This man can call forth the wind too!! (Laugh)
Is it only me who can laugh about that scene?

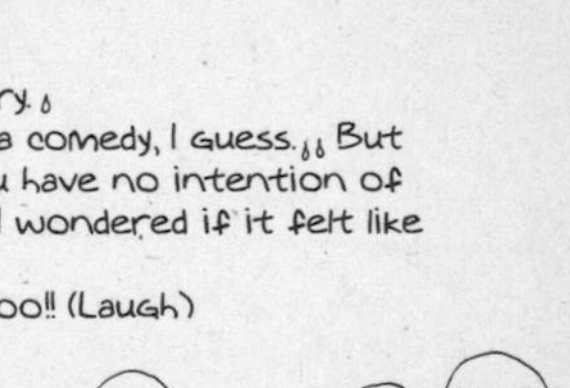
That was the wind from the ocean.
But maybe half of it was...
...your power.

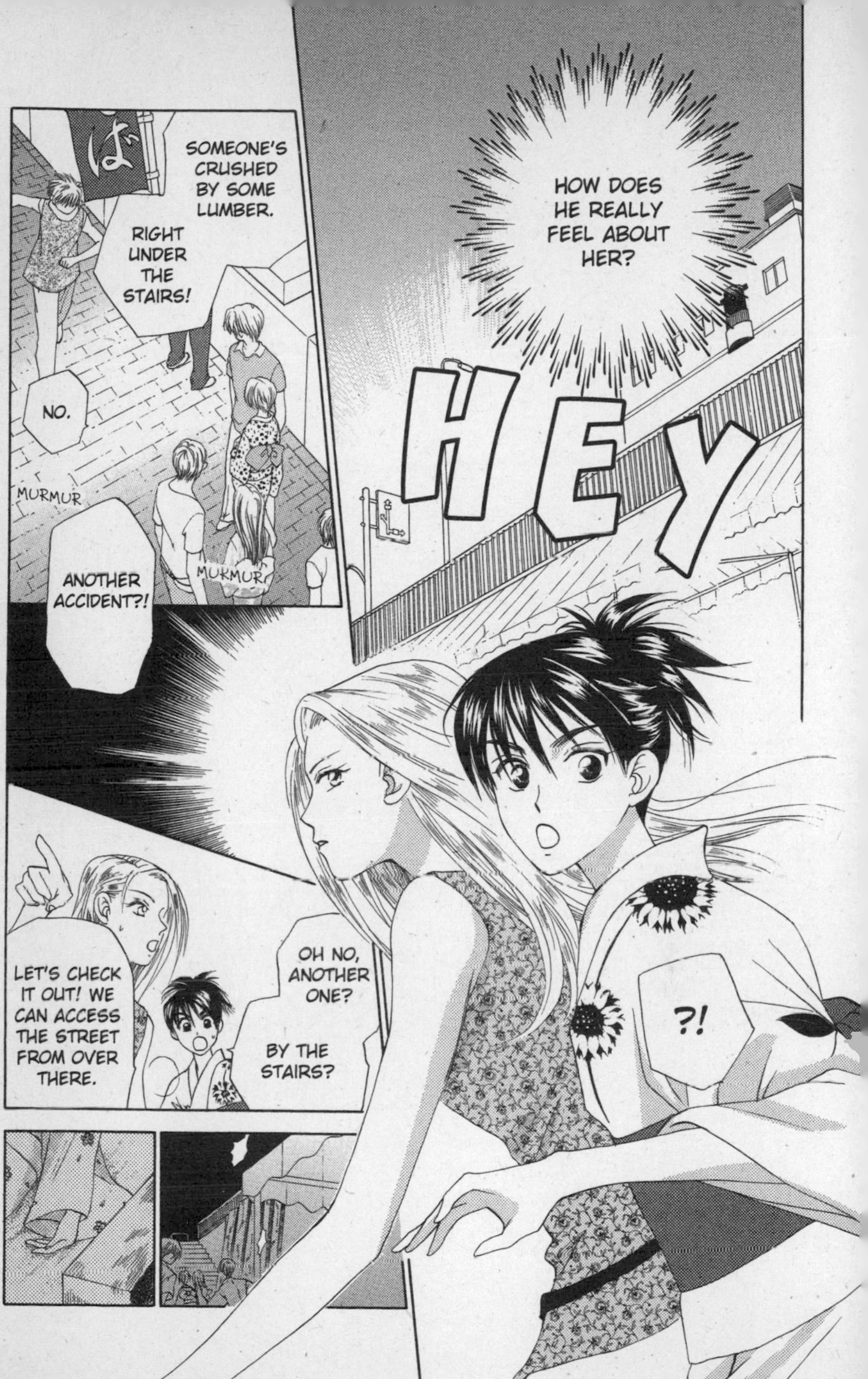
HOW DOES HE REALLY FEEL ABOUT HER?
HEY
SOMEONE'S CRUSHED BY SOME LUMBER.
RIGHT UNDER THE STAIRS!
NO.
MURMUR
MURMUR
ANOTHER ACCIDENT?!
?!
OH NO, ANOTHER ONE?
BY THE STAIRS?
LET'S CHECK IT OUT! WE CAN ACCESS THE STREET FROM OVER THERE.

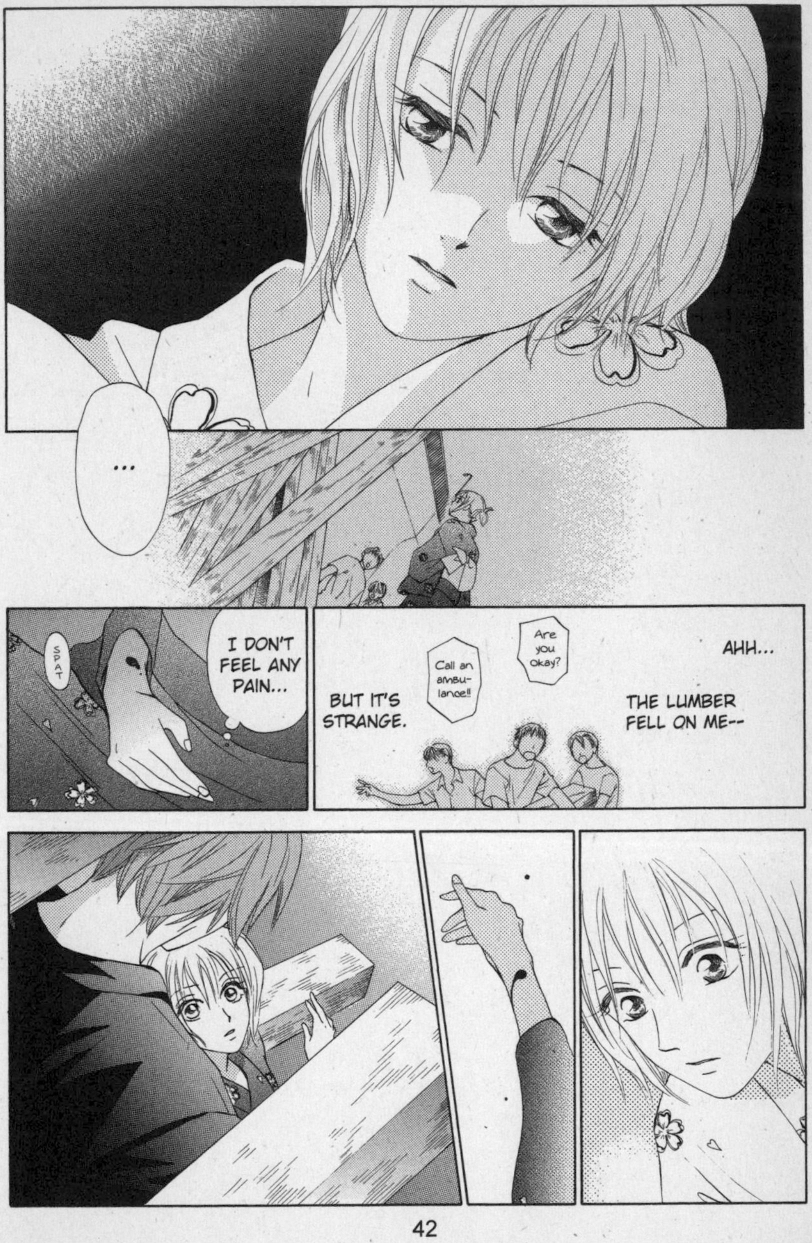
...
AHH...
Are you okay?
THE LUMBER FELL ON ME--
Call an ambulance!!
BUT IT'S STRANGE.
I DON'T FEEL ANY PAIN...
SPAT

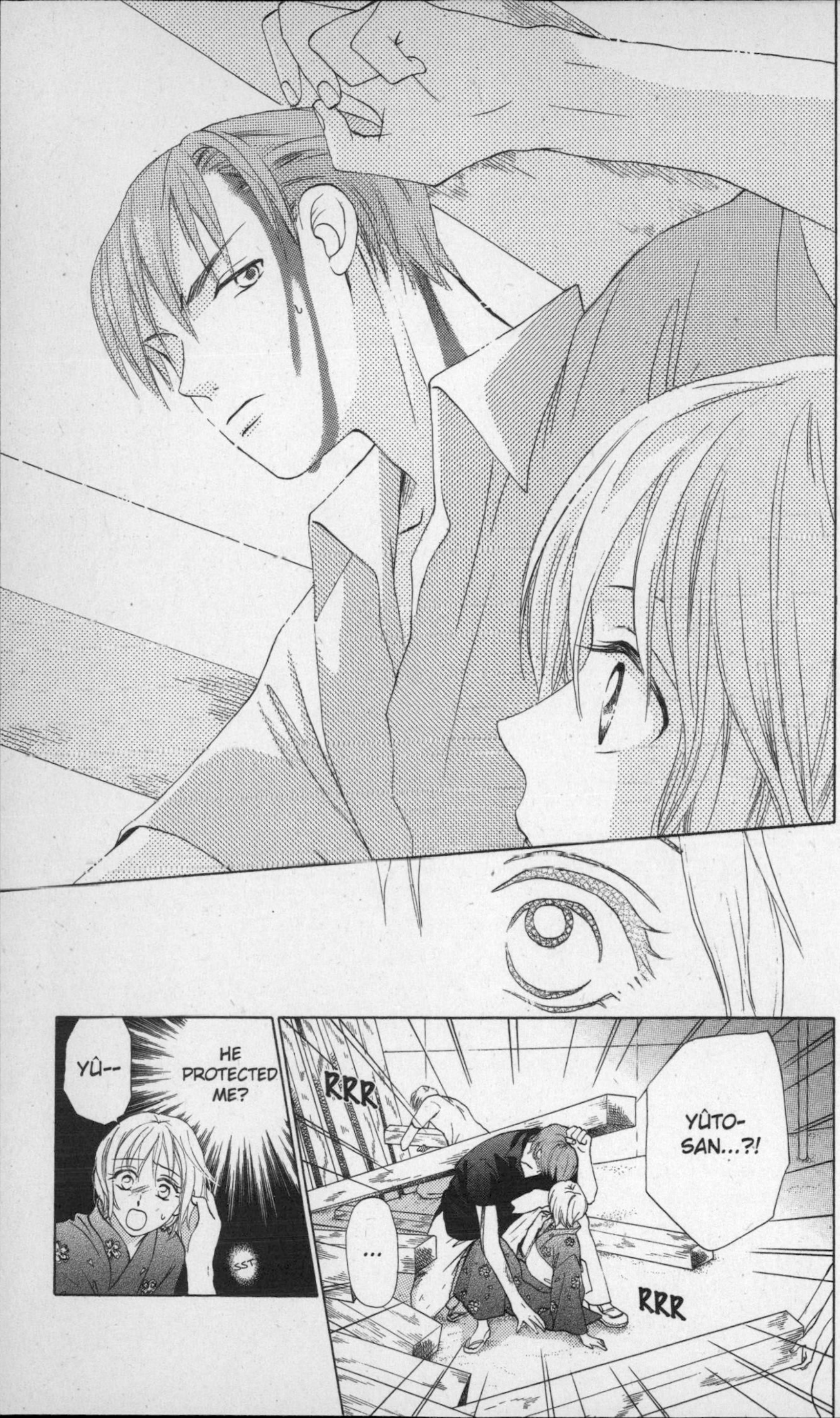
YÛTO-SAN...?!
RRR
...
RRR
HE PROTECTED ME?
YÛ--
SST

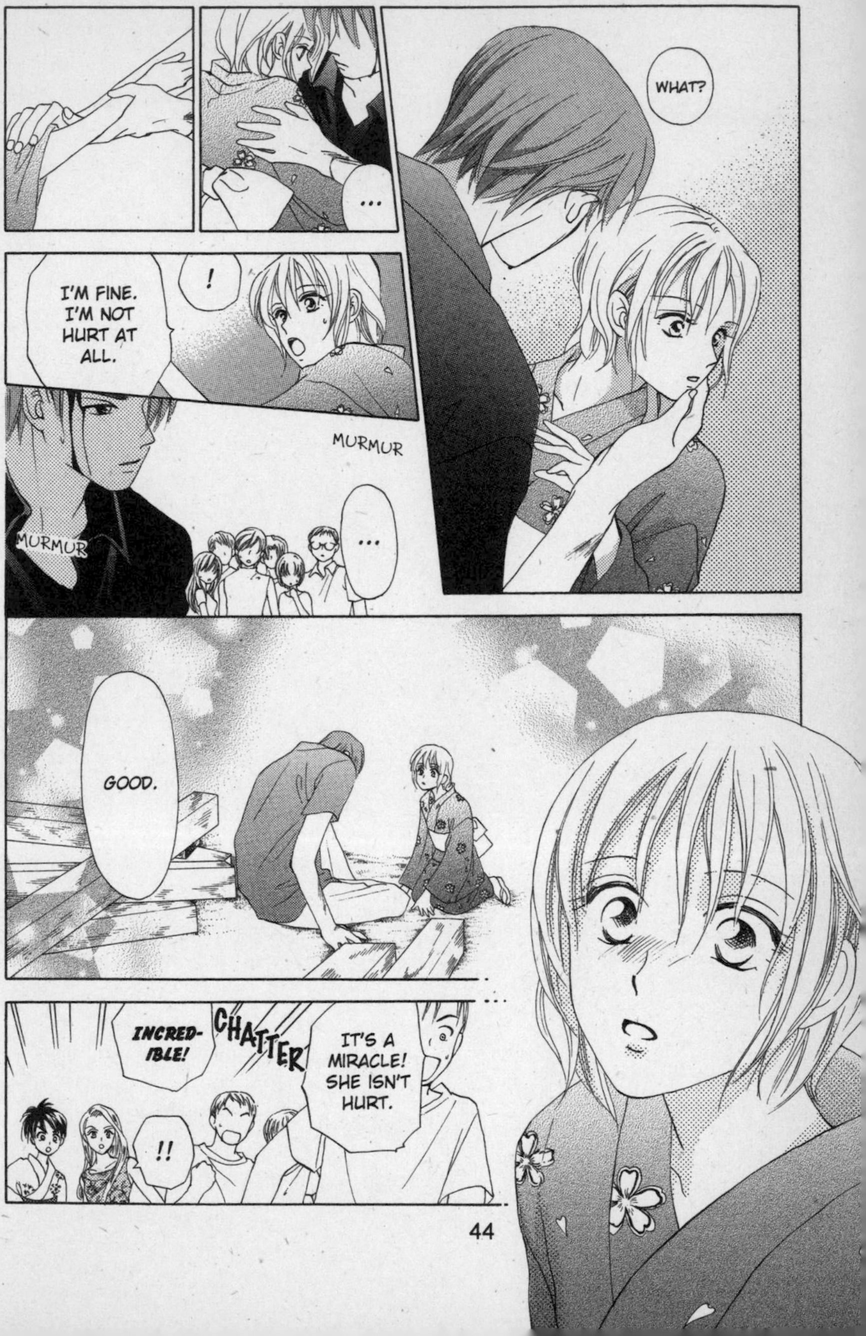
WHAT?
...
!
I'M FINE. I'M NOT HURT AT ALL.
MURMUR
...
MURMUR
...
GOOD.
IT'S A MIRACLE! SHE ISN'T HURT.
CHATTER
INCREDIBLE!
!!

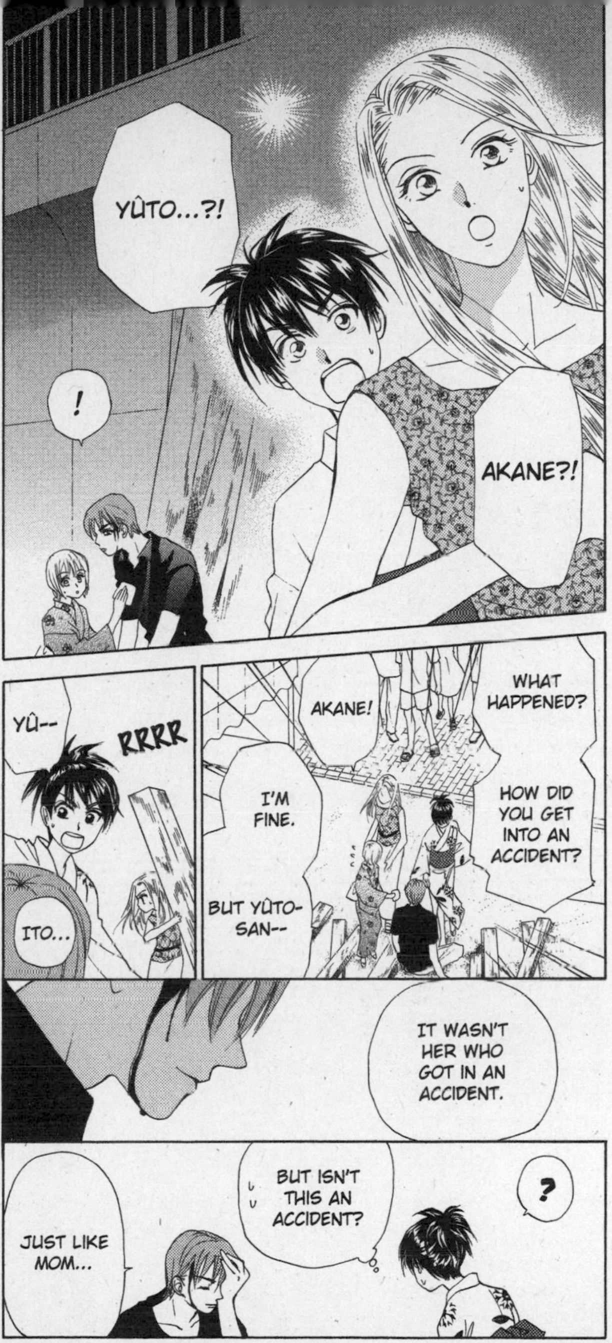
YÛTO...?!
AKANE?!
!
WHAT HAPPENED?
AKANE!
HOW DID YOU GET INTO AN ACCIDENT?
I'M FINE.
BUT YÛTO-SAN--
YÛ--
RRRR
ITO...
IT WASN'T HER WHO GOT IN AN ACCIDENT.
?
BUT ISN'T THIS AN ACCIDENT?
JUST LIKE MOM...

HOW MANY ASSISTANTS DO YOU HAVE?

Well, it depends on what I'm working on, but currently, I have about five regular assistants (including my sister).

*Shirômaru-san
*Taneda-san
*Sano-san
*Oono-san
*My sister, Sayaka

Although she's so busy that she's hard to get but I also have:
*Wakamatsu-san

(Note) It's only on the very last day before the work is due when all of them come in.

That makes four to six of us including me.

Everyone has a different schedule and some work as assistants to others too. That's why not all of us are working together all the time. The reality is, each of us takes on where the others leave off, and somehow we manage it all right.

If I find myself in a pinch and can't get enough assistants, I contact Mr. Editor-in-charge, who'll find me additional temporary assistants.

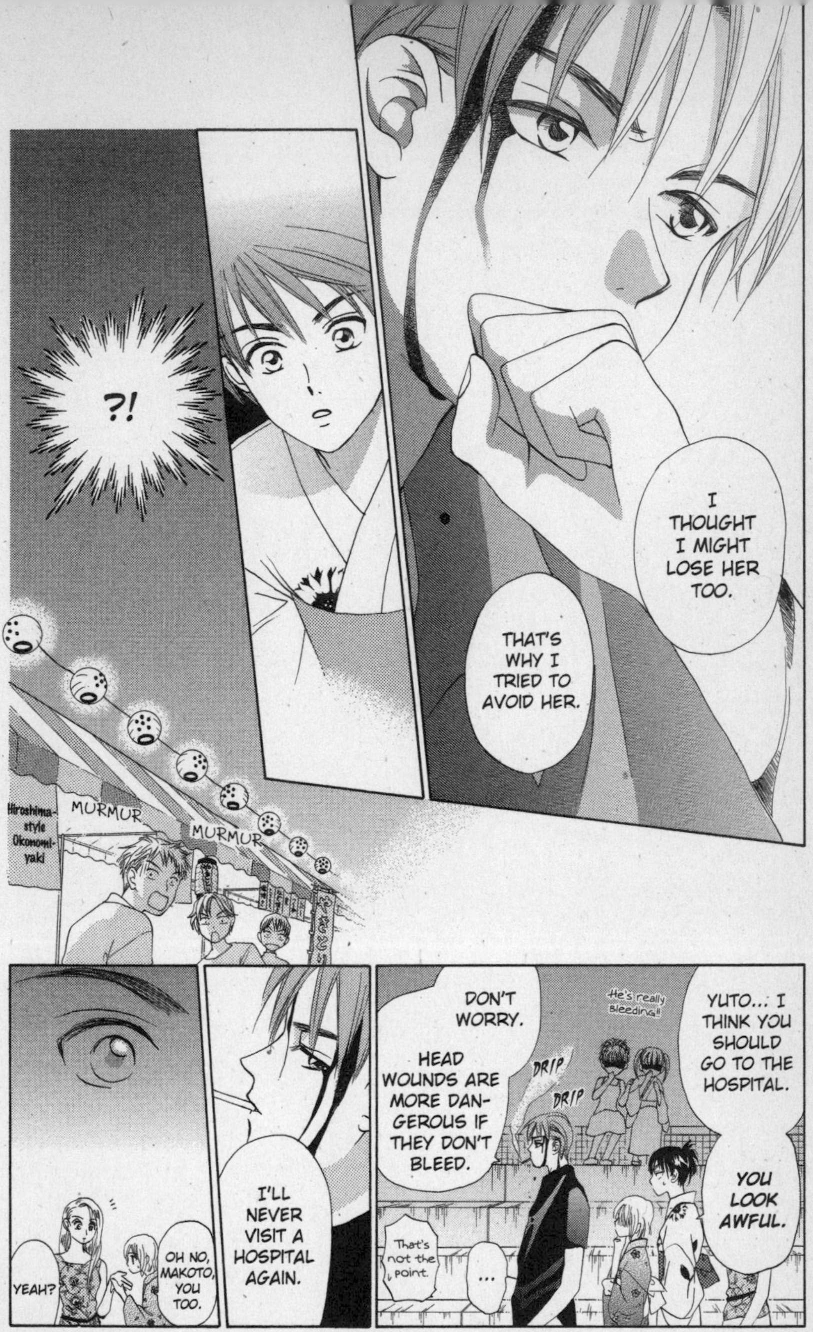
I THOUGHT I MIGHT LOSE HER TOO.
THAT'S WHY I TRIED TO AVOID HER.
?!
MURMUR
MURMUR
Hiroshima-style Okonomiyaki
YUTO...: I THINK YOU SHOULD GO TO THE HOSPITAL.
YOU LOOK AWFUL.
He's really bleeding!!
DRIP
DRIP
DON'T WORRY.
HEAD WOUNDS ARE MORE DAN-GEROUS IF THEY DON'T BLEED.
...
That's not the point.
I'LL NEVER VISIT A HOSPITAL AGAIN.
OH NO, MAKOTO, YOU TOO.
YEAH?

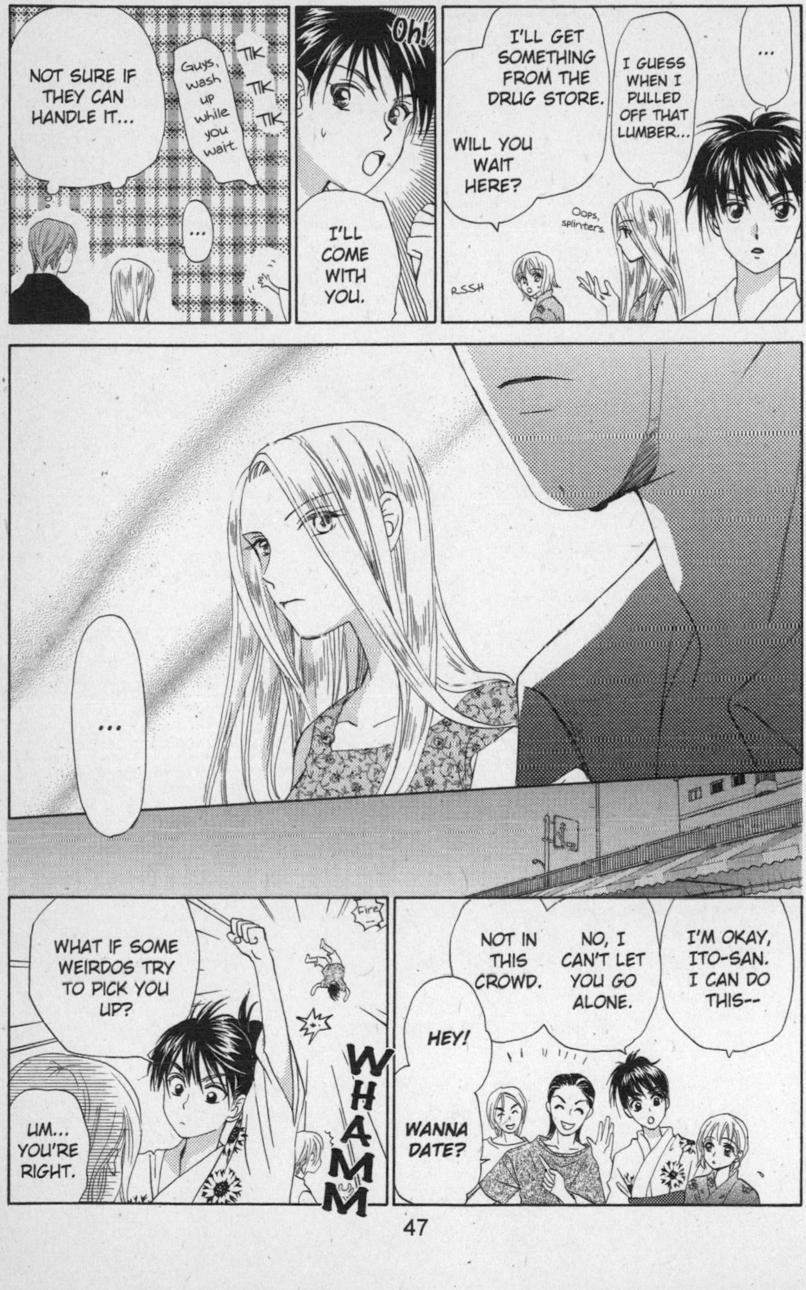
...
I GUESS WHEN I PULLED OFF THAT LUMBER...
Oops, splinters.
I'LL GET SOMETHING FROM THE DRUG STORE.
WILL YOU WAIT HERE?
RSSH
Oh!
I'LL COME WITH YOU.
TIK
TIK
TIK
Guys, wash up while you wait.
NOT SURE IF THEY CAN HANDLE IT...
...
...
I'M OKAY, ITO-SAN. I CAN DO THIS--
NO, I CAN'T LET YOU GO ALONE.
NOT IN THIS CROWD.
HEY!
WANNA DATE?
Fire
WHAT IF SOME WEIRDOS TRY TO PICK YOU UP?
WHAMM
UM... YOU'RE RIGHT.

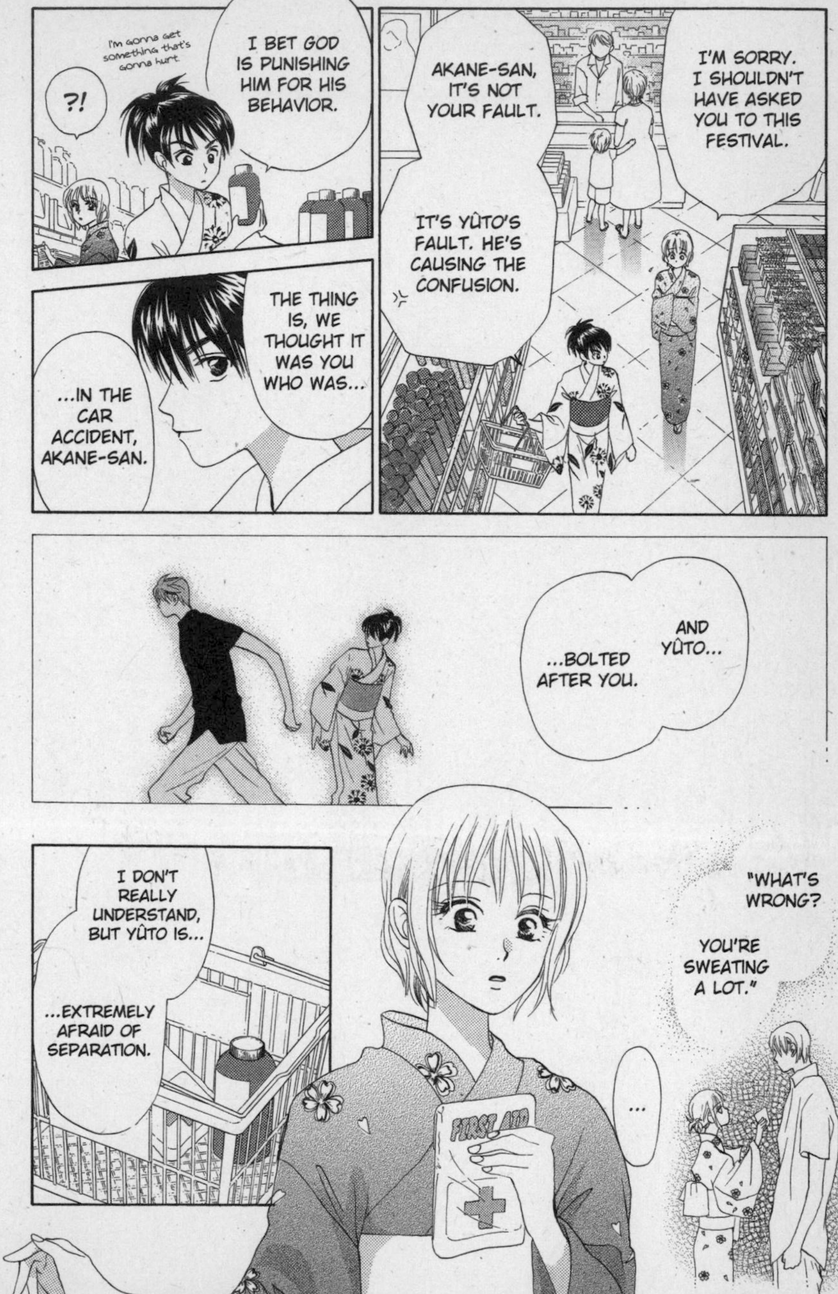
I'M SORRY. I SHOULDN'T HAVE ASKED YOU TO THIS FESTIVAL.
AKANE-SAN, IT'S NOT YOUR FAULT.
IT'S YÛTO'S FAULT. HE'S CAUSING THE CONFUSION.
I BET GOD IS PUNISHING HIM FOR HIS BEHAVIOR.
I'm gonna get something that's gonna hurt.
?!
THE THING IS, WE THOUGHT IT WAS YOU WHO WAS...
...IN THE CAR ACCIDENT, AKANE-SAN.
AND YÛTO...
...BOLTED AFTER YOU.
"WHAT'S WRONG?
YOU'RE SWEATING A LOT."
...
FIRST AID
I DON'T REALLY UNDERSTAND, BUT YÛTO IS...
...EXTREMELY AFRAID OF SEPARATION.

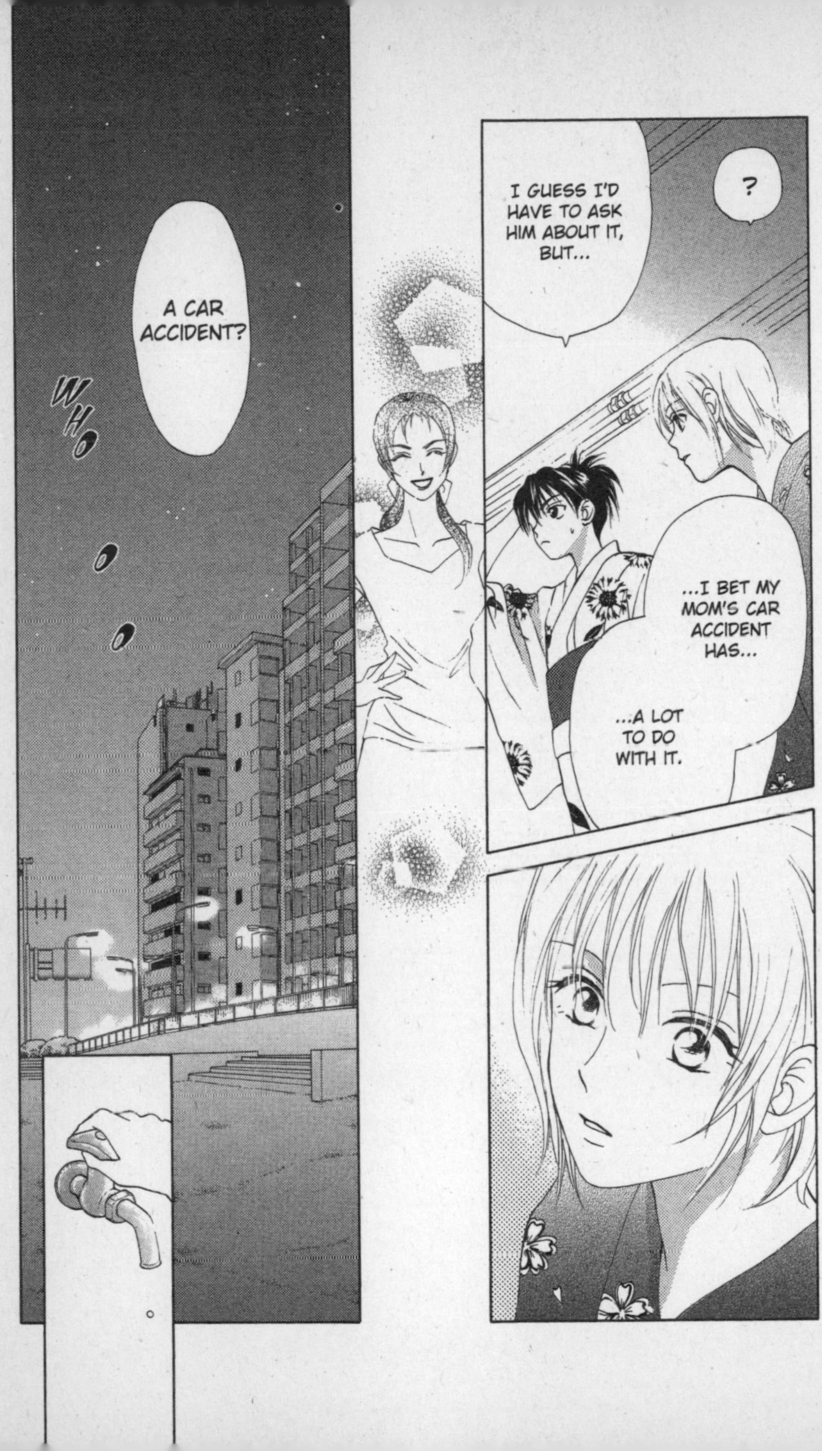
?
I GUESS I'D HAVE TO ASK HIM ABOUT IT, BUT...
...I BET MY MOM'S CAR ACCIDENT HAS...
...A LOT TO DO WITH IT.
A CAR ACCIDENT?
WHOOO

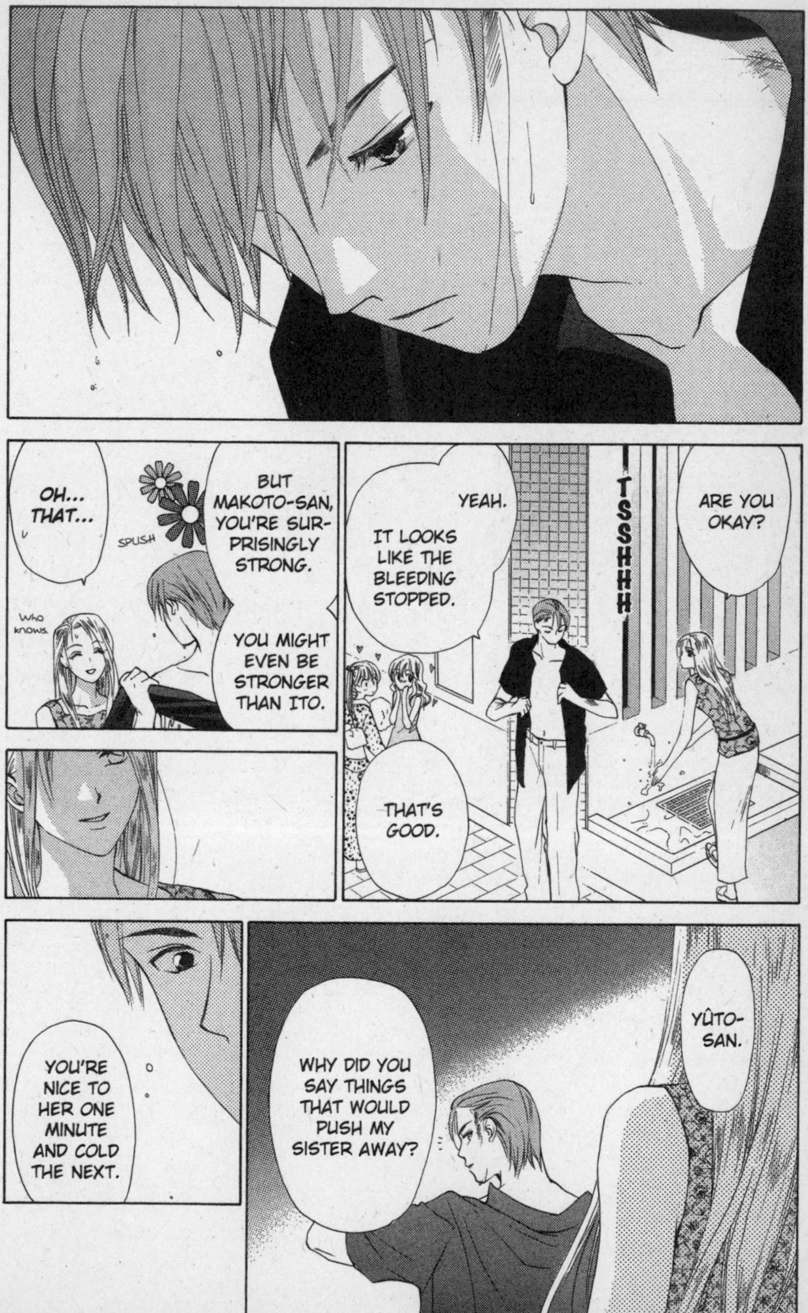
ARE YOU OKAY?
TSSHHH
YEAH.
IT LOOKS LIKE THE BLEEDING STOPPED.
THAT'S GOOD.
BUT MAKOTO-SAN, YOU'RE SURPRISINGLY STRONG.
YOU MIGHT EVEN BE STRONGER THAN ITO.
OH... THAT...
SPLISH
Who knows.
YÛTO-SAN.
WHY DID YOU SAY THINGS THAT WOULD PUSH MY SISTER AWAY?
YOU'RE NICE TO HER ONE MINUTE AND COLD THE NEXT.

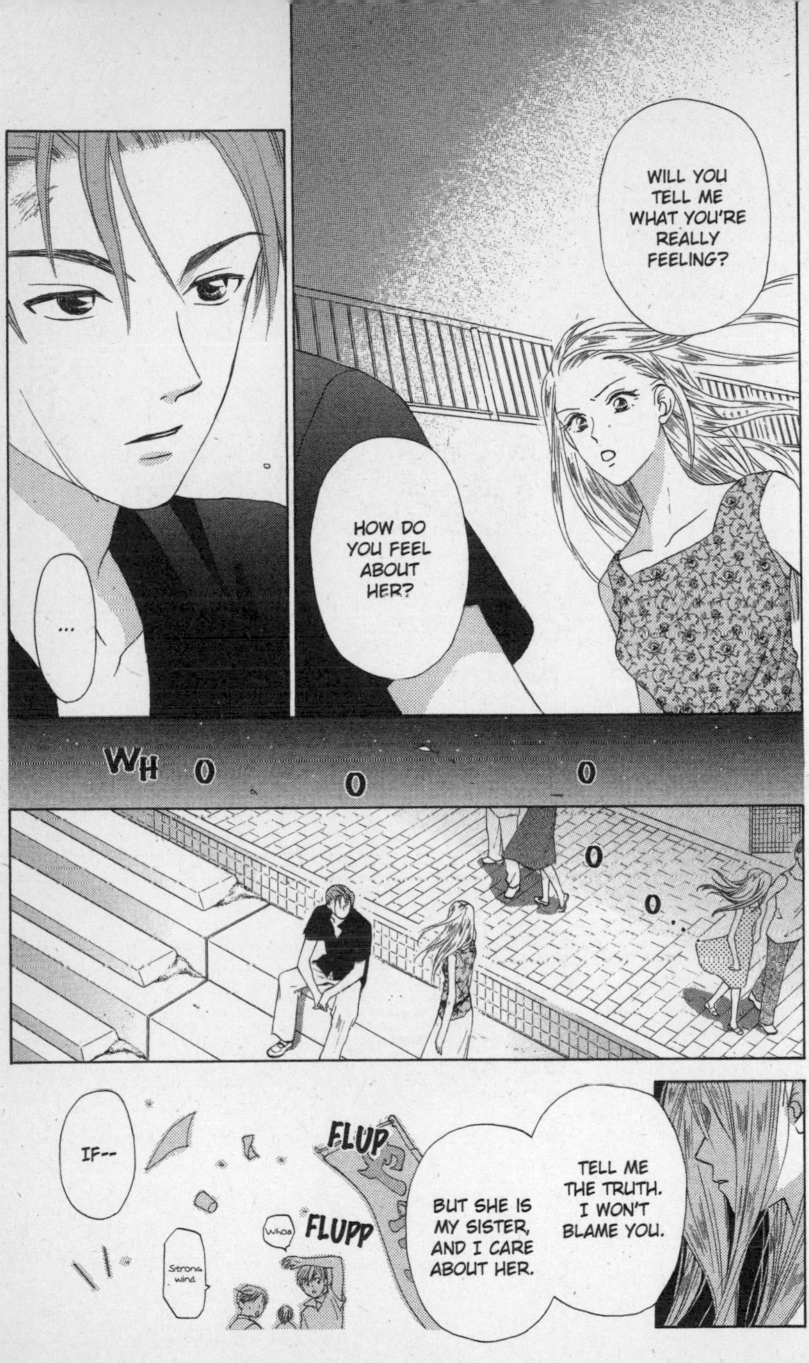
WILL YOU TELL ME WHAT YOU'RE REALLY FEELING?
HOW DO YOU FEEL ABOUT HER?
...
WHOOOOO...
TELL ME THE TRUTH. I WON'T BLAME YOU.
BUT SHE IS MY SISTER, AND I CARE ABOUT HER.
FLUP
FLUPP
Whoa
Strong wind
IF--

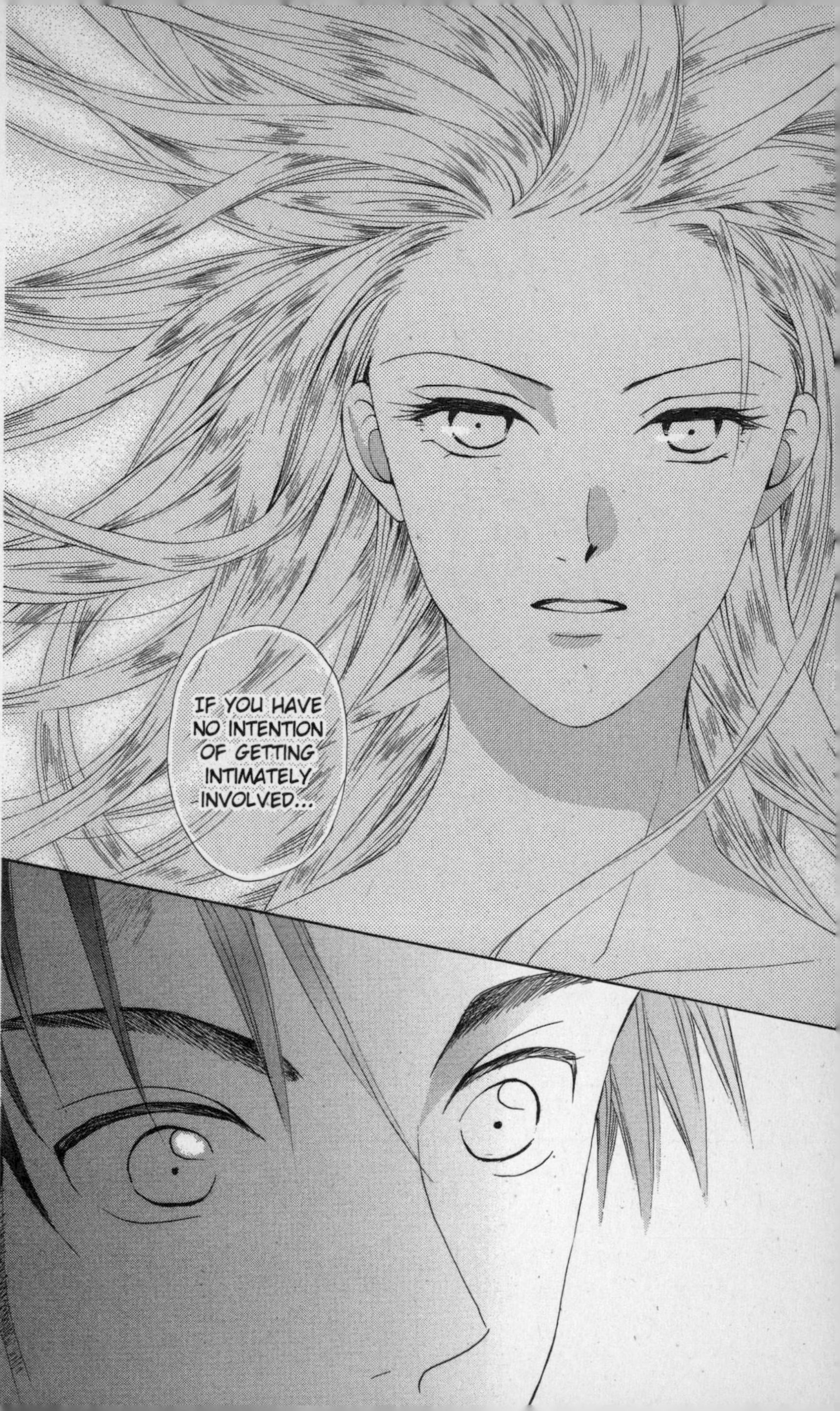
IF YOU HAVE NO INTENTION OF GETTING INTIMATELY INVOLVED...

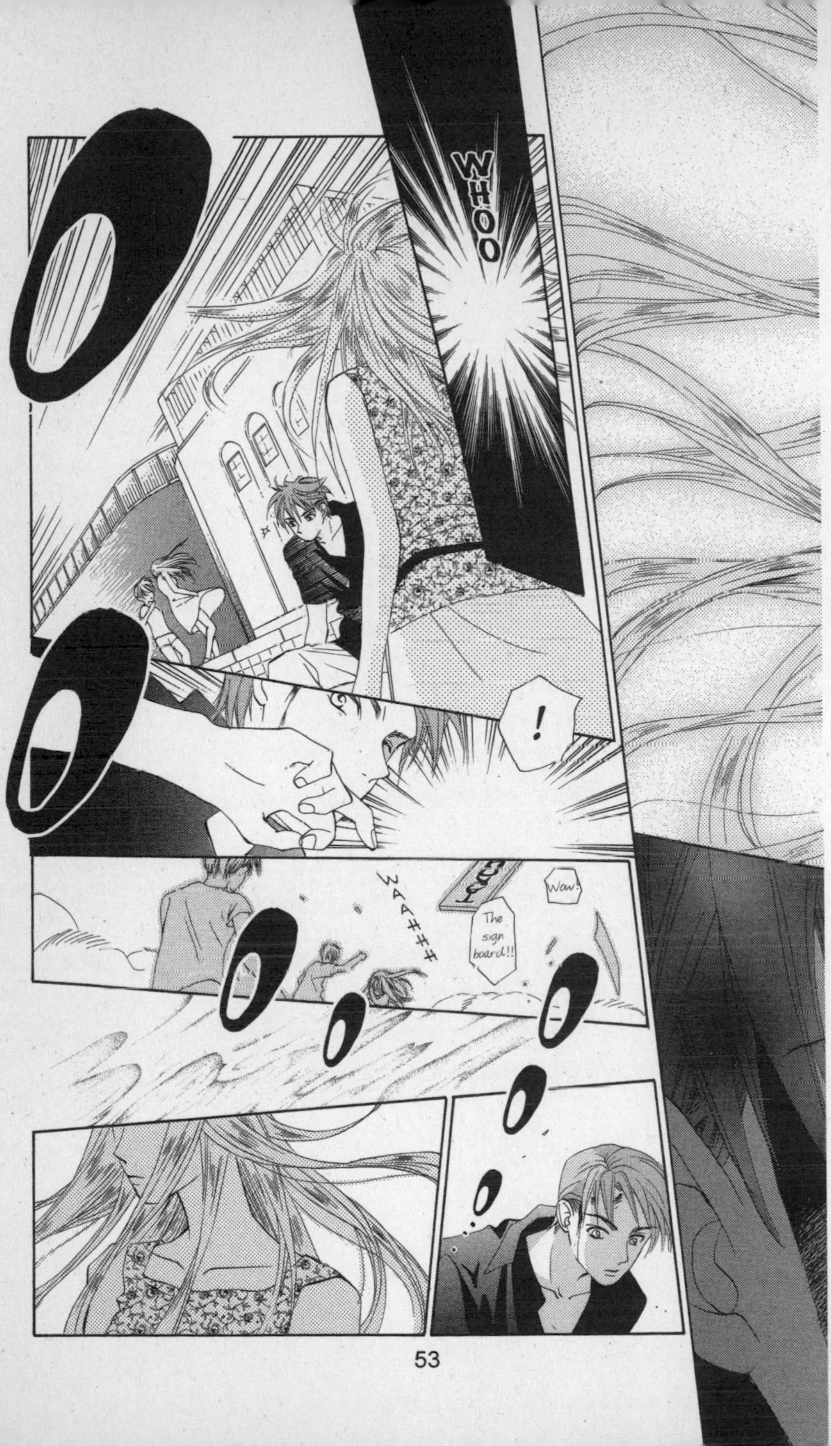
WHOO
!
Wow!
The sign board!!
WAAHHH

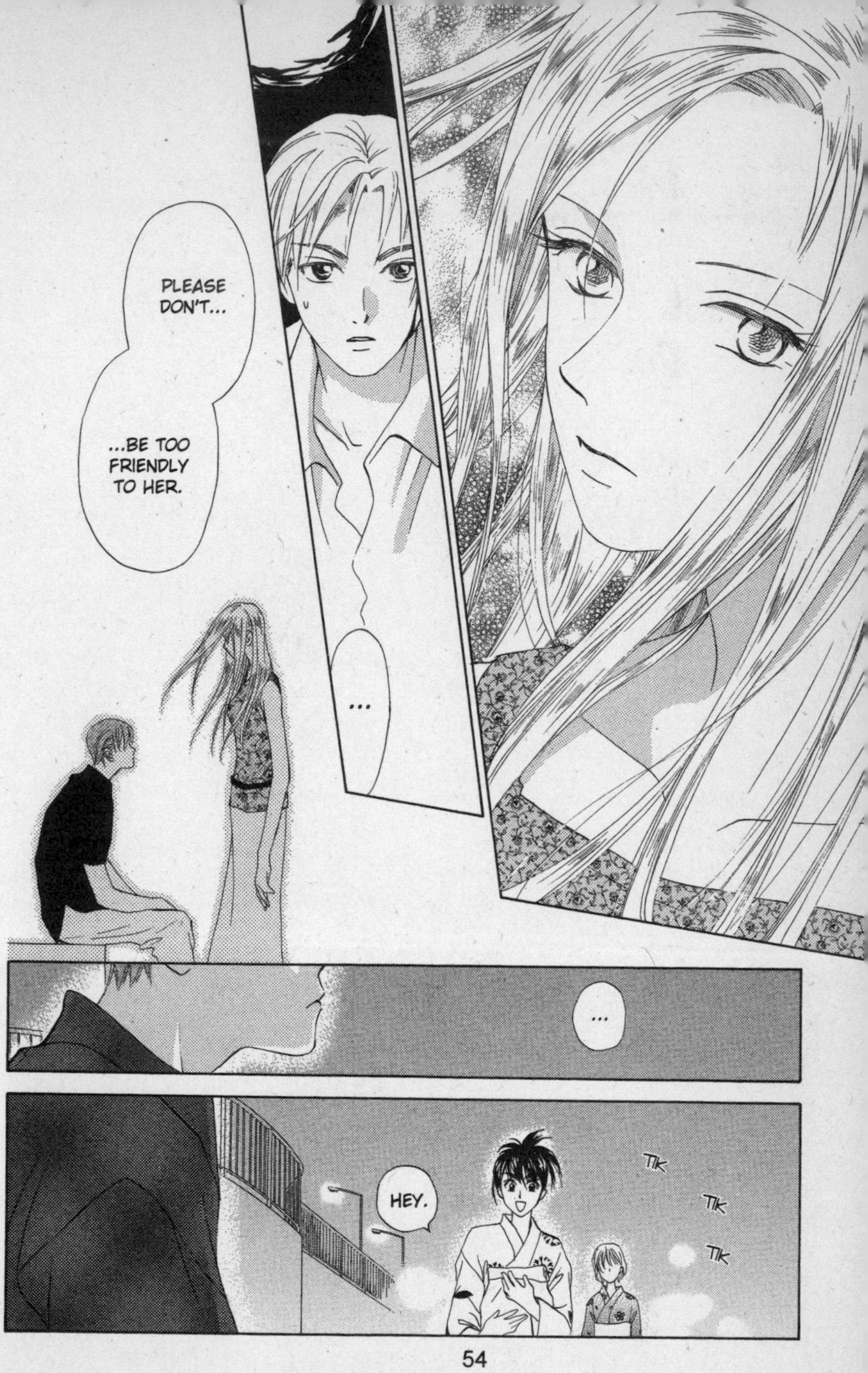
PLEASE DON'T...
...BE TOO FRIENDLY TO HER.
...
...
HEY.
TIK
TIK
TIK

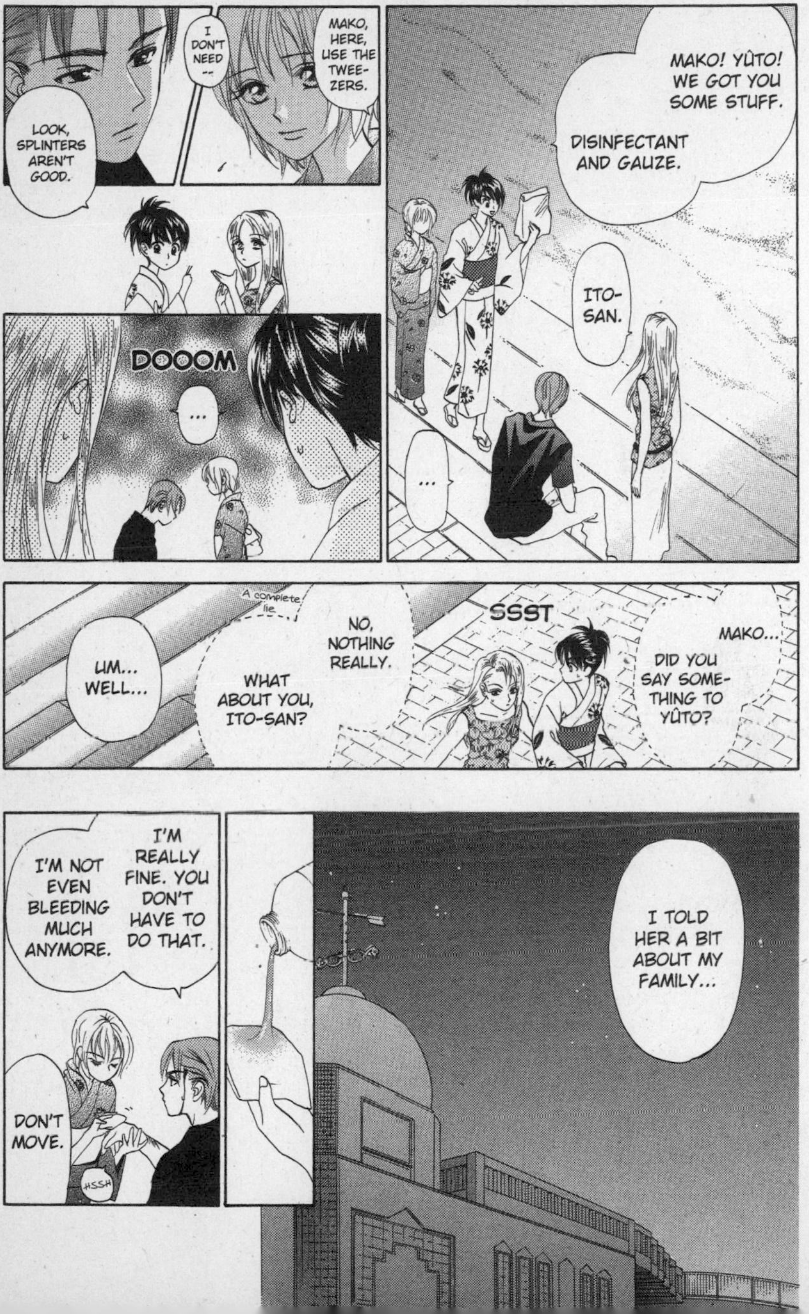
MAKO! YÛTO! WE GOT YOU SOME STUFF.
DISINFECTANT AND GAUZE.
ITO-SAN.
...
MAKO, HERE, USE THE TWEE-ZERS.
I DON'T NEED --
LOOK, SPLINTERS AREN'T GOOD.
DOOOM
...
MAKO...
DID YOU SAY SOME-THING TO YÛTO?
SSST
NO, NOTHING REALLY.
A complete lie.
WHAT ABOUT YOU, ITO-SAN?
UM... WELL...
I TOLD HER A BIT ABOUT MY FAMILY...
I'M REALLY FINE. YOU DON'T HAVE TO DO THAT.
I'M NOT EVEN BLEEDING MUCH ANYMORE.
DON'T MOVE.
HSSH

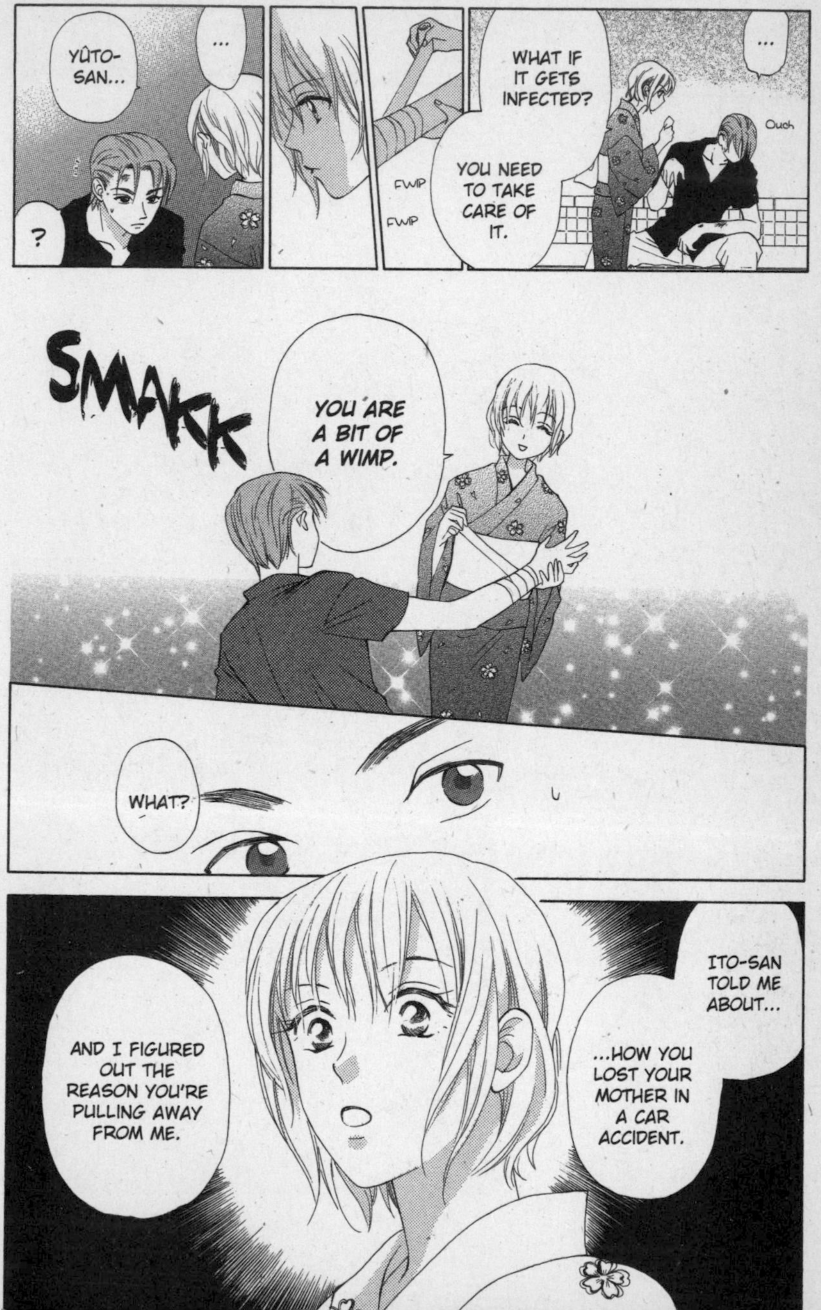
...
Ouch
WHAT IF IT GETS INFECTED?
YOU NEED TO TAKE CARE OF IT.
FWIP
FWIP
...
YÛTO-SAN...
?
SMAKK
YOU ARE A BIT OF A WIMP.
WHAT?
ITO-SAN TOLD ME ABOUT...
...HOW YOU LOST YOUR MOTHER IN A CAR ACCIDENT.
AND I FIGURED OUT THE REASON YOU'RE PULLING AWAY FROM ME.

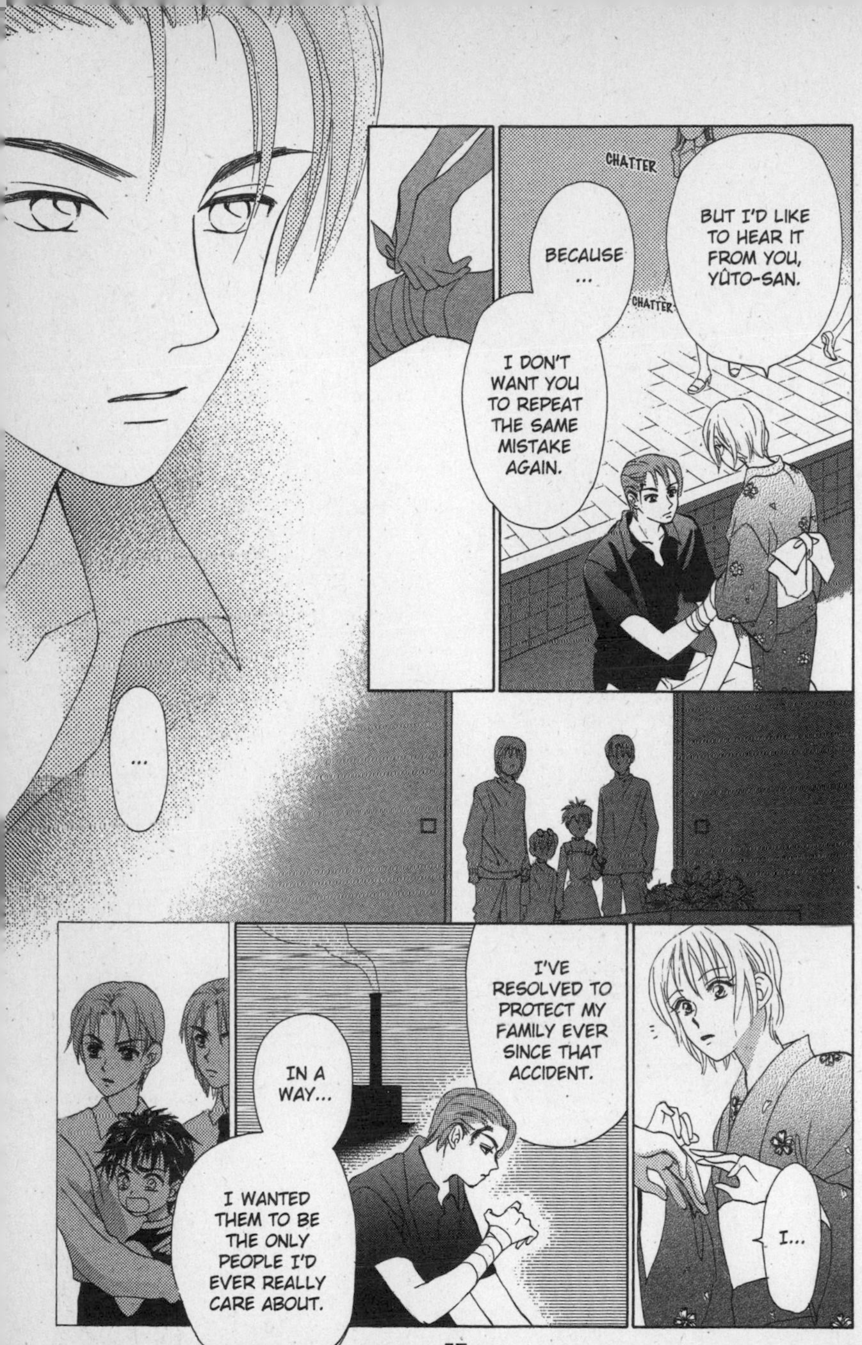
CHATTER
BUT I'D LIKE TO HEAR IT FROM YOU, YÛTO-SAN.
CHATTER
BECAUSE ...
I DON'T WANT YOU TO REPEAT THE SAME MISTAKE AGAIN.
...
I...
I'VE RESOLVED TO PROTECT MY FAMILY EVER SINCE THAT ACCIDENT.
IN A WAY...
I WANTED THEM TO BE THE ONLY PEOPLE I'D EVER REALLY CARE ABOUT.

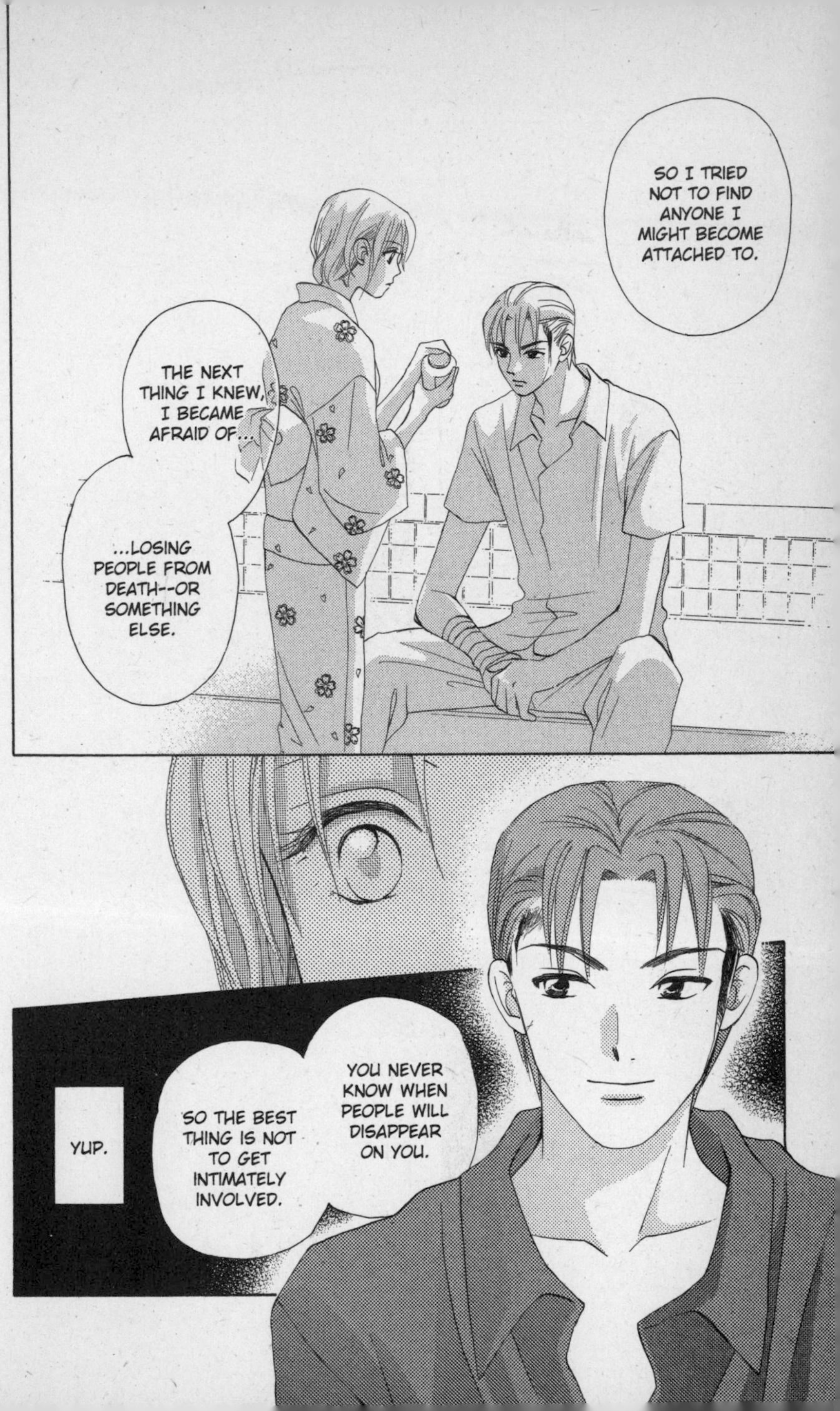
SO I TRIED NOT TO FIND ANYONE I MIGHT BECOME ATTACHED TO.
THE NEXT THING I KNEW, I BECAME AFRAID OF...
...LOSING PEOPLE FROM DEATH--OR SOMETHING ELSE.
YOU NEVER KNOW WHEN PEOPLE WILL DISAPPEAR ON YOU.
SO THE BEST THING IS NOT TO GET INTIMATELY INVOLVED.
YUP.

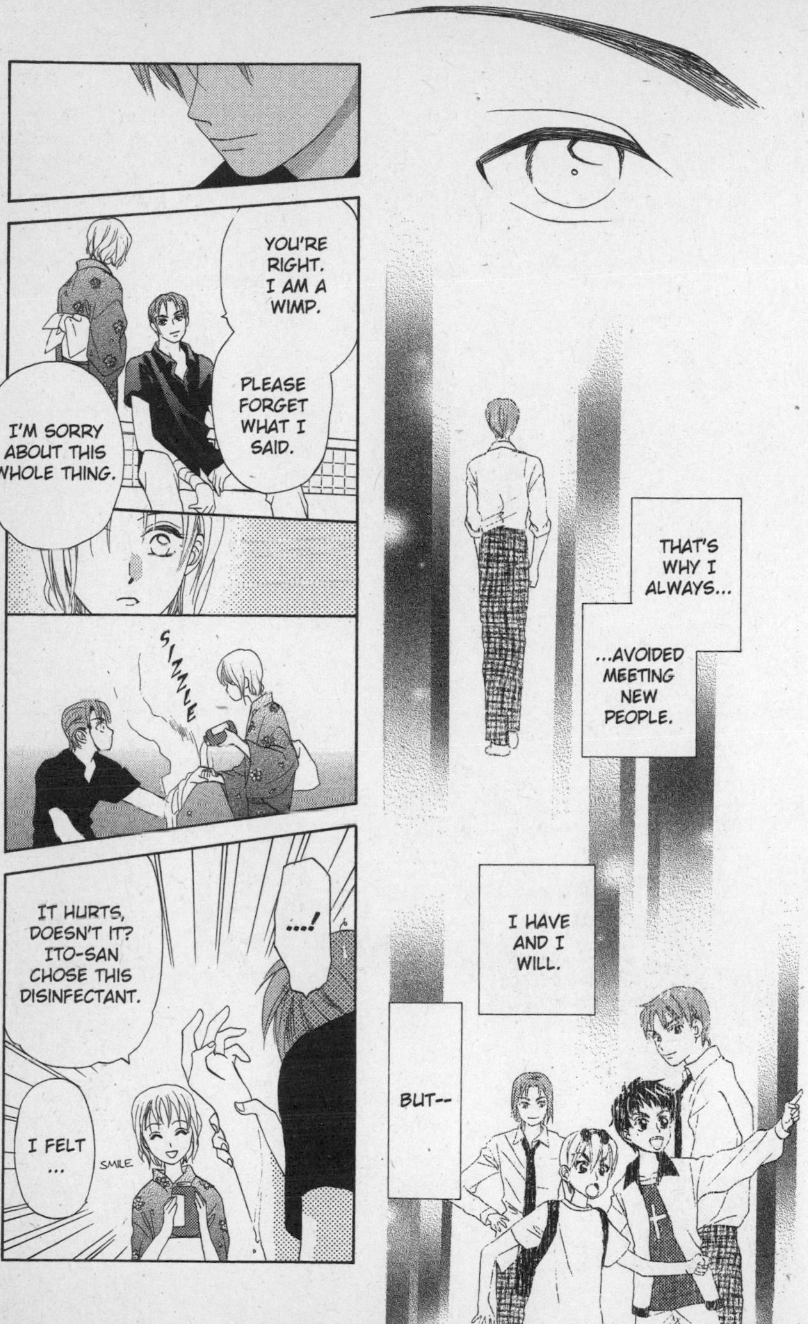
THAT'S WHY I ALWAYS...
...AVOIDED MEETING NEW PEOPLE.
I HAVE AND I WILL.
BUT--
YOU'RE RIGHT. I AM A WIMP.
PLEASE FORGET WHAT I SAID.
I'M SORRY ABOUT THIS WHOLE THING.
SIZZLE
...!
IT HURTS, DOESN'T IT? ITO-SAN CHOSE THIS DISINFECTANT.
I FELT ...
SMILE

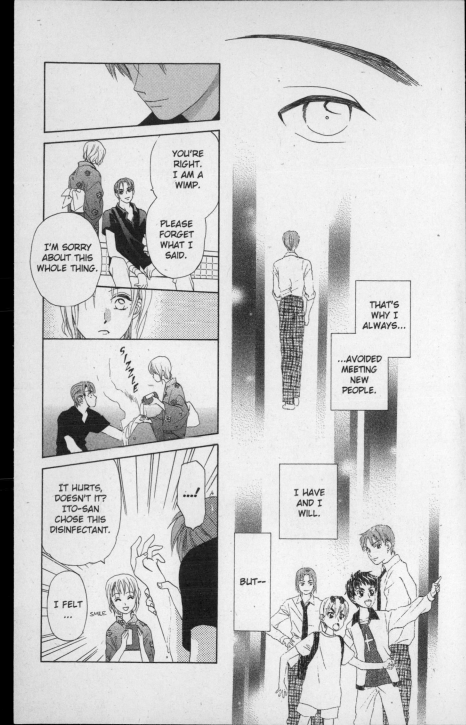

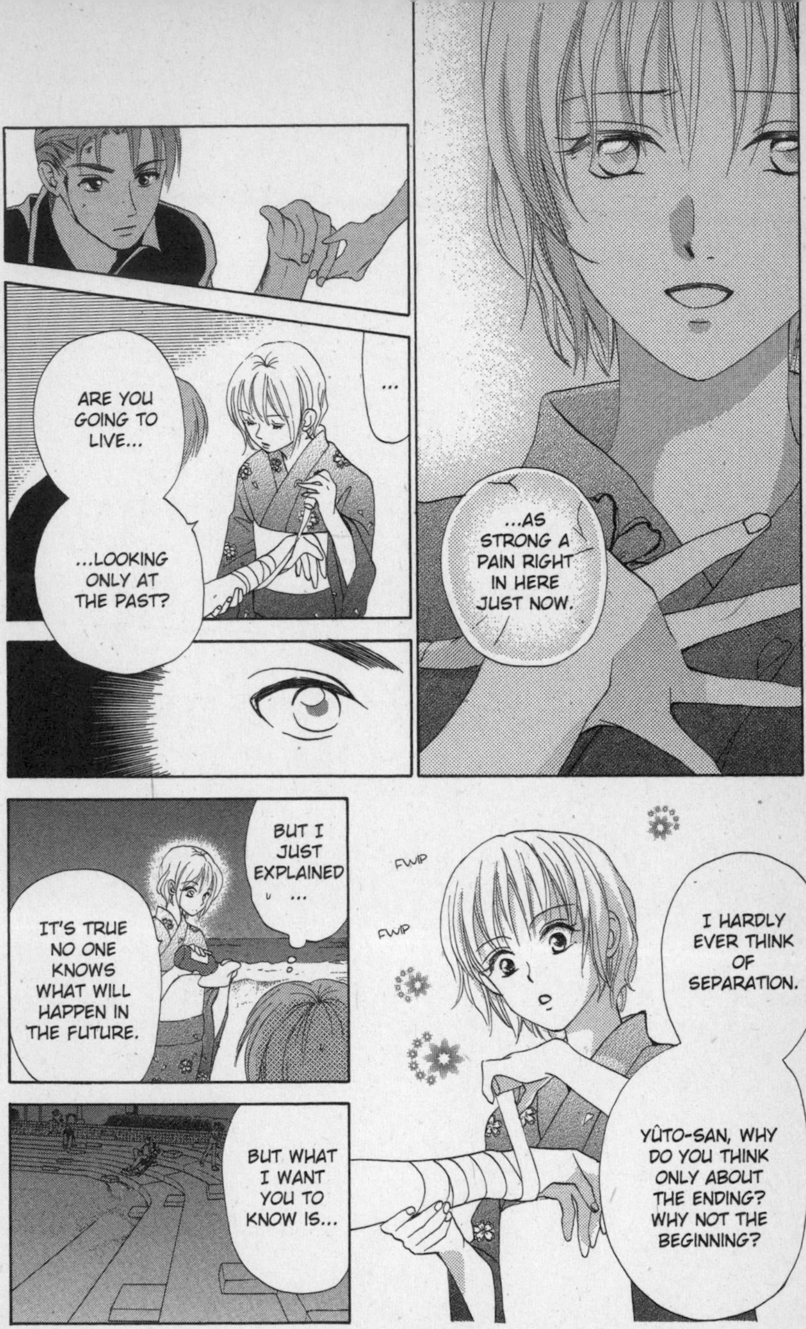
...AS STRONG A PAIN RIGHT IN HERE JUST NOW.
...
ARE YOU GOING TO LIVE...
...LOOKING ONLY AT THE PAST?
FWIP
FWIP
I HARDLY EVER THINK OF SEPARATION.
YÛTO-SAN, WHY DO YOU THINK ONLY ABOUT THE ENDING? WHY NOT THE BEGINNING?
BUT I JUST EXPLAINED ...
IT'S TRUE NO ONE KNOWS WHAT WILL HAPPEN IN THE FUTURE.
BUT WHAT I WANT YOU TO KNOW IS...

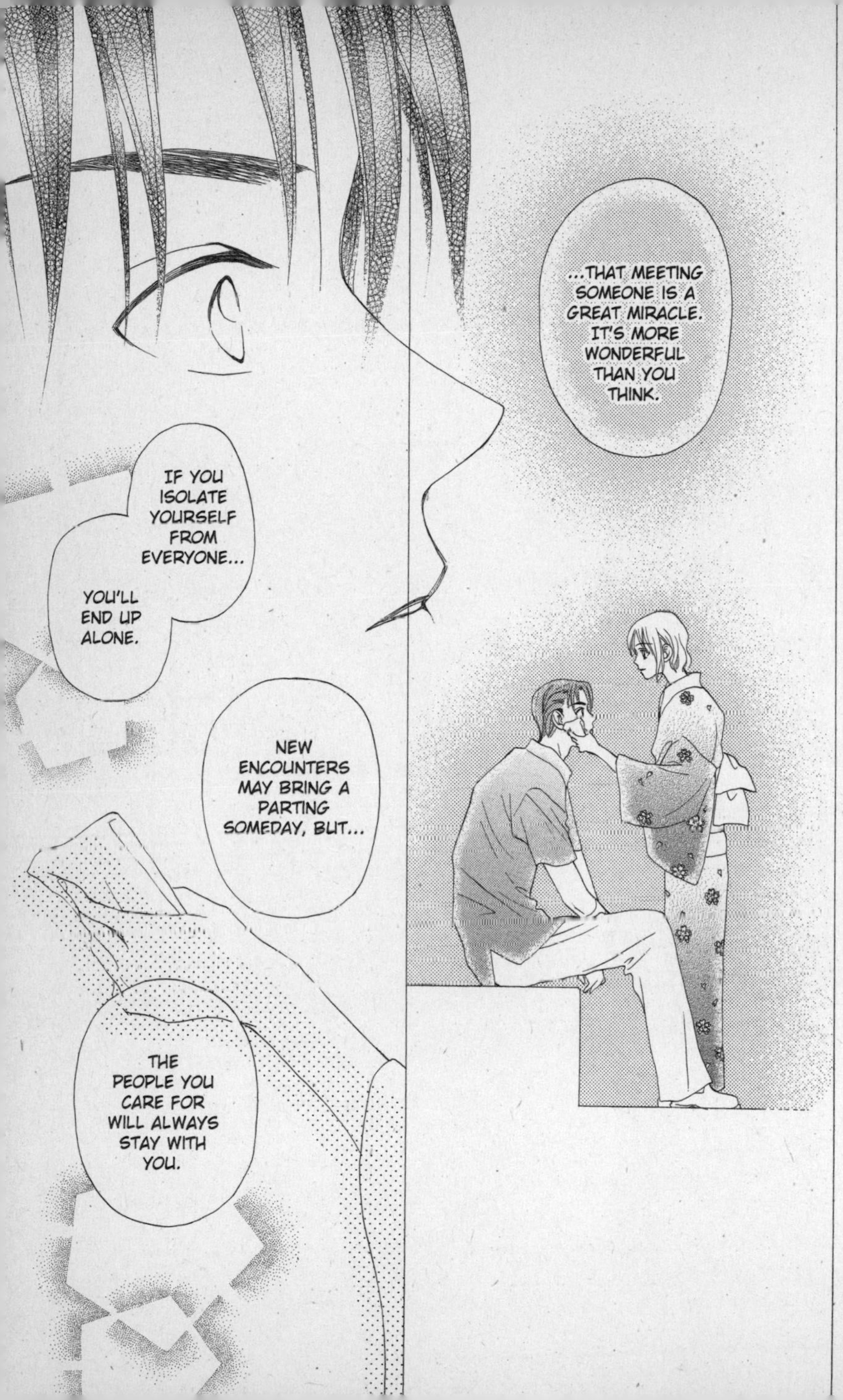
...THAT MEETING SOMEONE IS A GREAT MIRACLE. IT'S MORE WONDERFUL THAN YOU THINK.
IF YOU ISOLATE YOURSELF FROM EVERYONE...
YOU'LL END UP ALONE.
NEW ENCOUNTERS MAY BRING A PARTING SOMEDAY, BUT...
THE PEOPLE YOU CARE FOR WILL ALWAYS STAY WITH YOU.

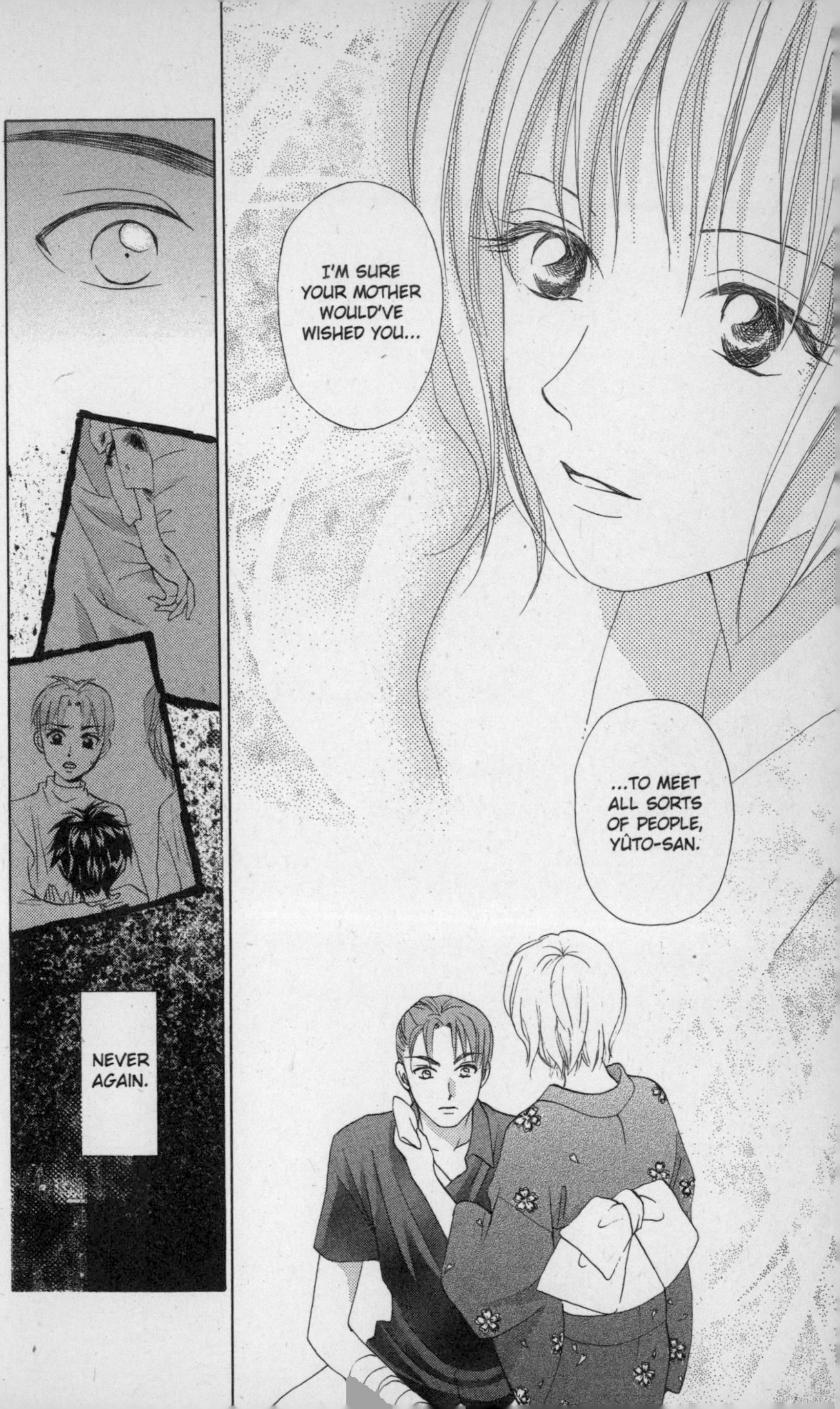
I'M SURE YOUR MOTHER WOULD'VE WISHED YOU...
...TO MEET ALL SORTS OF PEOPLE, YÛTO-SAN.
NEVER AGAIN.

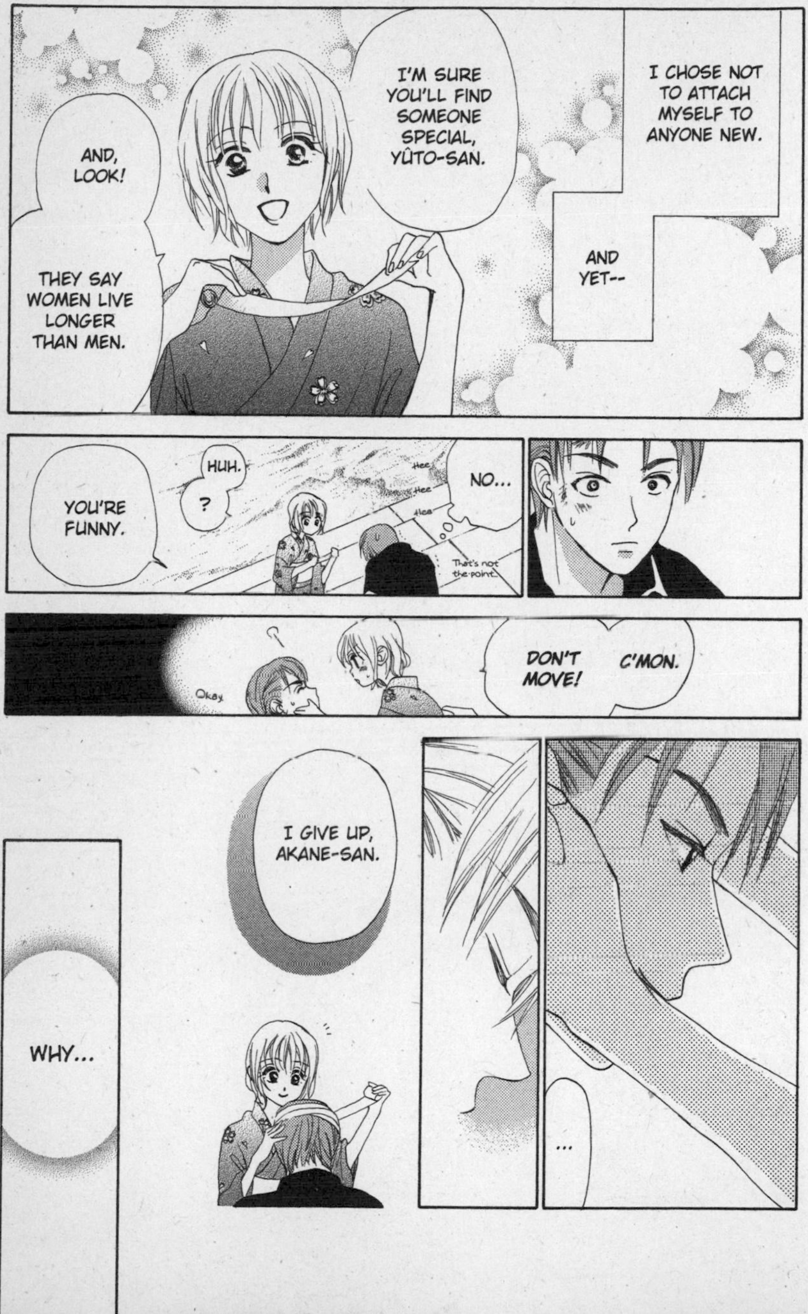
I CHOSE NOT TO ATTACH MYSELF TO ANYONE NEW.
AND YET--
I'M SURE YOU'LL FIND SOMEONE SPECIAL, YÛTO-SAN.
AND, LOOK!
THEY SAY WOMEN LIVE LONGER THAN MEN.
NO...
That's not the point...
Hee Hee Hee
HUH.
?
YOU'RE FUNNY.
C'MON.
DON'T MOVE!
Okay.
...
I GIVE UP, AKANE-SAN.
WHY...

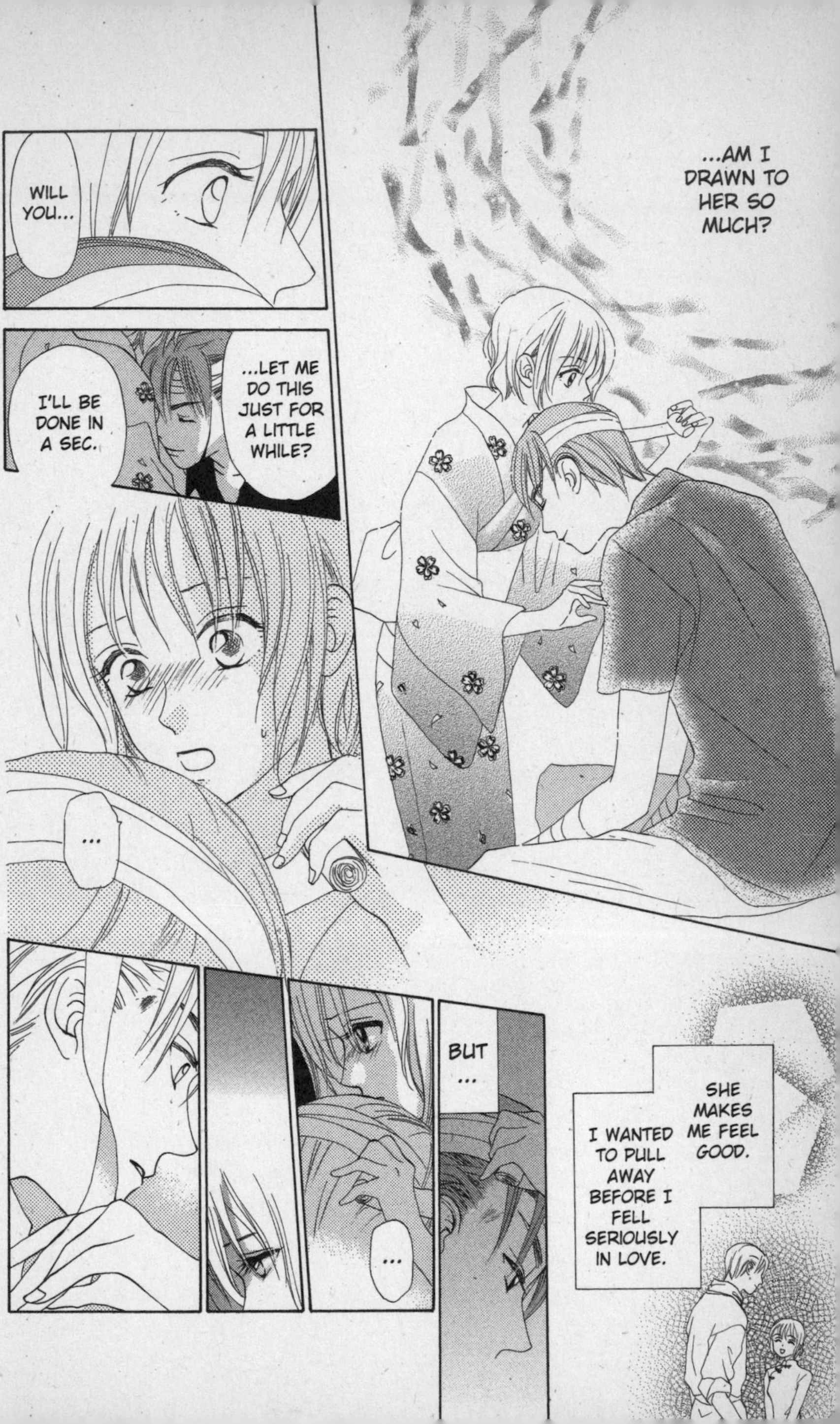
...AM I DRAWN TO HER SO MUCH?
WILL YOU...
...LET ME DO THIS JUST FOR A LITTLE WHILE?
I'LL BE DONE IN A SEC.
...
SHE MAKES ME FEEL GOOD.
I WANTED TO PULL AWAY BEFORE I FELL SERIOUSLY IN LOVE.
BUT ...
...

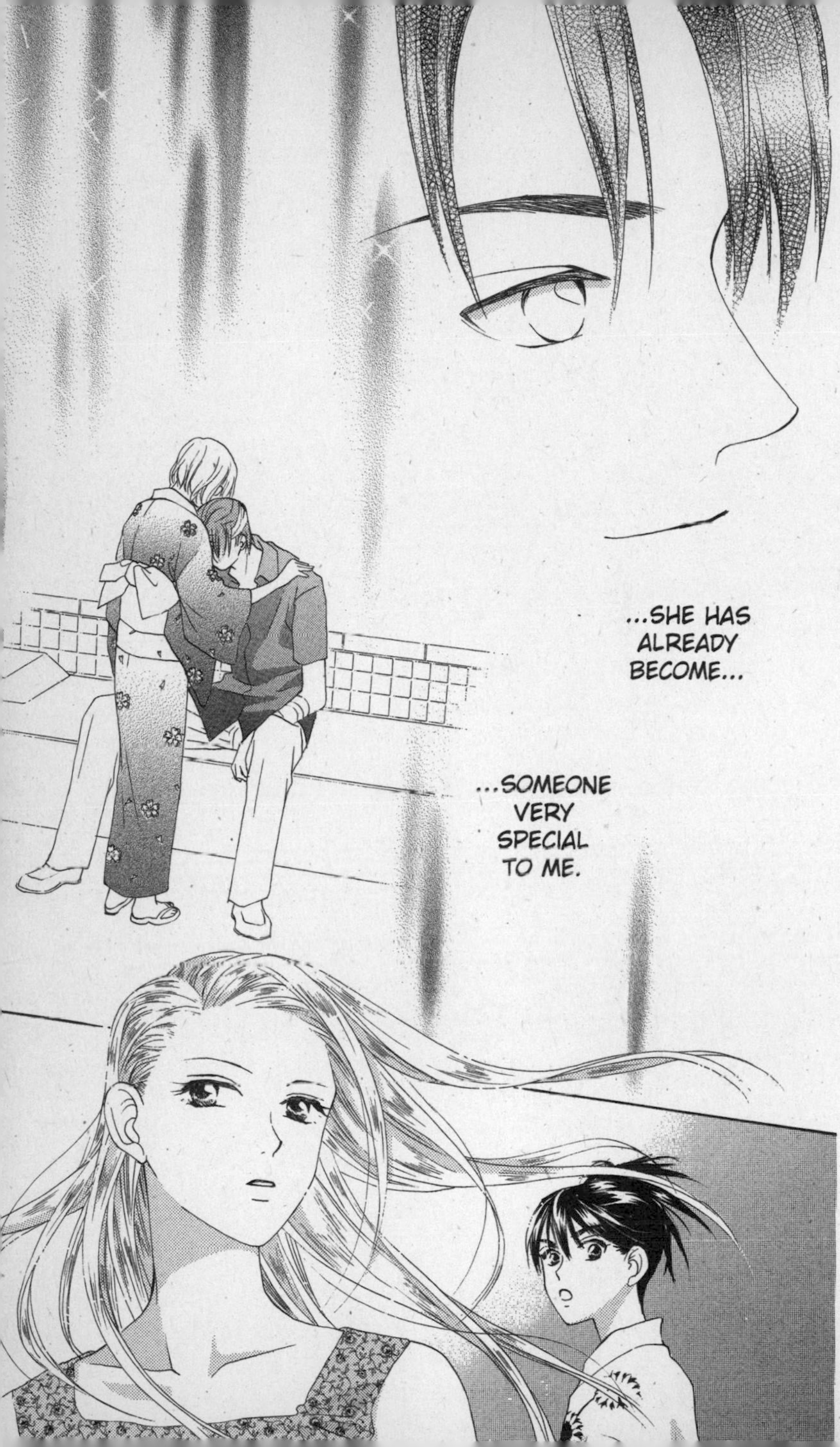
...SHE HAS ALREADY BECOME...
...SOMEONE VERY SPECIAL TO ME.

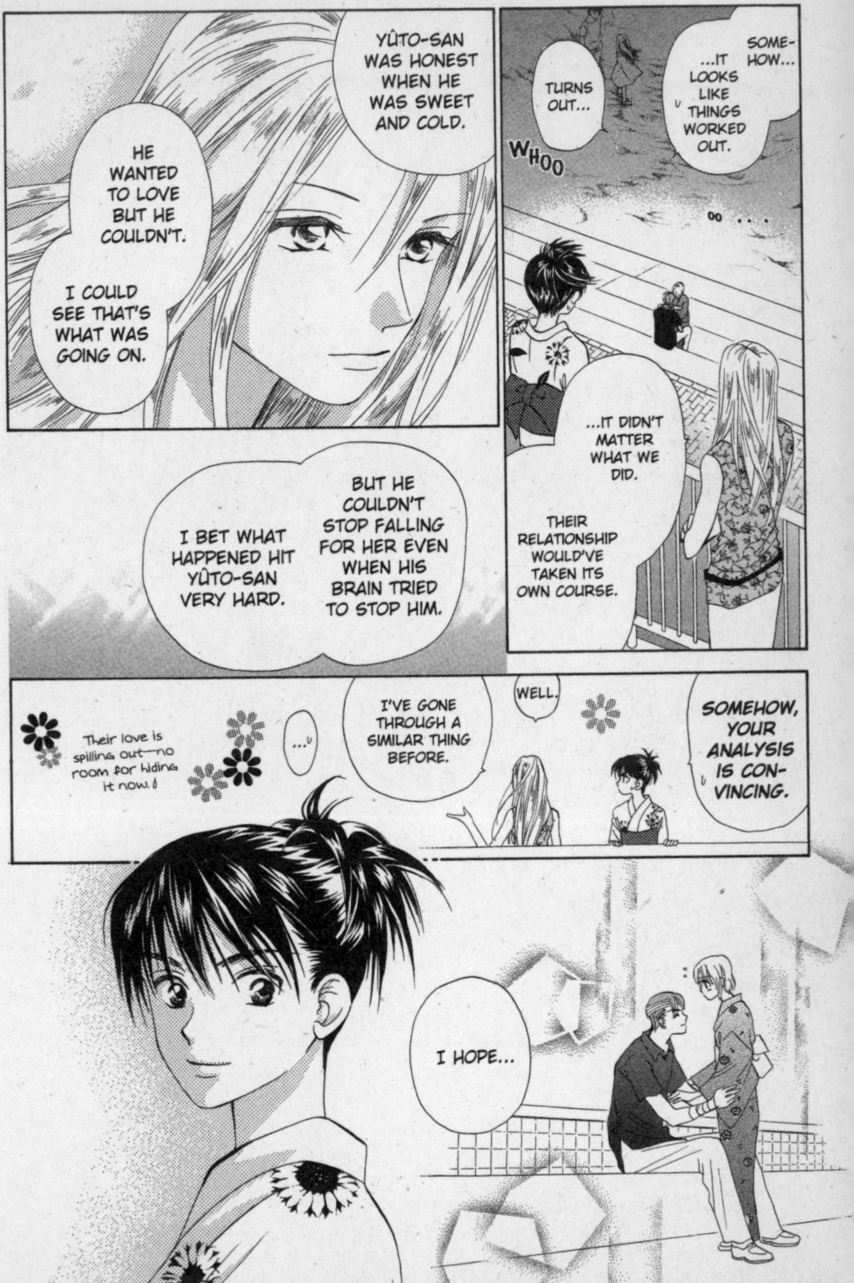
SOME-HOW...
...IT LOOKS LIKE THINGS WORKED OUT.
TURNS OUT...
WHOO
OO . . .
...IT DIDN'T MATTER WHAT WE DID.
THEIR RELATIONSHIP WOULD'VE TAKEN ITS OWN COURSE.
YÛTO-SAN WAS HONEST WHEN HE WAS SWEET AND COLD.
HE WANTED TO LOVE BUT HE COULDN'T.
I COULD SEE THAT'S WHAT WAS GOING ON.
BUT HE COULDN'T STOP FALLING FOR HER EVEN WHEN HIS BRAIN TRIED TO STOP HIM.
I BET WHAT HAPPENED HIT YÛTO-SAN VERY HARD.
SOMEHOW, YOUR ANALYSIS IS CON-VINCING.
WELL.
I'VE GONE THROUGH A SIMILAR THING BEFORE.
...
Their love is spilling out—no room for hiding it now.
I HOPE...

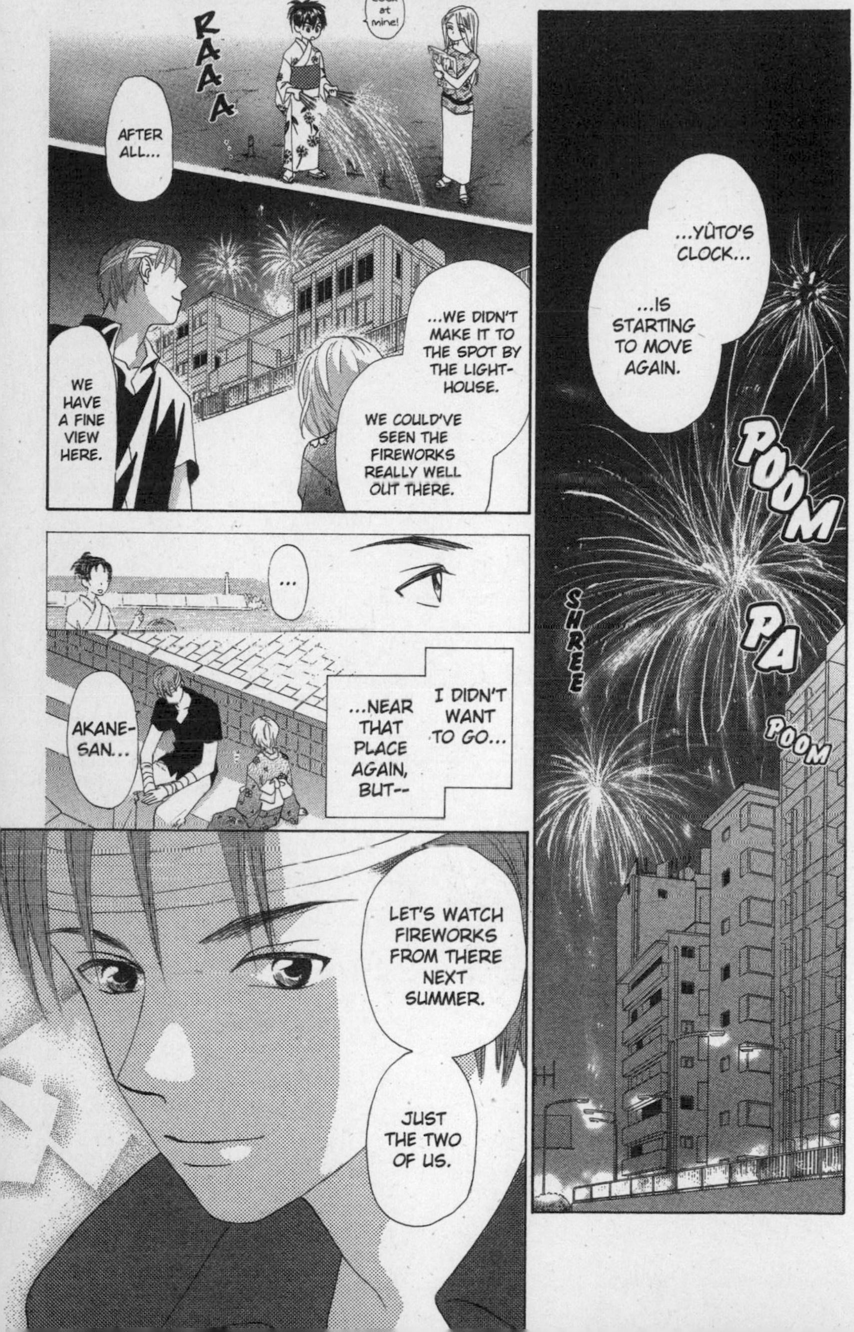
...YÛTO'S CLOCK...
...IS STARTING TO MOVE AGAIN.
POOM
SHREE
PA
POOM
Look at mine!
RAAA
AFTER ALL...
...WE DIDN'T MAKE IT TO THE SPOT BY THE LIGHT-HOUSE.
WE COULD'VE SEEN THE FIREWORKS REALLY WELL OUT THERE.
WE HAVE A FINE VIEW HERE.
...
I DIDN'T WANT TO GO...
...NEAR THAT PLACE AGAIN, BUT--
AKANE-SAN...
LET'S WATCH FIREWORKS FROM THERE NEXT SUMMER.
JUST THE TWO OF US.

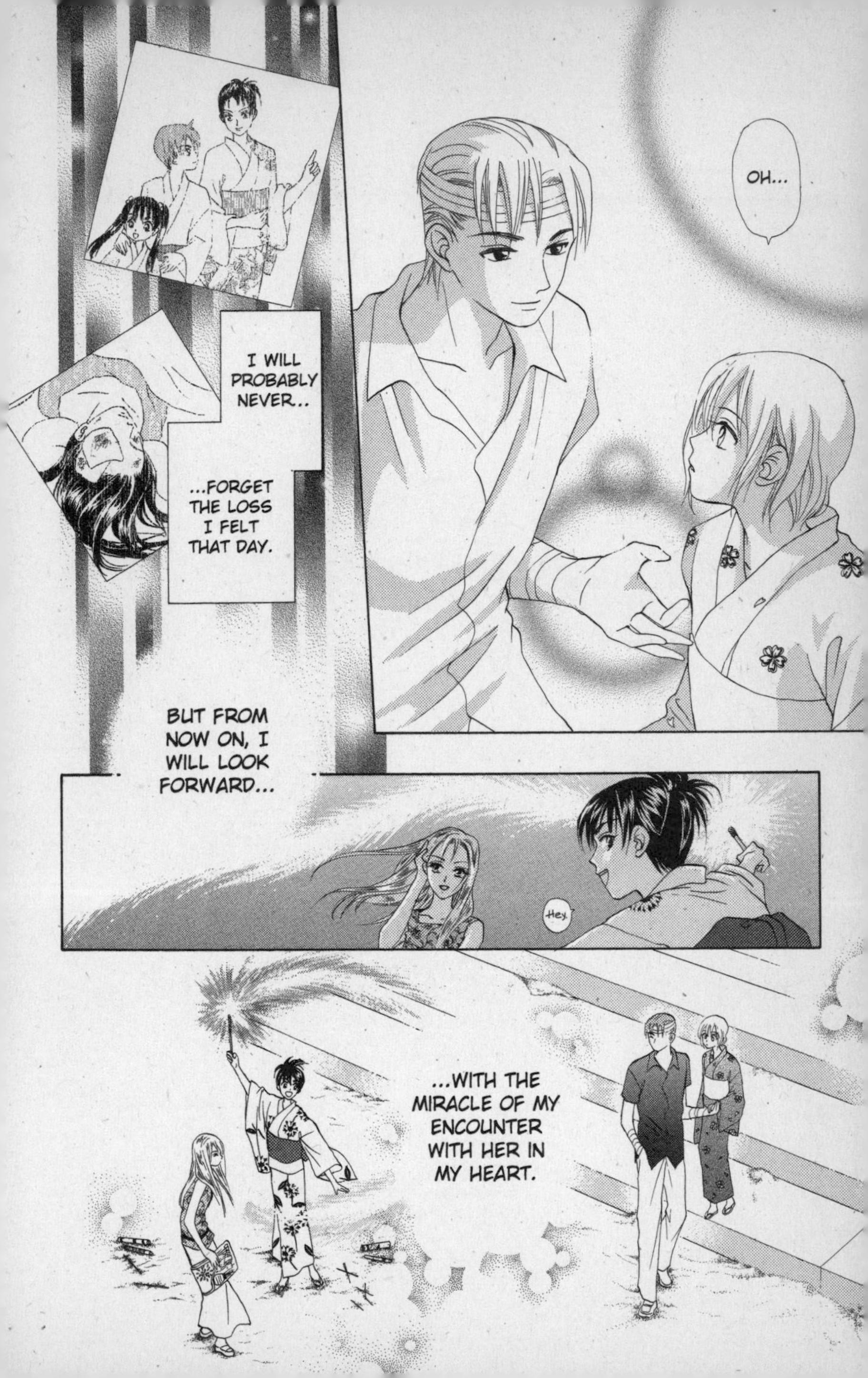
OH...
I WILL PROBABLY NEVER...
...FORGET THE LOSS I FELT THAT DAY.
BUT FROM NOW ON, I WILL LOOK FORWARD...
Hey.
...WITH THE MIRACLE OF MY ENCOUNTER WITH HER IN MY HEART.

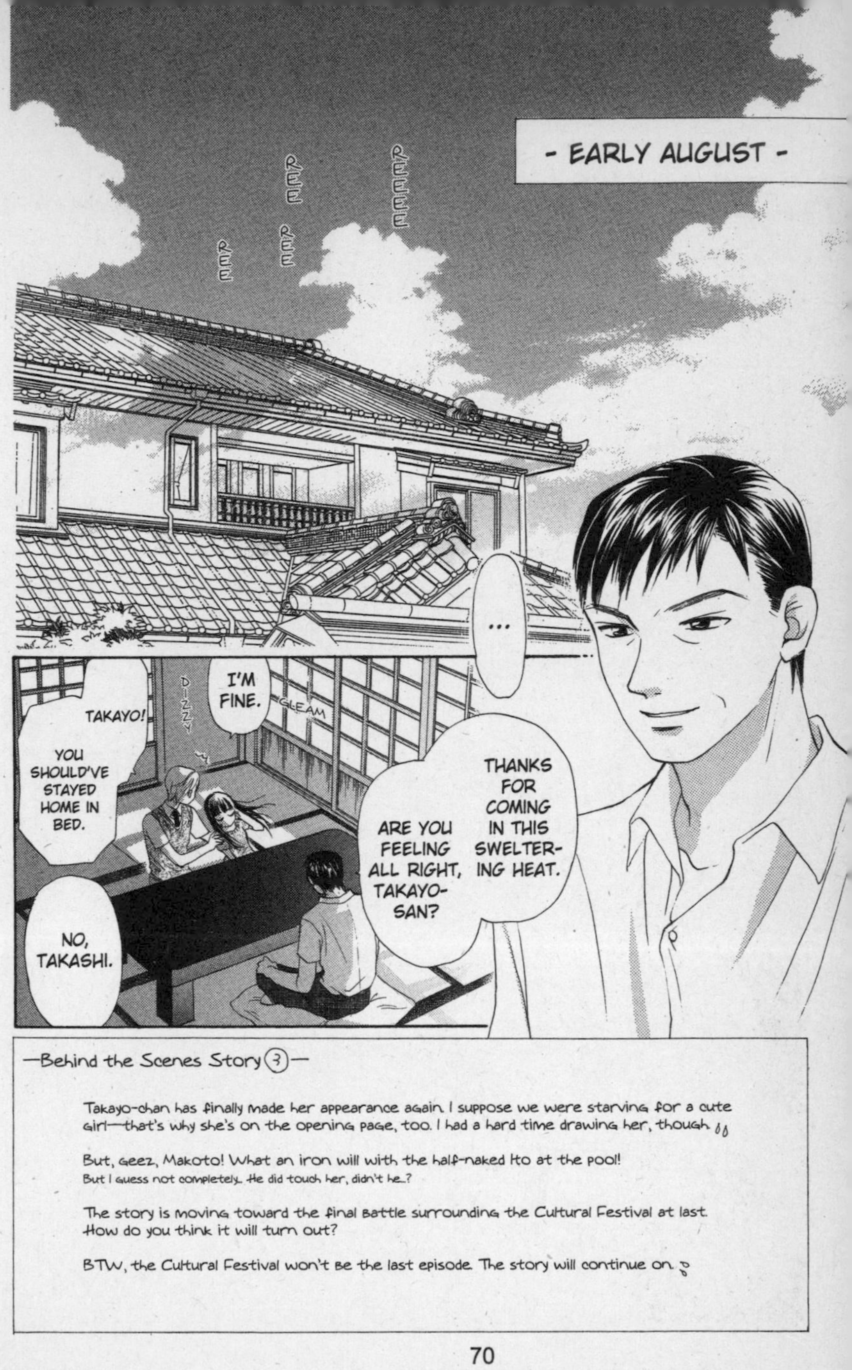
- EARLY AUGUST -
REEEEE
REE
REE
REE
...
THANKS FOR COMING IN THIS SWELTERING HEAT.
ARE YOU FEELING ALL RIGHT, TAKAYO-SAN?
I'M FINE.
GLEAM
DIZZY
TAKAYO!
YOU SHOULD'VE STAYED HOME IN BED.
NO, TAKASHI.

—Behind the Scenes Story ③—

Takayo-chan has finally made her appearance again. I suppose we were starving for a cute girl—that's why she's on the opening page, too. I had a hard time drawing her, though.

But, geez, Makoto! What an iron will with the half-naked Ito at the pool!
But I guess not completely. He did touch her, didn't he...?

The story is moving toward the final battle surrounding the Cultural Festival at last. How do you think it will turn out?

BTW, the Cultural Festival won't be the last episode. The story will continue on.

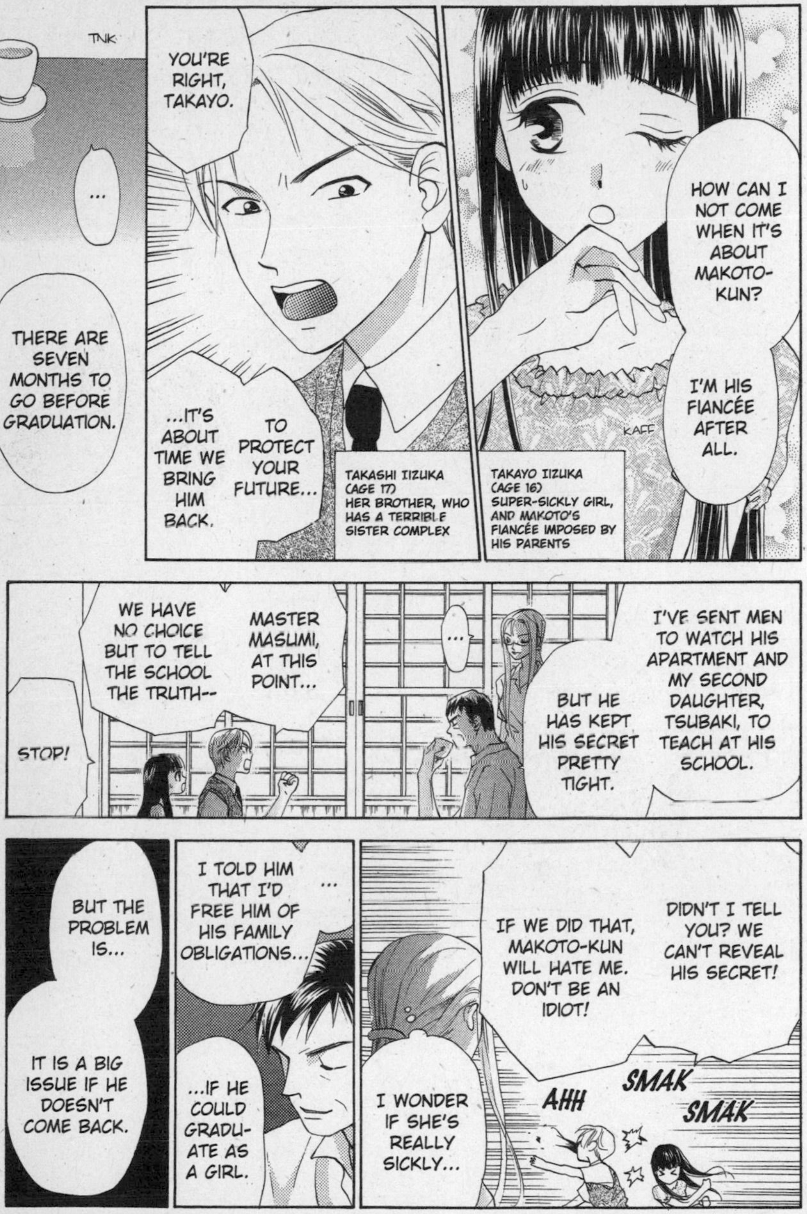
HOW CAN I NOT COME WHEN IT'S ABOUT MAKOTO-KUN?
I'M HIS FIANCÉE AFTER ALL.
KAFF
TAKAYO IIZUKA (AGE 16) SUPER-SICKLY GIRL, AND MAKOTO'S FIANCÉE IMPOSED BY HIS PARENTS
YOU'RE RIGHT, TAKAYO.
TO PROTECT YOUR FUTURE...
...IT'S ABOUT TIME WE BRING HIM BACK.
TAKASHI IIZUKA (AGE 17) HER BROTHER, WHO HAS A TERRIBLE SISTER COMPLEX
TNK
...
THERE ARE SEVEN MONTHS TO GO BEFORE GRADUATION.
I'VE SENT MEN TO WATCH HIS APARTMENT AND MY SECOND DAUGHTER, TSUBAKI, TO TEACH AT HIS SCHOOL.
BUT HE HAS KEPT HIS SECRET PRETTY TIGHT.
...
MASTER MASUMI, AT THIS POINT...
WE HAVE NO CHOICE BUT TO TELL THE SCHOOL THE TRUTH--
STOP!
DIDN'T I TELL YOU? WE CAN'T REVEAL HIS SECRET!
IF WE DID THAT, MAKOTO-KUN WILL HATE ME. DON'T BE AN IDIOT!
SMAK
SMAK
AHH
I WONDER IF SHE'S REALLY SICKLY...
...
I TOLD HIM THAT I'D FREE HIM OF HIS FAMILY OBLIGATIONS...
...IF HE COULD GRADUATE AS A GIRL.
BUT THE PROBLEM IS...
IT IS A BIG ISSUE IF HE DOESN'T COME BACK.

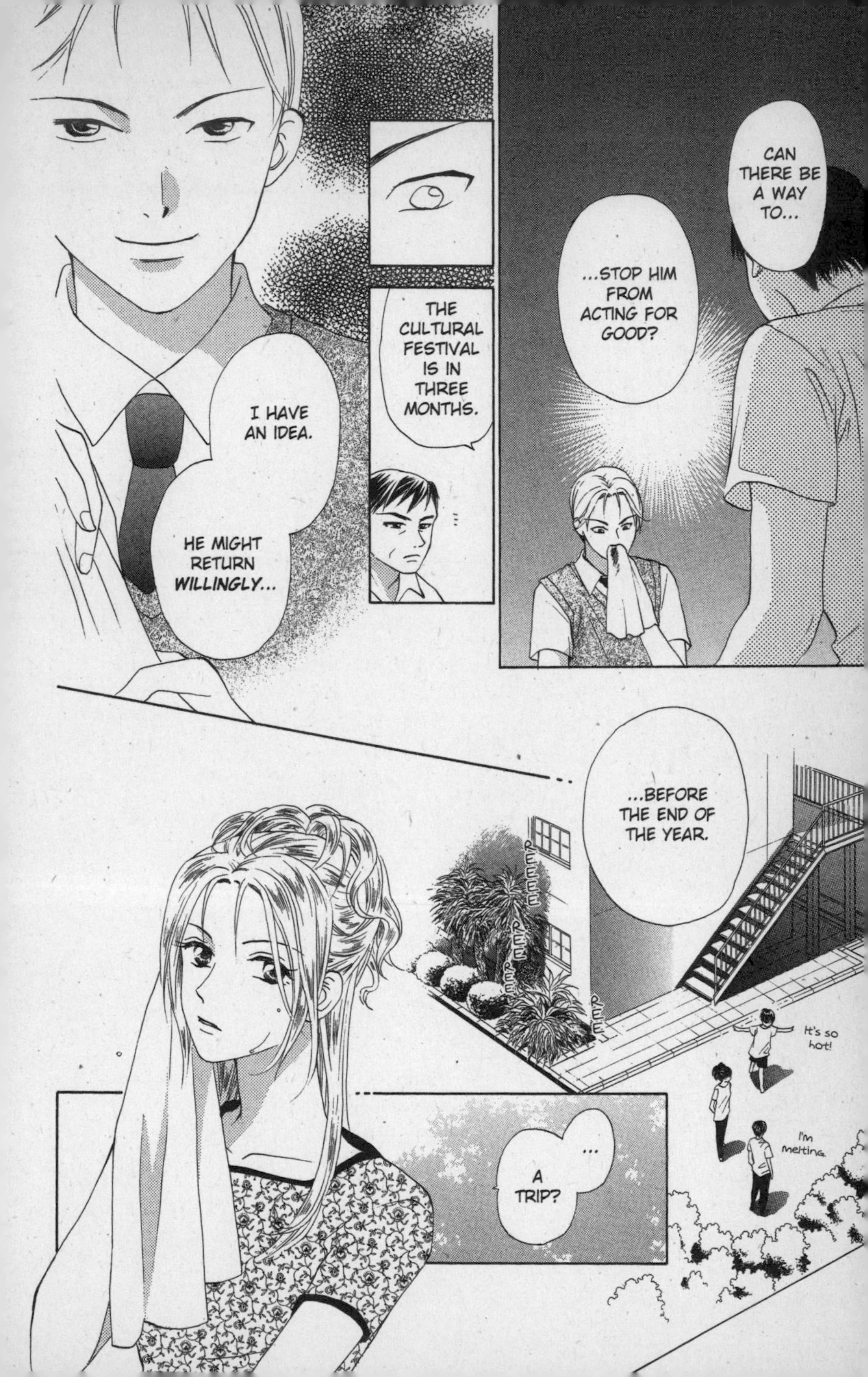
CAN THERE BE A WAY TO...
...STOP HIM FROM ACTING FOR GOOD?
THE CULTURAL FESTIVAL IS IN THREE MONTHS.
I HAVE AN IDEA.
HE MIGHT RETURN WILLINGLY...
...BEFORE THE END OF THE YEAR.
REEEE
REE
REE
REE
It's so hot!
I'm melting.
... A TRIP?

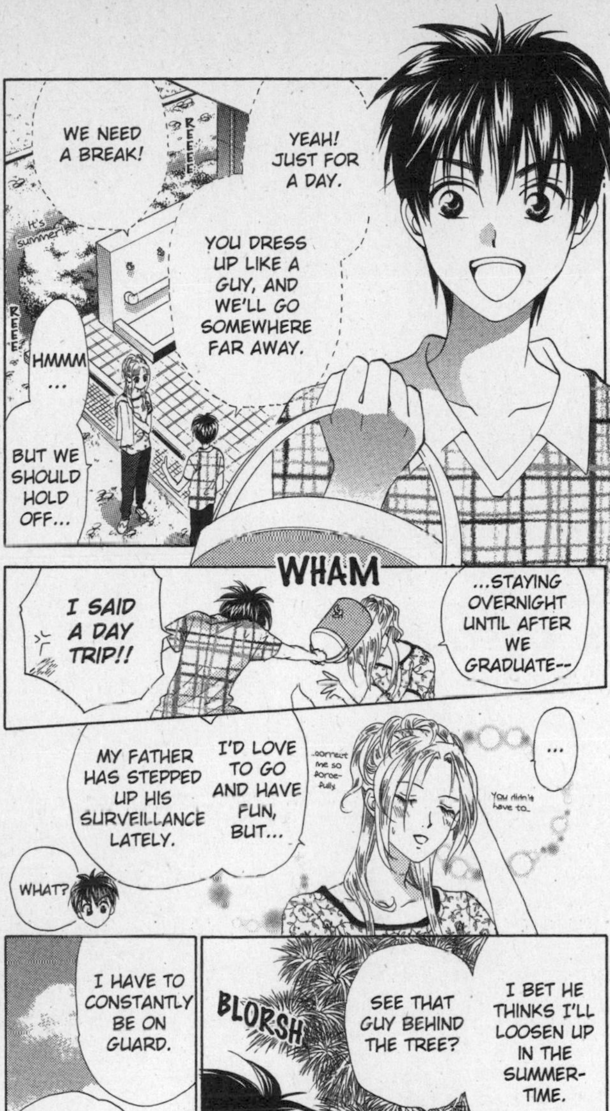
WE NEED A BREAK!
YEAH! JUST FOR A DAY.
YOU DRESS UP LIKE A GUY, AND WE'LL GO SOMEWHERE FAR AWAY.
REEEE
It's summer!
REEEE
HMMM...
BUT WE SHOULD HOLD OFF...
...STAYING OVERNIGHT UNTIL AFTER WE GRADUATE--
WHAM
I SAID A DAY TRIP!!
...
You didn't have to...
...correct me so force-fully.
I'D LOVE TO GO AND HAVE FUN, BUT...
MY FATHER HAS STEPPED UP HIS SURVEILLANCE LATELY.
WHAT?
I BET HE THINKS I'LL LOOSEN UP IN THE SUMMER-TIME.
SEE THAT GUY BEHIND THE TREE?
BLORSH
I HAVE TO CONSTANTLY BE ON GUARD.
SO, IT PROBABLY ISN'T A GOOD IDEA.

GODDESSES WANTED (LAUGH)

We usually ask the award winners of HMC, BC, and Athena, etc to come as temporary assistants (mainly during the finalizing stage). But when I'm in a real pinch and need "someone who's super-talented in drawing back-ground," we even beg new manga-ka who've already made their debut. And it happens more often than not... Sorry about that.

From around the Valentine's episode in volume 2 through volume 5 or 6, both Ayano Oguchi and Ryoko Fukuyama extended their helping hands. Thank you so much!! They're truly like Goddesses to me! And I still ask their help every so often. I'm so sorry to make you pull all-nighters. (Cry) And yes, earlier with my first series, Oguchi-san **commuted daily** when she lived three hours away! At the time, her parents did not allow her to sleep over.

It was a real pain. I caused so much trouble to the others...

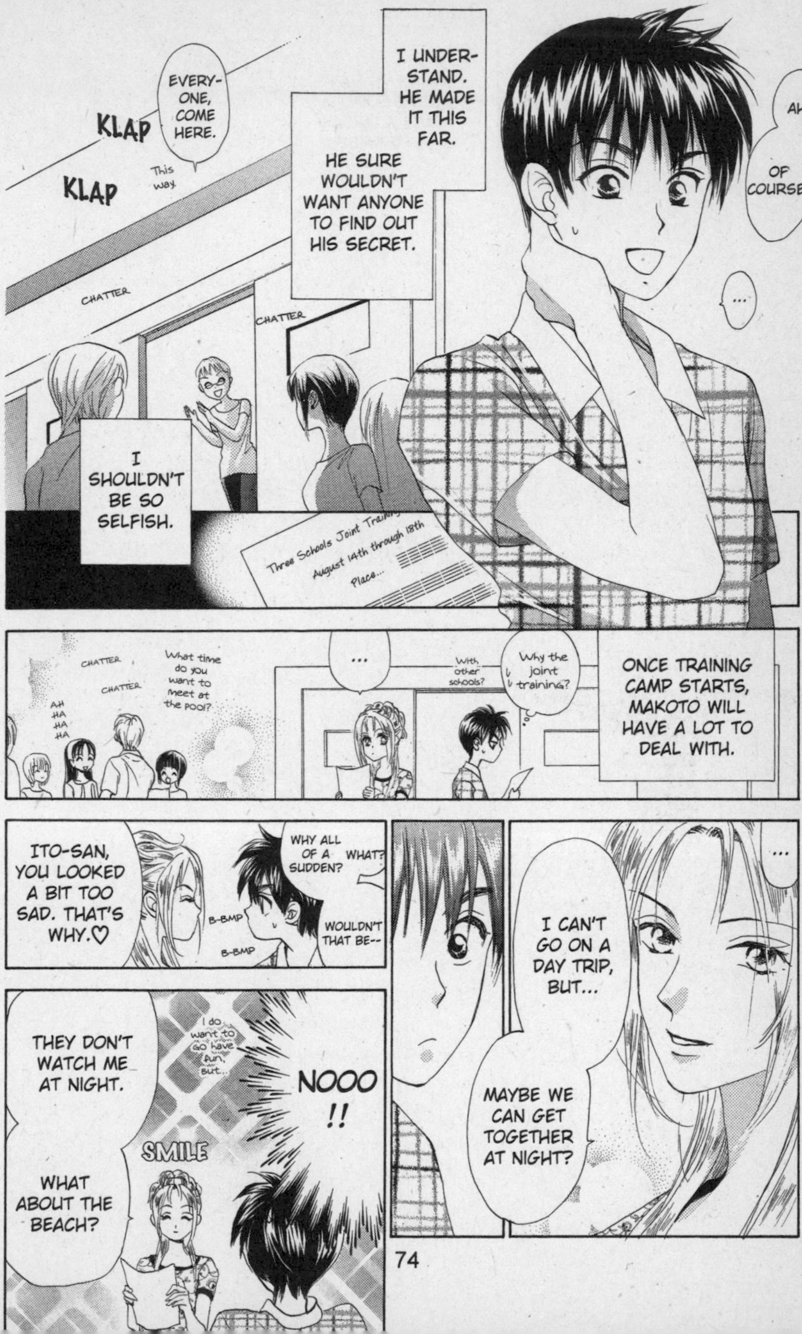
AH...
OF COURSE.
...
I UNDER-STAND. HE MADE IT THIS FAR.
HE SURE WOULDN'T WANT ANYONE TO FIND OUT HIS SECRET.
EVERY-ONE, COME HERE.
KLAP
KLAP
This way.
CHATTER
CHATTER
I SHOULDN'T BE SO SELFISH.
Three Schools Joint Training
August 14th through 18th
Place...
ONCE TRAINING CAMP STARTS, MAKOTO WILL HAVE A LOT TO DEAL WITH.
Why the joint training?
With other schools?
...
What time do you want to meet at the pool?
CHATTER
CHATTER
AH HA HA HA
...
I CAN'T GO ON A DAY TRIP, BUT...
MAYBE WE CAN GET TOGETHER AT NIGHT?
WHY ALL OF A SUDDEN?
WHAT?
WOULDN'T THAT BE--
B-BMP
B-BMP
ITO-SAN, YOU LOOKED A BIT TOO SAD. THAT'S WHY.♡
NOOO !!
I do want to go have fun, but...
THEY DON'T WATCH ME AT NIGHT.
SMILE
WHAT ABOUT THE BEACH?

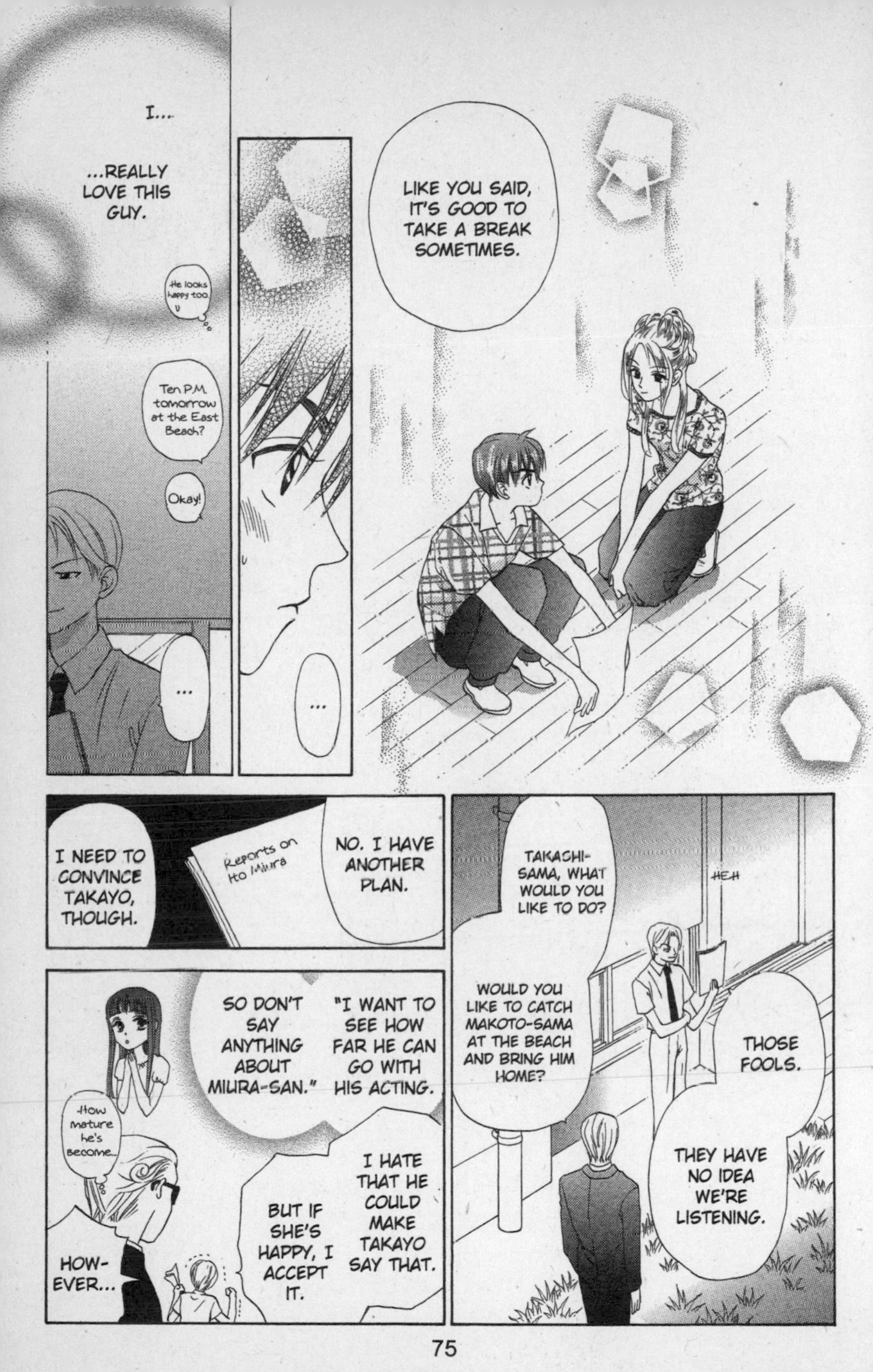
LIKE YOU SAID, IT'S GOOD TO TAKE A BREAK SOMETIMES.
...
I...
...REALLY LOVE THIS GUY.
He looks happy too.
Ten P.M. tomorrow at the East Beach?
Okay!
...
TAKASHI-SAMA, WHAT WOULD YOU LIKE TO DO?
HEH
WOULD YOU LIKE TO CATCH MAKOTO-SAMA AT THE BEACH AND BRING HIM HOME?
THOSE FOOLS.
THEY HAVE NO IDEA WE'RE LISTENING.
NO. I HAVE ANOTHER PLAN.
Reports on Ito Miura
I NEED TO CONVINCE TAKAYO, THOUGH.
"I WANT TO SEE HOW FAR HE CAN GO WITH HIS ACTING.
SO DON'T SAY ANYTHING ABOUT MIURA-SAN."
I HATE THAT HE COULD MAKE TAKAYO SAY THAT.
BUT IF SHE'S HAPPY, I ACCEPT IT.
How mature he's become...
HOW-EVER...

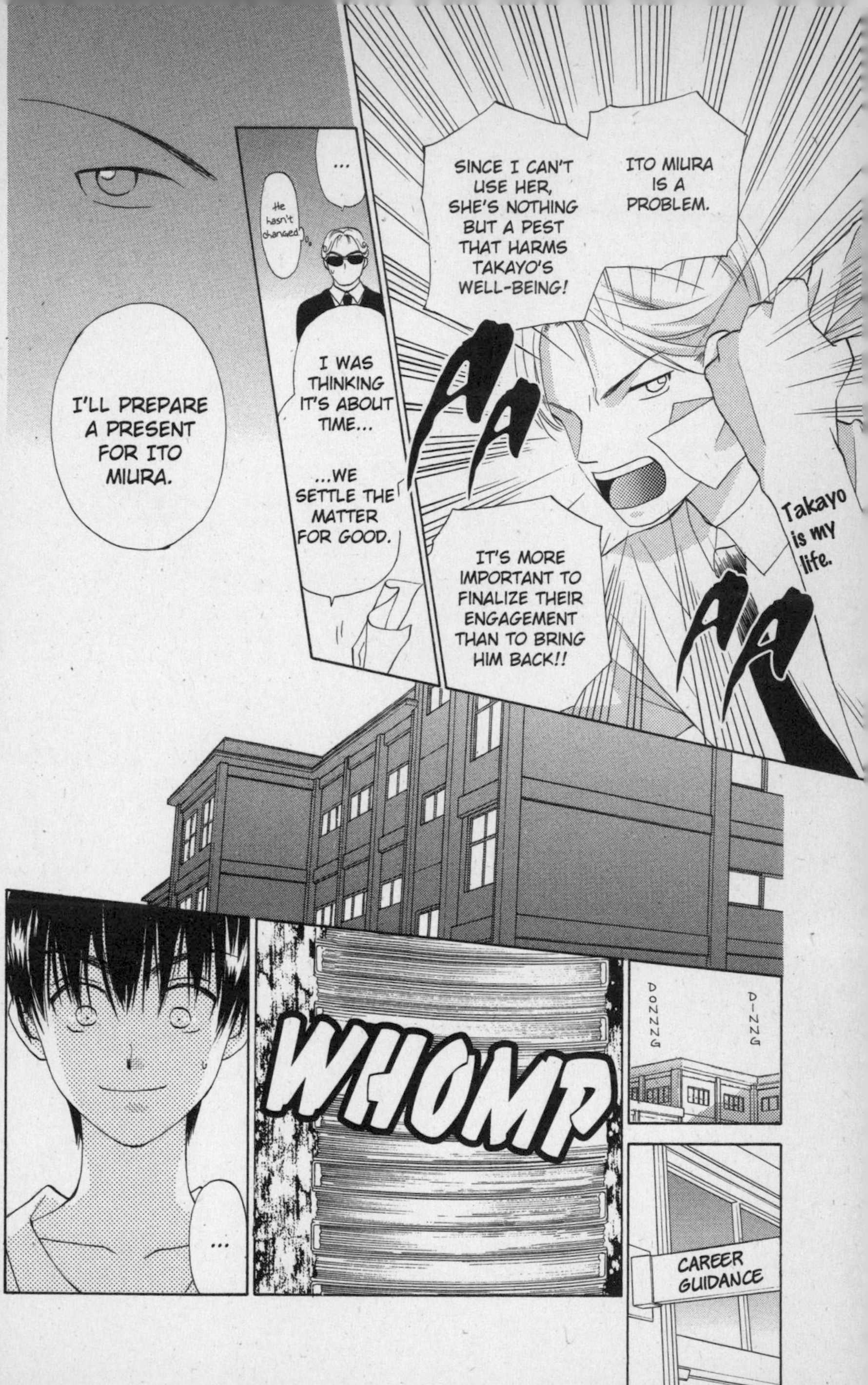
ITO MIURA IS A PROBLEM.
SINCE I CAN'T USE HER, SHE'S NOTHING BUT A PEST THAT HARMS TAKAYO'S WELL-BEING!
IT'S MORE IMPORTANT TO FINALIZE THEIR ENGAGEMENT THAN TO BRING HIM BACK!!
Takayo is my life.
...
He hasn't changed.
I WAS THINKING IT'S ABOUT TIME...
...WE SETTLE THE MATTER FOR GOOD.
I'LL PREPARE A PRESENT FOR ITO MIURA.
DINNG
DONNG
CAREER GUIDANCE
WHOMP
...

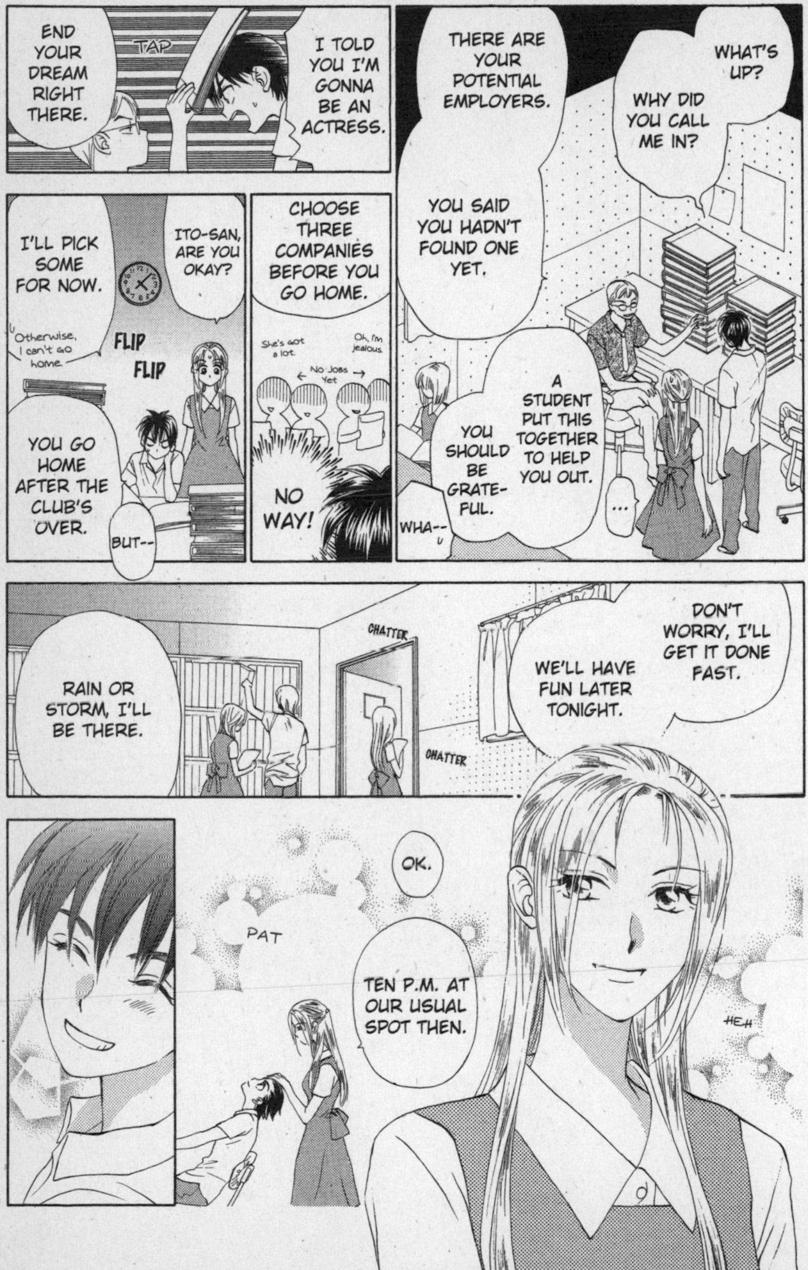
WHAT'S UP?
WHY DID YOU CALL ME IN?
THERE ARE YOUR POTENTIAL EMPLOYERS.
YOU SAID YOU HADN'T FOUND ONE YET.
A STUDENT PUT THIS TOGETHER TO HELP YOU OUT.
YOU SHOULD BE GRATEFUL.
...
WHA--
I TOLD YOU I'M GONNA BE AN ACTRESS.
TAP
END YOUR DREAM RIGHT THERE.
CHOOSE THREE COMPANIES BEFORE YOU GO HOME.
Oh, I'm jealous.
No Jobs Yet
She's got a lot.
NO WAY!
ITO-SAN, ARE YOU OKAY?
I'LL PICK SOME FOR NOW.
Otherwise, I can't go home.
FLIP
FLIP
YOU GO HOME AFTER THE CLUB'S OVER.
BUT--
DON'T WORRY, I'LL GET IT DONE FAST.
WE'LL HAVE FUN LATER TONIGHT.
CHATTER
CHATTER
RAIN OR STORM, I'LL BE THERE.
HEH
OK.
TEN P.M. AT OUR USUAL SPOT THEN.
PAT

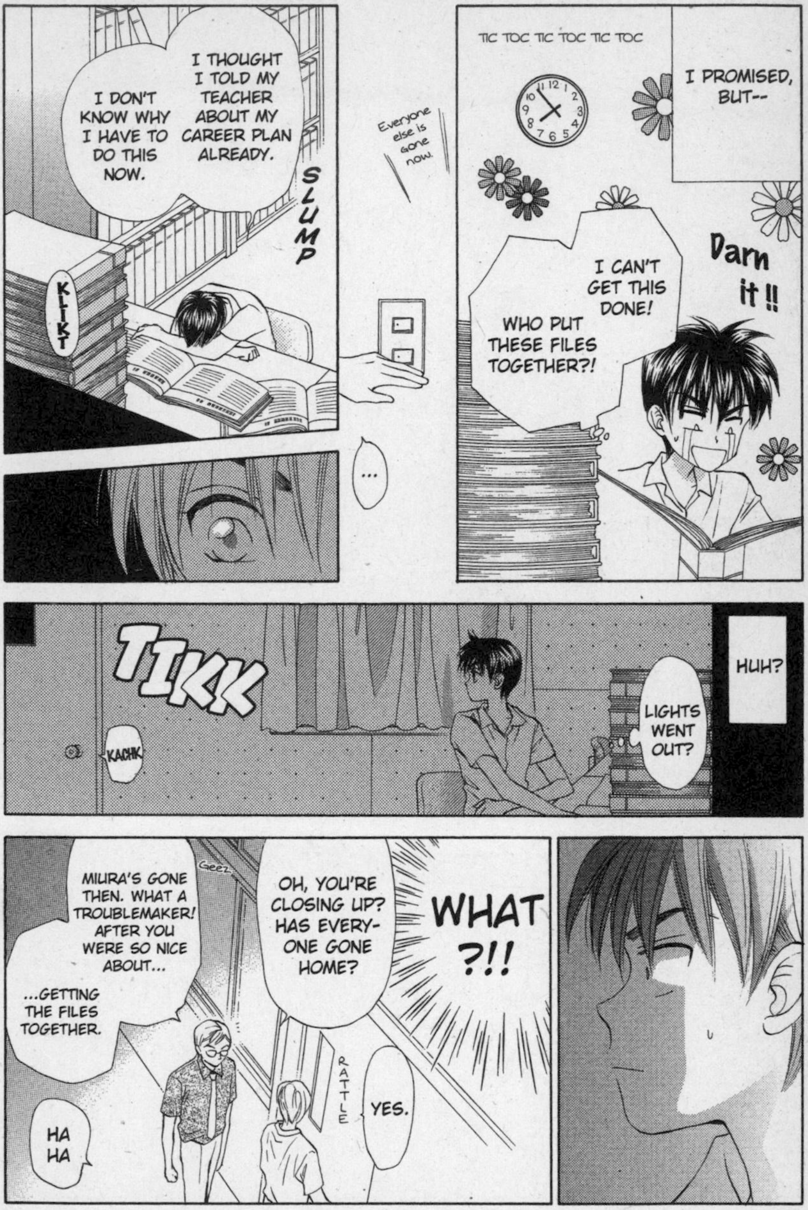
TIC TOC TIC TOC TIC TOC
I PROMISED, BUT--
Darn it !!
I CAN'T GET THIS DONE!
WHO PUT THESE FILES TOGETHER?!
Everyone else is gone now.
I THOUGHT I TOLD MY TEACHER ABOUT MY CAREER PLAN ALREADY.
I DON'T KNOW WHY I HAVE TO DO THIS NOW.
SLUMP
KLIKT
...
HUH?
LIGHTS WENT OUT?
TIKK
KACHK
WHAT ?!!
OH, YOU'RE CLOSING UP? HAS EVERY-ONE GONE HOME?
Geez
MIURA'S GONE THEN. WHAT A TROUBLEMAKER! AFTER YOU WERE SO NICE ABOUT...
...GETTING THE FILES TOGETHER.
RATTLE
YES.
HA HA

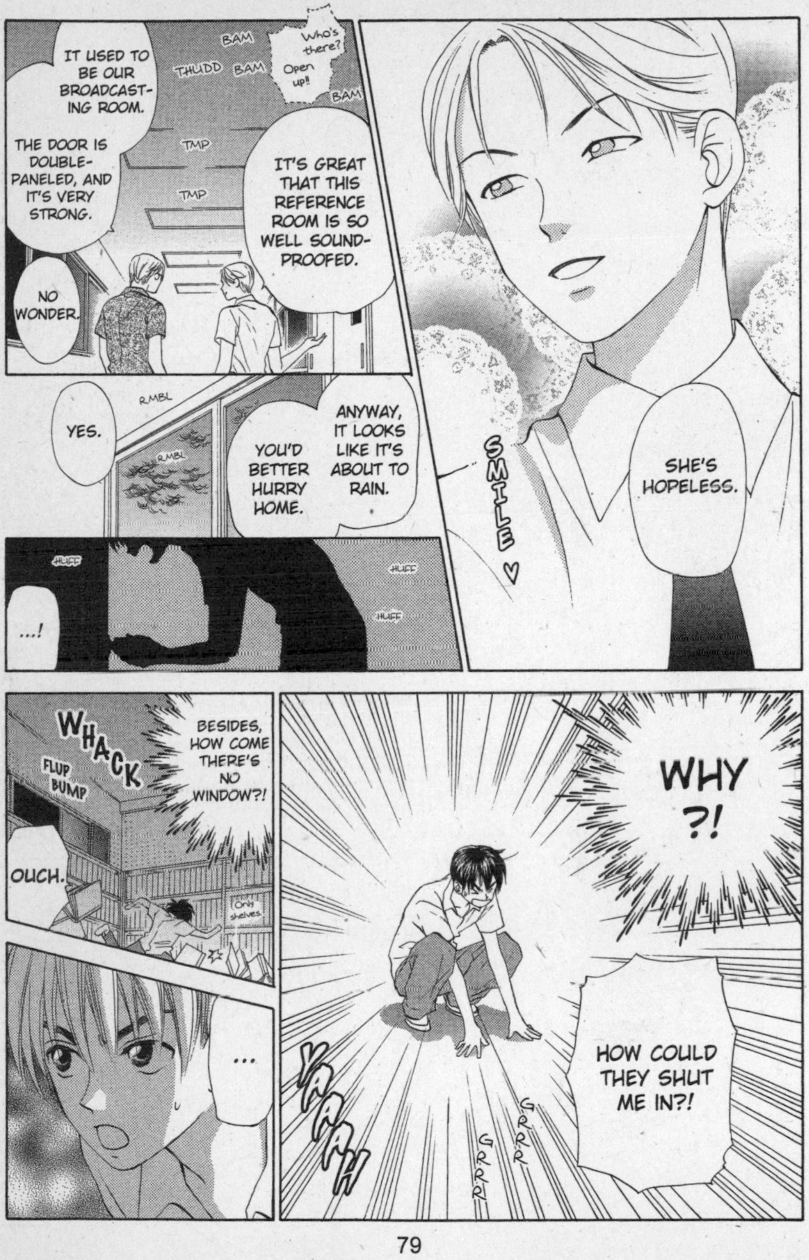

SHE'S HOPELESS.
SMILE ♥
Who's there? Open up!!
BAM
THUDD BAM
BAM
IT'S GREAT THAT THIS REFERENCE ROOM IS SO WELL SOUND-PROOFED.
IT USED TO BE OUR BROADCAST-ING ROOM.
THE DOOR IS DOUBLE-PANELED, AND IT'S VERY STRONG.
TMP
TMP
NO WONDER.
ANYWAY, IT LOOKS LIKE IT'S ABOUT TO RAIN.
YOU'D BETTER HURRY HOME.
RMBL
RMBL
YES.
HUFF
HUFF
HUFF
...!
WHY ?!
HOW COULD THEY SHUT ME IN?!
GRRR
GRRR
YAAAH
BESIDES, HOW COME THERE'S NO WINDOW?!
WHACK
FLUP
BUMP
OUCH.
Only shelves.
...

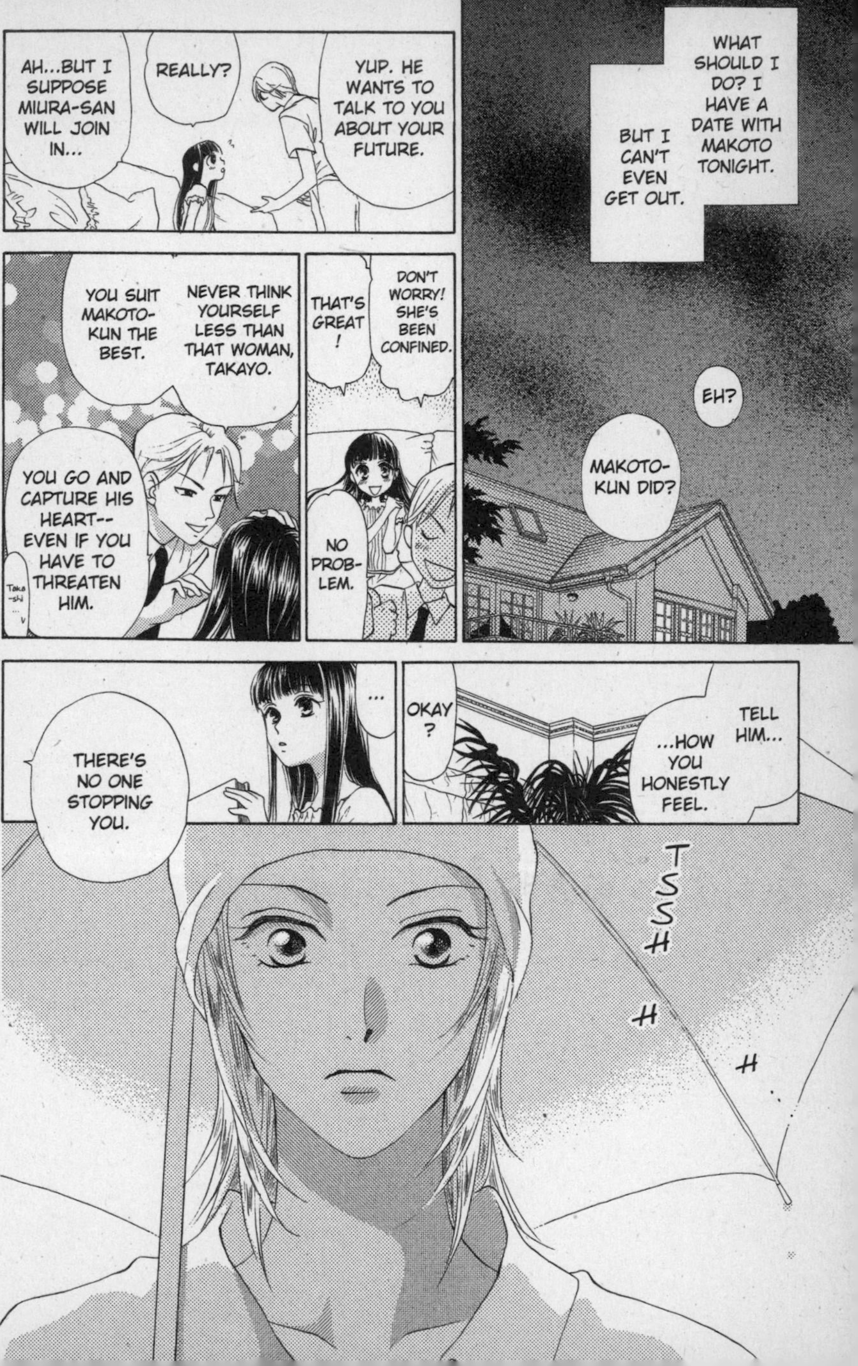
WHAT SHOULD I DO? I HAVE A DATE WITH MAKOTO TONIGHT.
BUT I CAN'T EVEN GET OUT.
EH?
MAKOTO-KUN DID?
YUP. HE WANTS TO TALK TO YOU ABOUT YOUR FUTURE.
REALLY?
AH...BUT I SUPPOSE MIURA-SAN WILL JOIN IN...
DON'T WORRY! SHE'S BEEN CONFINED.
THAT'S GREAT!
NO PROBLEM.
NEVER THINK YOURSELF LESS THAN THAT WOMAN, TAKAYO.
YOU SUIT MAKOTO-KUN THE BEST.
YOU GO AND CAPTURE HIS HEART--EVEN IF YOU HAVE TO THREATEN HIM.
Takashi...♥
TELL HIM...
...HOW YOU HONESTLY FEEL.
OKAY?
...
THERE'S NO ONE STOPPING YOU.
TSSH
H
H

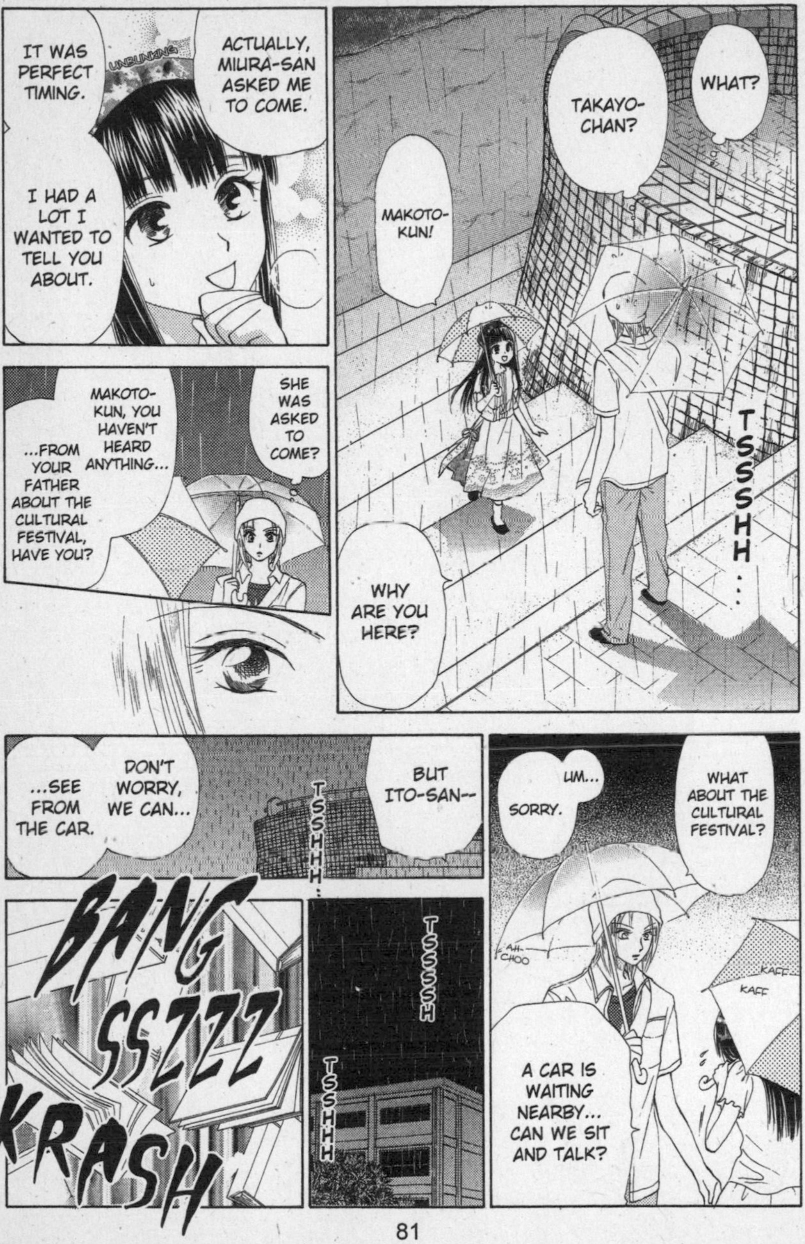
WHAT?
TAKAYO-CHAN?
MAKOTO-KUN!
TSSSHH...
WHY ARE YOU HERE?
ACTUALLY, MIURA-SAN ASKED ME TO COME.
UNBLINKING
IT WAS PERFECT TIMING.
I HAD A LOT I WANTED TO TELL YOU ABOUT.
SHE WAS ASKED TO COME?
MAKOTO-KUN, YOU HAVEN'T HEARD ANYTHING...
...FROM YOUR FATHER ABOUT THE CULTURAL FESTIVAL, HAVE YOU?
WHAT ABOUT THE CULTURAL FESTIVAL?
UM...
SORRY.
AH-CHOO
KAFF
KAFF
A CAR IS WAITING NEARBY... CAN WE SIT AND TALK?
BUT ITO-SAN--
TSSHHH...
DON'T WORRY, WE CAN...
...SEE FROM THE CAR.
TSSSSH
TSSHHH
BANG
SSZZZ
KRASH

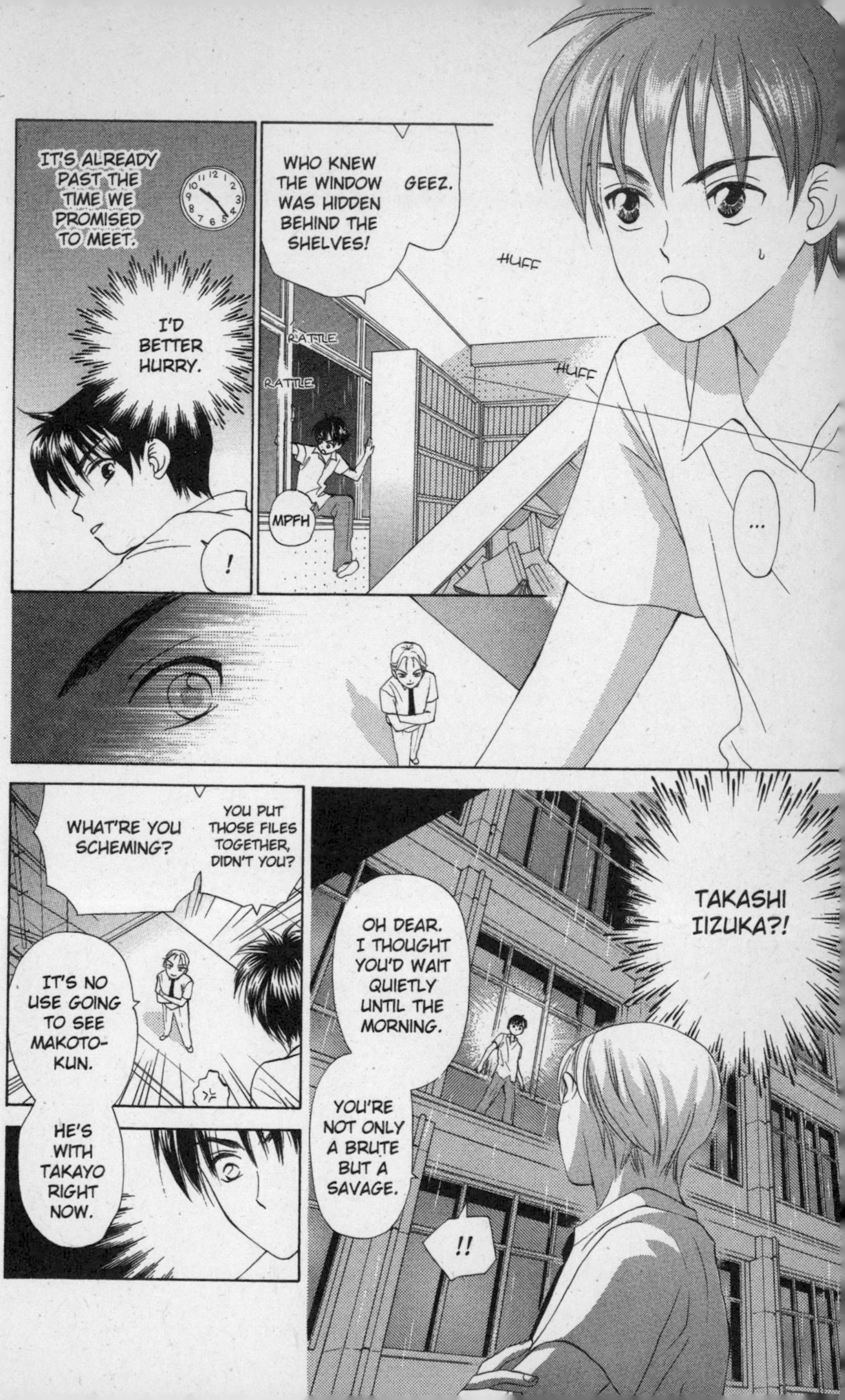
HUFF
HUFF
...
GEEZ.
WHO KNEW THE WINDOW WAS HIDDEN BEHIND THE SHELVES!
RATTLE
RATTLE
MPFH
IT'S ALREADY PAST THE TIME WE PROMISED TO MEET.
I'D BETTER HURRY.
!
TAKASHI IIZUKA?!
OH DEAR. I THOUGHT YOU'D WAIT QUIETLY UNTIL THE MORNING.
YOU'RE NOT ONLY A BRUTE BUT A SAVAGE.
!!
YOU PUT THOSE FILES TOGETHER, DIDN'T YOU?
WHAT'RE YOU SCHEMING?
IT'S NO USE GOING TO SEE MAKOTO-KUN.
HE'S WITH TAKAYO RIGHT NOW.

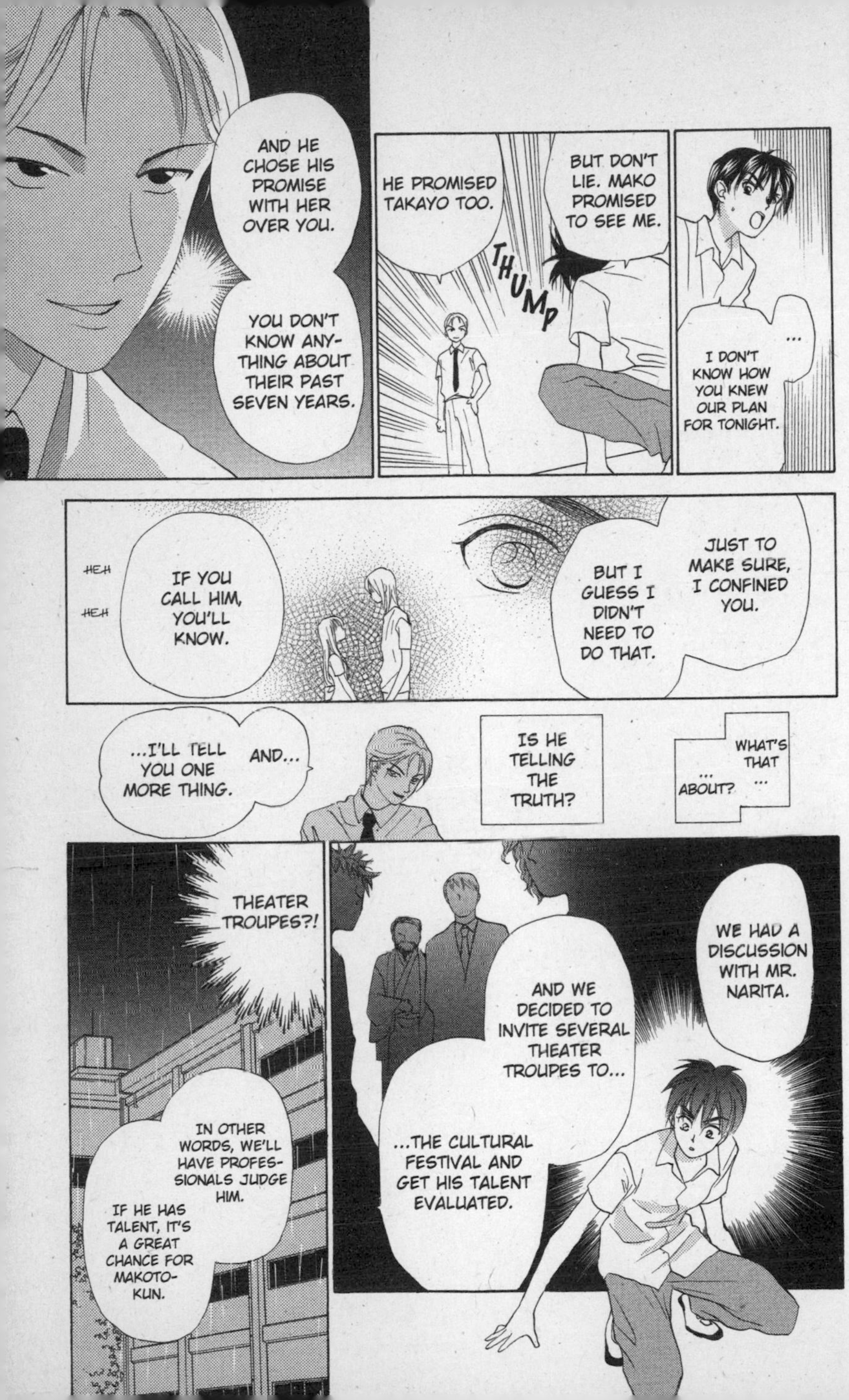
...
I DON'T KNOW HOW YOU KNEW OUR PLAN FOR TONIGHT.
BUT DON'T LIE. MAKO PROMISED TO SEE ME.
THUMP
HE PROMISED TAKAYO TOO.
AND HE CHOSE HIS PROMISE WITH HER OVER YOU.
YOU DON'T KNOW ANYTHING ABOUT THEIR PAST SEVEN YEARS.
JUST TO MAKE SURE, I CONFINED YOU.
BUT I GUESS I DIDN'T NEED TO DO THAT.
IF YOU CALL HIM, YOU'LL KNOW.
HEH
HEH
WHAT'S THAT ...
... ABOUT?
IS HE TELLING THE TRUTH?
AND...
...I'LL TELL YOU ONE MORE THING.
WE HAD A DISCUSSION WITH MR. NARITA.
AND WE DECIDED TO INVITE SEVERAL THEATER TROUPES TO...
...THE CULTURAL FESTIVAL AND GET HIS TALENT EVALUATED.
THEATER TROUPES?!
IN OTHER WORDS, WE'LL HAVE PROFESSIONALS JUDGE HIM.
IF HE HAS TALENT, IT'S A GREAT CHANCE FOR MAKOTO-KUN.

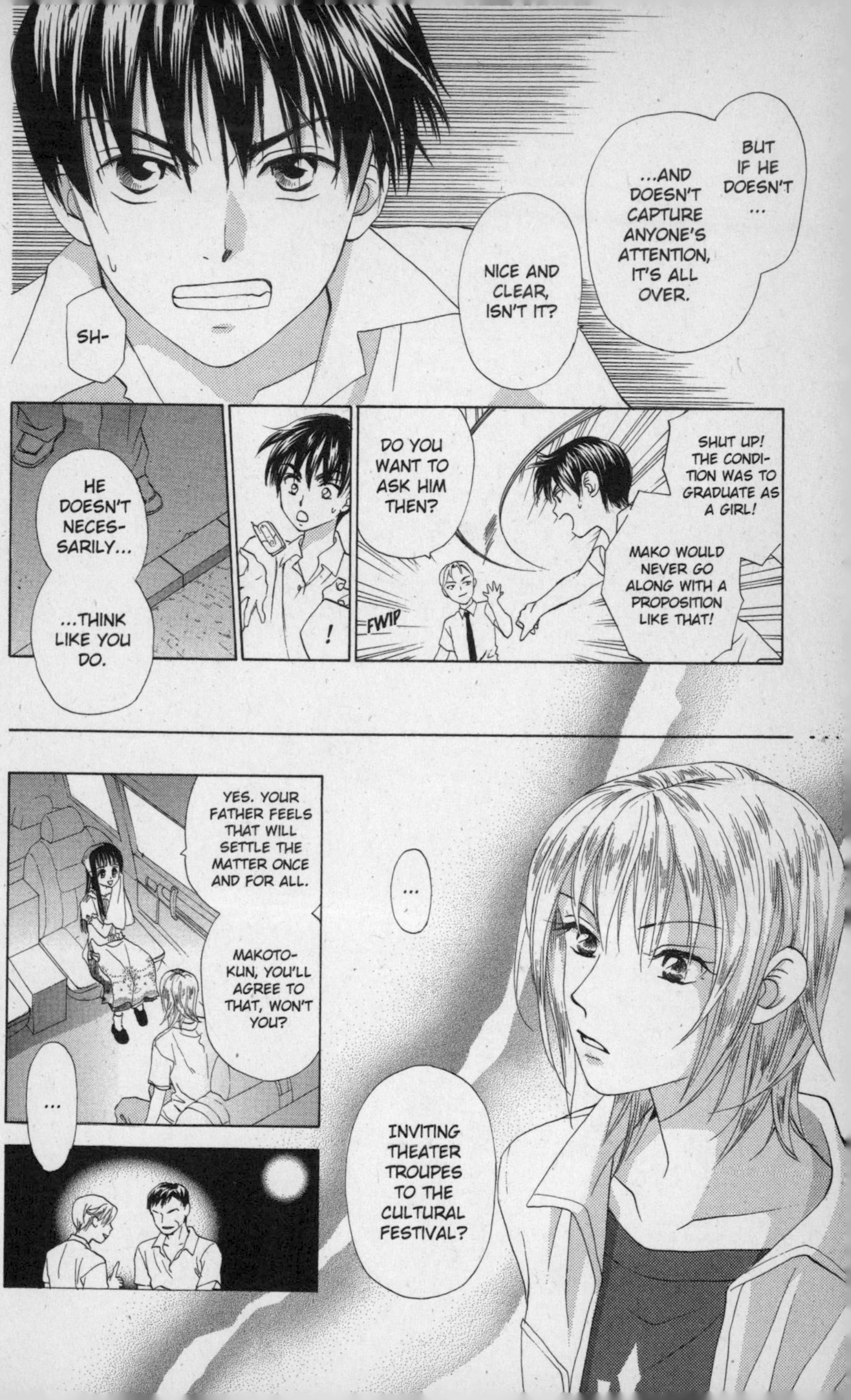
BUT IF HE DOESN'T ...
...AND DOESN'T CAPTURE ANYONE'S ATTENTION, IT'S ALL OVER.
NICE AND CLEAR, ISN'T IT?
SH-
SHUT UP! THE CONDITION WAS TO GRADUATE AS A GIRL!
MAKO WOULD NEVER GO ALONG WITH A PROPOSITION LIKE THAT!
DO YOU WANT TO ASK HIM THEN?
FWIP
!
HE DOESN'T NECES-SARILY...
...THINK LIKE YOU DO.
...
INVITING THEATER TROUPES TO THE CULTURAL FESTIVAL?
YES. YOUR FATHER FEELS THAT WILL SETTLE THE MATTER ONCE AND FOR ALL.
MAKOTO-KUN, YOU'LL AGREE TO THAT, WON'T YOU?
...

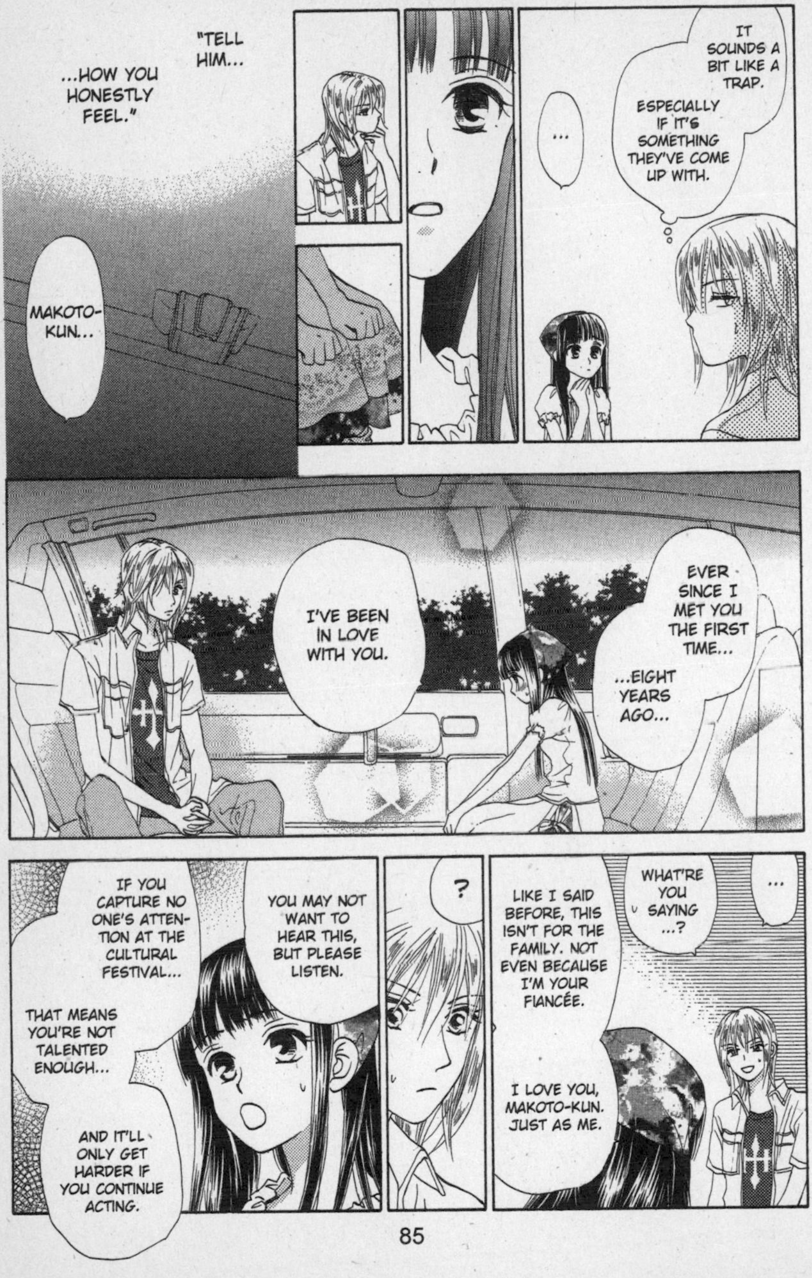
IT SOUNDS A BIT LIKE A TRAP.
ESPECIALLY IF IT'S SOMETHING THEY'VE COME UP WITH.
...
"TELL HIM...
...HOW YOU HONESTLY FEEL."
MAKOTO-KUN...
EVER SINCE I MET YOU THE FIRST TIME...
...EIGHT YEARS AGO...
I'VE BEEN IN LOVE WITH YOU.
...
WHAT'RE YOU SAYING ...?
LIKE I SAID BEFORE, THIS ISN'T FOR THE FAMILY. NOT EVEN BECAUSE I'M YOUR FIANCÉE.
I LOVE YOU, MAKOTO-KUN. JUST AS ME.
?
YOU MAY NOT WANT TO HEAR THIS, BUT PLEASE LISTEN.
IF YOU CAPTURE NO ONE'S ATTENTION AT THE CULTURAL FESTIVAL...
THAT MEANS YOU'RE NOT TALENTED ENOUGH...
AND IT'LL ONLY GET HARDER IF YOU CONTINUE ACTING.

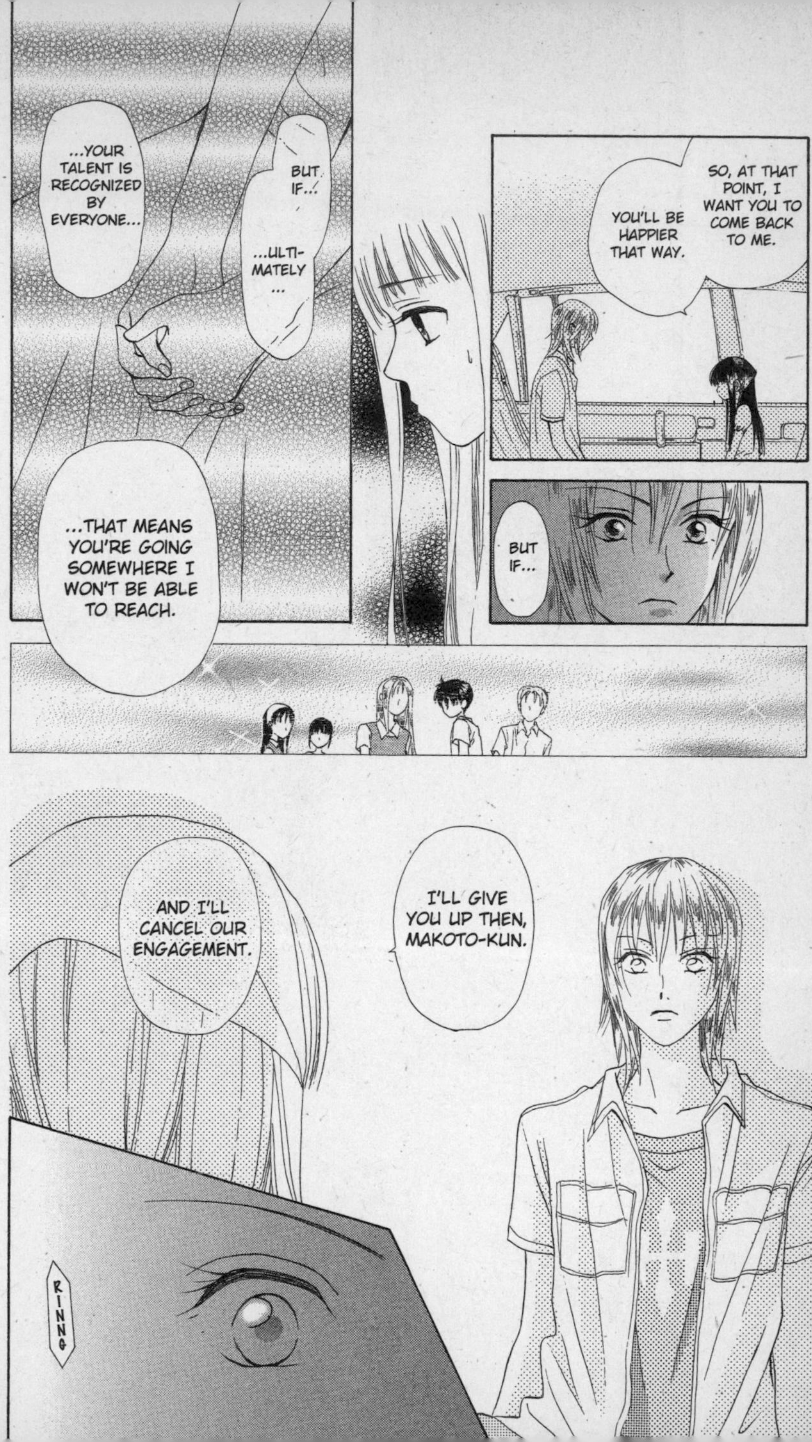
SO, AT THAT POINT, I WANT YOU TO COME BACK TO ME.
YOU'LL BE HAPPIER THAT WAY.
BUT IF...
BUT IF...
...ULTIMATELY...
...YOUR TALENT IS RECOGNIZED BY EVERYONE...
...THAT MEANS YOU'RE GOING SOMEWHERE I WON'T BE ABLE TO REACH.
I'LL GIVE YOU UP THEN, MAKOTO-KUN.
AND I'LL CANCEL OUR ENGAGEMENT.
RINNG

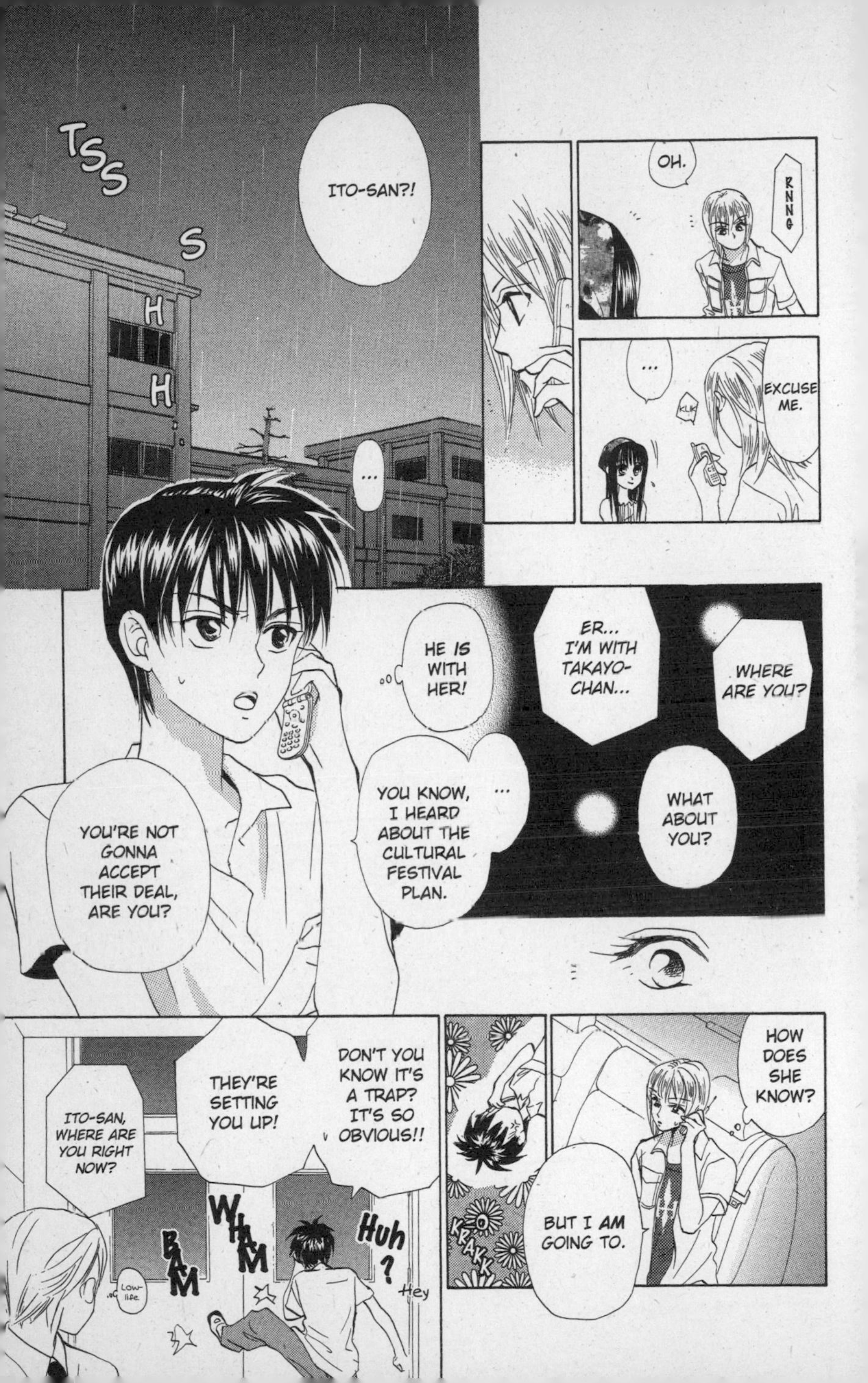
RNNG
OH.
EXCUSE ME.
KLIK
...
TSSSHH
ITO-SAN?!
...
WHERE ARE YOU?
ER... I'M WITH TAKAYO-CHAN...
WHAT ABOUT YOU?
HE IS WITH HER!
...
YOU KNOW, I HEARD ABOUT THE CULTURAL FESTIVAL PLAN.
YOU'RE NOT GONNA ACCEPT THEIR DEAL, ARE YOU?
HOW DOES SHE KNOW?
BUT I AM GOING TO.
KRAKK
DON'T YOU KNOW IT'S A TRAP? IT'S SO OBVIOUS!!
THEY'RE SETTING YOU UP!
ITO-SAN, WHERE ARE YOU RIGHT NOW?
Huh?
Hey
WHAM
BAM
Low life.

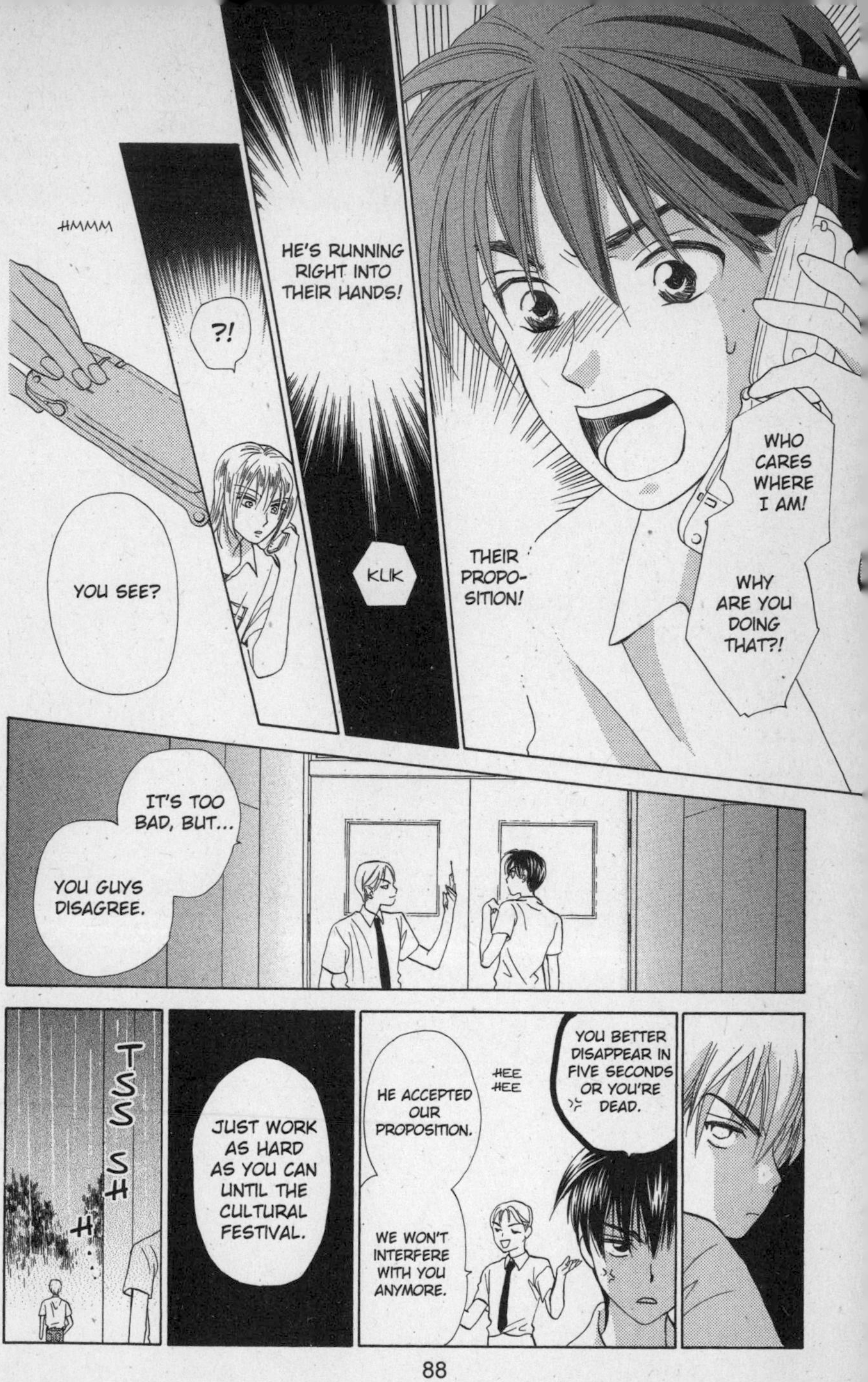
WHO CARES WHERE I AM!
WHY ARE YOU DOING THAT?!
THEIR PROPO-SITION!
HE'S RUNNING RIGHT INTO THEIR HANDS!
KLIK
?!
HMMM
YOU SEE?
IT'S TOO BAD, BUT...
YOU GUYS DISAGREE.
YOU BETTER DISAPPEAR IN FIVE SECONDS OR YOU'RE DEAD.
HEE HEE
HE ACCEPTED OUR PROPOSITION.
WE WON'T INTERFERE WITH YOU ANYMORE.
JUST WORK AS HARD AS YOU CAN UNTIL THE CULTURAL FESTIVAL.
TSS SH H...

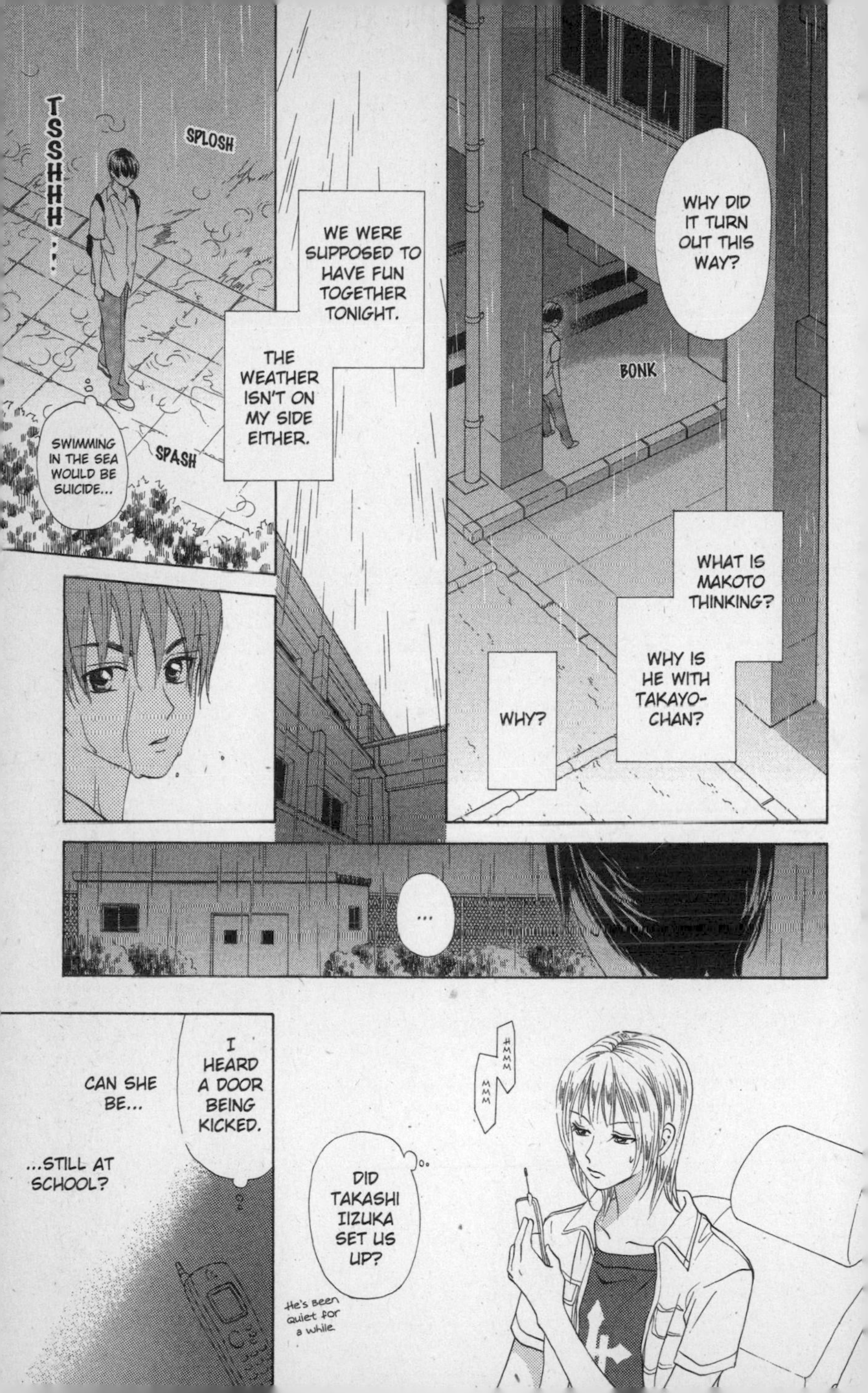
WHY DID IT TURN OUT THIS WAY?
BONK
WHAT IS MAKOTO THINKING?
WHY IS HE WITH TAKAYO-CHAN?
WHY?
WE WERE SUPPOSED TO HAVE FUN TOGETHER TONIGHT.
THE WEATHER ISN'T ON MY SIDE EITHER.
SPLOSH
TSSHHH...
SWIMMING IN THE SEA WOULD BE SUICIDE...
SPASH
...
HMMM
MMM
DID TAKASHI IIZUKA SET US UP?
He's been quiet for a while.
I HEARD A DOOR BEING KICKED.
CAN SHE BE...
...STILL AT SCHOOL?

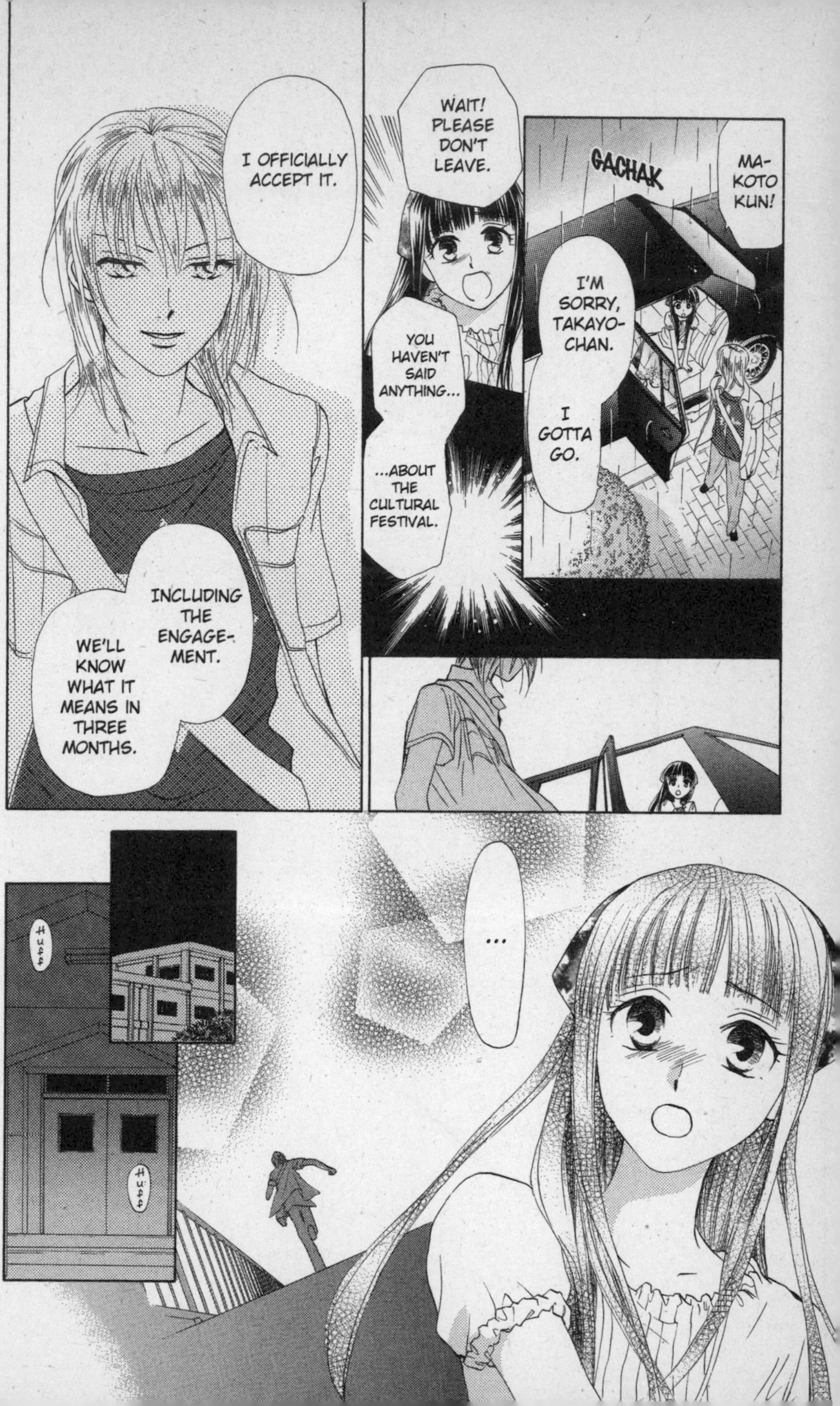
MA-KOTO KUN!
GACHAK
I'M SORRY, TAKAYO-CHAN.
I GOTTA GO.
WAIT! PLEASE DON'T LEAVE.
YOU HAVEN'T SAID ANYTHING...
...ABOUT THE CULTURAL FESTIVAL.
I OFFICIALLY ACCEPT IT.
INCLUDING THE ENGAGE-MENT.
WE'LL KNOW WHAT IT MEANS IN THREE MONTHS.
...
Huff
Huff

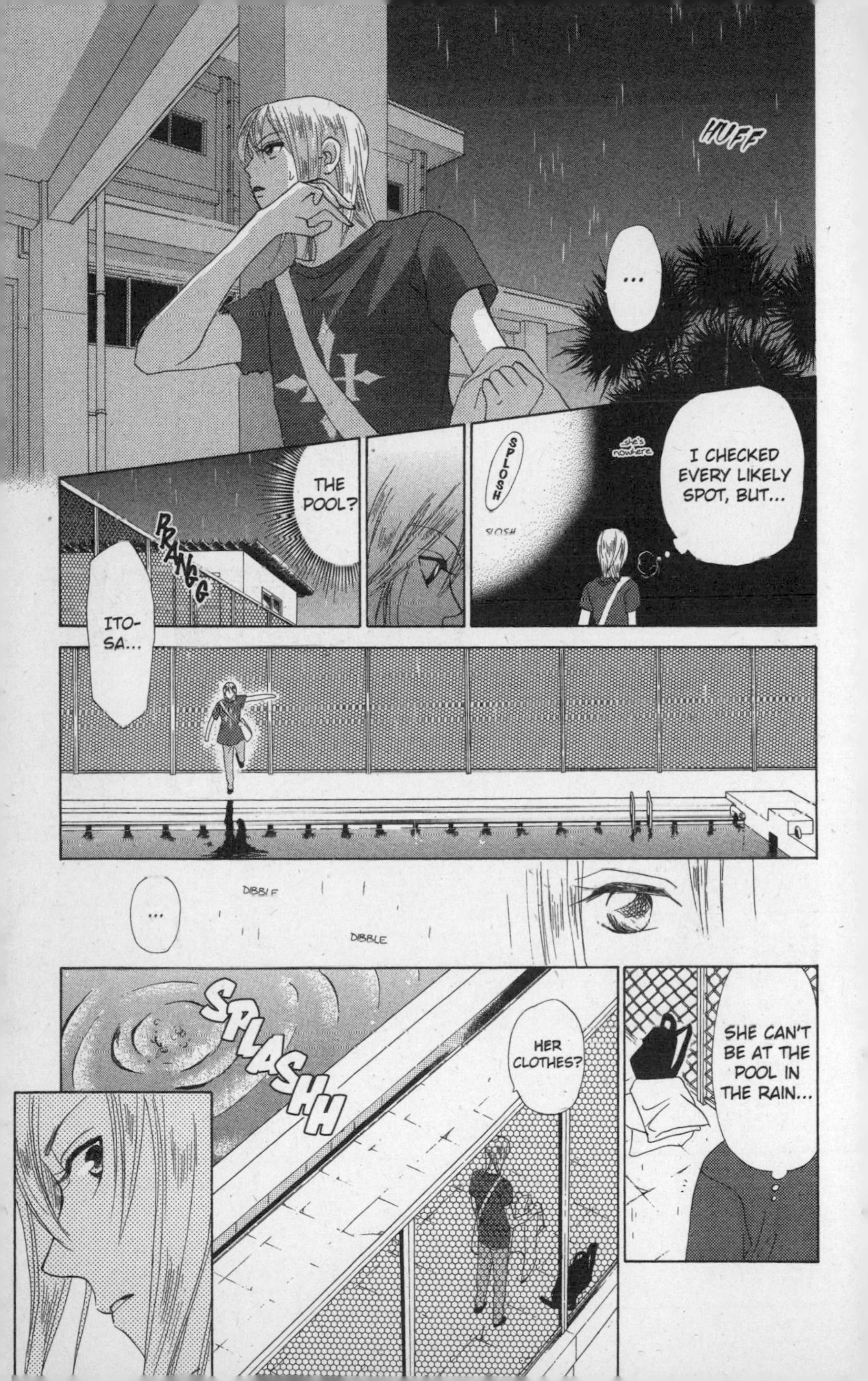
HUFF
...
I CHECKED EVERY LIKELY SPOT, BUT...
she's nowhere
SPLOSH
SLOSH
THE POOL?
RRANGG
ITO-SA...
DIBBLE
DIBBLE
...
SHE CAN'T BE AT THE POOL IN THE RAIN...
HER CLOTHES?
SPLASHH

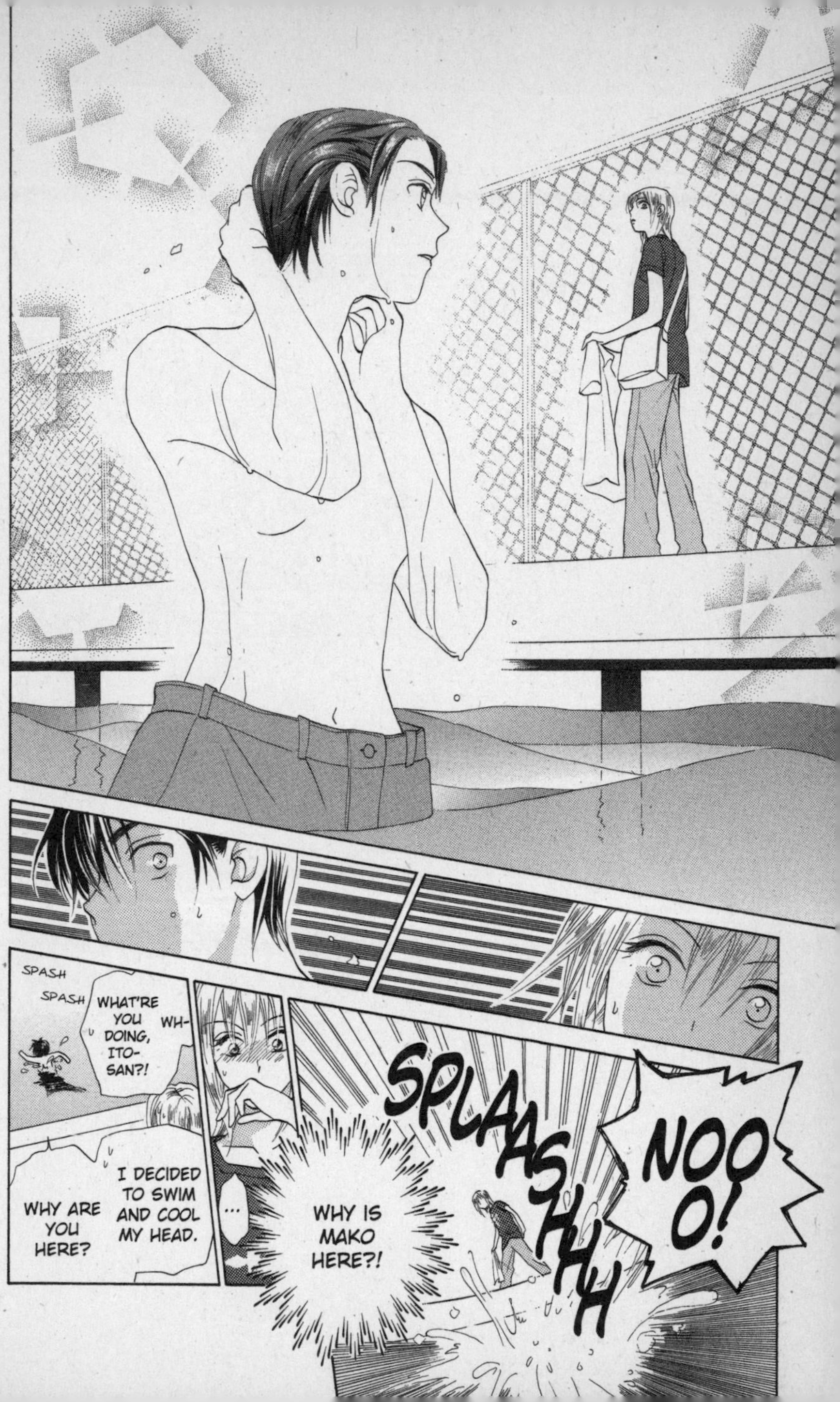
SPLAASHHH
NOOO!
WHY IS MAKO HERE?!
WH-
...
SPASH
SPASH
WHAT'RE YOU DOING, ITO-SAN?!
I DECIDED TO SWIM AND COOL MY HEAD.
WHY ARE YOU HERE?

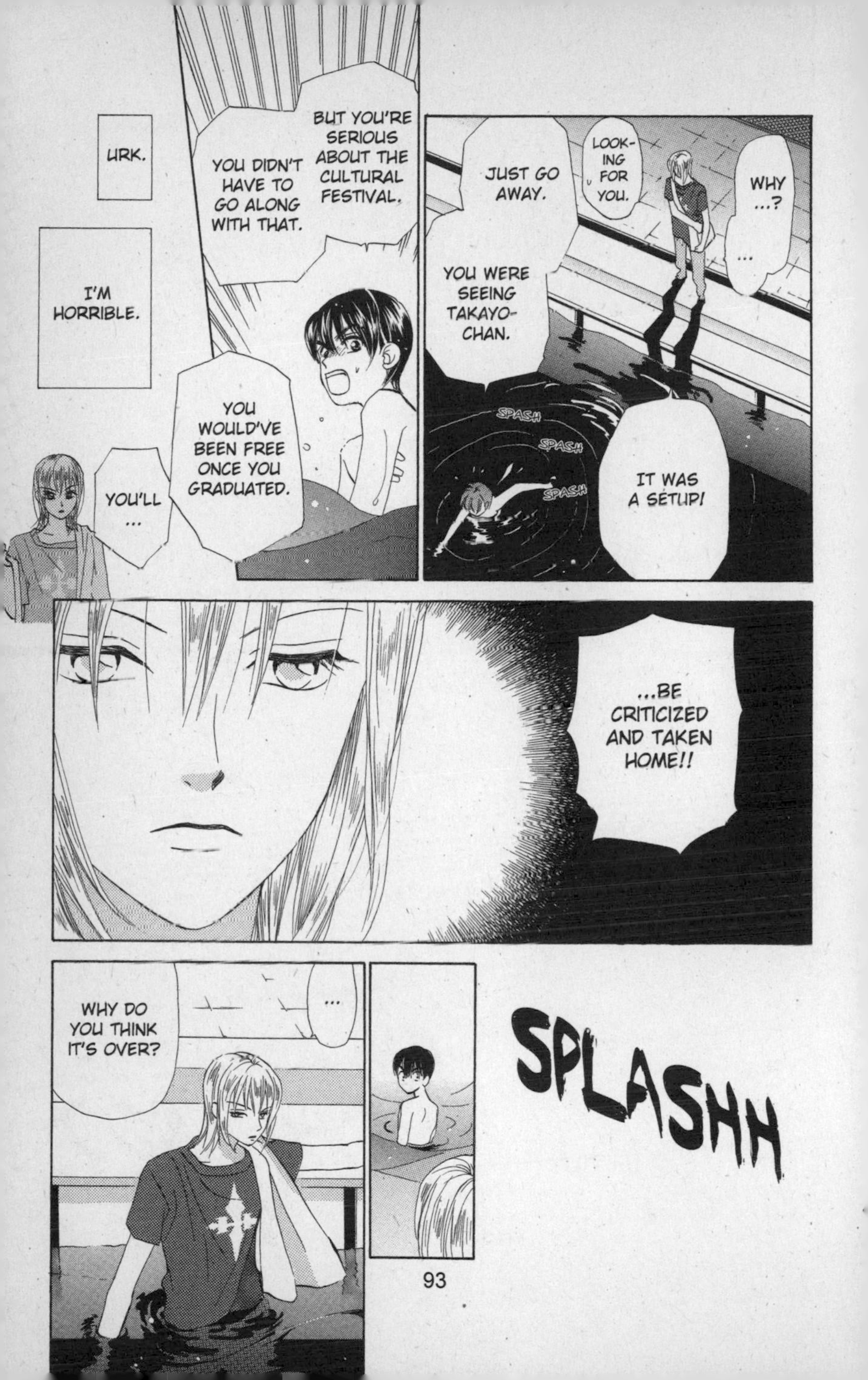
WHY ...?
...
LOOKING FOR YOU.
JUST GO AWAY.
YOU WERE SEEING TAKAYO-CHAN.
SPASH
SPASH
SPASH
IT WAS A SETUP!
BUT YOU'RE SERIOUS ABOUT THE CULTURAL FESTIVAL.
YOU DIDN'T HAVE TO GO ALONG WITH THAT.
URK.
I'M HORRIBLE.
YOU WOULD'VE BEEN FREE ONCE YOU GRADUATED.
YOU'LL ...
...BE CRITICIZED AND TAKEN HOME!!
SPLASHH
...
WHY DO YOU THINK IT'S OVER?

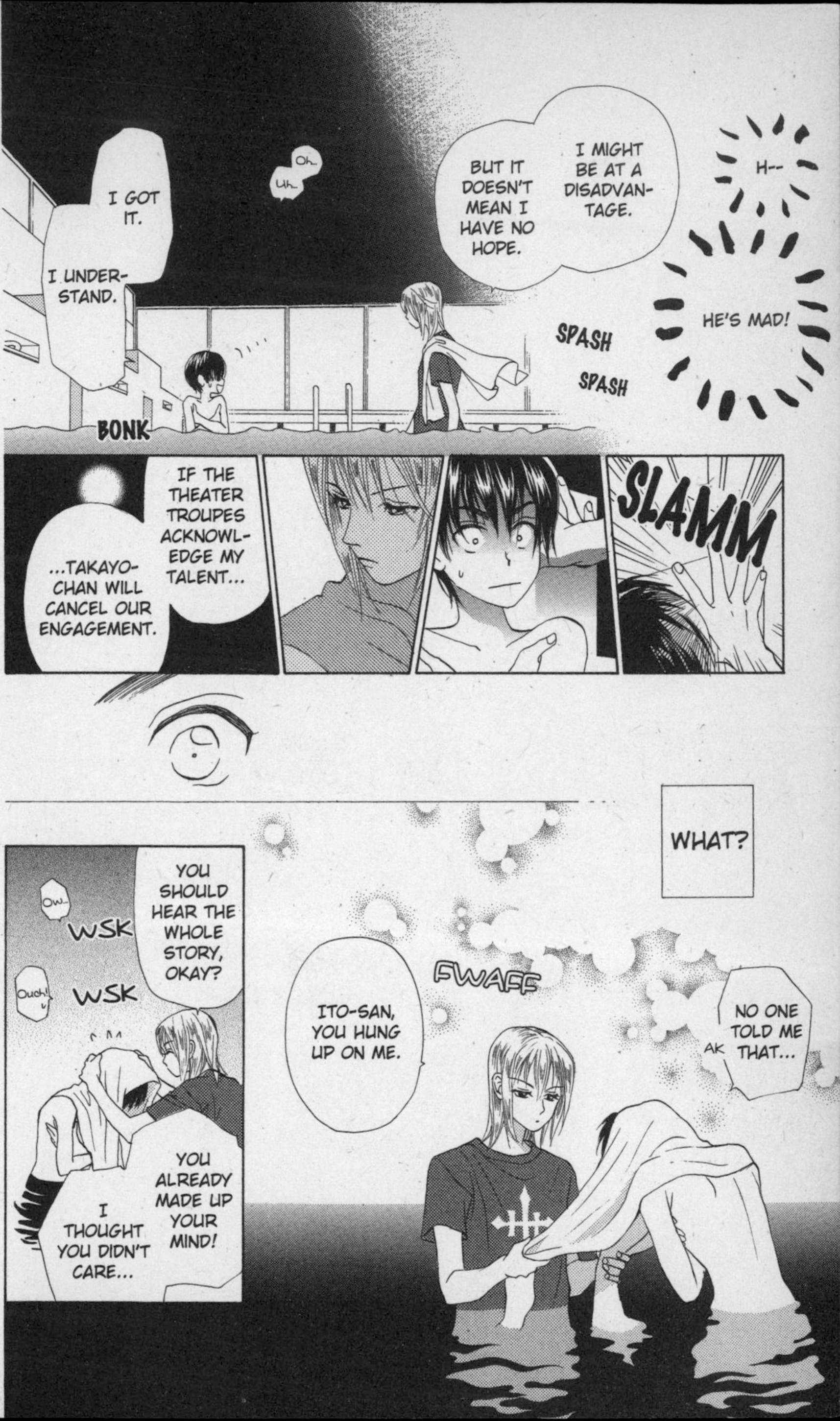
H--
HE'S MAD!
SPASH
SPASH
I MIGHT BE AT A DISADVANTAGE.
BUT IT DOESN'T MEAN I HAVE NO HOPE.
Oh..
Uh..
I GOT IT.
I UNDERSTAND.
BONK
SLAMM
IF THE THEATER TROUPES ACKNOWLEDGE MY TALENT...
...TAKAYO-CHAN WILL CANCEL OUR ENGAGEMENT.
WHAT?
NO ONE TOLD ME THAT...
AK
FWAFF
ITO-SAN, YOU HUNG UP ON ME.
YOU SHOULD HEAR THE WHOLE STORY, OKAY?
Ow..
WSK
Ouch!
WSK
YOU ALREADY MADE UP YOUR MIND!
I THOUGHT YOU DIDN'T CARE...

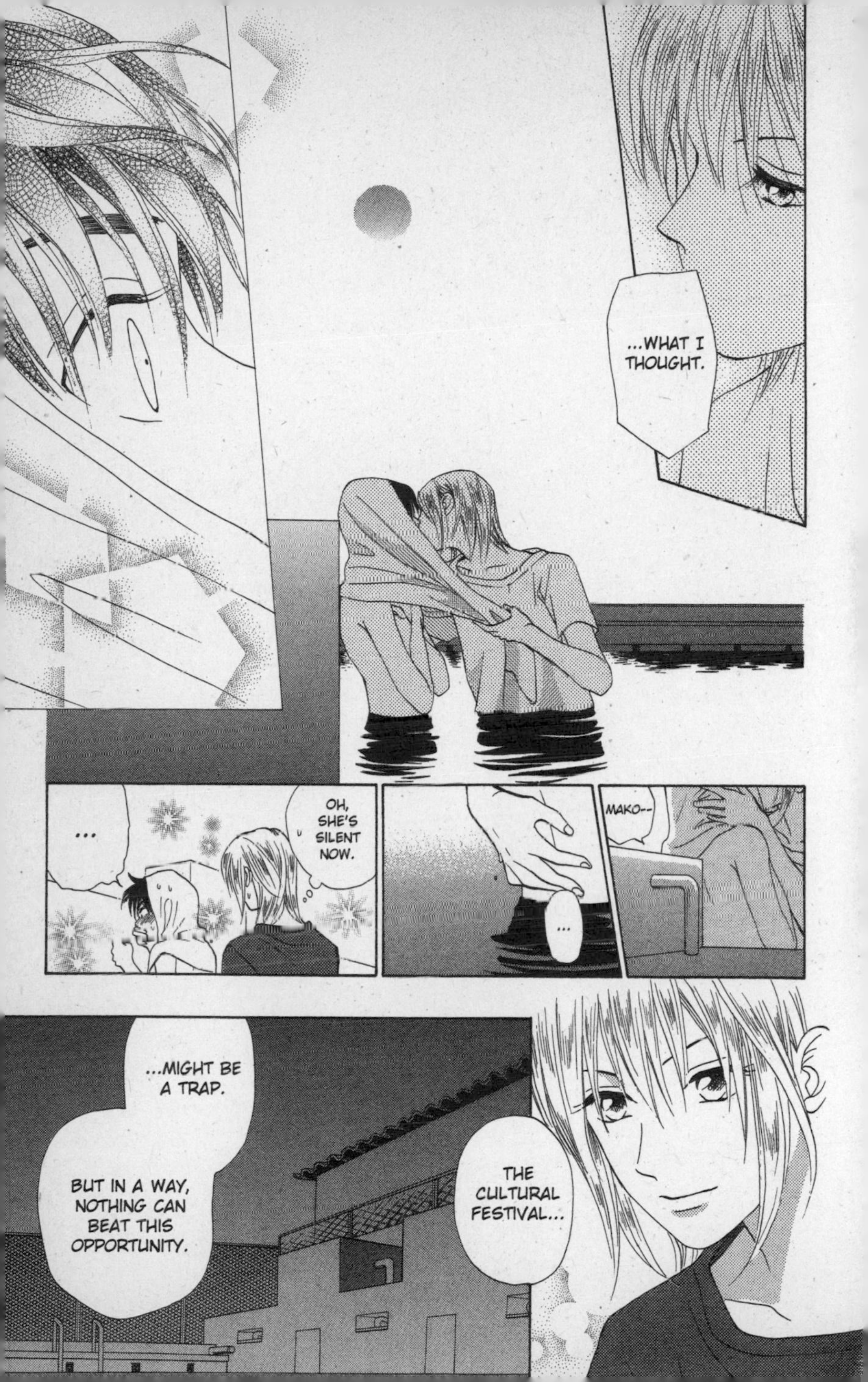
...WHAT I THOUGHT.
MAKO--
...
OH, SHE'S SILENT NOW.
...
THE CULTURAL FESTIVAL...
...MIGHT BE A TRAP.
BUT IN A WAY, NOTHING CAN BEAT THIS OPPORTUNITY.

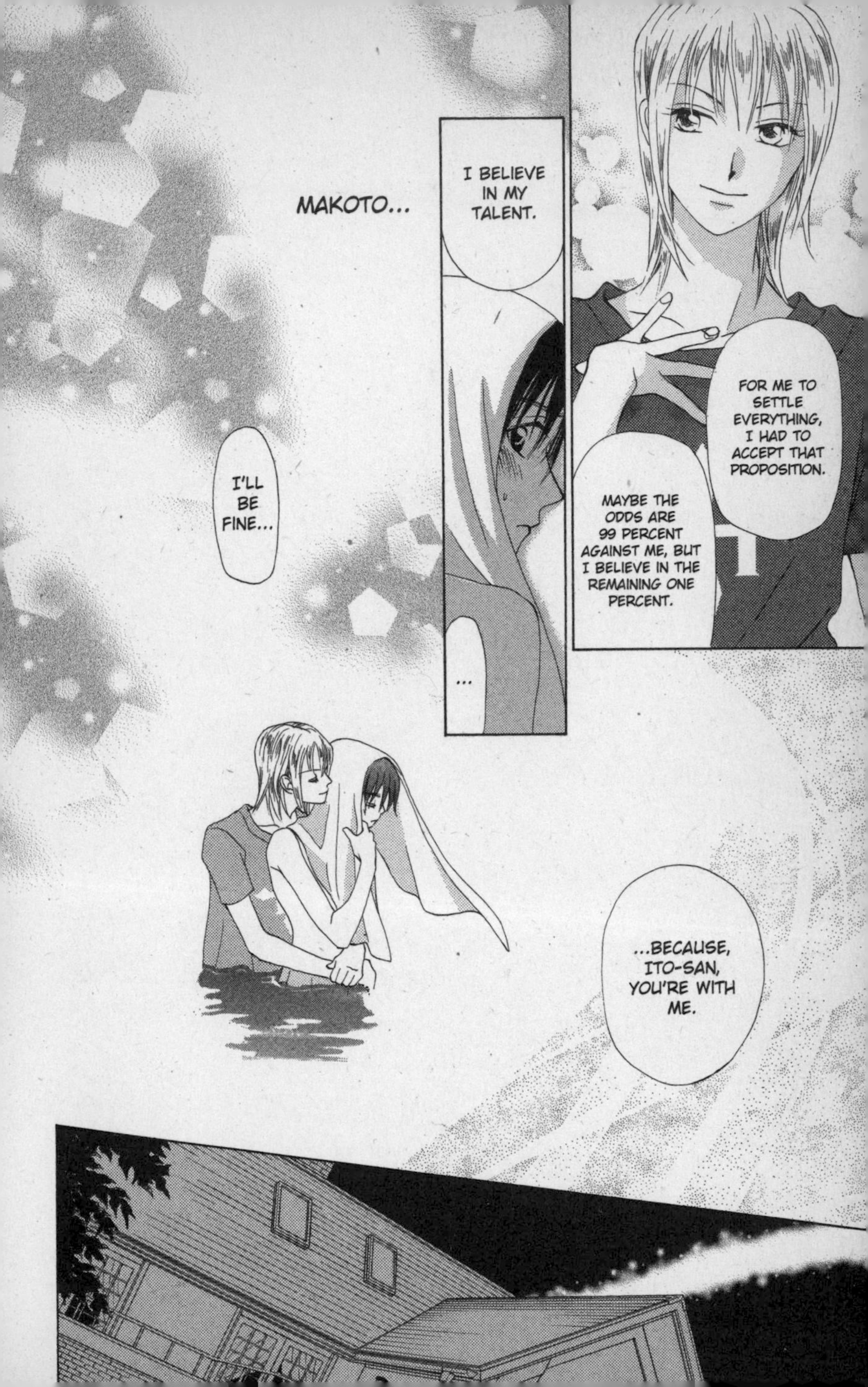
FOR ME TO SETTLE EVERYTHING, I HAD TO ACCEPT THAT PROPOSITION.
MAYBE THE ODDS ARE 99 PERCENT AGAINST ME, BUT I BELIEVE IN THE REMAINING ONE PERCENT.
I BELIEVE IN MY TALENT.
...
MAKOTO...
I'LL BE FINE...
...BECAUSE, ITO-SAN, YOU'RE WITH ME.

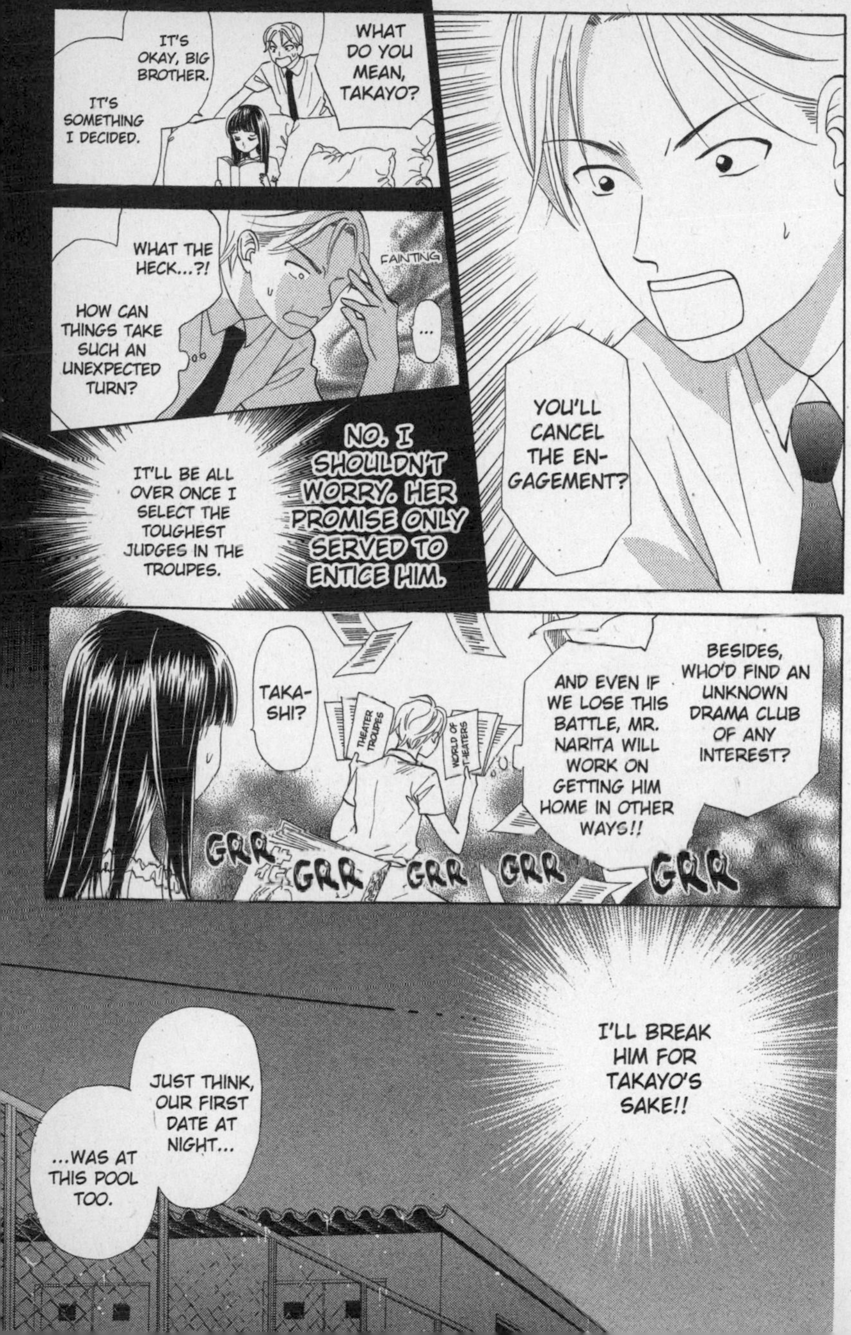
YOU'LL CANCEL THE EN-GAGEMENT?
WHAT DO YOU MEAN, TAKAYO?
IT'S OKAY, BIG BROTHER.
IT'S SOMETHING I DECIDED.
FAINTING
...
WHAT THE HECK...?!
HOW CAN THINGS TAKE SUCH AN UNEXPECTED TURN?
NO. I SHOULDN'T WORRY. HER PROMISE ONLY SERVED TO ENTICE HIM.
IT'LL BE ALL OVER ONCE I SELECT THE TOUGHEST JUDGES IN THE TROUPES.
BESIDES, WHO'D FIND AN UNKNOWN DRAMA CLUB OF ANY INTEREST?
AND EVEN IF WE LOSE THIS BATTLE, MR. NARITA WILL WORK ON GETTING HIM HOME IN OTHER WAYS!!
WORLD OF THEATERS
THEATER TROUPES
TAKA-SHI?
GRR GRR GRR GRR GRR
I'LL BREAK HIM FOR TAKAYO'S SAKE!!
JUST THINK, OUR FIRST DATE AT NIGHT...
...WAS AT THIS POOL TOO.

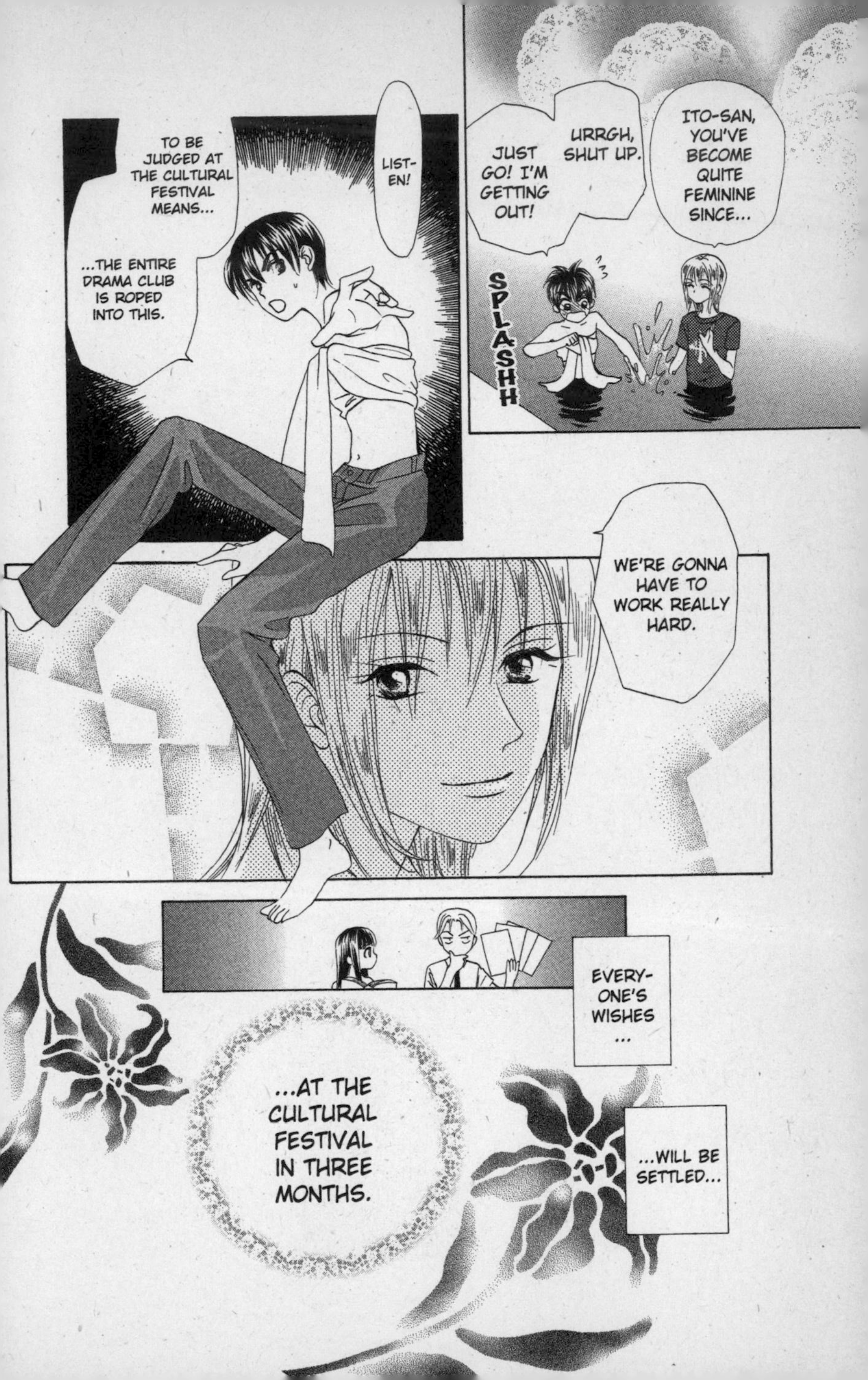
ITO-SAN, YOU'VE BECOME QUITE FEMININE SINCE...
URRGH, SHUT UP.
JUST GO! I'M GETTING OUT!
SPLASHH
LIST-EN!
TO BE JUDGED AT THE CULTURAL FESTIVAL MEANS...
...THE ENTIRE DRAMA CLUB IS ROPED INTO THIS.
WE'RE GONNA HAVE TO WORK REALLY HARD.
EVERY-ONE'S WISHES ...
...WILL BE SETTLED...
...AT THE CULTURAL FESTIVAL IN THREE MONTHS.

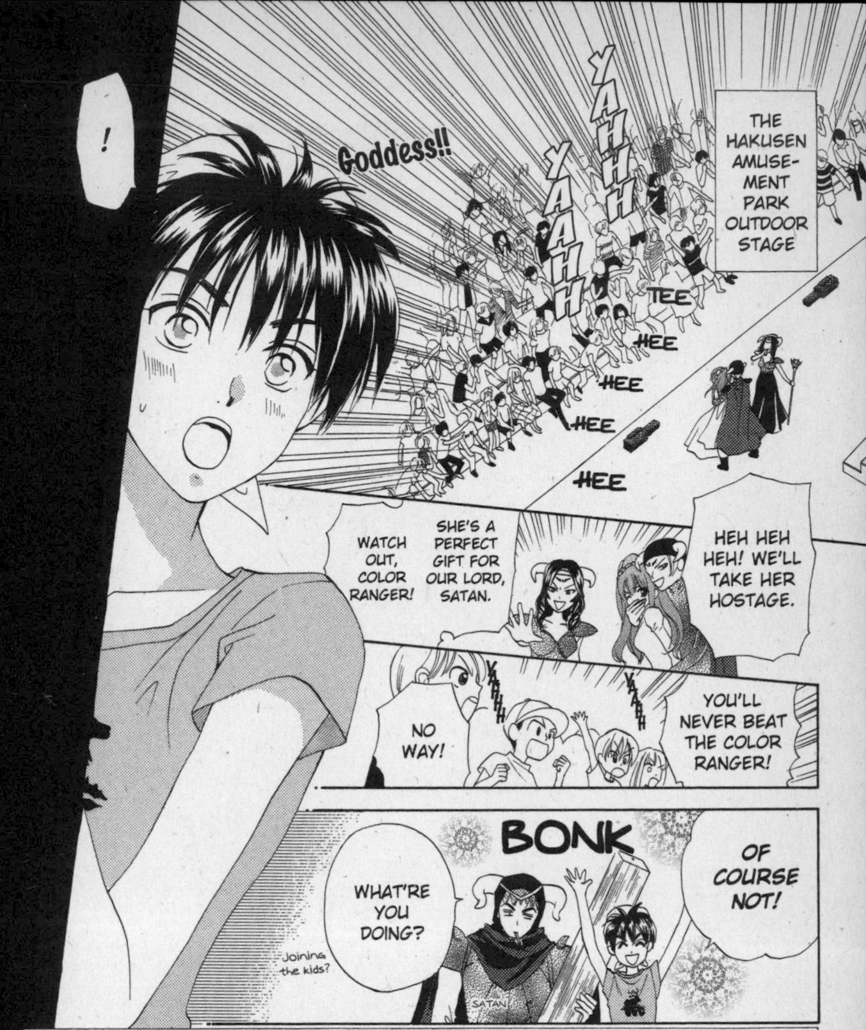
THE HAKUSEN AMUSEMENT PARK OUTDOOR STAGE
YAAHH
YAAHH
Goddess!!
TEE
HEE
HEE
HEE
HEE
HEH HEH HEH! WE'LL TAKE HER HOSTAGE.
SHE'S A PERFECT GIFT FOR OUR LORD, SATAN.
WATCH OUT, COLOR RANGER!
YOU'LL NEVER BEAT THE COLOR RANGER!
YAAHH
YAAHH
NO WAY!
OF COURSE NOT!
BONK
WHAT'RE YOU DOING?
Joining the kids?
SATAN
!

—Behind the Scenes Story ④—

The Japanese word "Megami" means "goddess," not "princess."
Ito sure doesn't seem to know that. But I suppose "Princess Kick" sounds better. Speaking of the kick, geez, it's awful. The drawing turned out horrendous!! I'll do better next time. BTW, I also received letters saying "Ito doesn't have to report everything to Makoto, does she?" You are absolutely right. She doesn't. But Ito felt uncomfortable, especially because of Toki-chan's track record.
He's like a beast in human clothes. Anyhow, it's good nothing bad happened in the end. (Laugh)

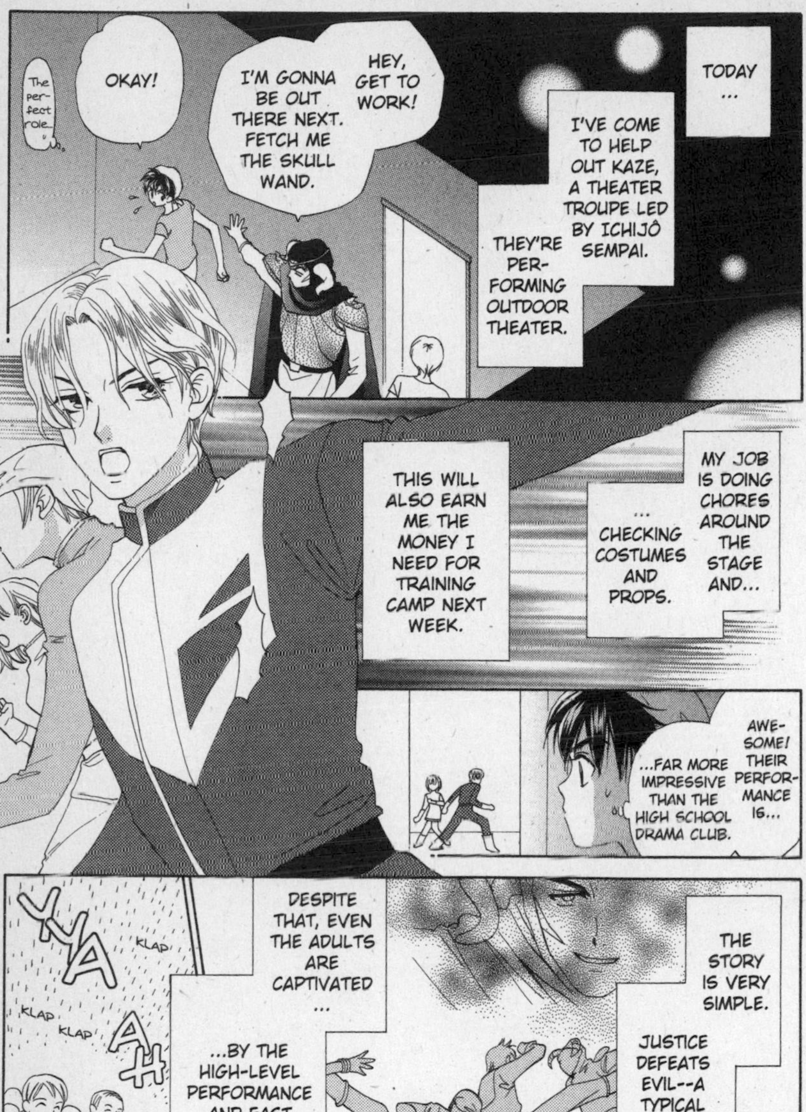
TODAY ...
I'VE COME TO HELP OUT KAZE, A THEATER TROUPE LED BY ICHIJÔ SEMPAI.
THEY'RE PER-FORMING OUTDOOR THEATER.
HEY, GET TO WORK!
I'M GONNA BE OUT THERE NEXT. FETCH ME THE SKULL WAND.
OKAY!
The per-fect role...
MY JOB IS DOING CHORES AROUND THE STAGE AND...
...CHECKING COSTUMES AND PROPS.
THIS WILL ALSO EARN ME THE MONEY I NEED FOR TRAINING CAMP NEXT WEEK.
AWE-SOME! THEIR PERFOR-MANCE IS...
...FAR MORE IMPRESSIVE THAN THE HIGH SCHOOL DRAMA CLUB.
THE STORY IS VERY SIMPLE.
JUSTICE DEFEATS EVIL--A TYPICAL ACTION SHOW.
DESPITE THAT, EVEN THE ADULTS ARE CAPTIVATED ...
...BY THE HIGH-LEVEL PERFORMANCE AND FAST PACE.
YAAHH
KLAP
KLAP
KLAP

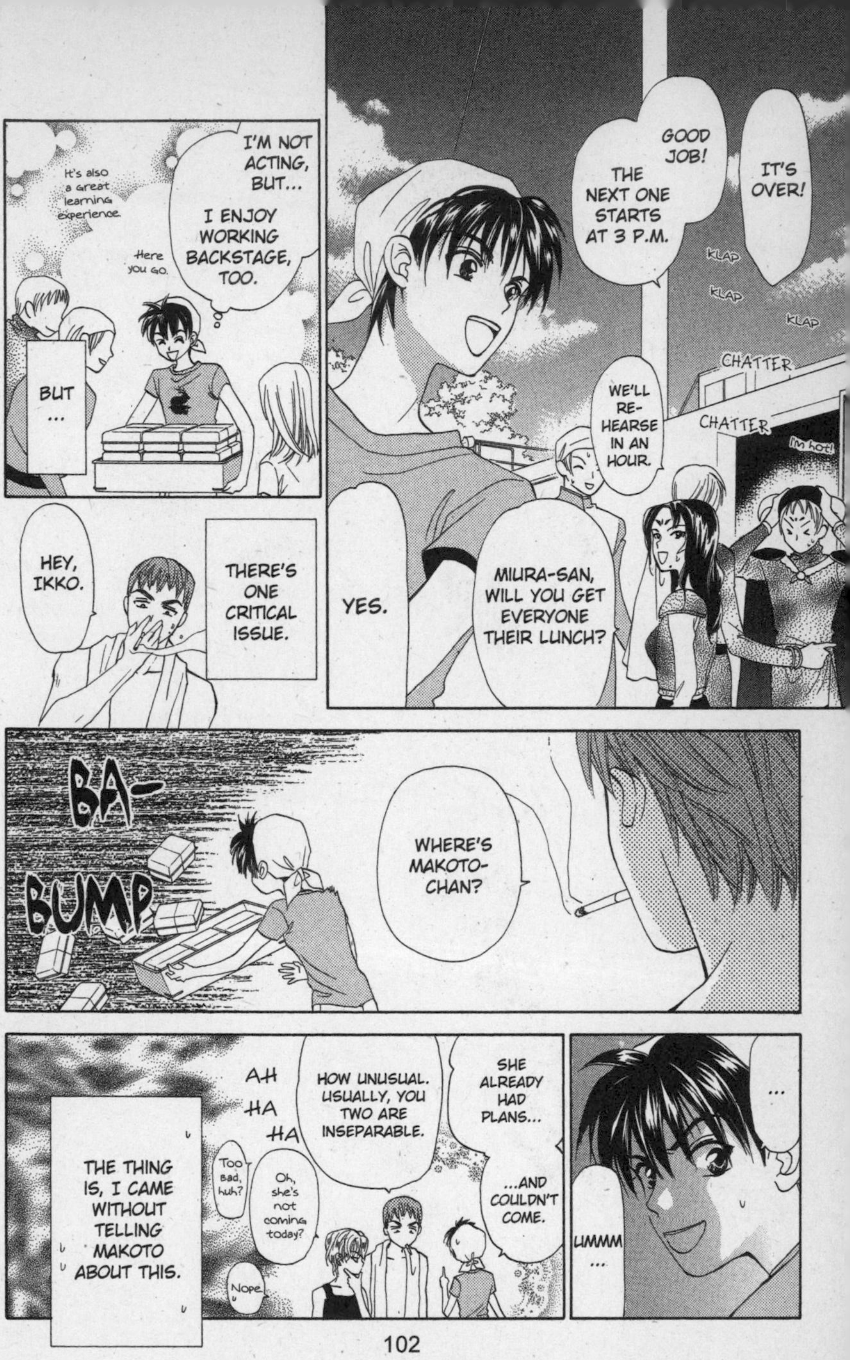
IT'S OVER!
GOOD JOB! THE NEXT ONE STARTS AT 3 P.M.
KLAP
KLAP
KLAP
CHATTER
CHATTER
I'm hot!
WE'LL RE-HEARSE IN AN HOUR.
MIURA-SAN, WILL YOU GET EVERYONE THEIR LUNCH?
YES.
I'M NOT ACTING, BUT...
I ENJOY WORKING BACKSTAGE, TOO.
It's also a great learning experience.
Here you go.
BUT ...
THERE'S ONE CRITICAL ISSUE.
HEY, IKKO.
WHERE'S MAKOTO-CHAN?
BA-BUMP
...
UMMM ...
SHE ALREADY HAD PLANS...
...AND COULDN'T COME.
HOW UNUSUAL. USUALLY, YOU TWO ARE INSEPARABLE.
AH HA HA
Oh, she's not coming today?
Too bad, huh?
Nope.
THE THING IS, I CAME WITHOUT TELLING MAKOTO ABOUT THIS.

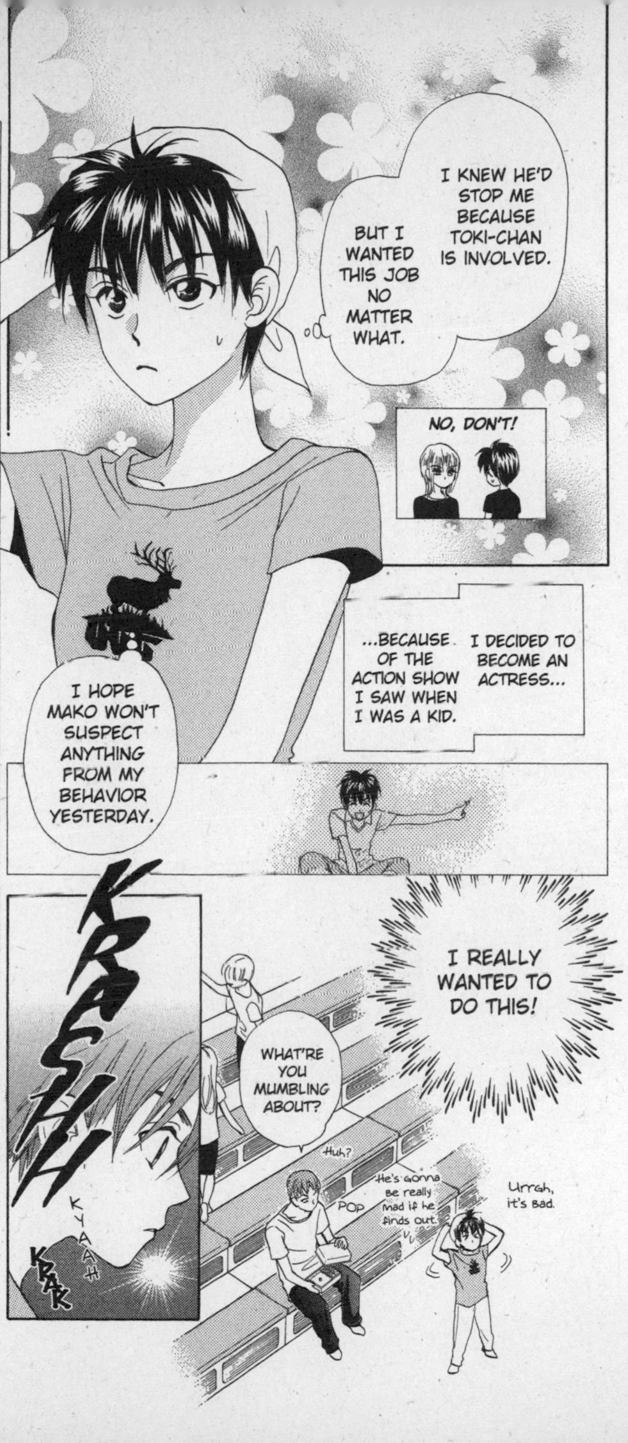
I KNEW HE'D STOP ME BECAUSE TOKI-CHAN IS INVOLVED.
BUT I WANTED THIS JOB NO MATTER WHAT.
NO, DON'T!
I HOPE MAKO WON'T SUSPECT ANYTHING FROM MY BEHAVIOR YESTERDAY.
I DECIDED TO BECOME AN ACTRESS...
...BECAUSE OF THE ACTION SHOW I SAW WHEN I WAS A KID.
I REALLY WANTED TO DO THIS!
KRASHH
KYAAAH
KRAK
WHAT'RE YOU MUMBLING ABOUT?
Huh?
POP
He's gonna be really mad if he finds out.
Urrgh, it's bad.

And Shirômaru-san has been helping me out from the get-go! She was introduced to me through Oguchi-san and came as a temporary assistant at first. But I fell in love with her work, and I've been asking her to come as a regular member ever since. She takes on my unreasonable requests right away and finishes them as if they're nothing. Without her, I'm dead. (Laugh)

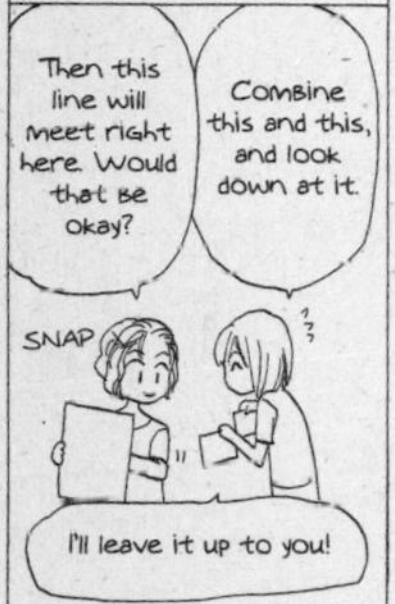
Combine this and this, and look down at it.
Then this line will meet right here. Would that be okay?
SNAP
I'll leave it up to you!

I'm the one who's clueless about parsing lines.

Among my assistants, she's been with me the longest, and she's the best! The most complex background always gets handed to her. (Laugh)

Sorry, and thanks so much!

Let's go out for some drinks again!!

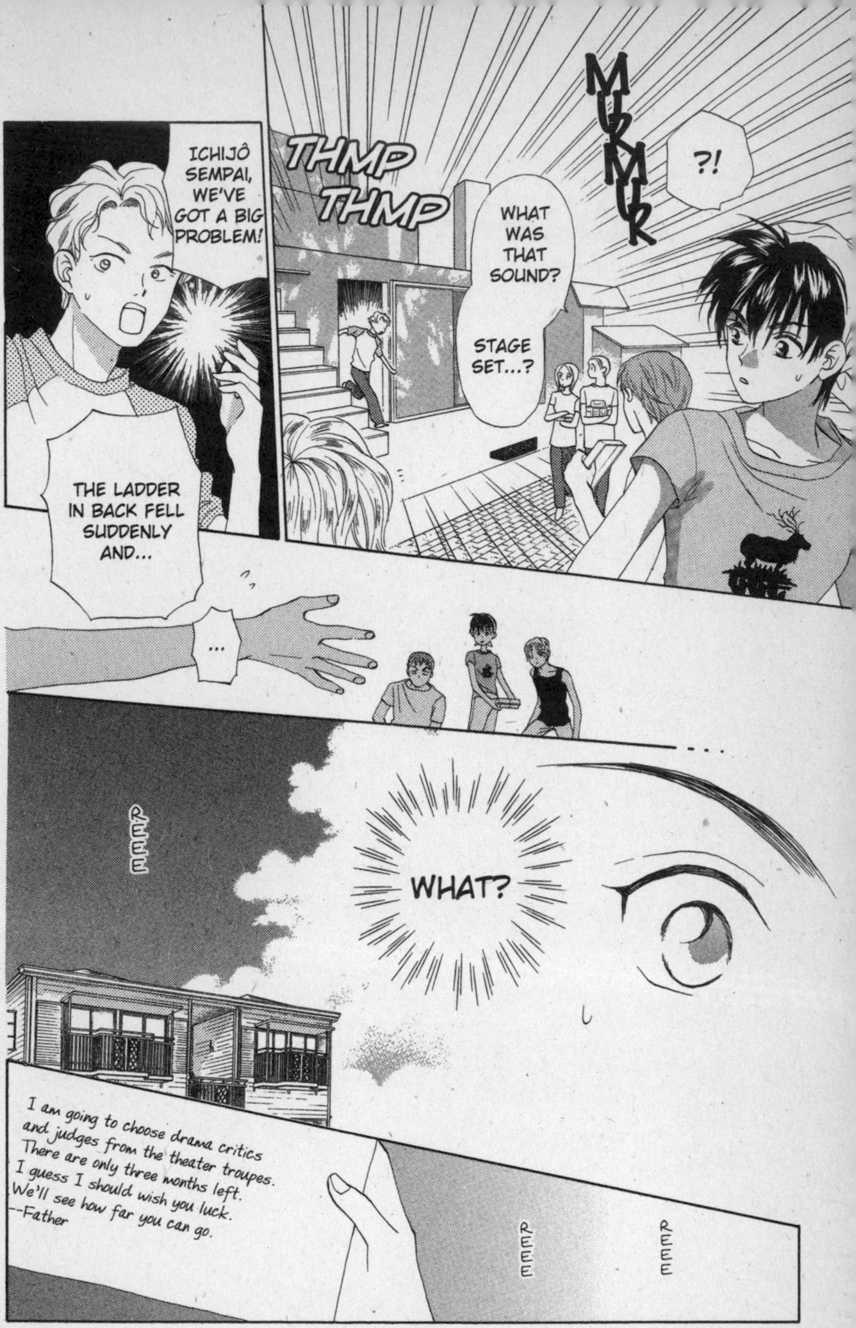
MURMUR
?!
THMP THMP
WHAT WAS THAT SOUND?
STAGE SET...?
ICHIJÔ SEMPAI, WE'VE GOT A BIG PROBLEM!
THE LADDER IN BACK FELL SUDDENLY AND...
...
WHAT?
REEE
I am going to choose drama critics and judges from the theater troupes.
There are only three months left.
I guess I should wish you luck.
We'll see how far you can go.
--Father
REEE
REEE

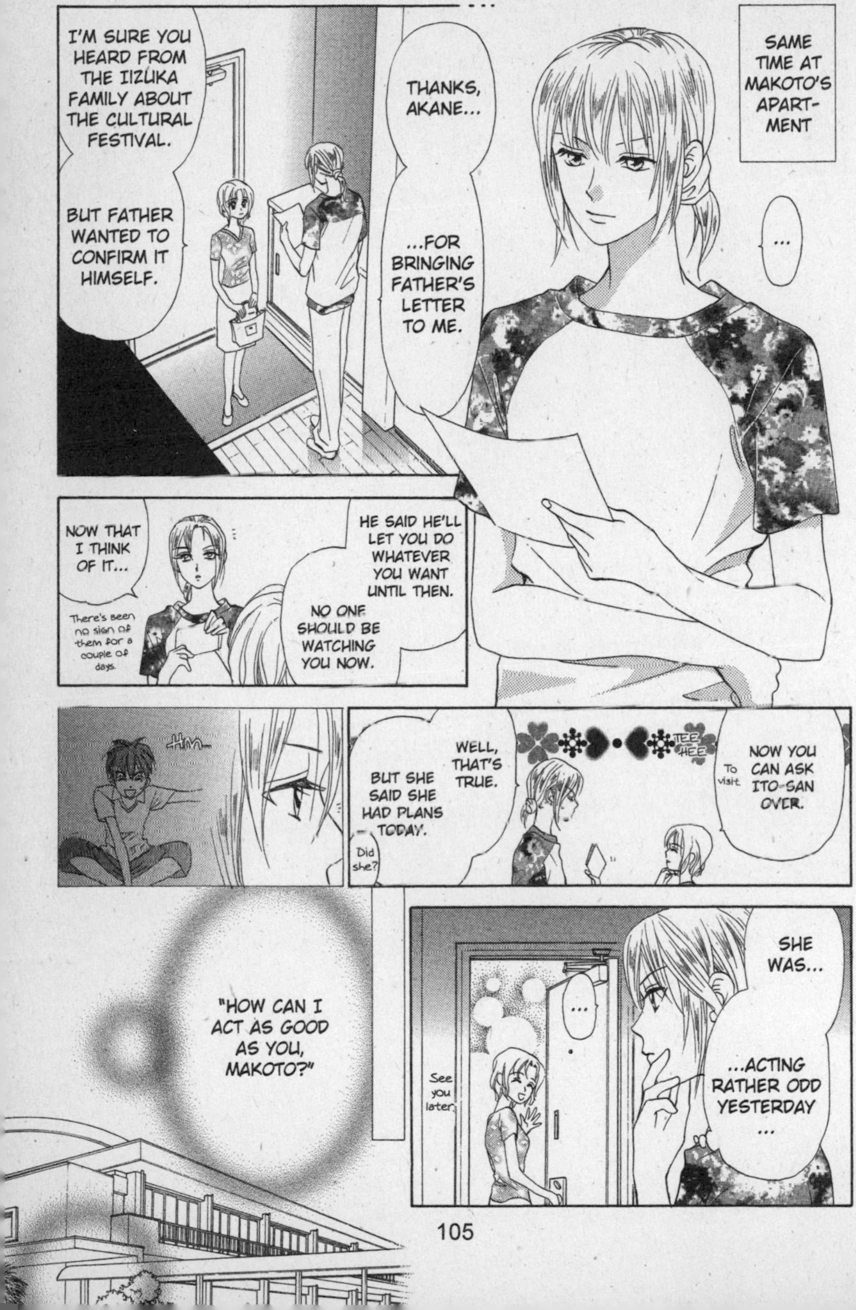
SAME TIME AT MAKOTO'S APART-MENT
...
THANKS, AKANE...
...FOR BRINGING FATHER'S LETTER TO ME.
I'M SURE YOU HEARD FROM THE IIZUKA FAMILY ABOUT THE CULTURAL FESTIVAL.
BUT FATHER WANTED TO CONFIRM IT HIMSELF.
HE SAID HE'LL LET YOU DO WHATEVER YOU WANT UNTIL THEN.
NO ONE SHOULD BE WATCHING YOU NOW.
NOW THAT I THINK OF IT...
There's been no sign of them for a couple of days.
NOW YOU CAN ASK ITO-SAN OVER.
To visit.
TEE HEE
WELL, THAT'S TRUE.
BUT SHE SAID SHE HAD PLANS TODAY.
Did she?
Hm
SHE WAS...
...
...ACTING RATHER ODD YESTERDAY ...
See you later.
"HOW CAN I ACT AS GOOD AS YOU, MAKOTO?"

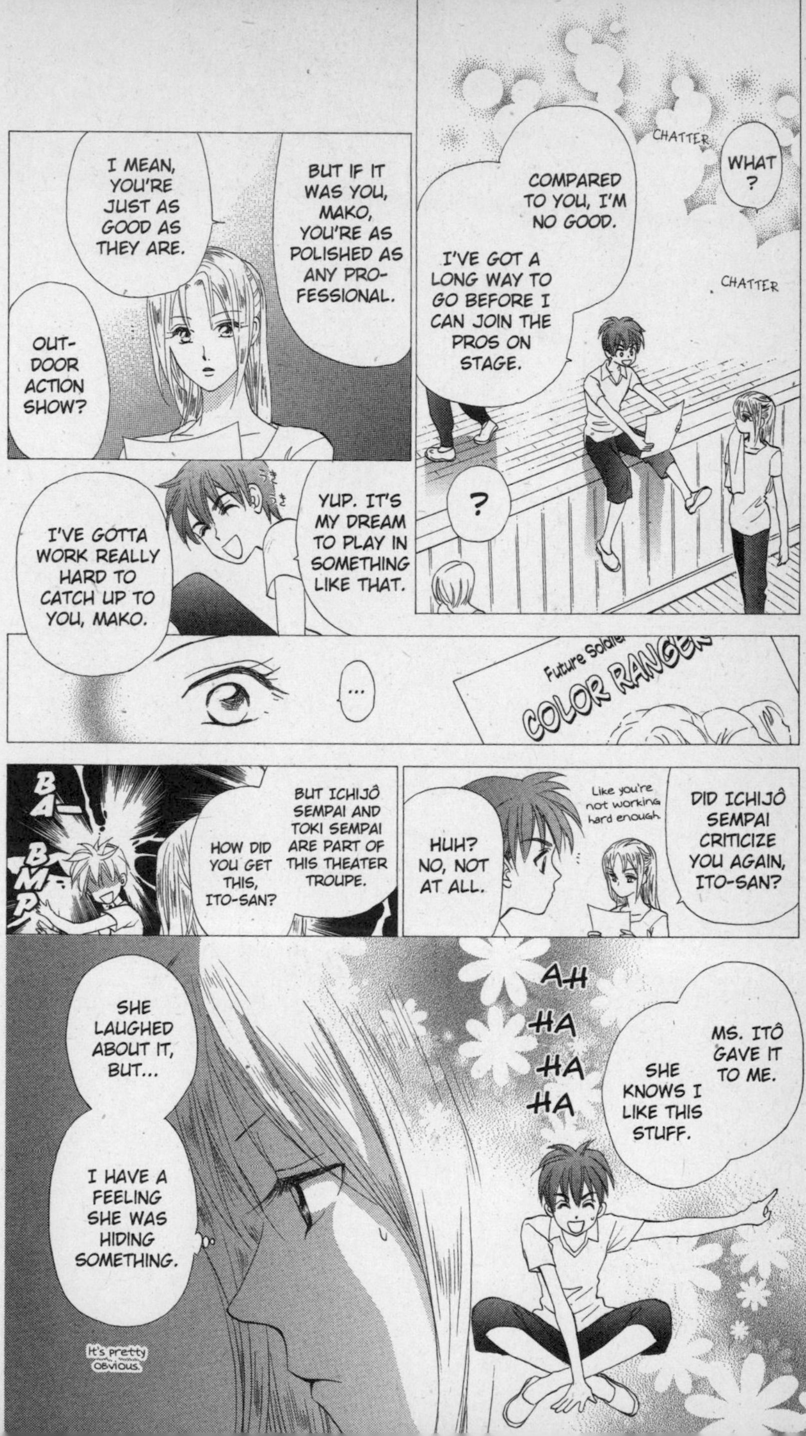
WHAT?
CHATTER
COMPARED TO YOU, I'M NO GOOD.
I'VE GOT A LONG WAY TO GO BEFORE I CAN JOIN THE PROS ON STAGE.
CHATTER
?
BUT IF IT WAS YOU, MAKO, YOU'RE AS POLISHED AS ANY PRO-FESSIONAL.
I MEAN, YOU'RE JUST AS GOOD AS THEY ARE.
OUT-DOOR ACTION SHOW?
YUP. IT'S MY DREAM TO PLAY IN SOMETHING LIKE THAT.
I'VE GOTTA WORK REALLY HARD TO CATCH UP TO YOU, MAKO.
Future Soldier
COLOR RANGER
...
DID ICHIJÔ SEMPAI CRITICIZE YOU AGAIN, ITO-SAN?
Like you're not working hard enough.
HUH? NO, NOT AT ALL.
BUT ICHIJÔ SEMPAI AND TOKI SEMPAI ARE PART OF THIS THEATER TROUPE.
HOW DID YOU GET THIS, ITO-SAN?
BA-BMP
MS. ITÔ GAVE IT TO ME.
SHE KNOWS I LIKE THIS STUFF.
AH HA HA HA
SHE LAUGHED ABOUT IT, BUT...
I HAVE A FEELING SHE WAS HIDING SOMETHING.
It's pretty obvious.

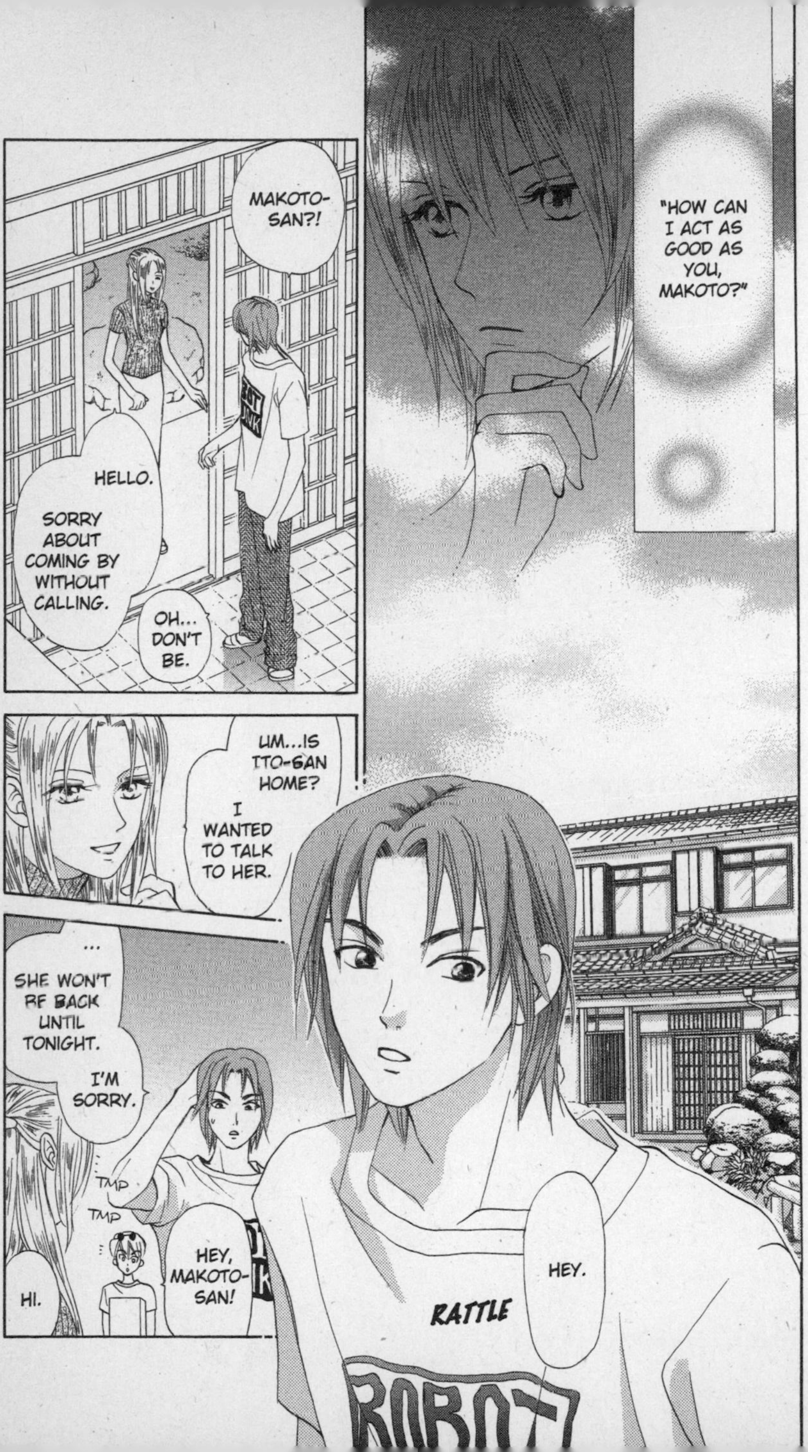
"HOW CAN I ACT AS GOOD AS YOU, MAKOTO?"
MAKOTO-SAN?!
HELLO.
SORRY ABOUT COMING BY WITHOUT CALLING.
OH... DON'T BE.
UM...IS ITO-SAN HOME?
I WANTED TO TALK TO HER.
...
SHE WON'T BE BACK UNTIL TONIGHT.
I'M SORRY.
TMP
TMP
HEY, MAKOTO-SAN!
HI.
RATTLE
HEY.

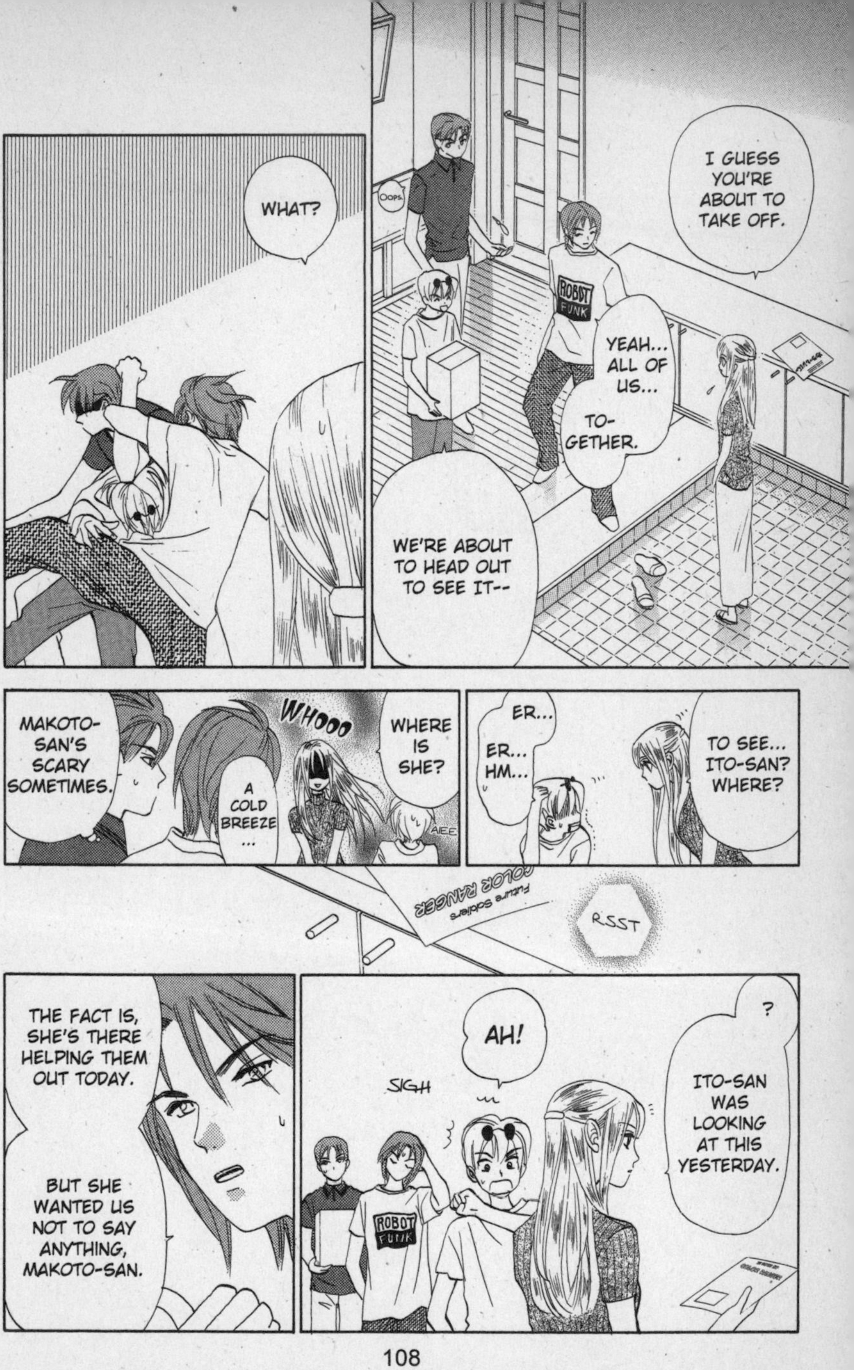
Oops.
I GUESS YOU'RE ABOUT TO TAKE OFF.
YEAH... ALL OF US...
TO-GETHER.
WE'RE ABOUT TO HEAD OUT TO SEE IT--
WHAT?
TO SEE... ITO-SAN? WHERE?
ER...
ER... HM...
WHERE IS SHE?
WHOOO
AEE
A COLD BREEZE ...
MAKOTO-SAN'S SCARY SOMETIMES.
Future Soldier's
COLOR RANGER
RSST
?
ITO-SAN WAS LOOKING AT THIS YESTERDAY.
AH!
SIGH
THE FACT IS, SHE'S THERE HELPING THEM OUT TODAY.
BUT SHE WANTED US NOT TO SAY ANYTHING, MAKOTO-SAN.

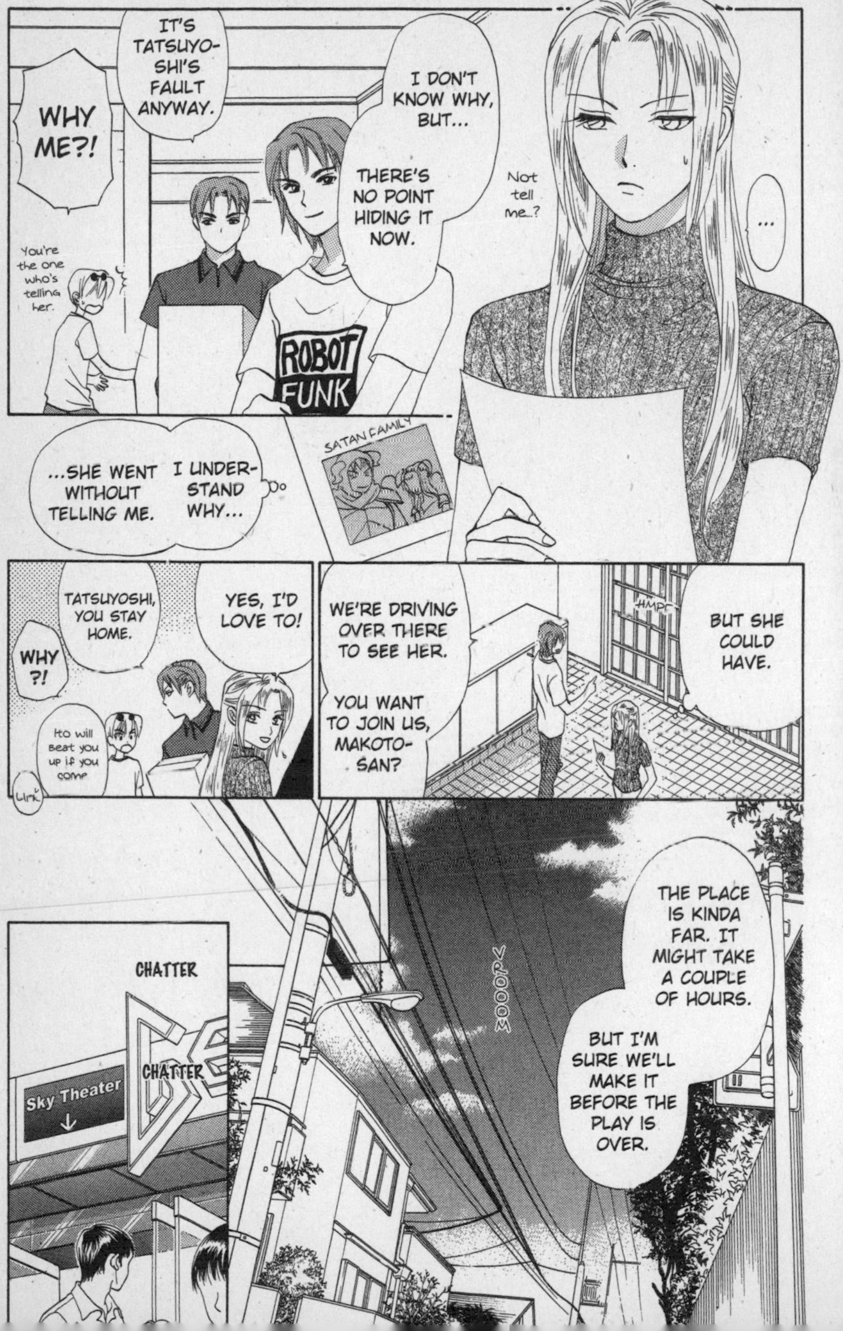
...
Not tell me..?
SATAN FAMILY
I DON'T KNOW WHY, BUT...
THERE'S NO POINT HIDING IT NOW.
ROBOT FUNK
IT'S TATSUYOSHI'S FAULT ANYWAY.
WHY ME?!
You're the one who's telling her.
I UNDERSTAND WHY...
...SHE WENT WITHOUT TELLING ME.
BUT SHE COULD HAVE.
HMPF
WE'RE DRIVING OVER THERE TO SEE HER.
YOU WANT TO JOIN US, MAKOTO-SAN?
YES, I'D LOVE TO!
TATSUYOSHI, YOU STAY HOME.
WHY?!
Ito will beat you up if you come
Urk
THE PLACE IS KINDA FAR. IT MIGHT TAKE A COUPLE OF HOURS.
BUT I'M SURE WE'LL MAKE IT BEFORE THE PLAY IS OVER.
VROOOM
CHATTER
Sky Theater
CHATTER

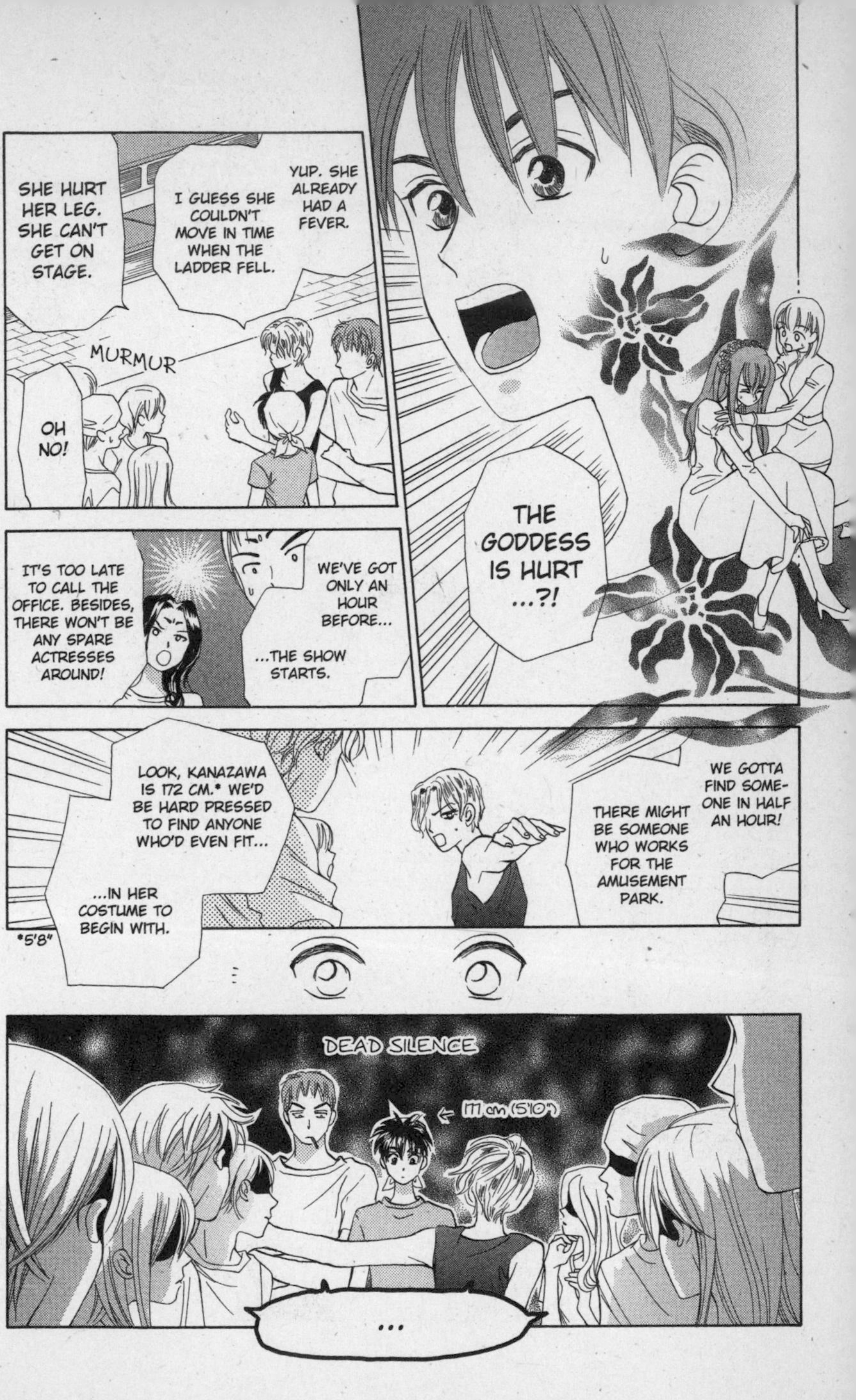
THE GODDESS IS HURT ...?!
YUP. SHE ALREADY HAD A FEVER.
I GUESS SHE COULDN'T MOVE IN TIME WHEN THE LADDER FELL.
SHE HURT HER LEG. SHE CAN'T GET ON STAGE.
MURMUR
OH NO!
WE'VE GOT ONLY AN HOUR BEFORE...
...THE SHOW STARTS.
IT'S TOO LATE TO CALL THE OFFICE. BESIDES, THERE WON'T BE ANY SPARE ACTRESSES AROUND!
WE GOTTA FIND SOMEONE IN HALF AN HOUR!
THERE MIGHT BE SOMEONE WHO WORKS FOR THE AMUSEMENT PARK.
LOOK, KANAZAWA IS 172 CM.* WE'D BE HARD PRESSED TO FIND ANYONE WHO'D EVEN FIT...
...IN HER COSTUME TO BEGIN WITH.
*5'8"
DEAD SILENCE
177 cm (5'10")
...

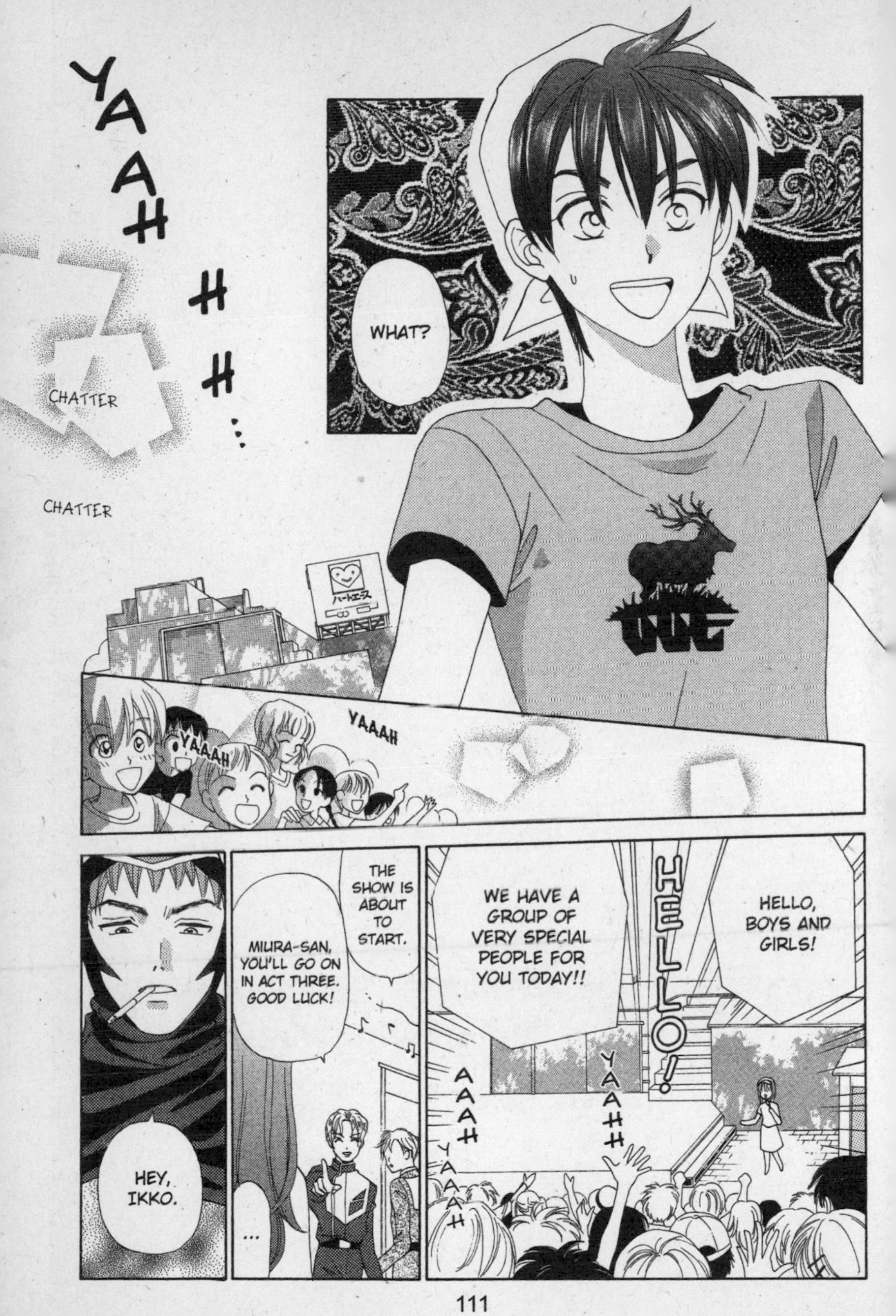
WHAT?
YAAAHHH...
CHATTER
CHATTER
YAAAH
YAAAH
HELLO, BOYS AND GIRLS!
HELLO!
WE HAVE A GROUP OF VERY SPECIAL PEOPLE FOR YOU TODAY!!
YAAAHH
AAAAH
YAAAAH
THE SHOW IS ABOUT TO START.
MIURA-SAN, YOU'LL GO ON IN ACT THREE. GOOD LUCK!
...
HEY, IKKO.

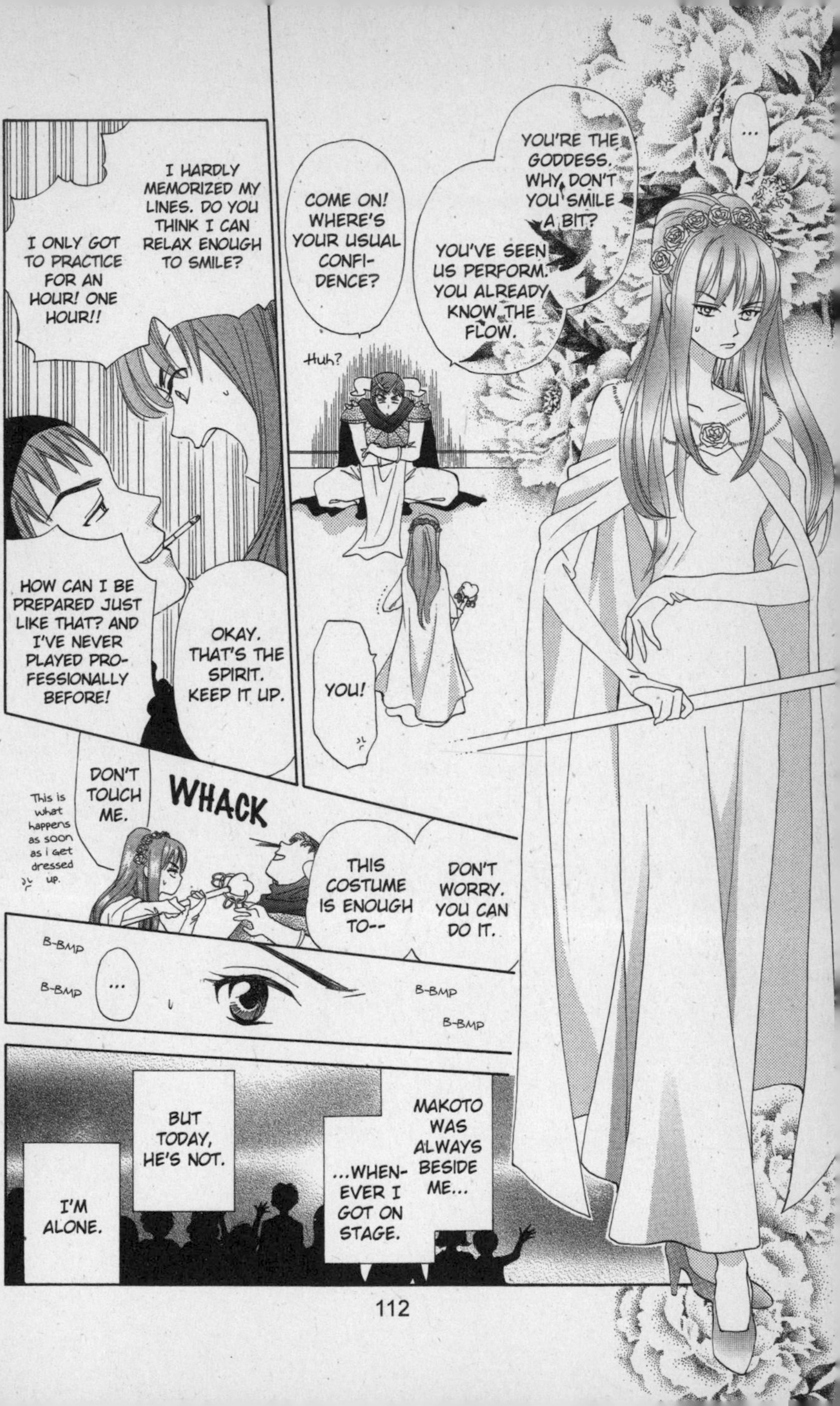
...
YOU'RE THE GODDESS. WHY DON'T YOU SMILE A BIT?
YOU'VE SEEN US PERFORM. YOU ALREADY KNOW THE FLOW.
COME ON! WHERE'S YOUR USUAL CONFIDENCE?
Huh?
YOU!
I HARDLY MEMORIZED MY LINES. DO YOU THINK I CAN RELAX ENOUGH TO SMILE?
I ONLY GOT TO PRACTICE FOR AN HOUR! ONE HOUR!!
OKAY. THAT'S THE SPIRIT. KEEP IT UP.
HOW CAN I BE PREPARED JUST LIKE THAT? AND I'VE NEVER PLAYED PROFESSIONALLY BEFORE!
DON'T WORRY. YOU CAN DO IT.
THIS COSTUME IS ENOUGH TO--
WHACK
DON'T TOUCH ME.
This is what happens as soon as I get dressed up.
B-BMP
B-BMP
...
B-BMP
B-BMP
MAKOTO WAS ALWAYS BESIDE ME...
...WHENEVER I GOT ON STAGE.
BUT TODAY, HE'S NOT.
I'M ALONE.

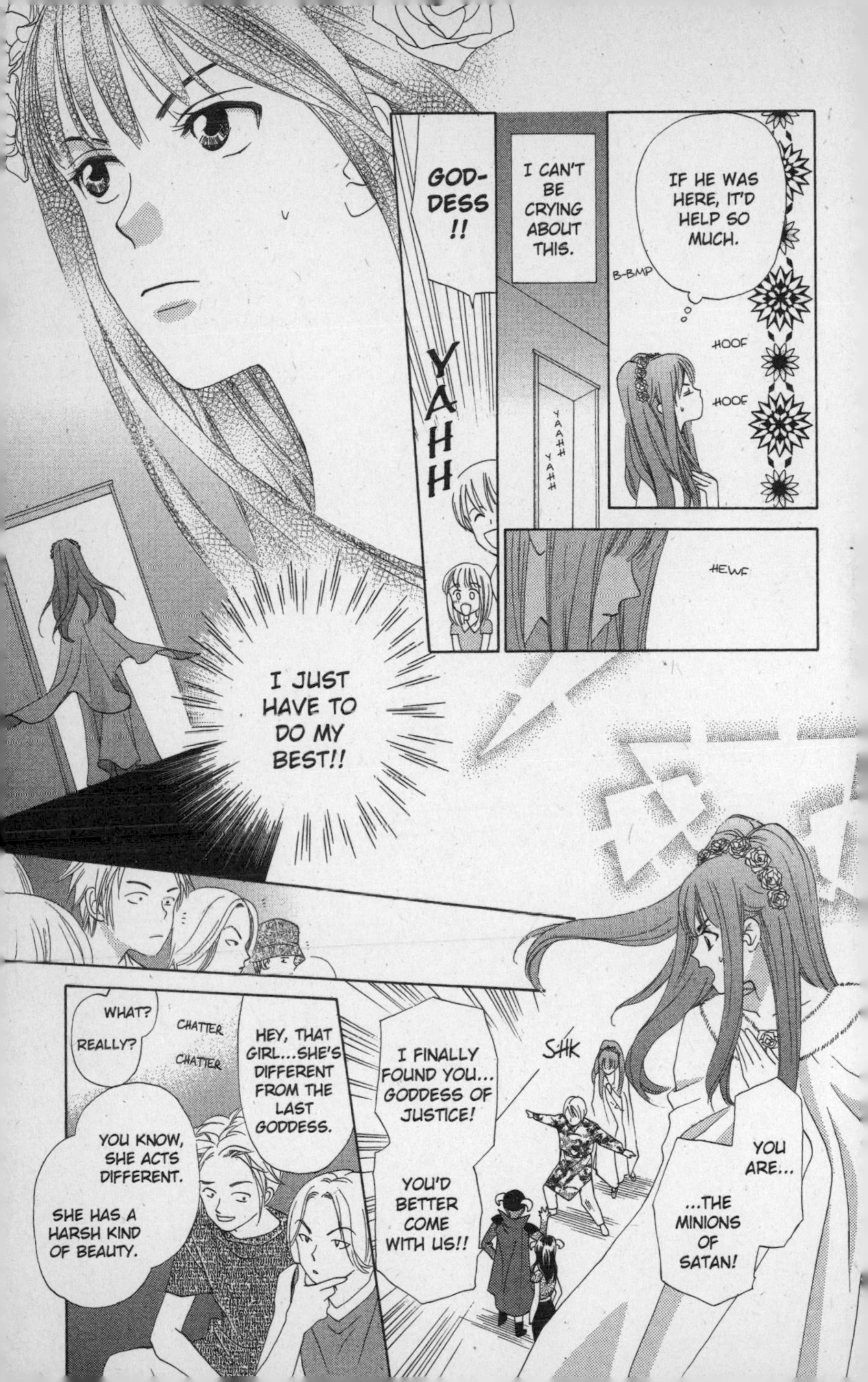
IF HE WAS HERE, IT'D HELP SO MUCH.
B-BMP
HOOF
HOOF
I CAN'T BE CRYING ABOUT THIS.
GOD-DESS!!
YAHH
YAAHH
YAHH
HEWF
I JUST HAVE TO DO MY BEST!!
SHK
YOU ARE...
...THE MINIONS OF SATAN!
I FINALLY FOUND YOU... GODDESS OF JUSTICE!
YOU'D BETTER COME WITH US!!
HEY, THAT GIRL...SHE'S DIFFERENT FROM THE LAST GODDESS.
CHATTER
CHATTER
WHAT?
REALLY?
YOU KNOW, SHE ACTS DIFFERENT.
SHE HAS A HARSH KIND OF BEAUTY.

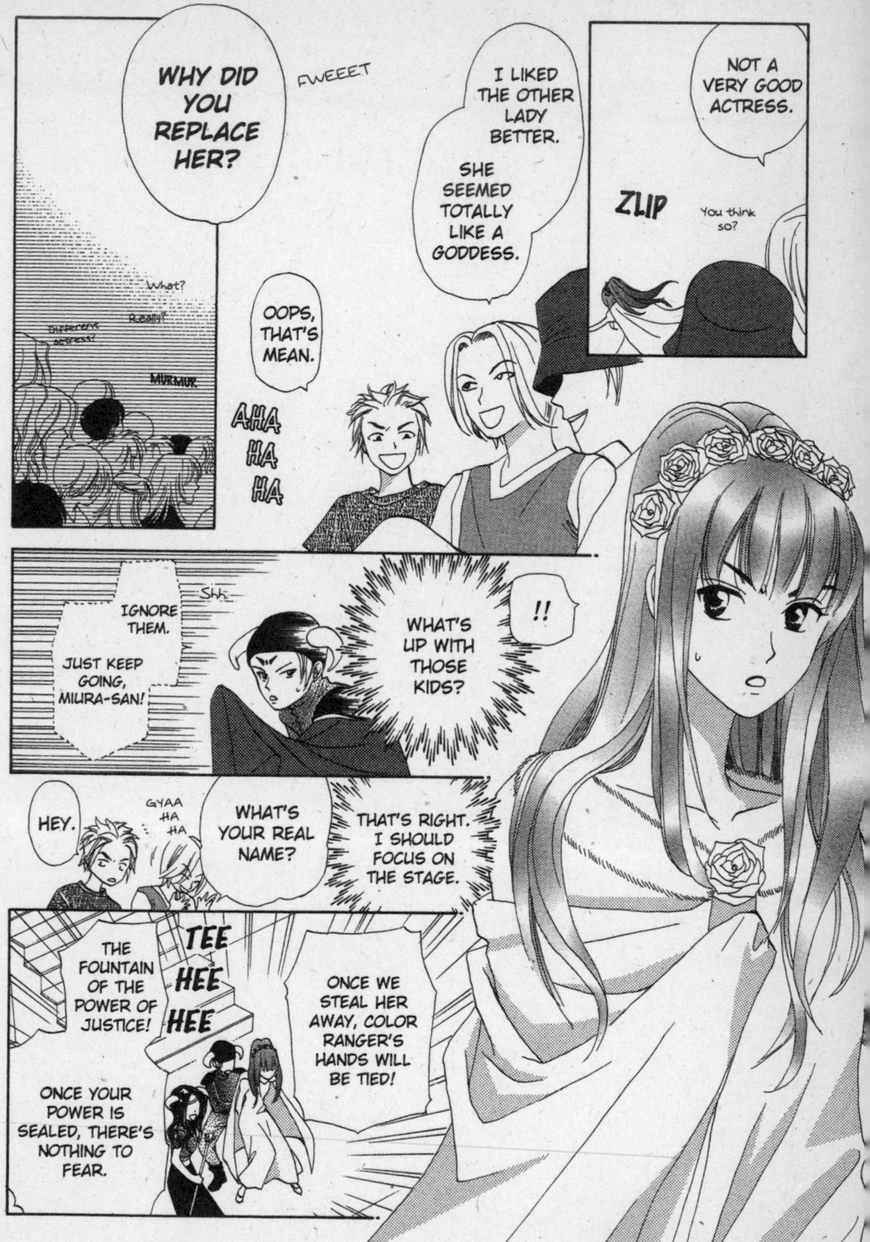

NOT A VERY GOOD ACTRESS.
ZLIP
You think so?
I LIKED THE OTHER LADY BETTER.
SHE SEEMED TOTALLY LIKE A GODDESS.
OOPS, THAT'S MEAN.
AHA HA HA
FWEEET
WHY DID YOU REPLACE HER?
What?
Really?
Different actress?
MURMUR
!!
WHAT'S UP WITH THOSE KIDS?
Shh
IGNORE THEM.
JUST KEEP GOING, MIURA-SAN!
THAT'S RIGHT. I SHOULD FOCUS ON THE STAGE.
WHAT'S YOUR REAL NAME?
GYAA HA HA
HEY.
ONCE WE STEAL HER AWAY, COLOR RANGER'S HANDS WILL BE TIED!
TEE HEE HEE
THE FOUNTAIN OF THE POWER OF JUSTICE!
ONCE YOUR POWER IS SEALED, THERE'S NOTHING TO FEAR.

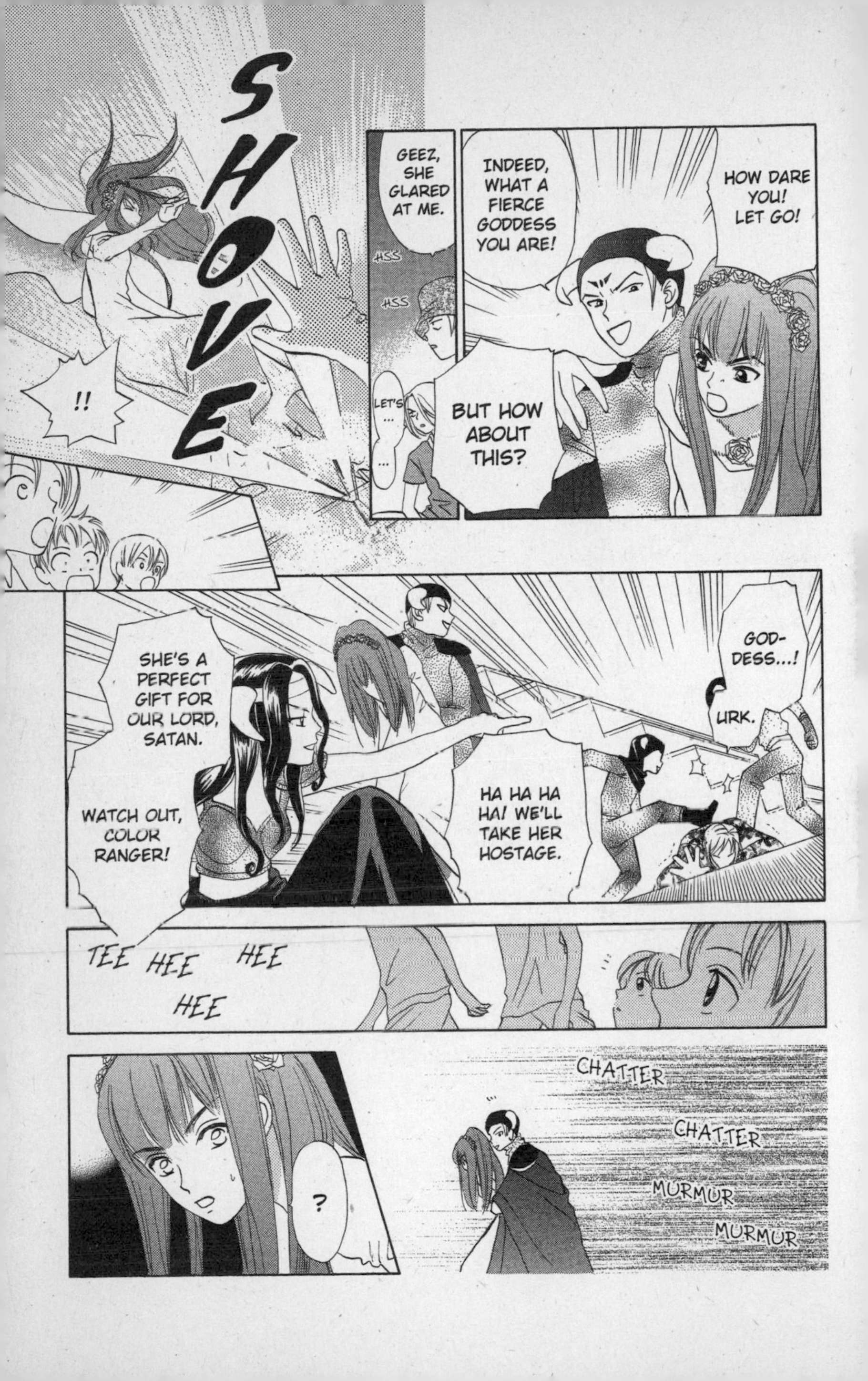
HOW DARE YOU! LET GO!
INDEED, WHAT A FIERCE GODDESS YOU ARE!
BUT HOW ABOUT THIS?
GEEZ, SHE GLARED AT ME.
HSS
HSS
LET'S ...
...
SHOVE
!!
GOD-DESS...!
URK.
HA HA HA HA! WE'LL TAKE HER HOSTAGE.
SHE'S A PERFECT GIFT FOR OUR LORD, SATAN.
WATCH OUT, COLOR RANGER!
TEE HEE HEE HEE
CHATTER
CHATTER
MURMUR
MURMUR
?

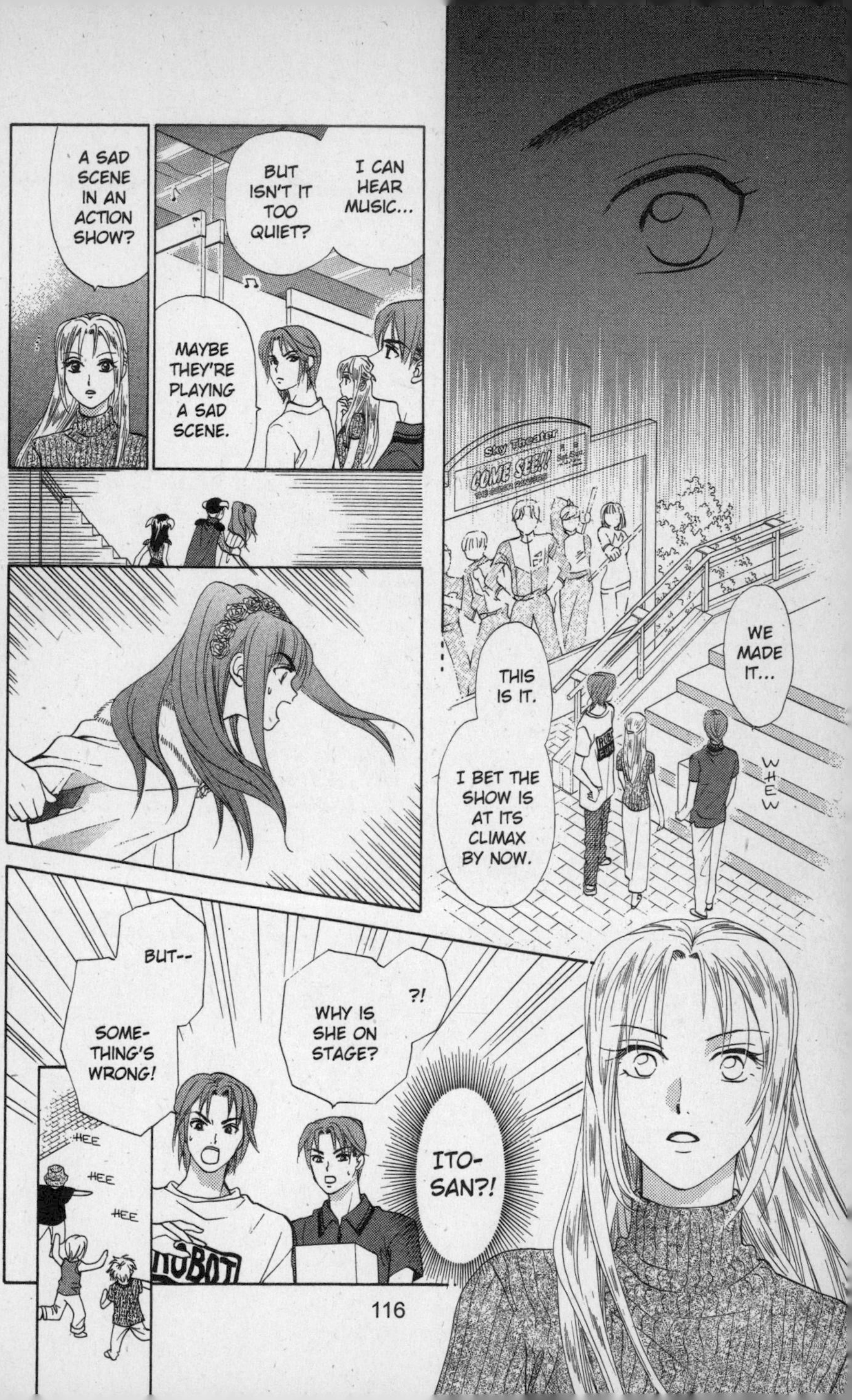
Sky Theater
COME SEE!!
WE MADE IT...
WHEW
THIS IS IT.
I BET THE SHOW IS AT ITS CLIMAX BY NOW.
I CAN HEAR MUSIC...
BUT ISN'T IT TOO QUIET?
MAYBE THEY'RE PLAYING A SAD SCENE.
A SAD SCENE IN AN ACTION SHOW?
ITO-SAN?!
?!
WHY IS SHE ON STAGE?
BUT--
SOME-THING'S WRONG!
HEE
HEE
HEE

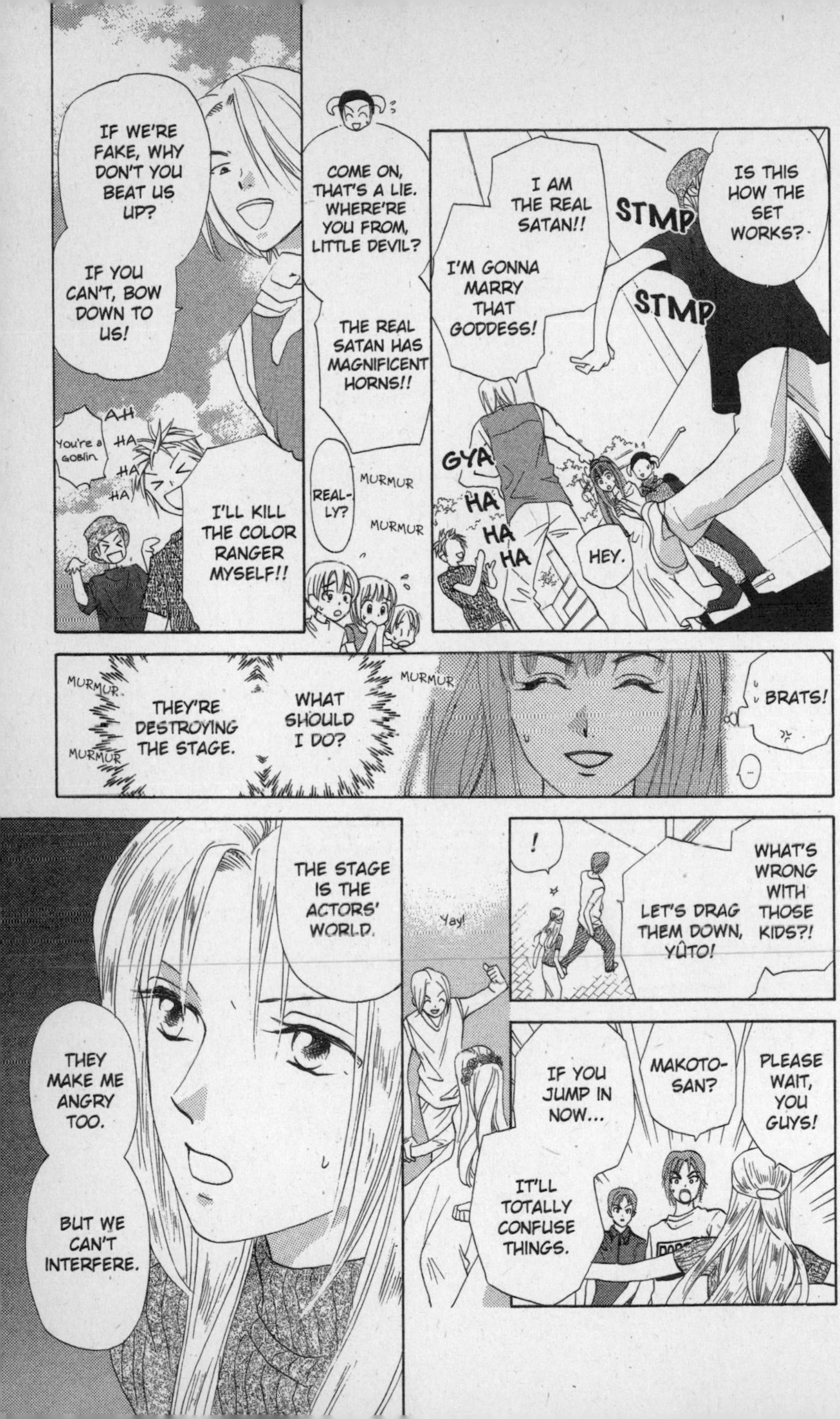
IS THIS HOW THE SET WORKS?
STMP
STMP
I AM THE REAL SATAN!!
I'M GONNA MARRY THAT GODDESS!
GYA HA HA HA
HEY.
COME ON, THAT'S A LIE. WHERE'RE YOU FROM, LITTLE DEVIL?
THE REAL SATAN HAS MAGNIFICENT HORNS!!
MURMUR
REAL-LY?
MURMUR
IF WE'RE FAKE, WHY DON'T YOU BEAT US UP?
IF YOU CAN'T, BOW DOWN TO US!
AH HA HA HA
You're a goblin.
I'LL KILL THE COLOR RANGER MYSELF!!
BRATS!
...
MURMUR
WHAT SHOULD I DO?
THEY'RE DESTROYING THE STAGE.
MURMUR
MURMUR
WHAT'S WRONG WITH THOSE KIDS?!
LET'S DRAG THEM DOWN, YÛTO!
!
PLEASE WAIT, YOU GUYS!
MAKOTO-SAN?
IF YOU JUMP IN NOW...
IT'LL TOTALLY CONFUSE THINGS.
THE STAGE IS THE ACTORS' WORLD.
Yay!
THEY MAKE ME ANGRY TOO.
BUT WE CAN'T INTERFERE.

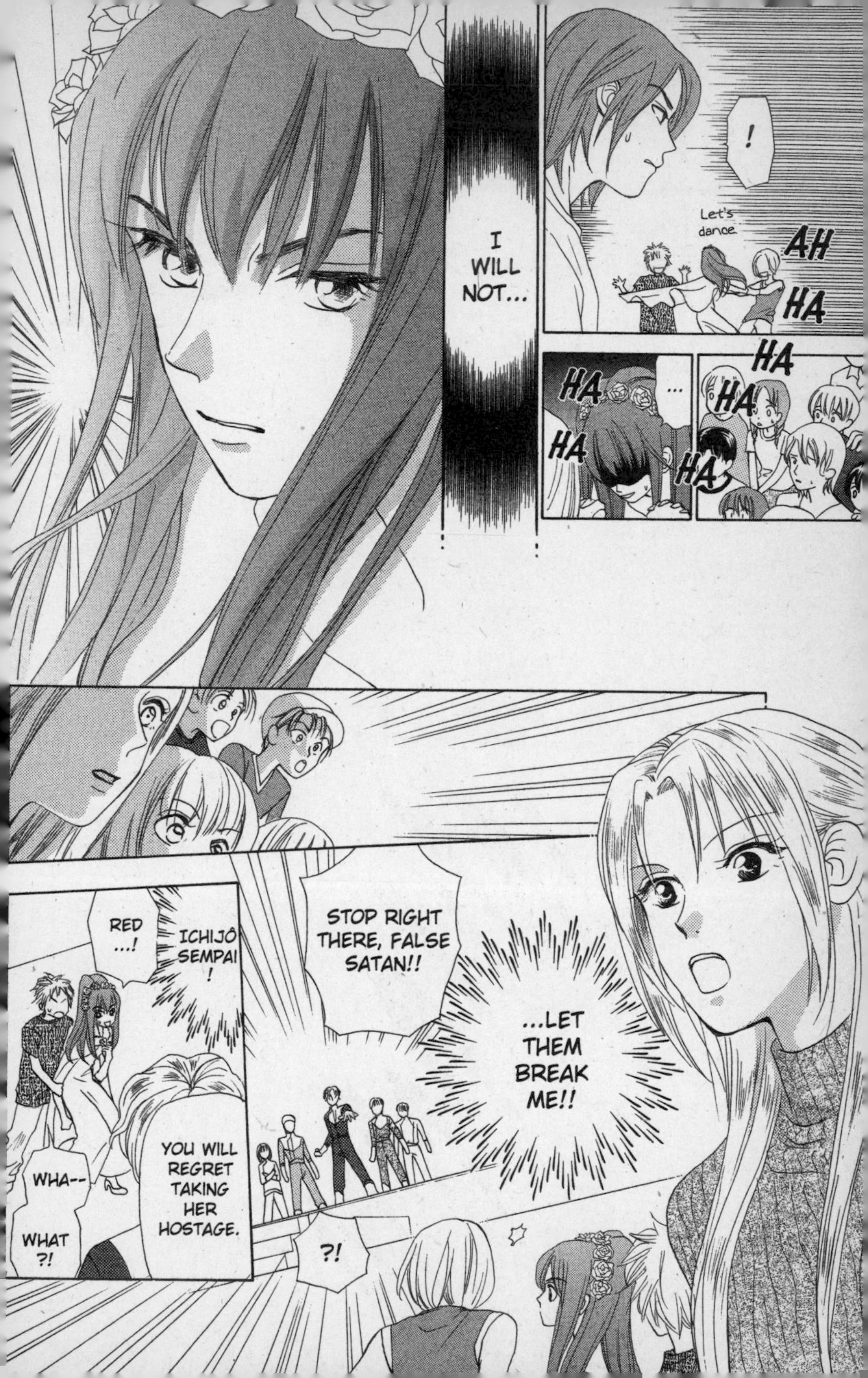
!
Let's dance.
AH HA HA
HA HA
...
HA HA
I WILL NOT...
STOP RIGHT THERE, FALSE SATAN!!
...LET THEM BREAK ME!!
?!
ICHIJÔ SEMPAI!
RED ...!
YOU WILL REGRET TAKING HER HOSTAGE.
WHA--
WHAT ?!

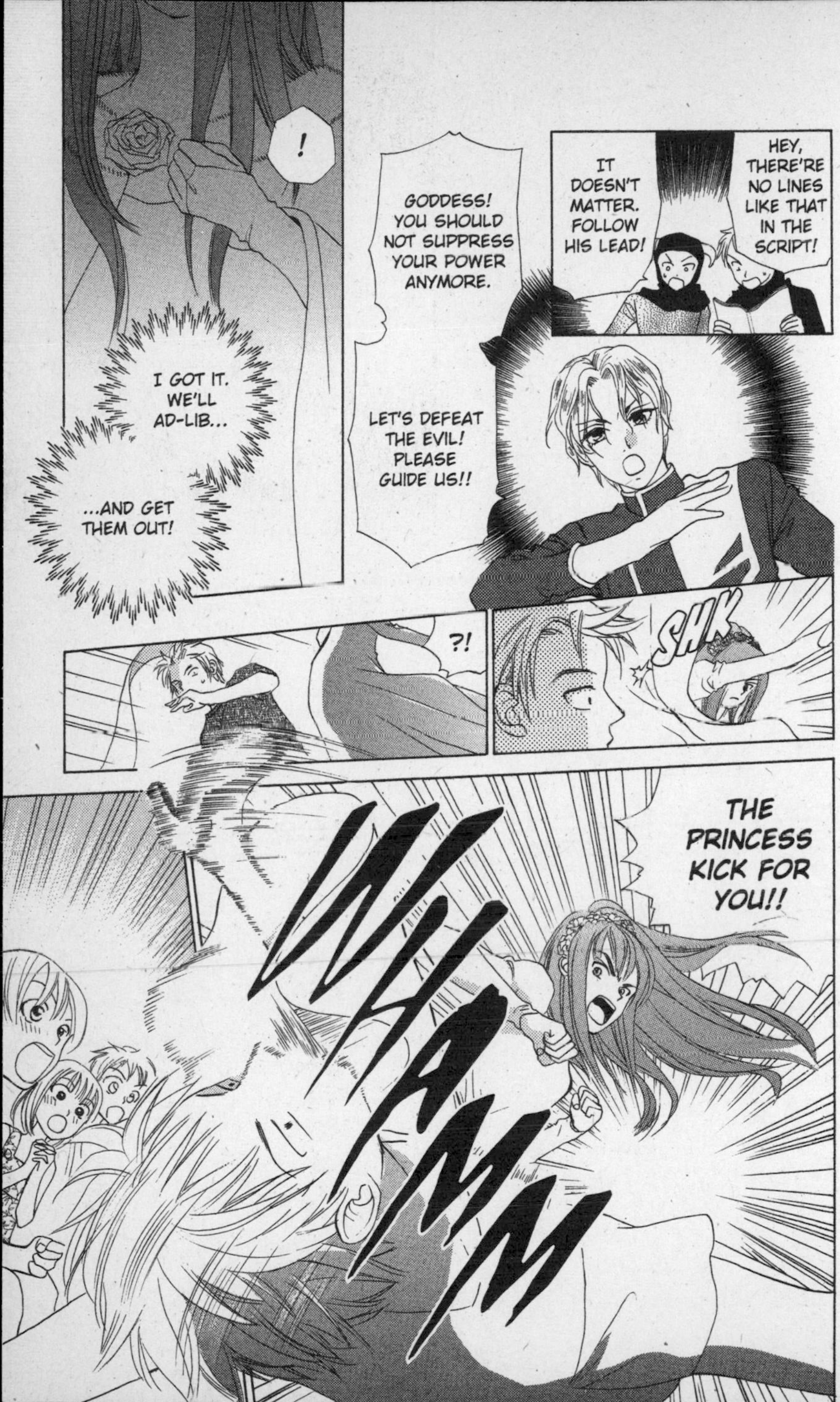
HEY, THERE'RE NO LINES LIKE THAT IN THE SCRIPT!
IT DOESN'T MATTER. FOLLOW HIS LEAD!
GODDESS! YOU SHOULD NOT SUPPRESS YOUR POWER ANYMORE.
LET'S DEFEAT THE EVIL! PLEASE GUIDE US!!
!
I GOT IT. WE'LL AD-LIB...
...AND GET THEM OUT!
SHK
?!
THE PRINCESS KICK FOR YOU!!
WHAMM

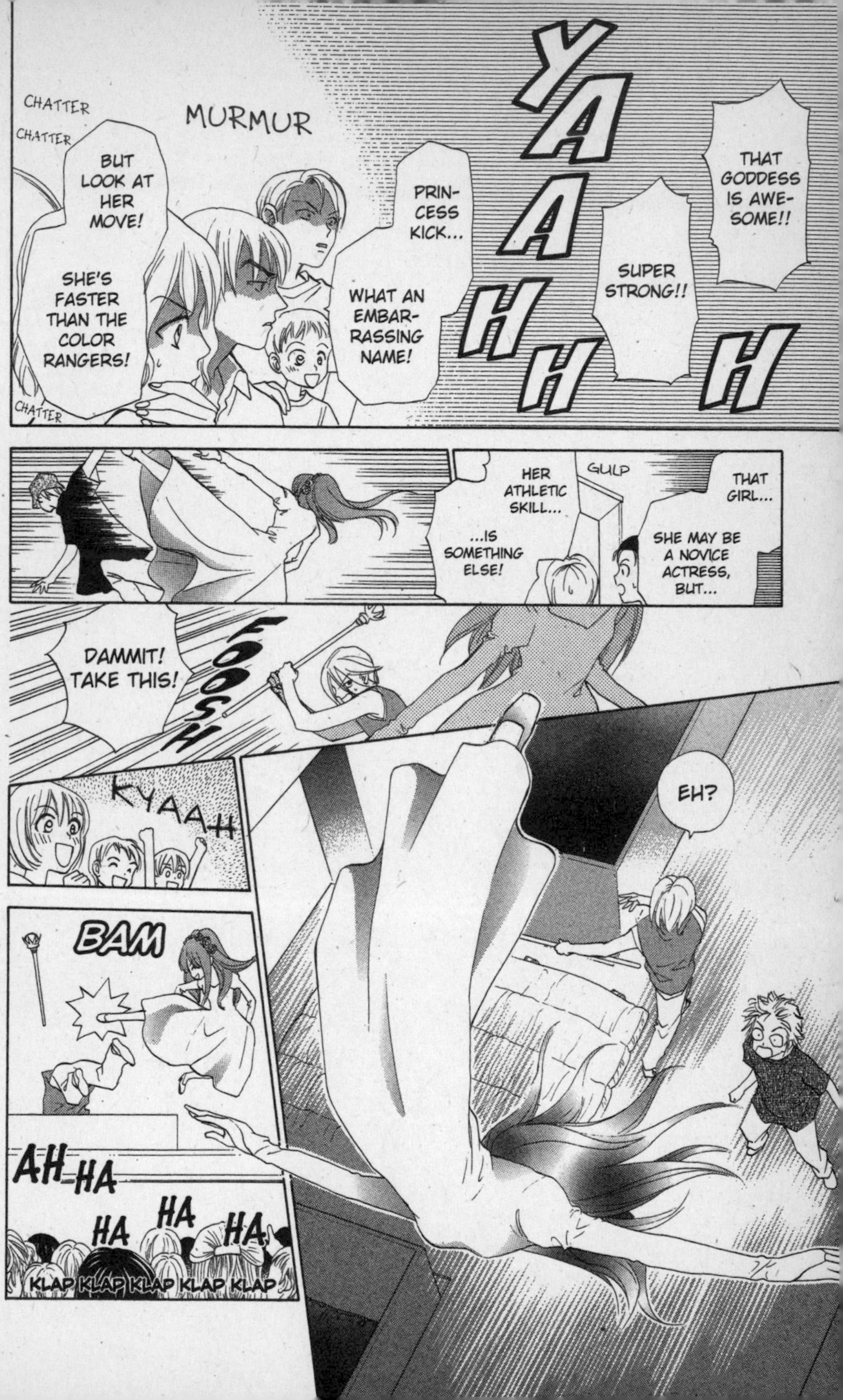
YAAHHH
THAT GODDESS IS AWE-SOME!!
SUPER STRONG!!
PRIN-CESS KICK...
WHAT AN EMBAR-RASSING NAME!
MURMUR
BUT LOOK AT HER MOVE!
SHE'S FASTER THAN THE COLOR RANGERS!
CHATTER
CHATTER
CHATTER
THAT GIRL...
SHE MAY BE A NOVICE ACTRESS, BUT...
GULP
HER ATHLETIC SKILL...
...IS SOMETHING ELSE!
DAMMIT! TAKE THIS!
FOOOSH
EH?
KYAAAH
BAM
AH-HA
HA
HA
HA
KLAP KLAP KLAP KLAP KLAP

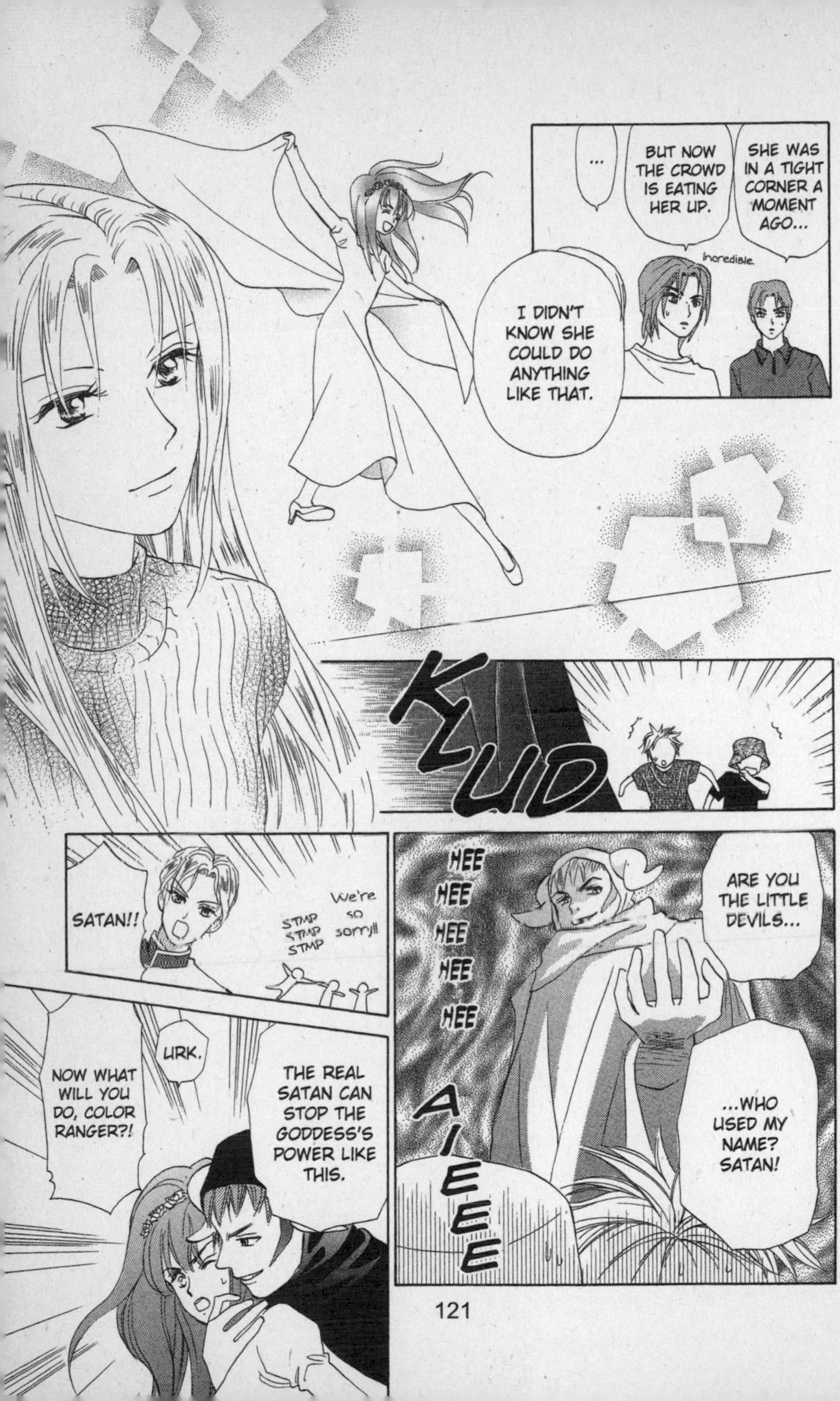
SHE WAS IN A TIGHT CORNER A MOMENT AGO...
BUT NOW THE CROWD IS EATING HER UP.
...
Incredible.
I DIDN'T KNOW SHE COULD DO ANYTHING LIKE THAT.
KLUD
HEE HEE HEE HEE HEE
ARE YOU THE LITTLE DEVILS...
...WHO USED MY NAME? SATAN!
AIEEE
SATAN!!
We're so sorry!!
STMP STMP STMP
URK.
THE REAL SATAN CAN STOP THE GODDESS'S POWER LIKE THIS.
NOW WHAT WILL YOU DO, COLOR RANGER?!

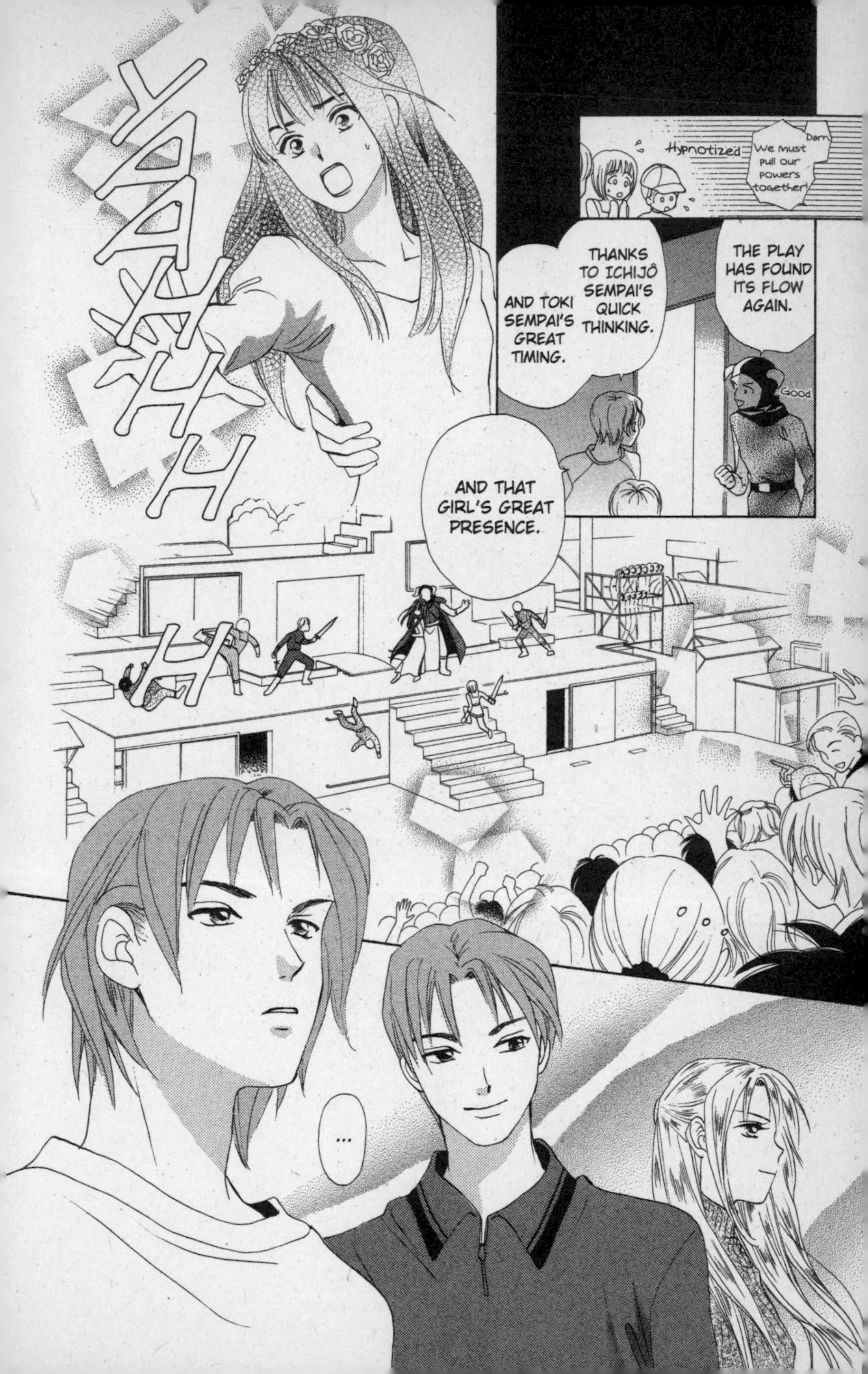
Hypnotized
Damn
We must pull our powers together!
THE PLAY HAS FOUND ITS FLOW AGAIN.
Good.
THANKS TO ICHIJÔ SEMPAI'S QUICK THINKING.
AND TOKI SEMPAI'S GREAT TIMING.
YAAHHHH
AND THAT GIRL'S GREAT PRESENCE.
...

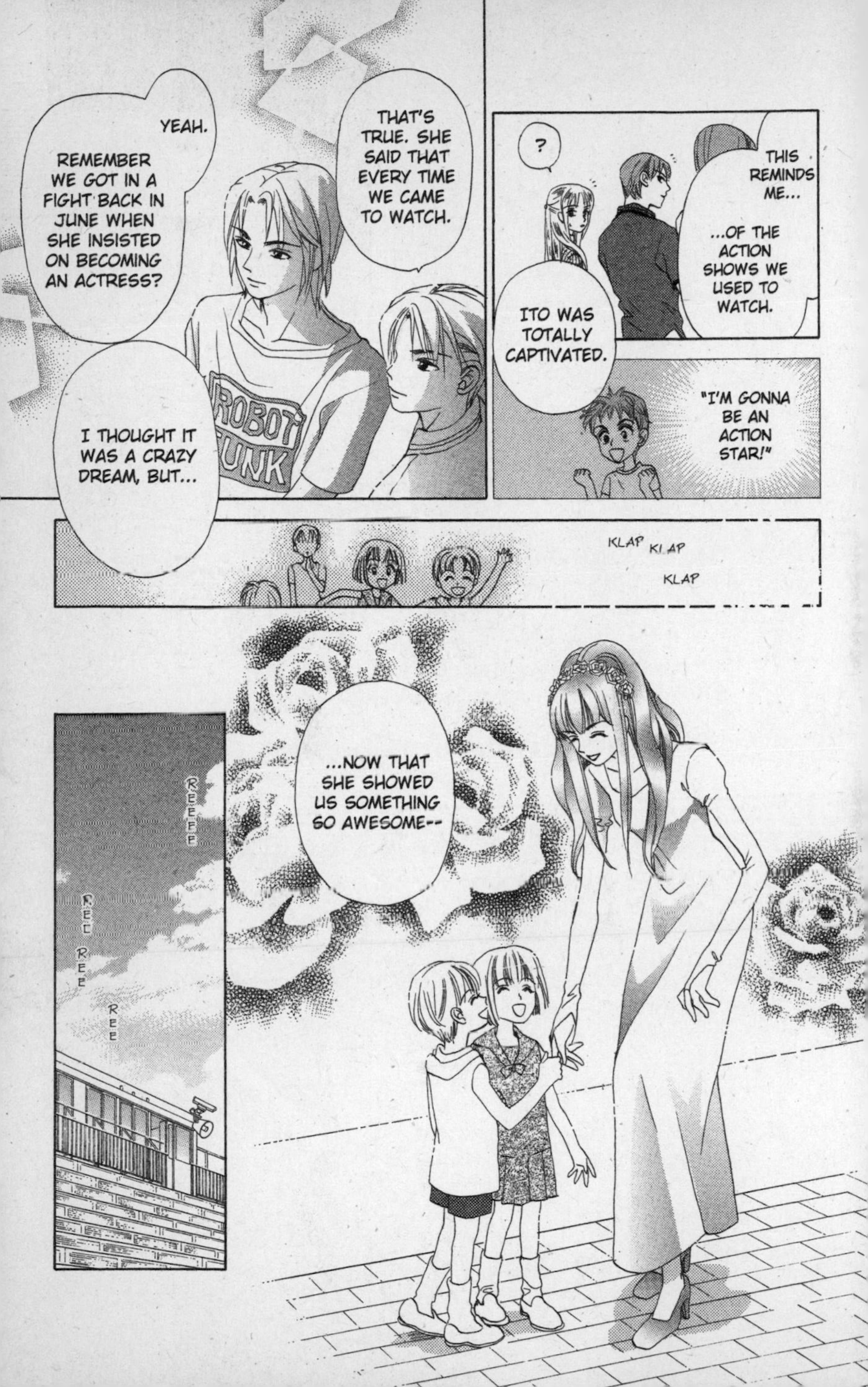
?
THIS REMINDS ME...
...OF THE ACTION SHOWS WE USED TO WATCH.
ITO WAS TOTALLY CAPTIVATED.
"I'M GONNA BE AN ACTION STAR!"
THAT'S TRUE. SHE SAID THAT EVERY TIME WE CAME TO WATCH.
YEAH.
REMEMBER WE GOT IN A FIGHT BACK IN JUNE WHEN SHE INSISTED ON BECOMING AN ACTRESS?
I THOUGHT IT WAS A CRAZY DREAM, BUT...
KLAP KLAP
KLAP
...NOW THAT SHE SHOWED US SOMETHING SO AWESOME--
REEEE
REE
REE
REE

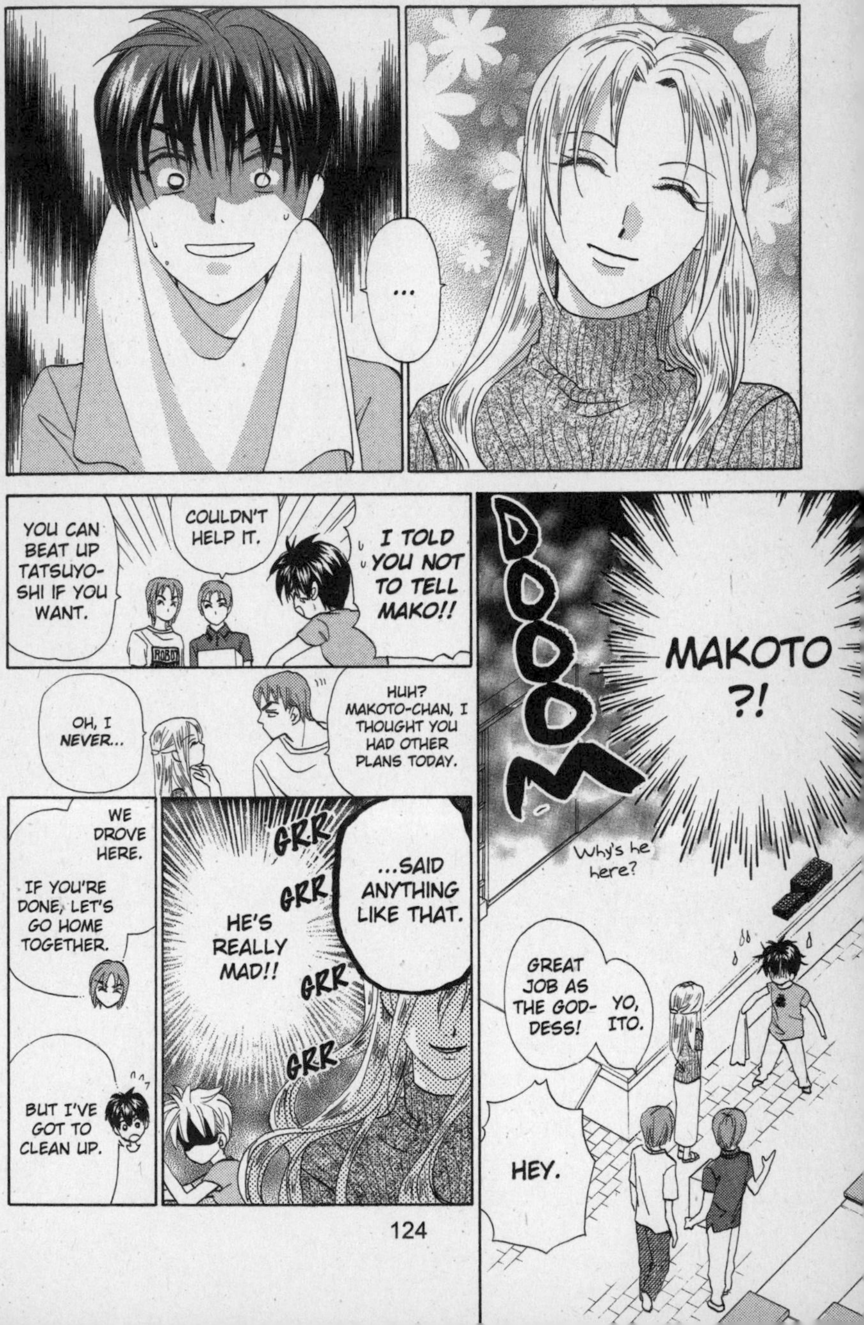
...
DOOOM
MAKOTO ?!
Why's he here?
YO, ITO.
GREAT JOB AS THE GOD-DESS!
HEY.
I TOLD YOU NOT TO TELL MAKO!!
COULDN'T HELP IT.
YOU CAN BEAT UP TATSUYO-SHI IF YOU WANT.
HUH? MAKOTO-CHAN, I THOUGHT YOU HAD OTHER PLANS TODAY.
OH, I NEVER...
...SAID ANYTHING LIKE THAT.
GRR
GRR
HE'S REALLY MAD!!
GRR
GRR
WE DROVE HERE.
IF YOU'RE DONE, LET'S GO HOME TOGETHER.
BUT I'VE GOT TO CLEAN UP.

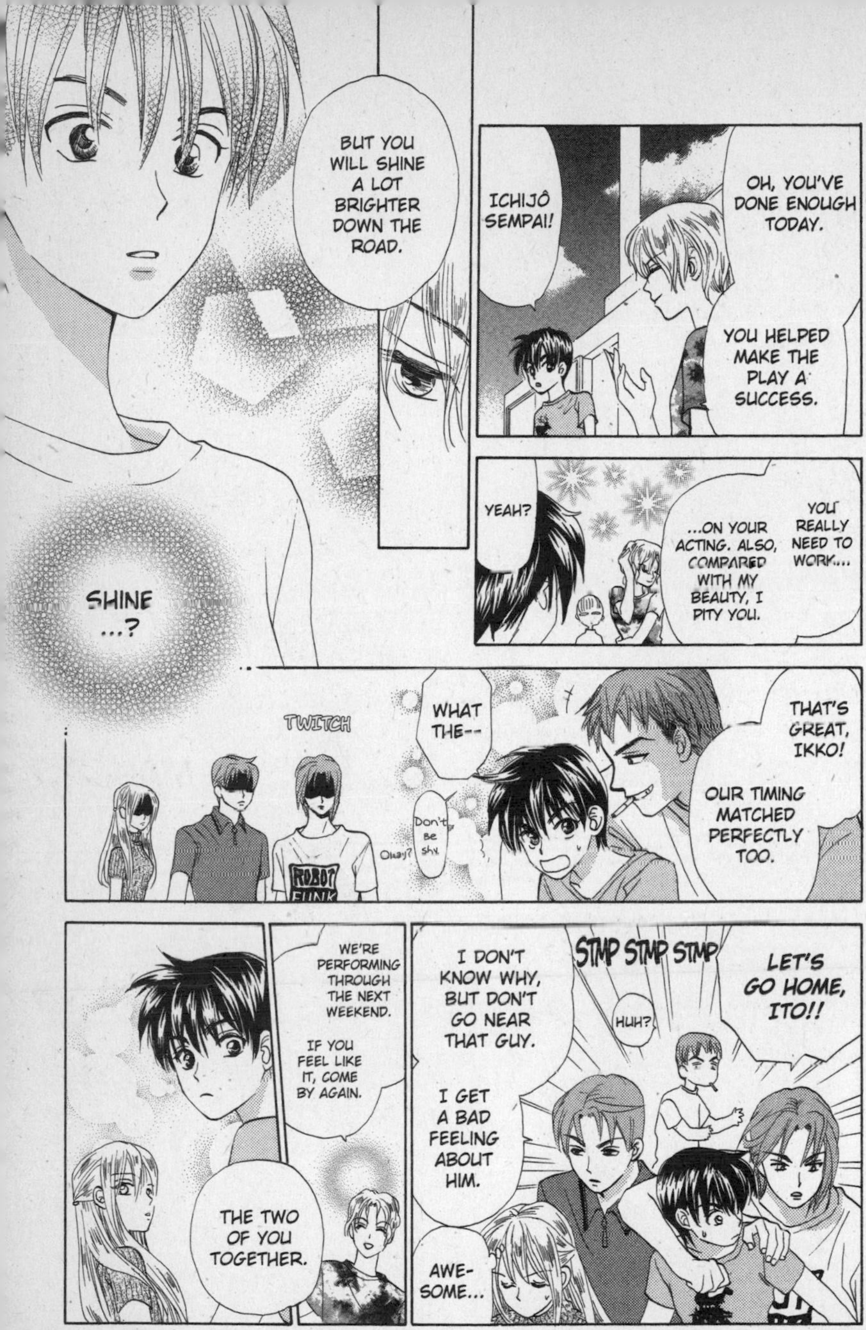
OH, YOU'VE DONE ENOUGH TODAY.
YOU HELPED MAKE THE PLAY A SUCCESS.
ICHIJÔ SEMPAI!
YOU REALLY NEED TO WORK...
...ON YOUR ACTING. ALSO, COMPARED WITH MY BEAUTY, I PITY YOU.
YEAH?
BUT YOU WILL SHINE A LOT BRIGHTER DOWN THE ROAD.
SHINE ...?
THAT'S GREAT, IKKO!
OUR TIMING MATCHED PERFECTLY TOO.
WHAT THE--
Don't be shy.
Okay?
TWITCH
LET'S GO HOME, ITO!!
STMP STMP STMP
HUH?
I DON'T KNOW WHY, BUT DON'T GO NEAR THAT GUY.
I GET A BAD FEELING ABOUT HIM.
AWE-SOME...
WE'RE PERFORMING THROUGH THE NEXT WEEKEND.
IF YOU FEEL LIKE IT, COME BY AGAIN.
THE TWO OF YOU TOGETHER.

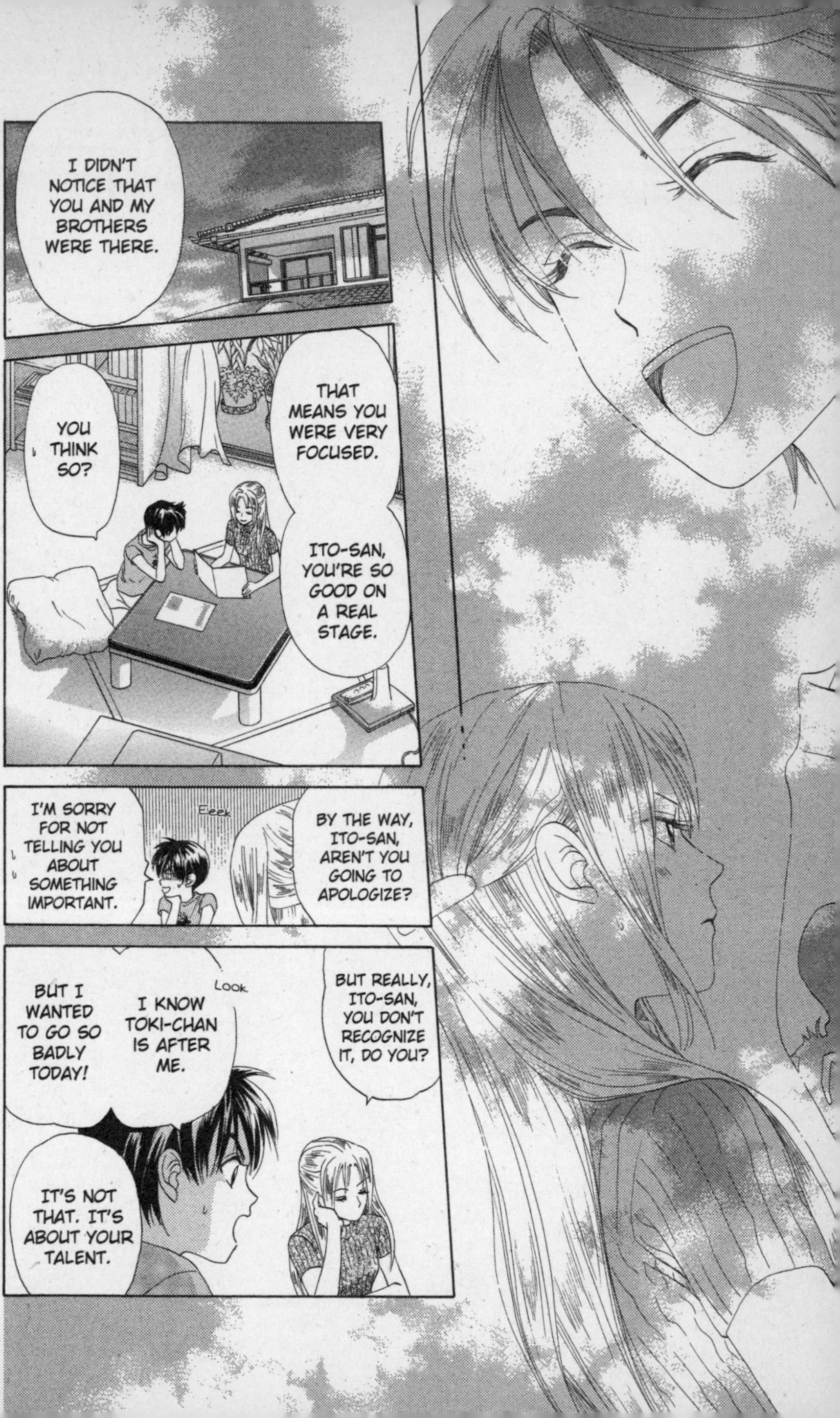
I DIDN'T NOTICE THAT YOU AND MY BROTHERS WERE THERE.
THAT MEANS YOU WERE VERY FOCUSED.
ITO-SAN, YOU'RE SO GOOD ON A REAL STAGE.
YOU THINK SO?
BY THE WAY, ITO-SAN, AREN'T YOU GOING TO APOLOGIZE?
Eeek
I'M SORRY FOR NOT TELLING YOU ABOUT SOMETHING IMPORTANT.
BUT REALLY, ITO-SAN, YOU DON'T RECOGNIZE IT, DO YOU?
Look
I KNOW TOKI-CHAN IS AFTER ME.
BUT I WANTED TO GO SO BADLY TODAY!
IT'S NOT THAT. IT'S ABOUT YOUR TALENT.

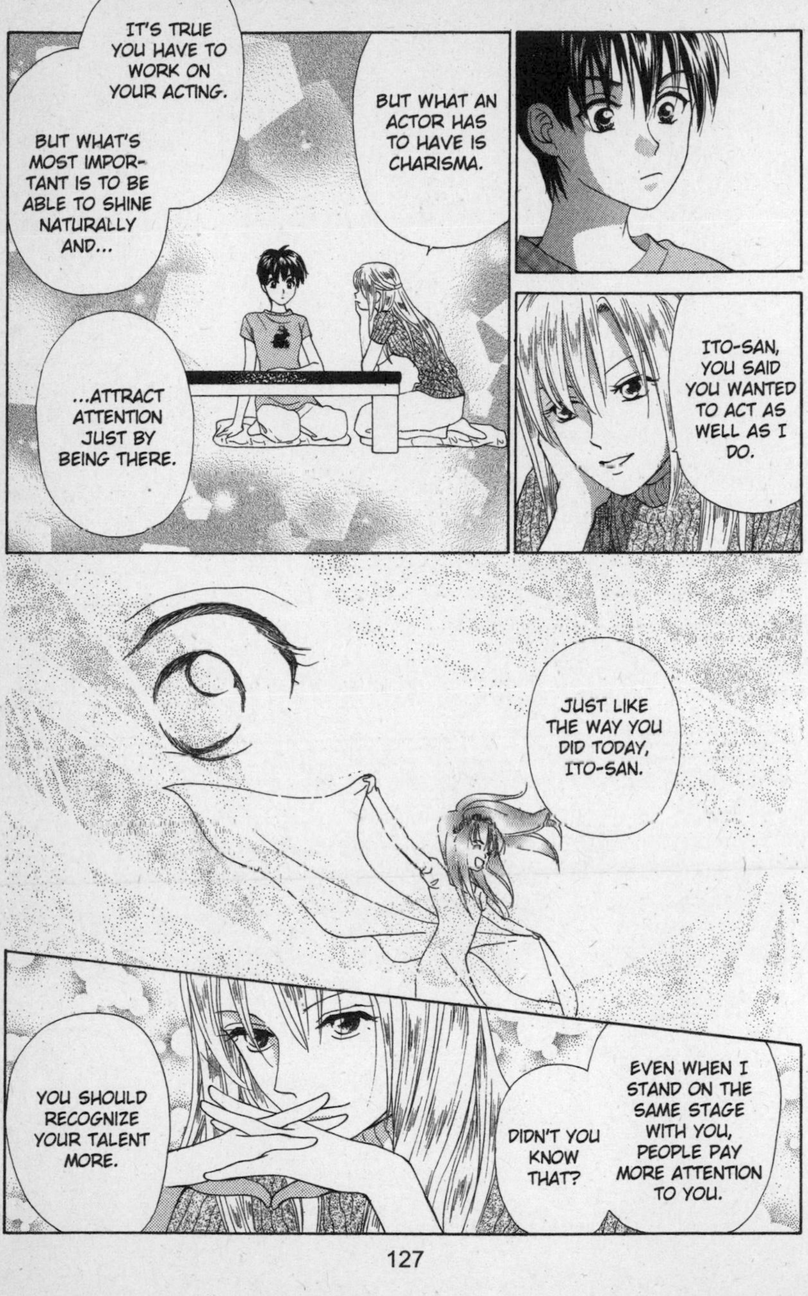
ITO-SAN, YOU SAID YOU WANTED TO ACT AS WELL AS I DO.
IT'S TRUE YOU HAVE TO WORK ON YOUR ACTING.
BUT WHAT AN ACTOR HAS TO HAVE IS CHARISMA.
BUT WHAT'S MOST IMPOR-TANT IS TO BE ABLE TO SHINE NATURALLY AND...
...ATTRACT ATTENTION JUST BY BEING THERE.
JUST LIKE THE WAY YOU DID TODAY, ITO-SAN.
EVEN WHEN I STAND ON THE SAME STAGE WITH YOU, PEOPLE PAY MORE ATTENTION TO YOU.
DIDN'T YOU KNOW THAT?
YOU SHOULD RECOGNIZE YOUR TALENT MORE.

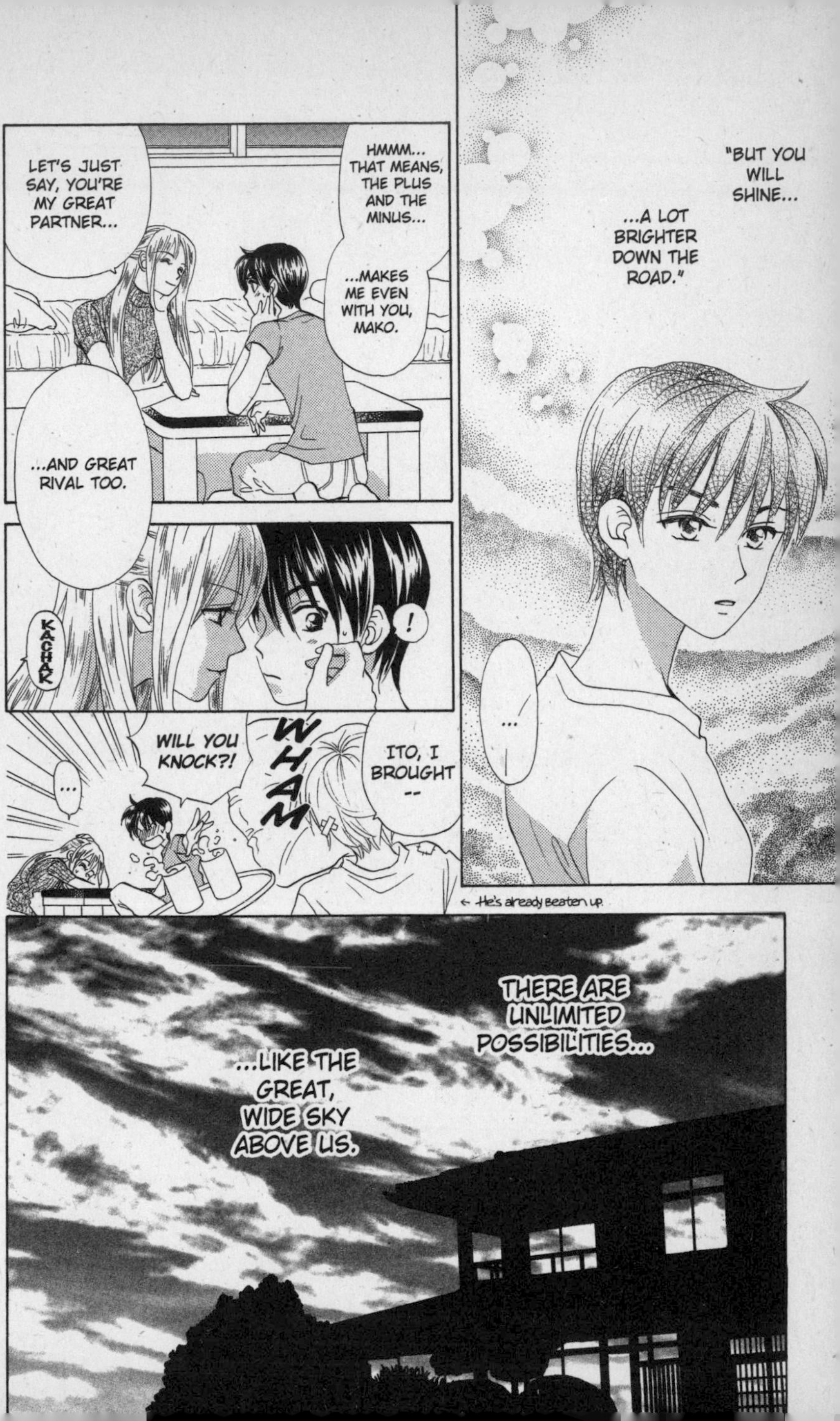
"BUT YOU WILL SHINE...
...A LOT BRIGHTER DOWN THE ROAD."
...
HMMM... THAT MEANS, THE PLUS AND THE MINUS...
LET'S JUST SAY, YOU'RE MY GREAT PARTNER...
...MAKES ME EVEN WITH YOU, MAKO.
...AND GREAT RIVAL TOO.
!
KACHAK
ITO, I BROUGHT --
WHAM
WILL YOU KNOCK?!
...
← He's already beaten up.
THERE ARE UNLIMITED POSSIBILITIES...
...LIKE THE GREAT, WIDE SKY ABOVE US.

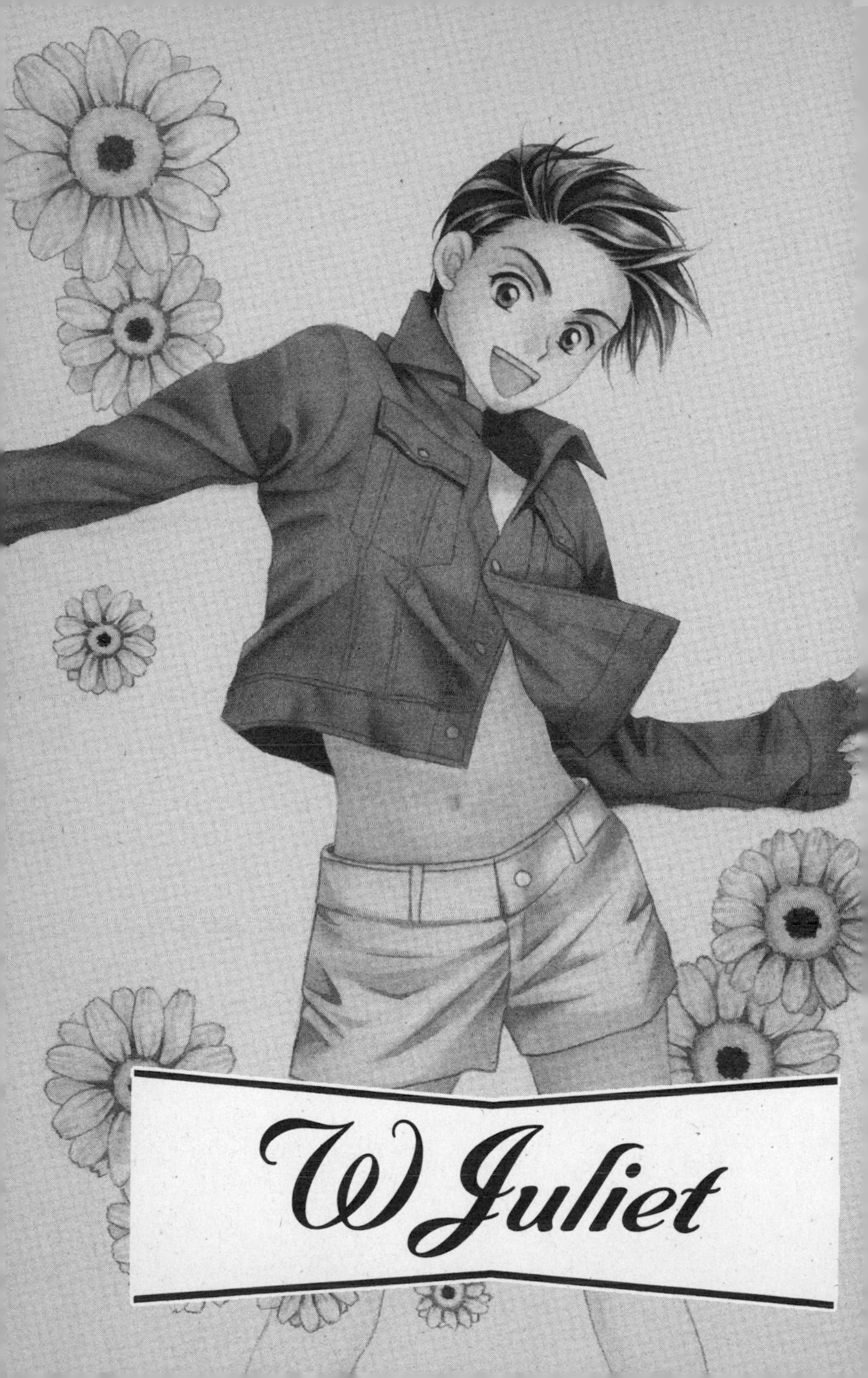
W Juliet

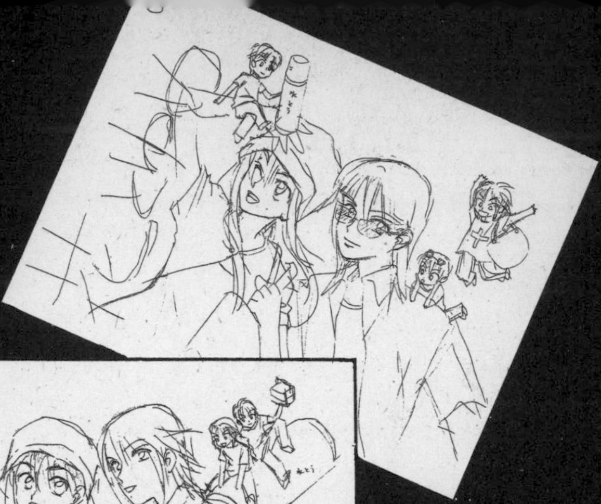

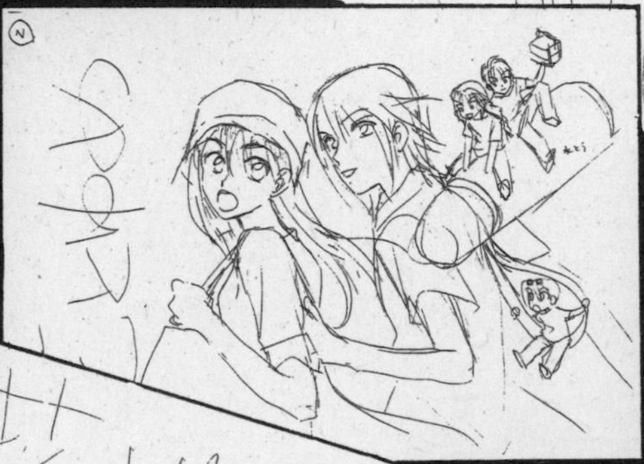

2001
Hana to Yume No. 10
Cover art. Draft (B5 size)
"Please provide a horizontal layout too." Since I was asked, I drew them. But the one they actually used was the vertical illustration only.

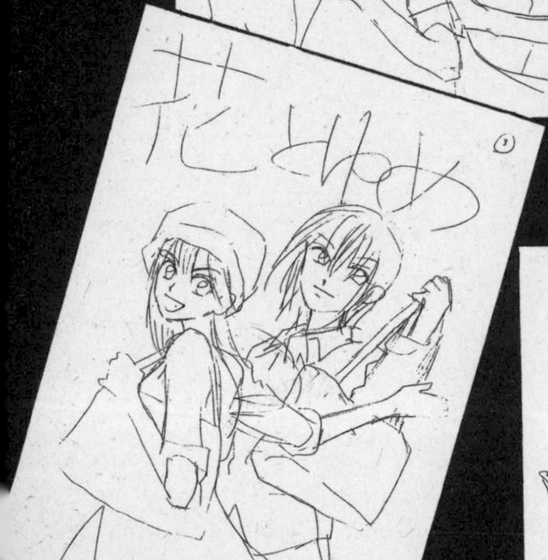
花とゆめ

Final draft
↳
Draft (B4 size)

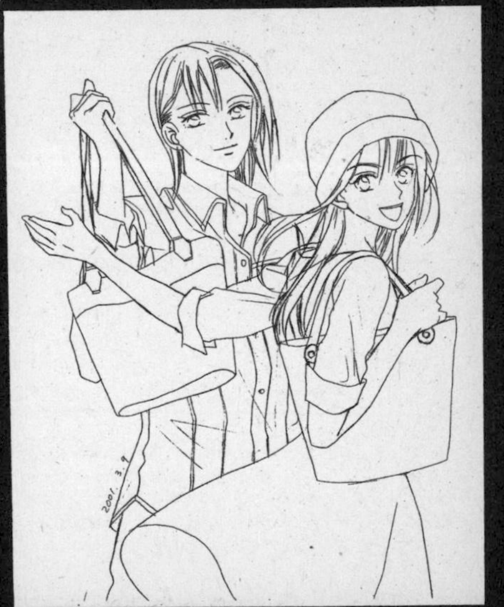
2001. 3. 9

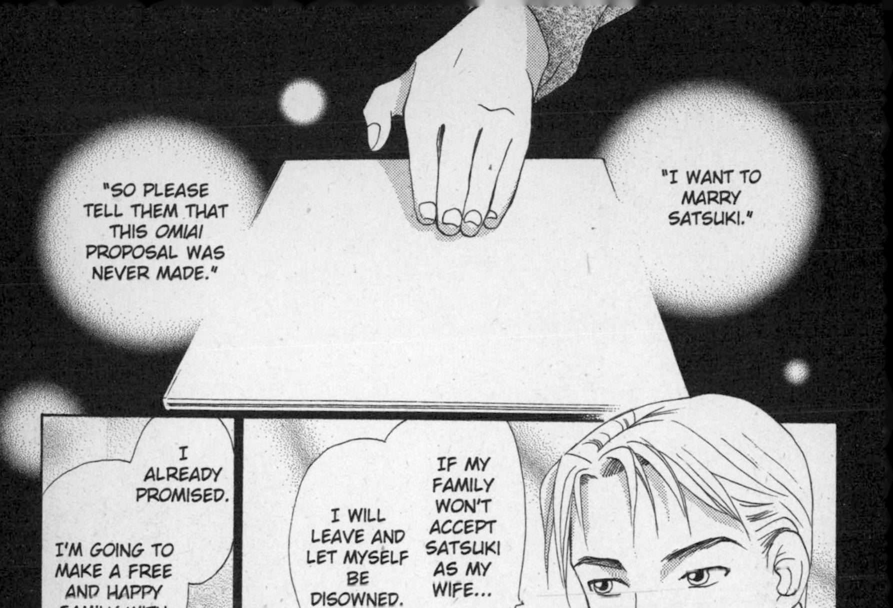
"I WANT TO MARRY SATSUKI."
"SO PLEASE TELL THEM THAT THIS *OMIAI* PROPOSAL WAS NEVER MADE."
IF MY FAMILY WON'T ACCEPT SATSUKI AS MY WIFE...
I WILL LEAVE AND LET MYSELF BE DISOWNED.
GORÔ!
YOU CAN'T STOP ME, MOTHER.
I ALREADY PROMISED.
I'M GOING TO MAKE A FREE AND HAPPY FAMILY WITH HER.
I AM...

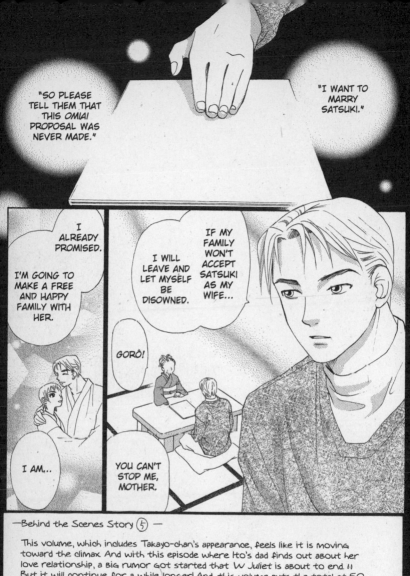

—Behind the Scenes Story ⑤ —

This volume, which includes Takayo-chan's appearance, feels like it is moving toward the climax And with this episode where Ito's dad finds out about her love relationship, a big rumor got started that W Juliet is about to end. ıı But it will continue for a while longer! And, this volume puts the total at 50 installments since the series started. ∴ As a matter of fact, there was a typo in the magazine (showing the wrong number), which prompted many inquiry letters asking if this really made the total 50. Mr. Editor-in-Charge and I counted to make sure and confirmed that the total is indeed 50! (Including the special episodes.) I noticed the typo along the way and requested a correction.

	Vol 4 - 6 episodes	Vol 8 - 6 episodes
Vol 1 - 4 episodes	Vol 5 - 6 episodes	Vol 9 - 6 episodes
Vol 2 - 5 episodes	Vol 6 - 6 episodes	
Vol 3 - 5 episodes	Vol 7 - 6 episodes	50 episodes total!

I'm sorry about this. We might have confused those of you who have been reading the magazine installments. So, sorry!

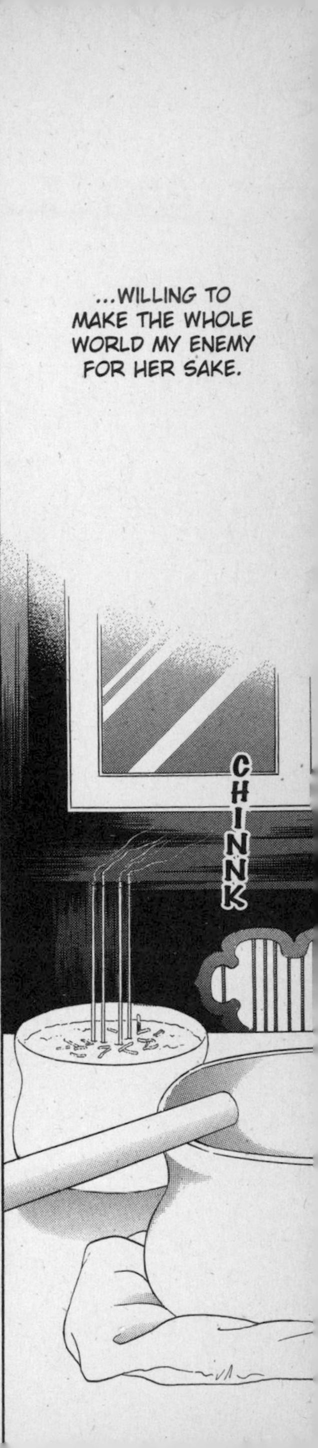
...WILLING TO MAKE THE WHOLE WORLD MY ENEMY FOR HER SAKE.
CHINNK

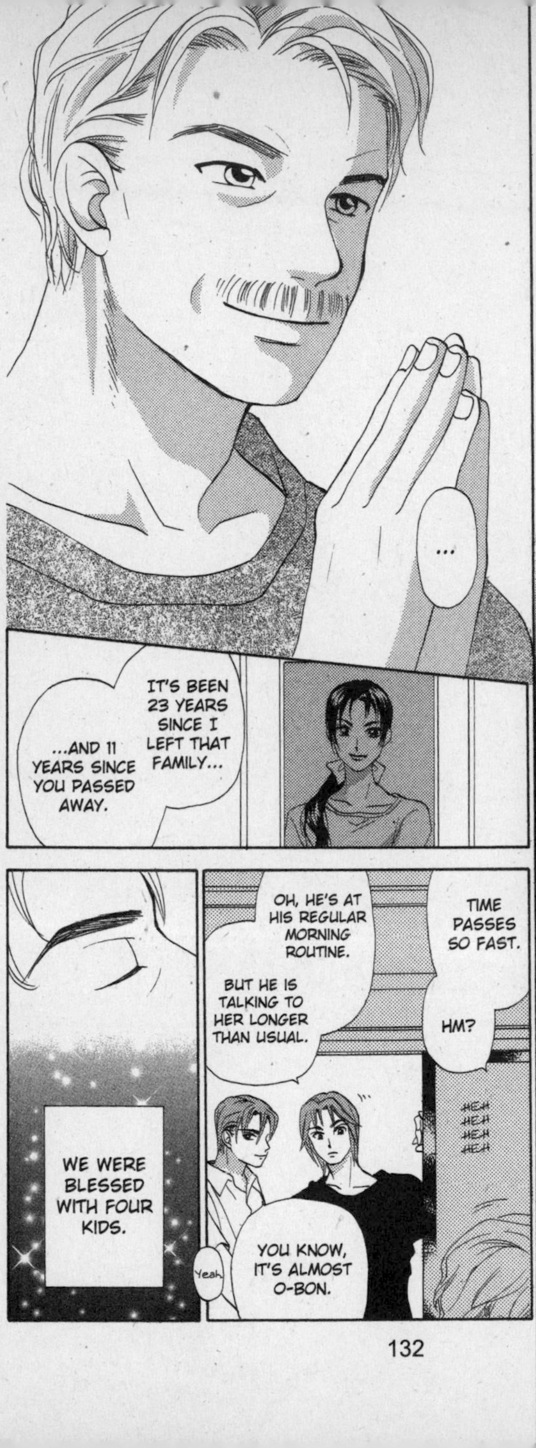
...
IT'S BEEN 23 YEARS SINCE I LEFT THAT FAMILY...
...AND 11 YEARS SINCE YOU PASSED AWAY.
TIME PASSES SO FAST.
HM?
OH, HE'S AT HIS REGULAR MORNING ROUTINE.
BUT HE IS TALKING TO HER LONGER THAN USUAL.
HEH HEH HEH HEH
YOU KNOW, IT'S ALMOST O-BON.
Yeah
WE WERE BLESSED WITH FOUR KIDS.

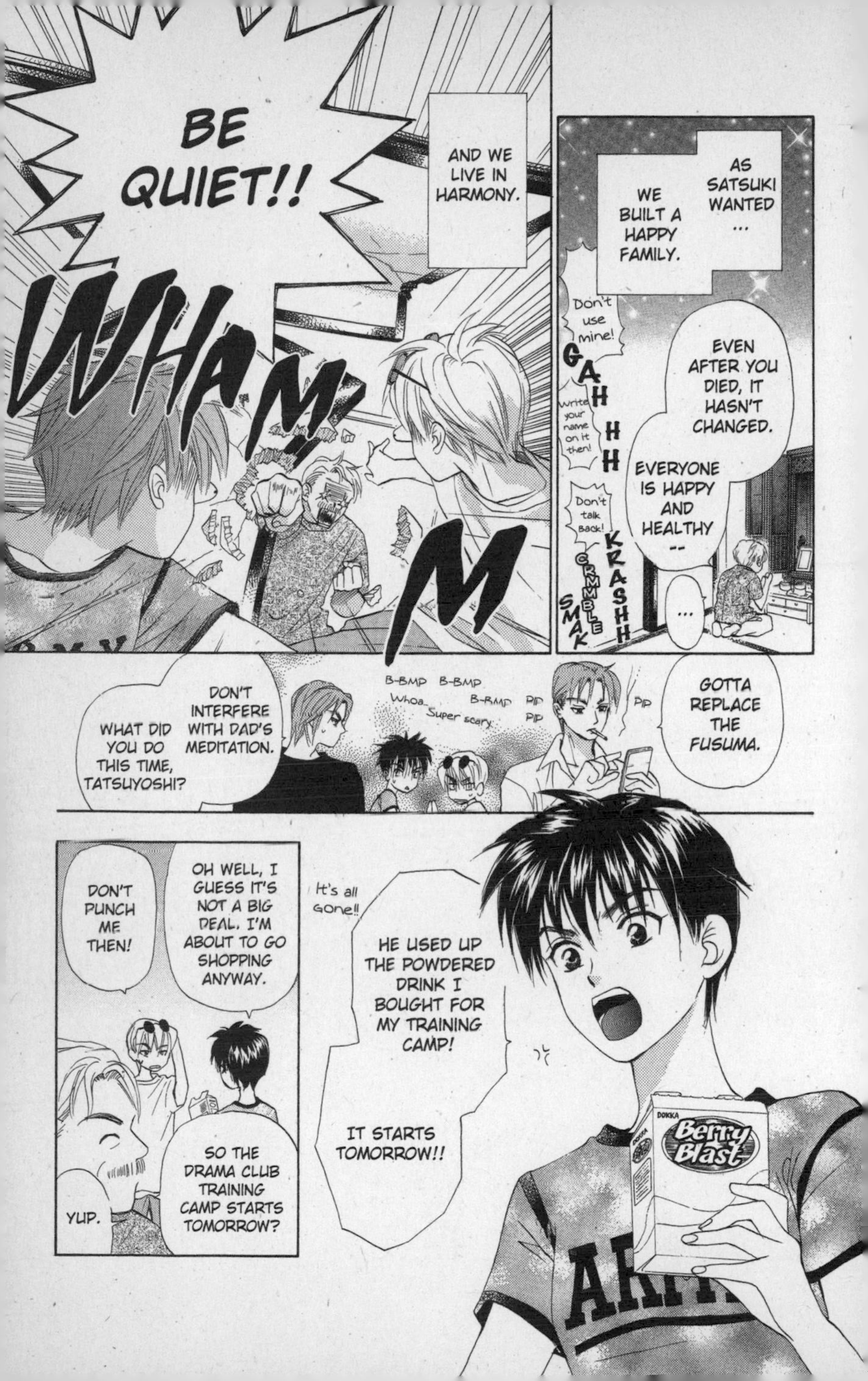
AS SATSUKI WANTED...
WE BUILT A HAPPY FAMILY.
Don't use mine!
GAHHH
Write your name on it then!
EVEN AFTER YOU DIED, IT HASN'T CHANGED.
EVERYONE IS HAPPY AND HEALTHY --
Don't talk back!
KRASHH
CRMMBLE
SMAK
...
AND WE LIVE IN HARMONY.
BE QUIET!!
WHAMM
GOTTA REPLACE THE FUSUMA.
PIP PIP PIP
B-BMP B-BMP B-BMP
Whoa... Super scary.
DON'T INTERFERE WITH DAD'S MEDITATION.
WHAT DID YOU DO THIS TIME, TATSUYOSHI?
HE USED UP THE POWDERED DRINK I BOUGHT FOR MY TRAINING CAMP!
It's all Gone!!
IT STARTS TOMORROW!!
DOKKA
Berry Blast
OH WELL, I GUESS IT'S NOT A BIG DEAL. I'M ABOUT TO GO SHOPPING ANYWAY.
DON'T PUNCH ME THEN!
SO THE DRAMA CLUB TRAINING CAMP STARTS TOMORROW?
YUP.

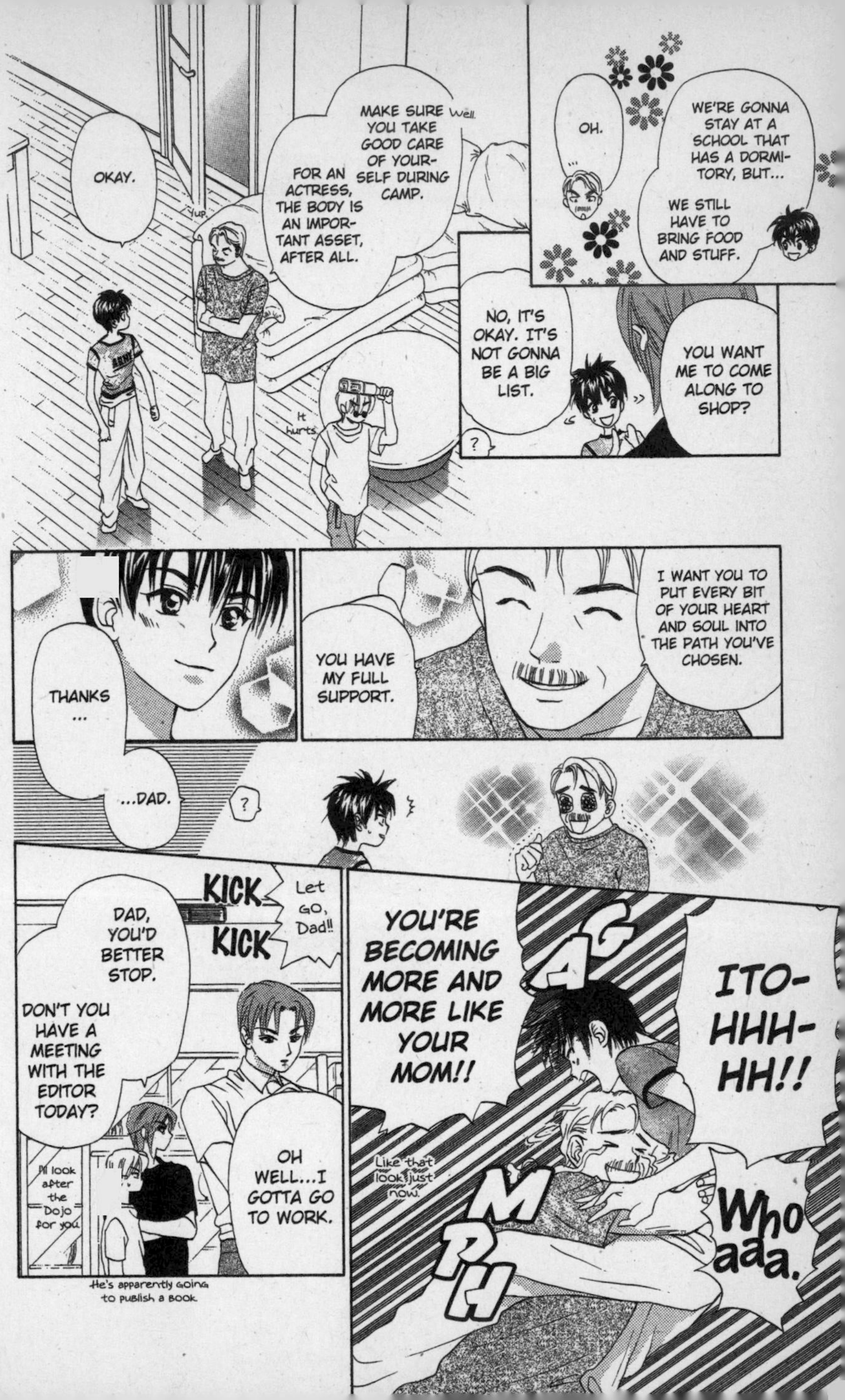
WE'RE GONNA STAY AT A SCHOOL THAT HAS A DORMITORY, BUT...
OH.
...
WE STILL HAVE TO BRING FOOD AND STUFF.
YOU WANT ME TO COME ALONG TO SHOP?
NO, IT'S OKAY. IT'S NOT GONNA BE A BIG LIST.
?
MAKE SURE YOU TAKE GOOD CARE OF YOURSELF DURING CAMP.
Well.
FOR AN ACTRESS, THE BODY IS AN IMPORTANT ASSET, AFTER ALL.
It hurts.
OKAY.
Yup.
I WANT YOU TO PUT EVERY BIT OF YOUR HEART AND SOUL INTO THE PATH YOU'VE CHOSEN.
YOU HAVE MY FULL SUPPORT.
THANKS...
...DAD.
?
ITO-HHHHH!!
YOU'RE BECOMING MORE AND MORE LIKE YOUR MOM!!
GA
Whoaaa.
MPH
Like that look just now.
Let GO, Dad!!
KICK
KICK
DAD, YOU'D BETTER STOP.
DON'T YOU HAVE A MEETING WITH THE EDITOR TODAY?
OH WELL...I GOTTA GO TO WORK.
I'll look after the Dojo for you
He's apparently going to publish a book

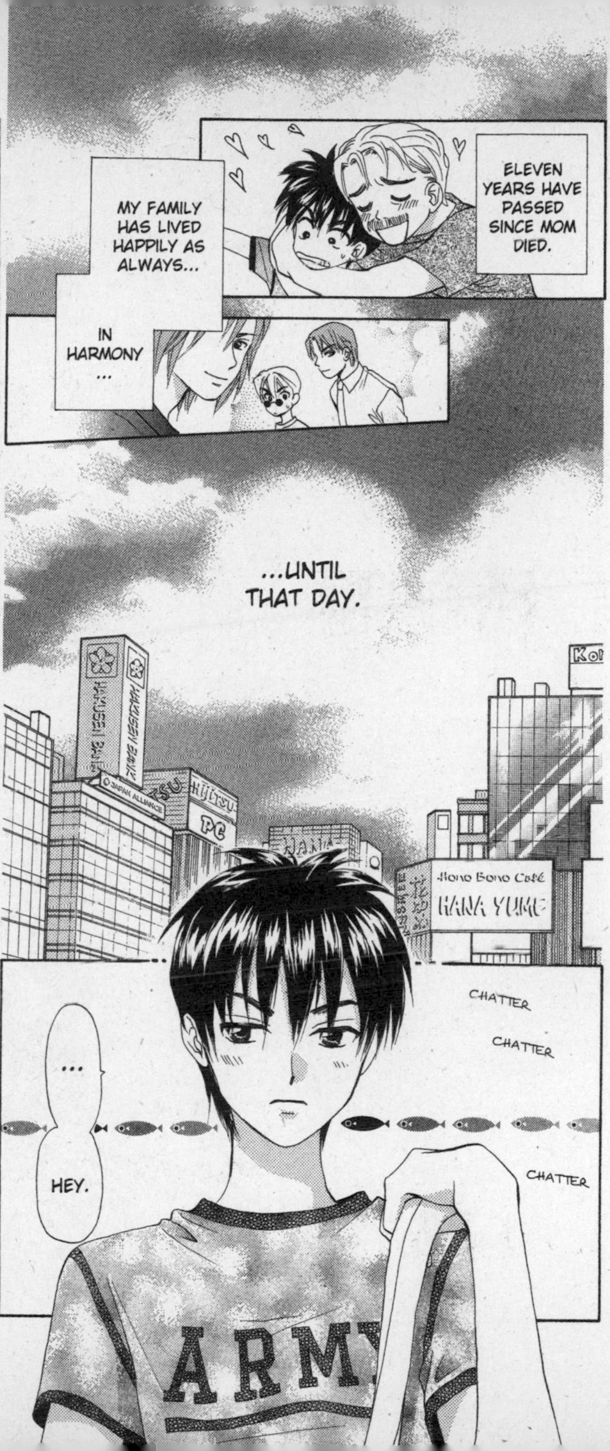
ELEVEN YEARS HAVE PASSED SINCE MOM DIED.
MY FAMILY HAS LIVED HAPPILY AS ALWAYS...
IN HARMONY ...
...UNTIL THAT DAY.
HAKUSEN BANK
JAPAN ALLIANCE
PC
Hono Bono Café HANA YUME
CHATTER
CHATTER
CHATTER
...
HEY.
ARMY

Let me talk about Wakamatsu-san next. She's been coming to help since volume 3. She is super duper fast. And very good!

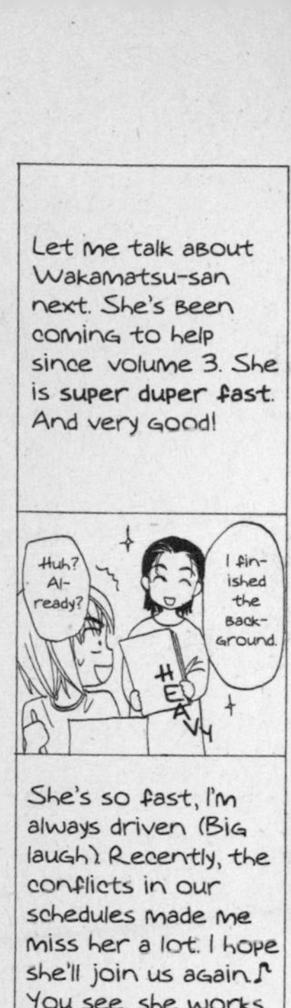
I finished the background.
Huh? Already?
HEAVY

She's so fast, I'm always driven (Big laugh) Recently, the conflicts in our schedules made me miss her a lot. I hope she'll join us again.♪ You see, she works as an assistant to many others too.

And Taneda-san has been assisting me since volume 6. She is the queen of tones. Her technique is awesome!! Gorgeous! Thanks to her, we have more tones since volume 6. Now everyone gives her the critical scenes to work on. (Laugh) Heh heh heh...

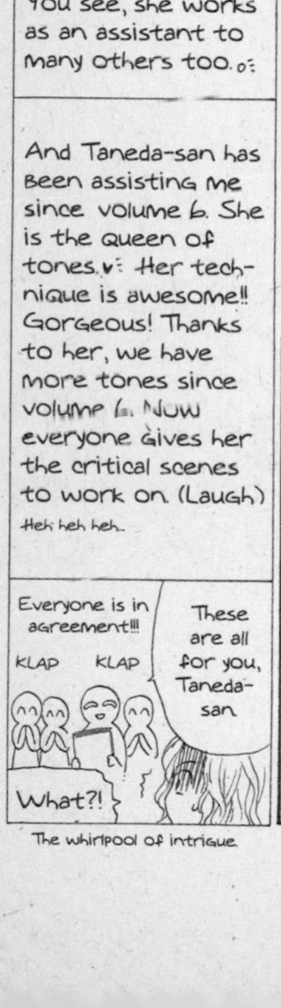
These are all for you, Taneda-san.
Everyone is in agreement!!!
KLAP KLAP
What?!

The whirlpool of intrigue

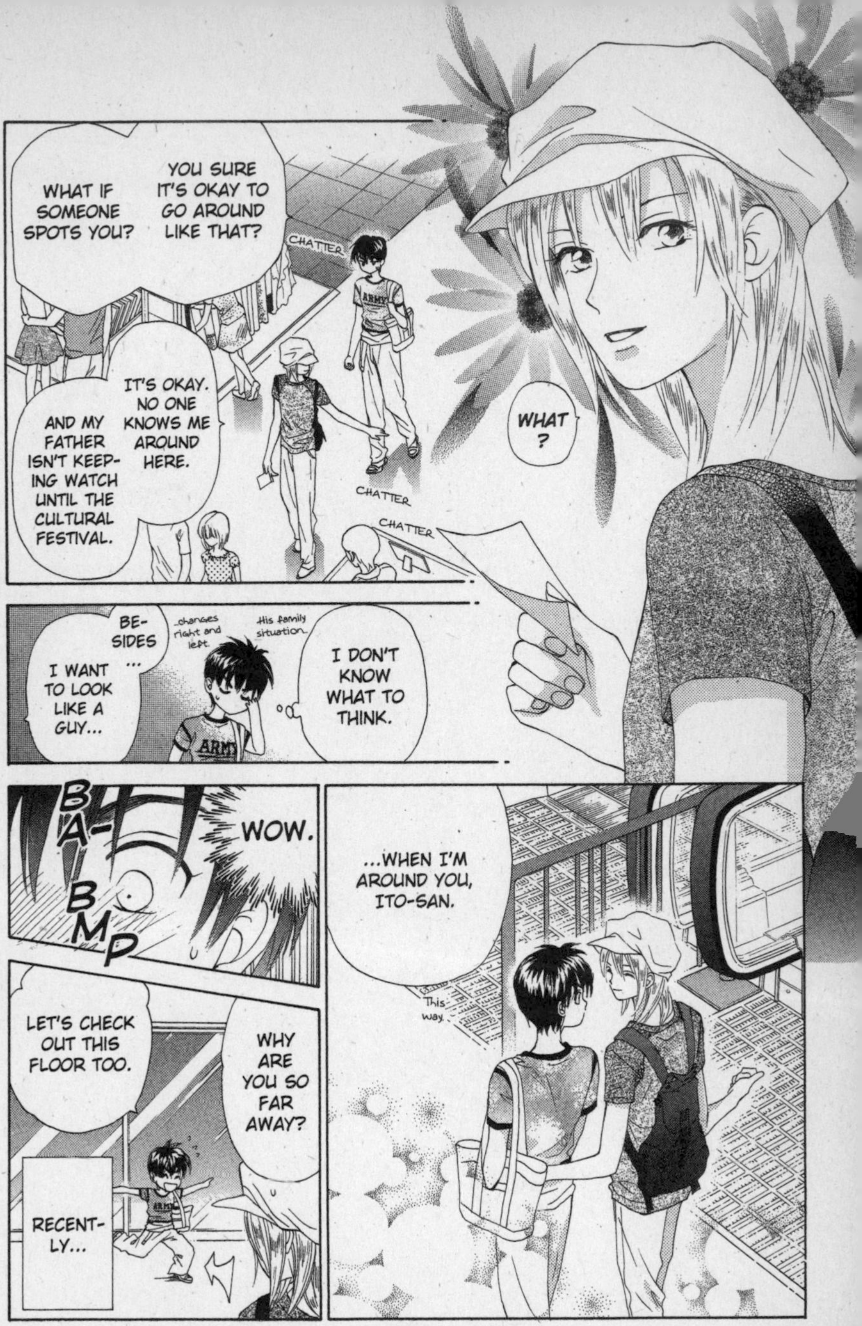
WHAT?
YOU SURE IT'S OKAY TO GO AROUND LIKE THAT?
WHAT IF SOMEONE SPOTS YOU?
CHATTER
IT'S OKAY. NO ONE KNOWS ME AROUND HERE.
AND MY FATHER ISN'T KEEPING WATCH UNTIL THE CULTURAL FESTIVAL.
CHATTER
CHATTER
I DON'T KNOW WHAT TO THINK.
His family situation...
...changes right and left.
BESIDES...
I WANT TO LOOK LIKE A GUY...
...WHEN I'M AROUND YOU, ITO-SAN.
This way.
WOW.
BA-BMP
WHY ARE YOU SO FAR AWAY?
LET'S CHECK OUT THIS FLOOR TOO.
RECENTLY...

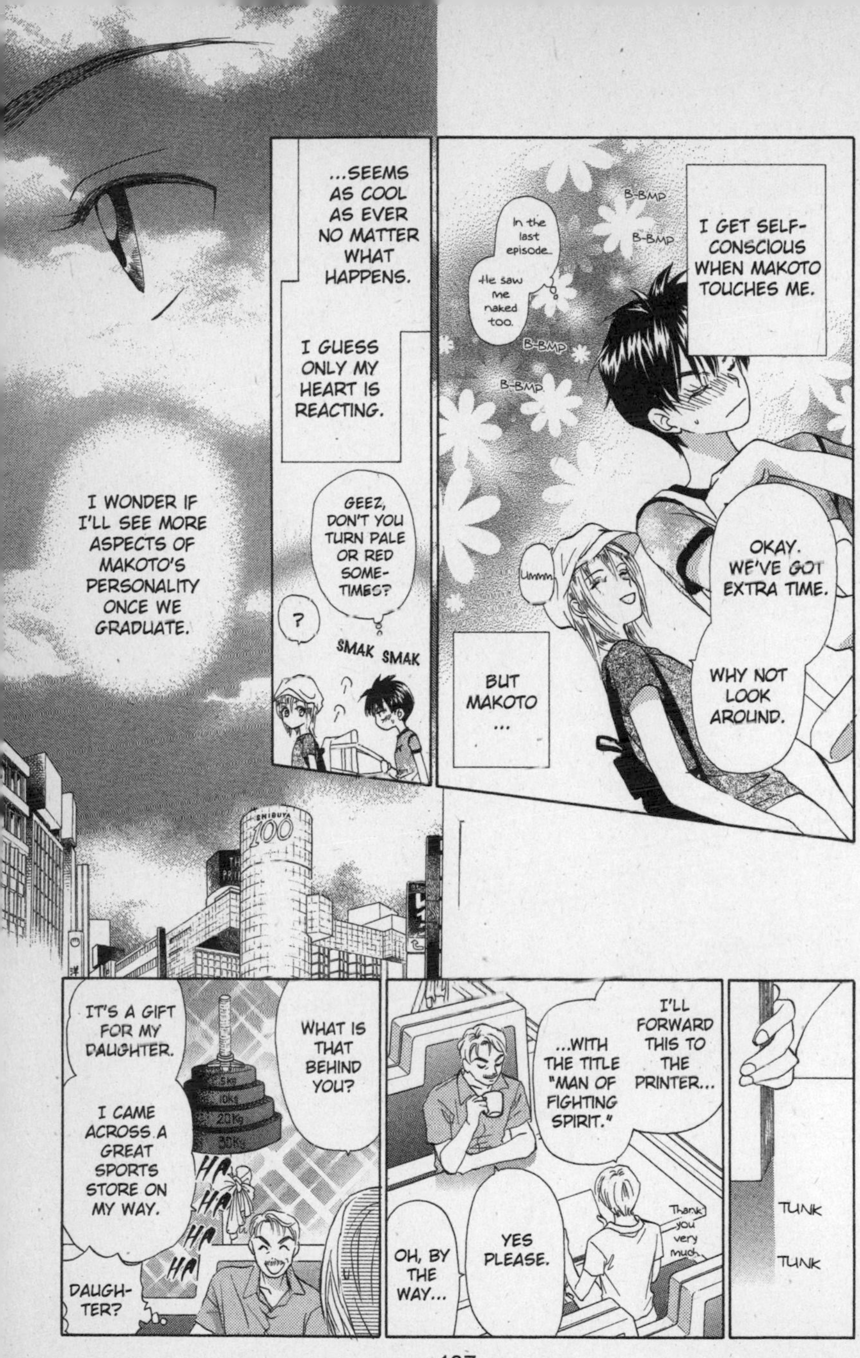
I GET SELF-CONSCIOUS WHEN MAKOTO TOUCHES ME.
B-BMP
B-BMP
In the last episode...
He saw me naked too.
B-BMP
B-BMP
OKAY. WE'VE GOT EXTRA TIME.
WHY NOT LOOK AROUND.
Ummm.
BUT MAKOTO ...
...SEEMS AS COOL AS EVER NO MATTER WHAT HAPPENS.
I GUESS ONLY MY HEART IS REACTING.
GEEZ, DON'T YOU TURN PALE OR RED SOME-TIMES?
?
SMAK SMAK
I WONDER IF I'LL SEE MORE ASPECTS OF MAKOTO'S PERSONALITY ONCE WE GRADUATE.
SHIBUYA 100
TUNK
TUNK
I'LL FORWARD THIS TO THE PRINTER...
...WITH THE TITLE "MAN OF FIGHTING SPIRIT."
Thank you very much.
YES PLEASE.
OH, BY THE WAY...
WHAT IS THAT BEHIND YOU?
IT'S A GIFT FOR MY DAUGHTER.
5kg
10kg
20kg
30kg
I CAME ACROSS A GREAT SPORTS STORE ON MY WAY.
HA HA HA HA
DAUGH-TER?

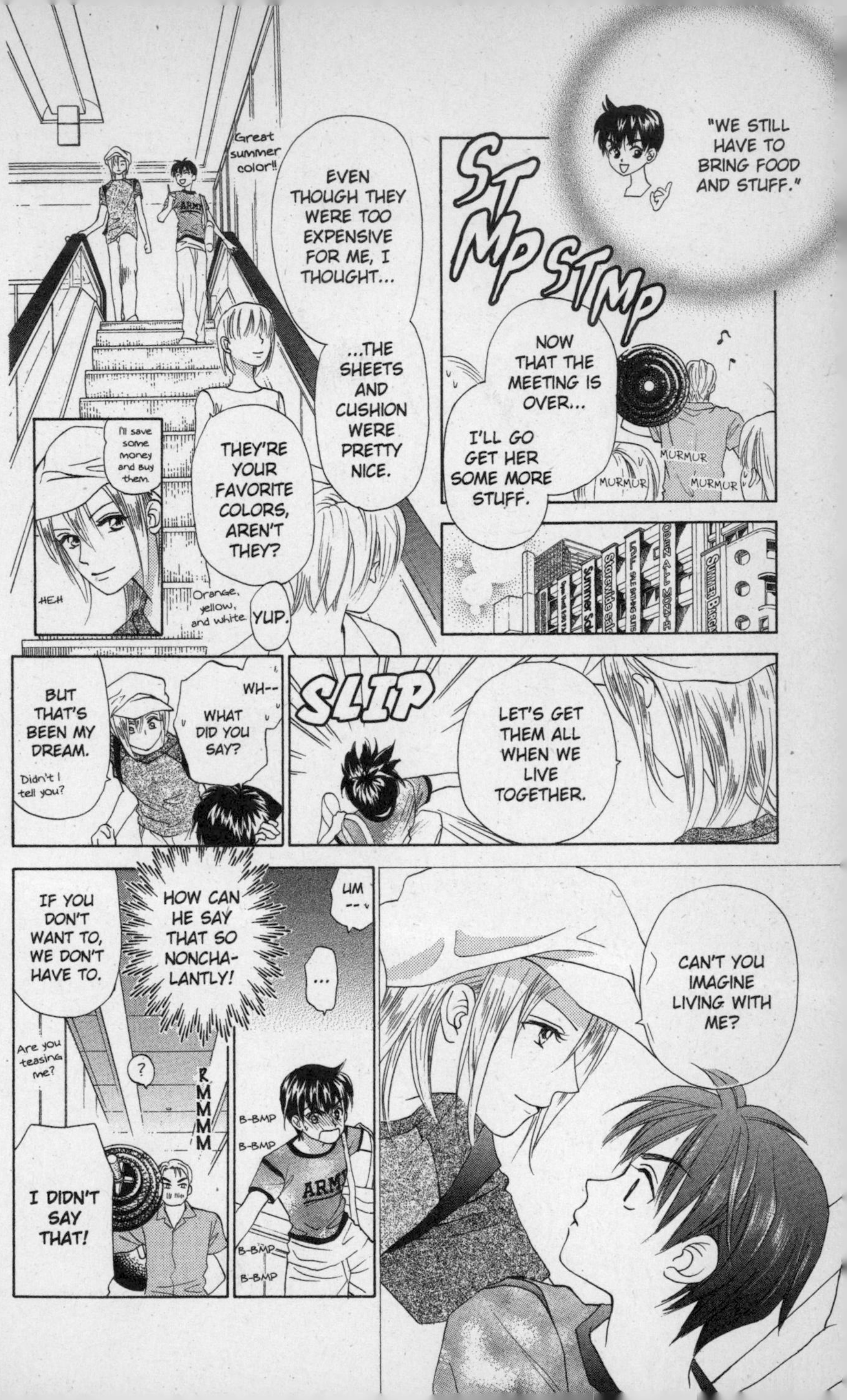
"WE STILL HAVE TO BRING FOOD AND STUFF."
STMP STMP
NOW THAT THE MEETING IS OVER...
I'LL GO GET HER SOME MORE STUFF.
MURMUR
MURMUR
MURMUR
Great summer color!!
EVEN THOUGH THEY WERE TOO EXPENSIVE FOR ME, I THOUGHT...
...THE SHEETS AND CUSHION WERE PRETTY NICE.
THEY'RE YOUR FAVORITE COLORS, AREN'T THEY?
Orange, yellow, and white.
YUP.
I'll save some money and buy them.
HEH
SLIP
LET'S GET THEM ALL WHEN WE LIVE TOGETHER.
WH--
WHAT DID YOU SAY?
BUT THAT'S BEEN MY DREAM.
Didn't I tell you?
CAN'T YOU IMAGINE LIVING WITH ME?
UM--
...
HOW CAN HE SAY THAT SO NONCHALANTLY!
B-BMP
B-BMP
B-BMP
B-BMP
RMMMM
IF YOU DON'T WANT TO, WE DON'T HAVE TO.
?
Are you teasing me?
I DIDN'T SAY THAT!

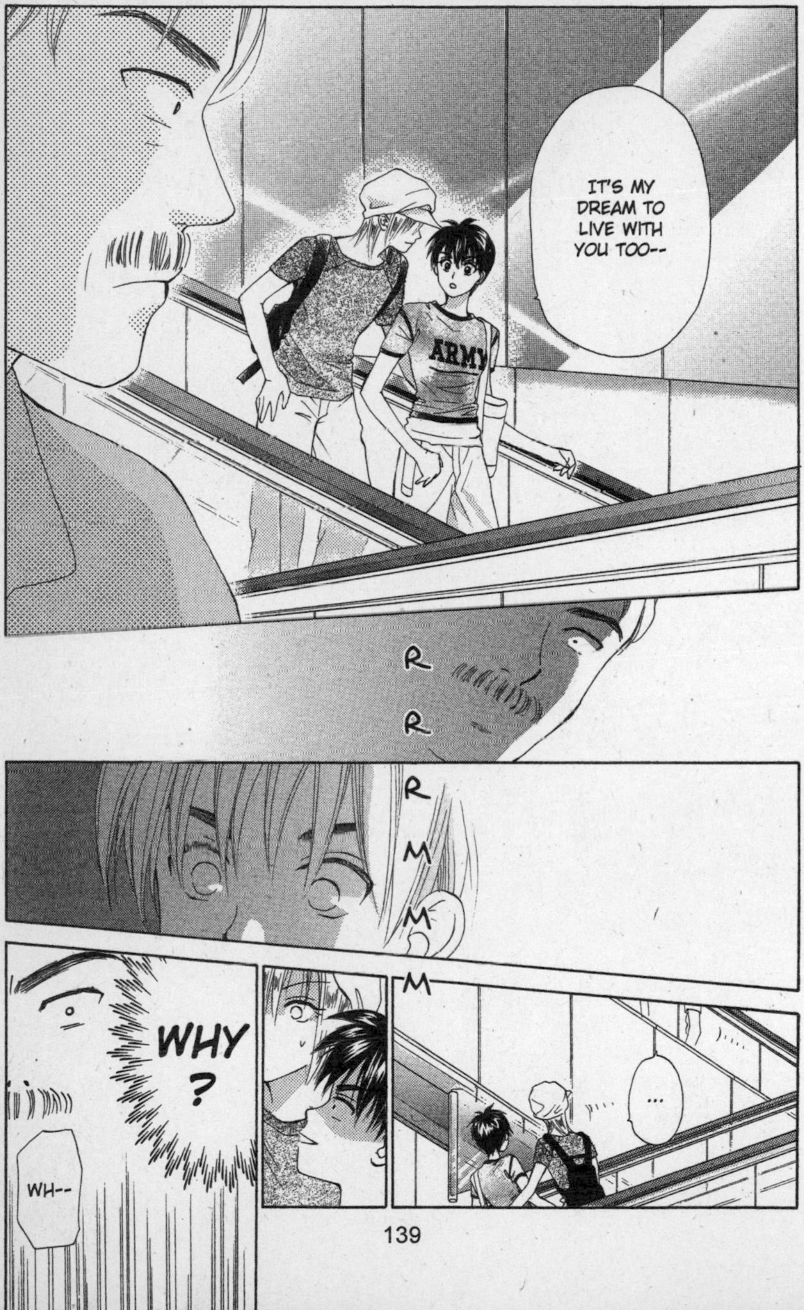
IT'S MY DREAM TO LIVE WITH YOU TOO--
RRRMMM
...
WHY?
WH--

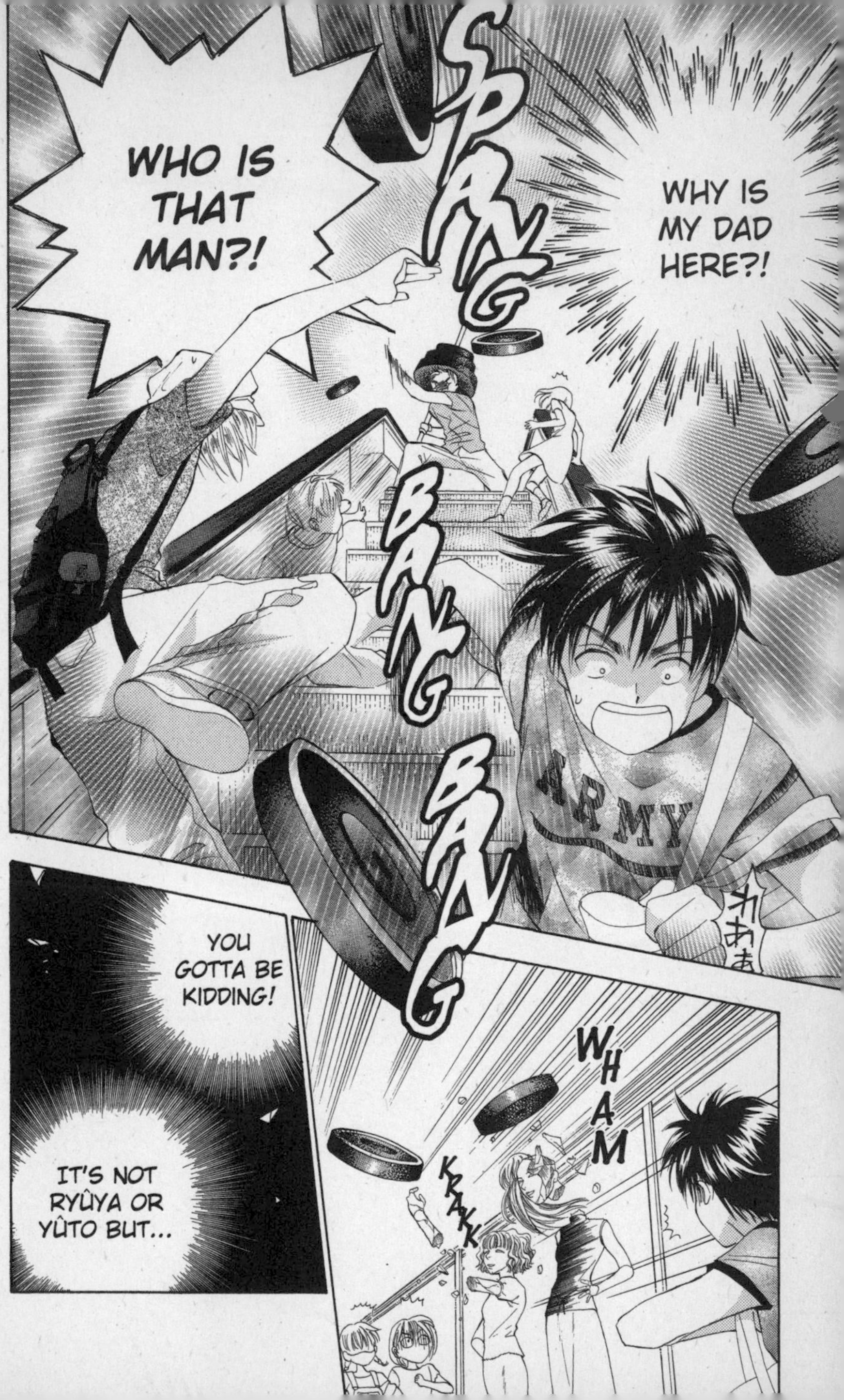
WHY IS MY DAD HERE?!
SPANG
WHO IS THAT MAN?!
BANG
BANG
WHAM
KRAKK
YOU GOTTA BE KIDDING!
IT'S NOT RYÛYA OR YÛTO BUT...

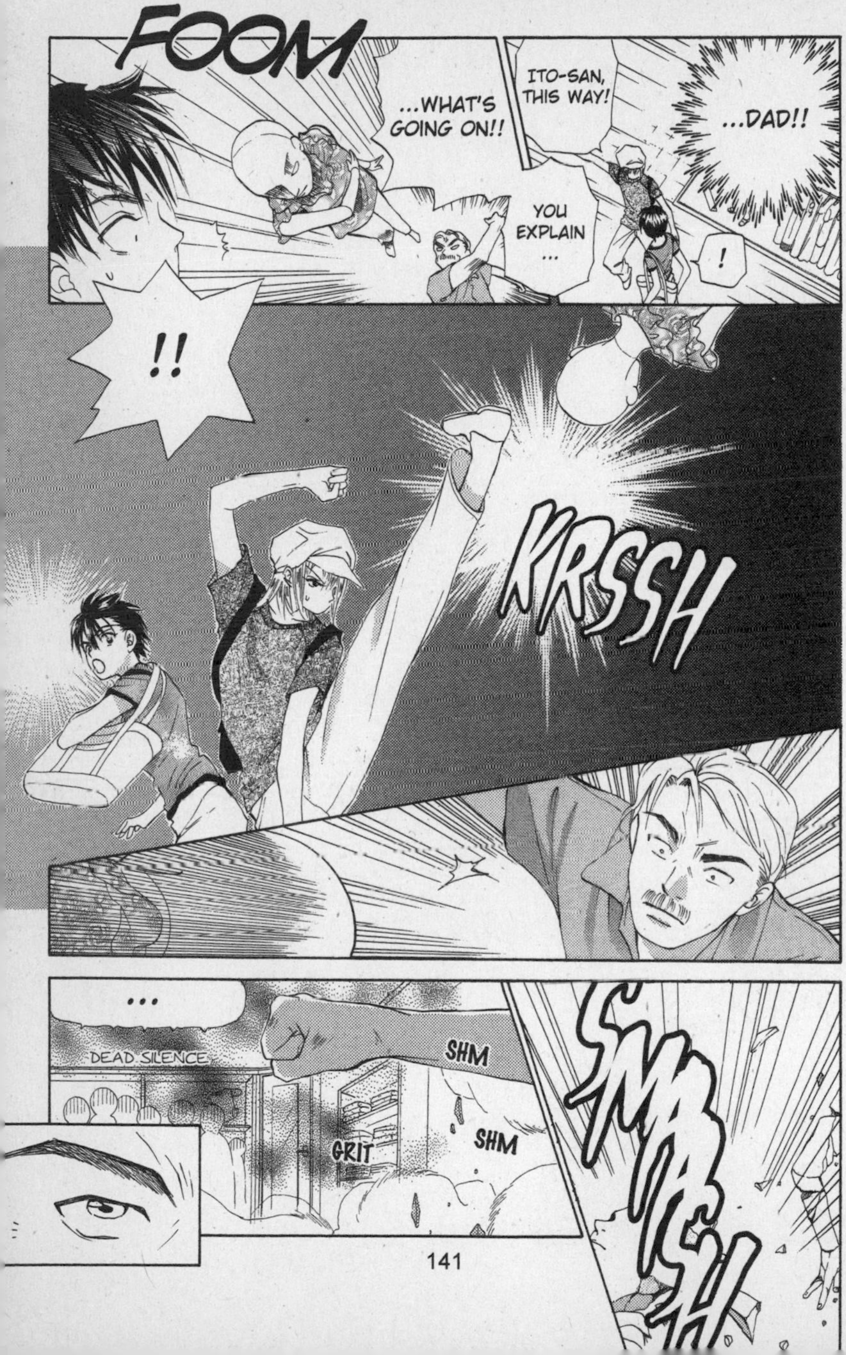
ITO-SAN, THIS WAY!
...DAD!!
!
FOOM
...WHAT'S GOING ON!!
YOU EXPLAIN ...
!!
KRSSH
SMASH
...
DEAD SILENCE
SHM
SHM
GRIT

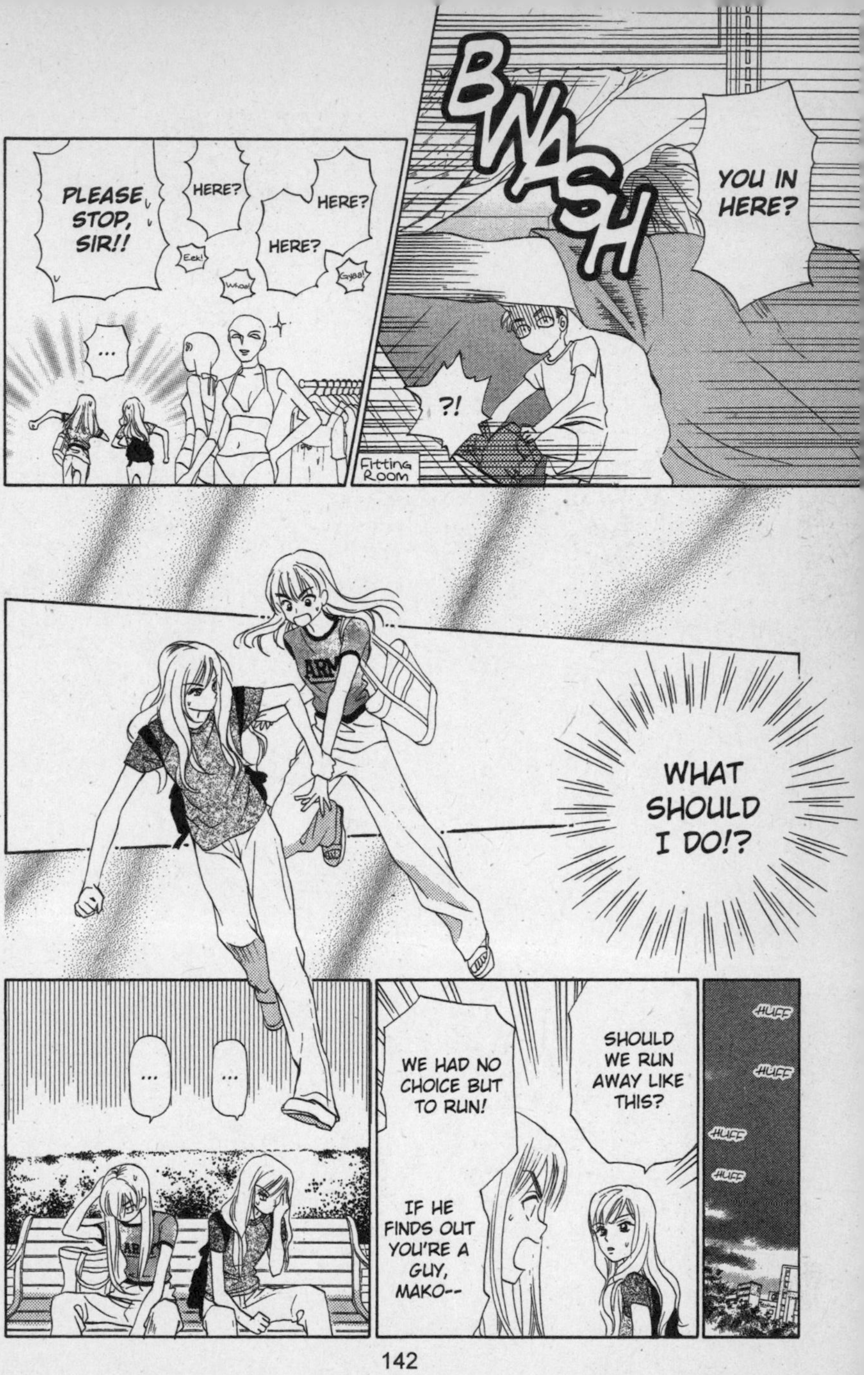
BWASH
YOU IN HERE?
?!
Fitting Room
HERE?
Gyaa!
HERE?
Whoa!
HERE?
Eek!
PLEASE STOP, SIR!!
...
WHAT SHOULD I DO!?
HUFF
HUFF
HUFF
HUFF
SHOULD WE RUN AWAY LIKE THIS?
WE HAD NO CHOICE BUT TO RUN!
IF HE FINDS OUT YOU'RE A GUY, MAKO--
...
...

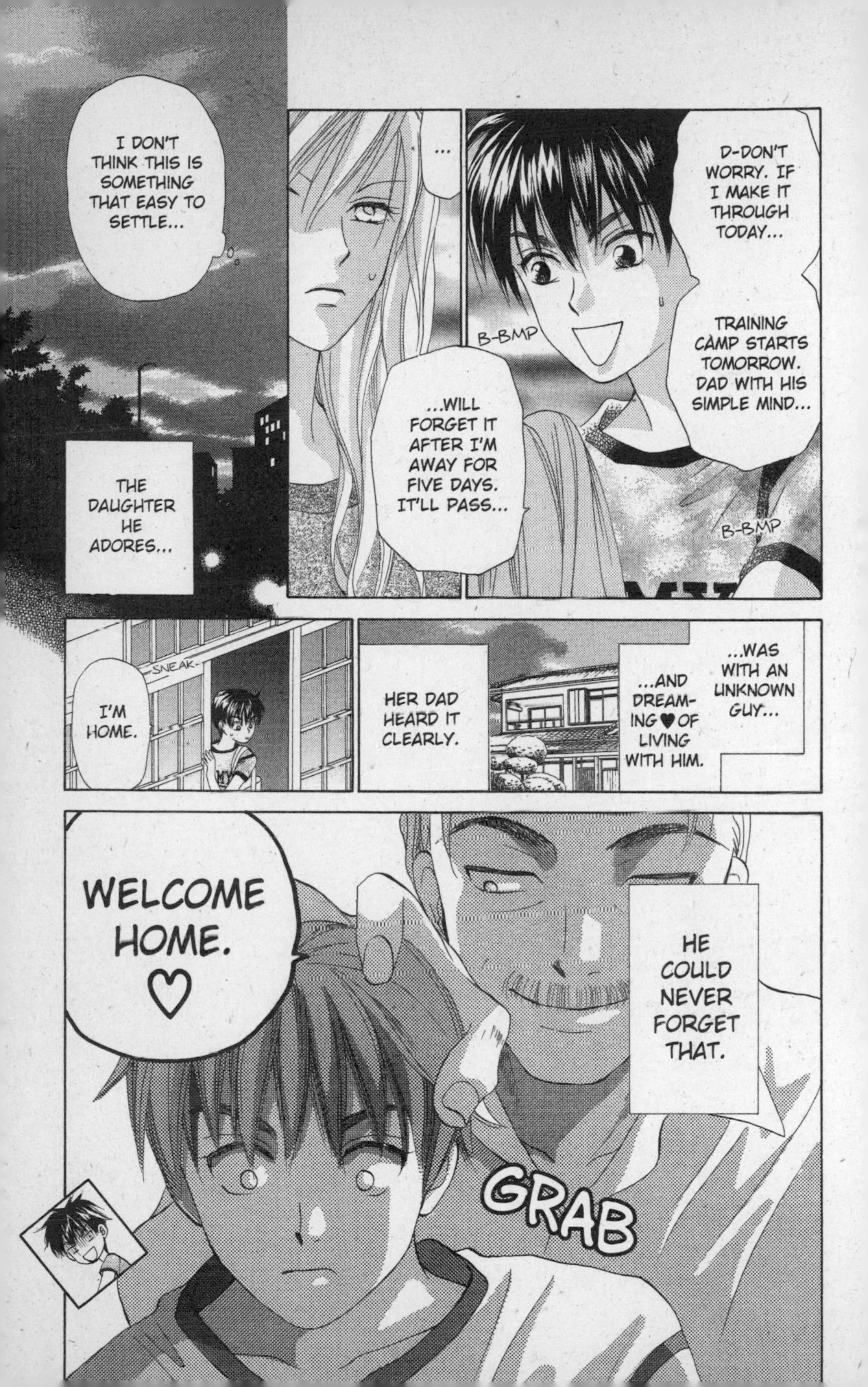
D-DON'T WORRY. IF I MAKE IT THROUGH TODAY...
TRAINING CAMP STARTS TOMORROW. DAD WITH HIS SIMPLE MIND...
B-BMP
...WILL FORGET IT AFTER I'M AWAY FOR FIVE DAYS. IT'LL PASS...
B-BMP
...
I DON'T THINK THIS IS SOMETHING THAT EASY TO SETTLE...
THE DAUGHTER HE ADORES...
...WAS WITH AN UNKNOWN GUY...
...AND DREAM-ING ♥ OF LIVING WITH HIM.
HER DAD HEARD IT CLEARLY.
SNEAK
I'M HOME.
WELCOME HOME. ♡
HE COULD NEVER FORGET THAT.
GRAB

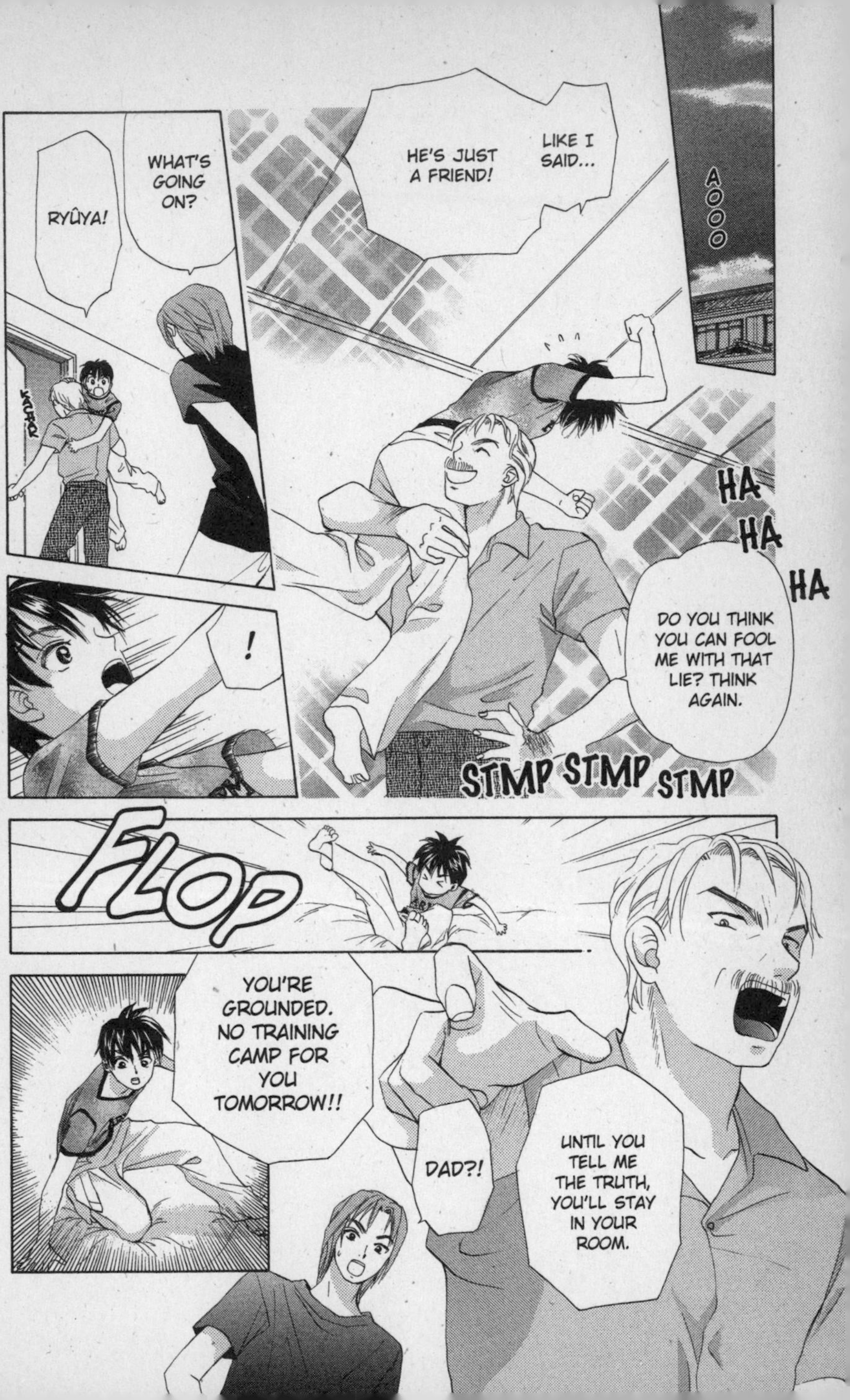
AOOO
LIKE I SAID...
HE'S JUST A FRIEND!
HA HA HA
DO YOU THINK YOU CAN FOOL ME WITH THAT LIE? THINK AGAIN.
STMP STMP STMP
WHAT'S GOING ON?
RYÛYA!
!
FLOP
YOU'RE GROUNDED. NO TRAINING CAMP FOR YOU TOMORROW!!
UNTIL YOU TELL ME THE TRUTH, YOU'LL STAY IN YOUR ROOM.
DAD?!

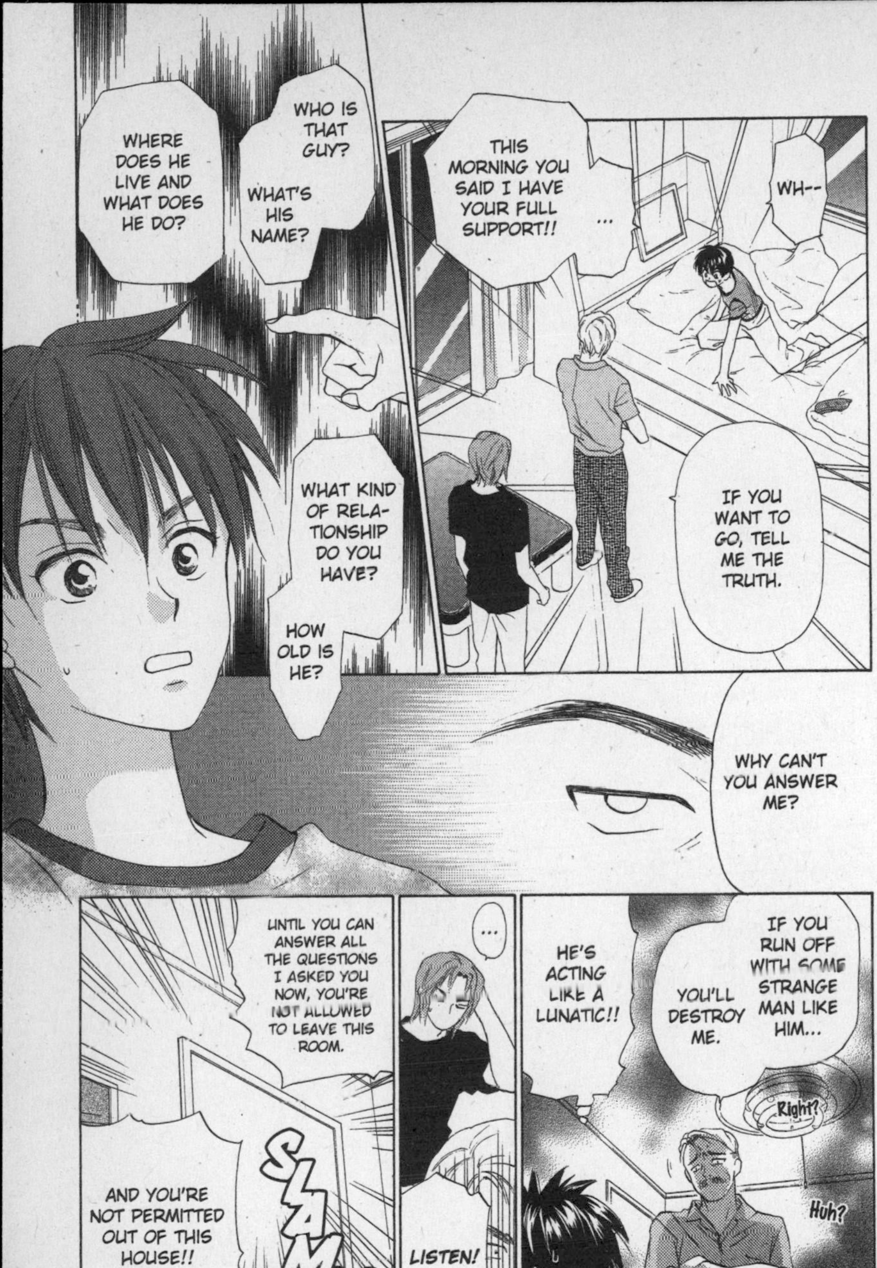
WH--
THIS MORNING YOU SAID I HAVE YOUR FULL SUPPORT!!
...
IF YOU WANT TO GO, TELL ME THE TRUTH.
WHO IS THAT GUY?
WHAT'S HIS NAME?
WHERE DOES HE LIVE AND WHAT DOES HE DO?
WHAT KIND OF RELA-TIONSHIP DO YOU HAVE?
HOW OLD IS HE?
WHY CAN'T YOU ANSWER ME?
IF YOU RUN OFF WITH SOME STRANGE MAN LIKE HIM...
YOU'LL DESTROY ME.
Right?
HE'S ACTING LIKE A LUNATIC!!
Huh?
...
LISTEN!
UNTIL YOU CAN ANSWER ALL THE QUESTIONS I ASKED YOU NOW, YOU'RE NOT ALLOWED TO LEAVE THIS ROOM.
SLAMM
AND YOU'RE NOT PERMITTED OUT OF THIS HOUSE!!

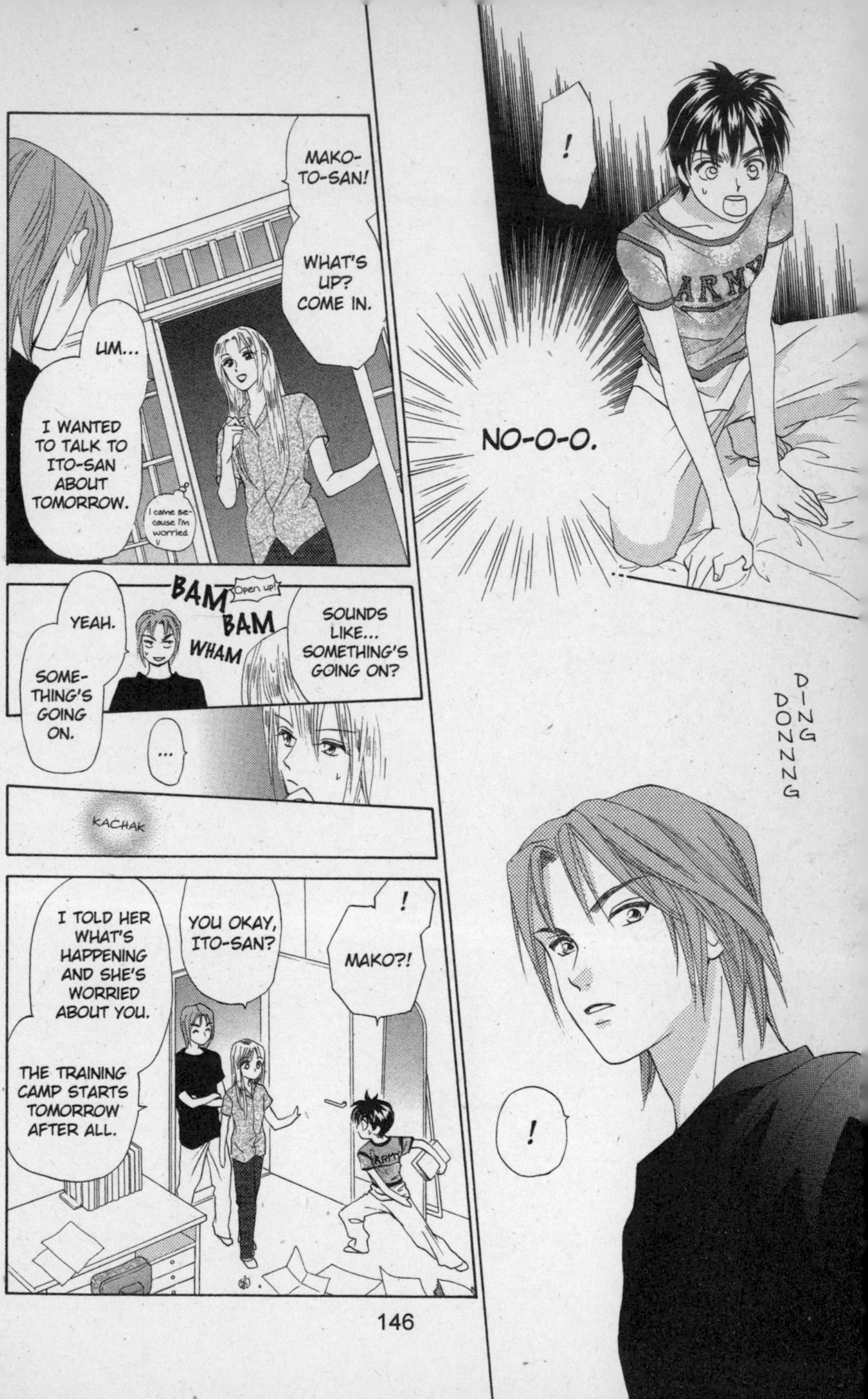
!
NO-O-O.
...
DING
DONNNG
!
MAKO-TO-SAN!
WHAT'S UP? COME IN.
UM...
I WANTED TO TALK TO ITO-SAN ABOUT TOMORROW.
I came because I'm worried
SOUNDS LIKE... SOMETHING'S GOING ON?
Open up!
BAM BAM WHAM
YEAH.
SOMETHING'S GOING ON.
...
KACHAK
!
MAKO?!
YOU OKAY, ITO-SAN?
I TOLD HER WHAT'S HAPPENING AND SHE'S WORRIED ABOUT YOU.
THE TRAINING CAMP STARTS TOMORROW AFTER ALL.

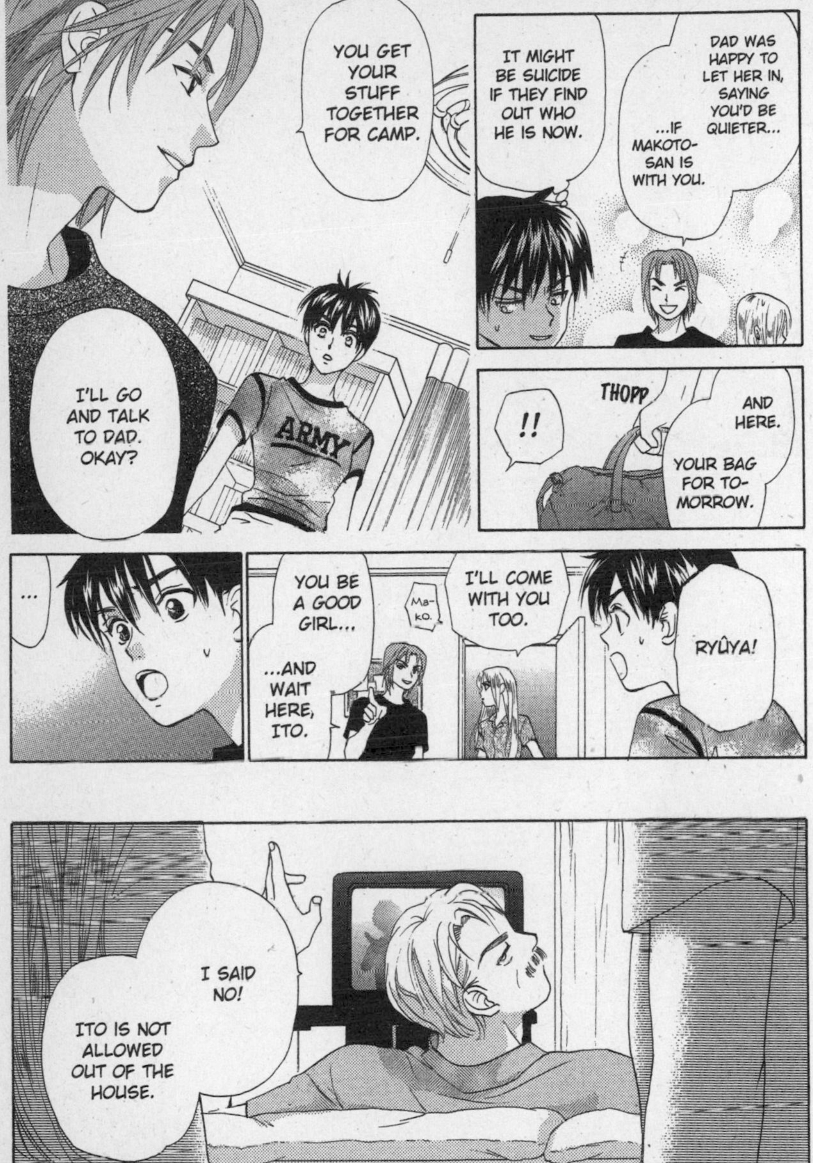
DAD WAS HAPPY TO LET HER IN, SAYING YOU'D BE QUIETER...
...IF MAKOTO-SAN IS WITH YOU.
IT MIGHT BE SUICIDE IF THEY FIND OUT WHO HE IS NOW.
AND HERE.
YOUR BAG FOR TO-MORROW.
THOPP
!!
YOU GET YOUR STUFF TOGETHER FOR CAMP.
I'LL GO AND TALK TO DAD. OKAY?
RYÛYA!
I'LL COME WITH YOU TOO.
Ma-ko.
YOU BE A GOOD GIRL...
...AND WAIT HERE, ITO.
...
I SAID NO!
ITO IS NOT ALLOWED OUT OF THE HOUSE.

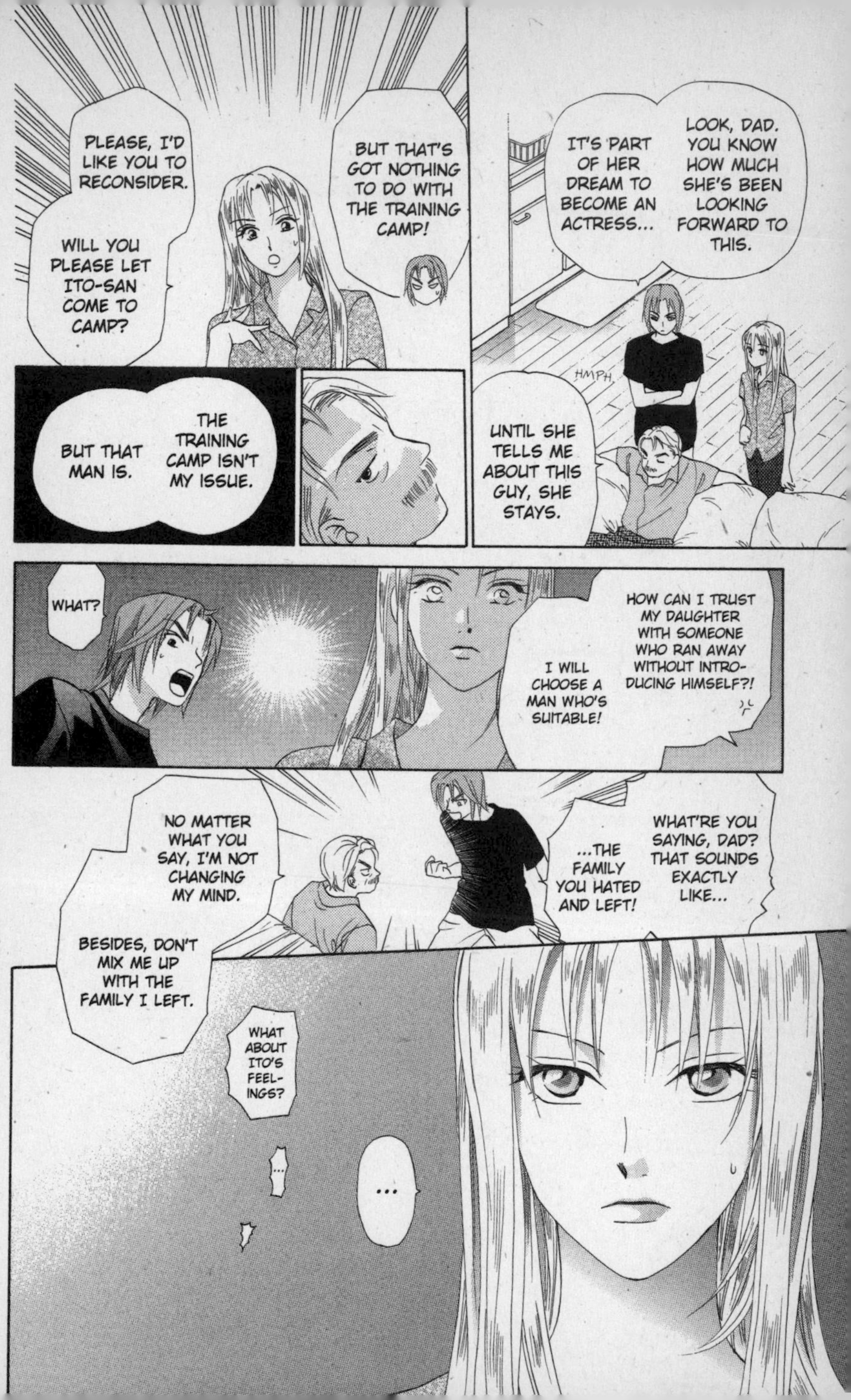
LOOK, DAD. YOU KNOW HOW MUCH SHE'S BEEN LOOKING FORWARD TO THIS.
IT'S PART OF HER DREAM TO BECOME AN ACTRESS...
HMPH
UNTIL SHE TELLS ME ABOUT THIS GUY, SHE STAYS.
BUT THAT'S GOT NOTHING TO DO WITH THE TRAINING CAMP!
PLEASE, I'D LIKE YOU TO RECONSIDER.
WILL YOU PLEASE LET ITO-SAN COME TO CAMP?
THE TRAINING CAMP ISN'T MY ISSUE.
BUT THAT MAN IS.
HOW CAN I TRUST MY DAUGHTER WITH SOMEONE WHO RAN AWAY WITHOUT INTRO-DUCING HIMSELF?!
I WILL CHOOSE A MAN WHO'S SUITABLE!
WHAT?
WHAT'RE YOU SAYING, DAD? THAT SOUNDS EXACTLY LIKE...
...THE FAMILY YOU HATED AND LEFT!
NO MATTER WHAT YOU SAY, I'M NOT CHANGING MY MIND.
BESIDES, DON'T MIX ME UP WITH THE FAMILY I LEFT.
WHAT ABOUT ITO'S FEEL-INGS?
...
...

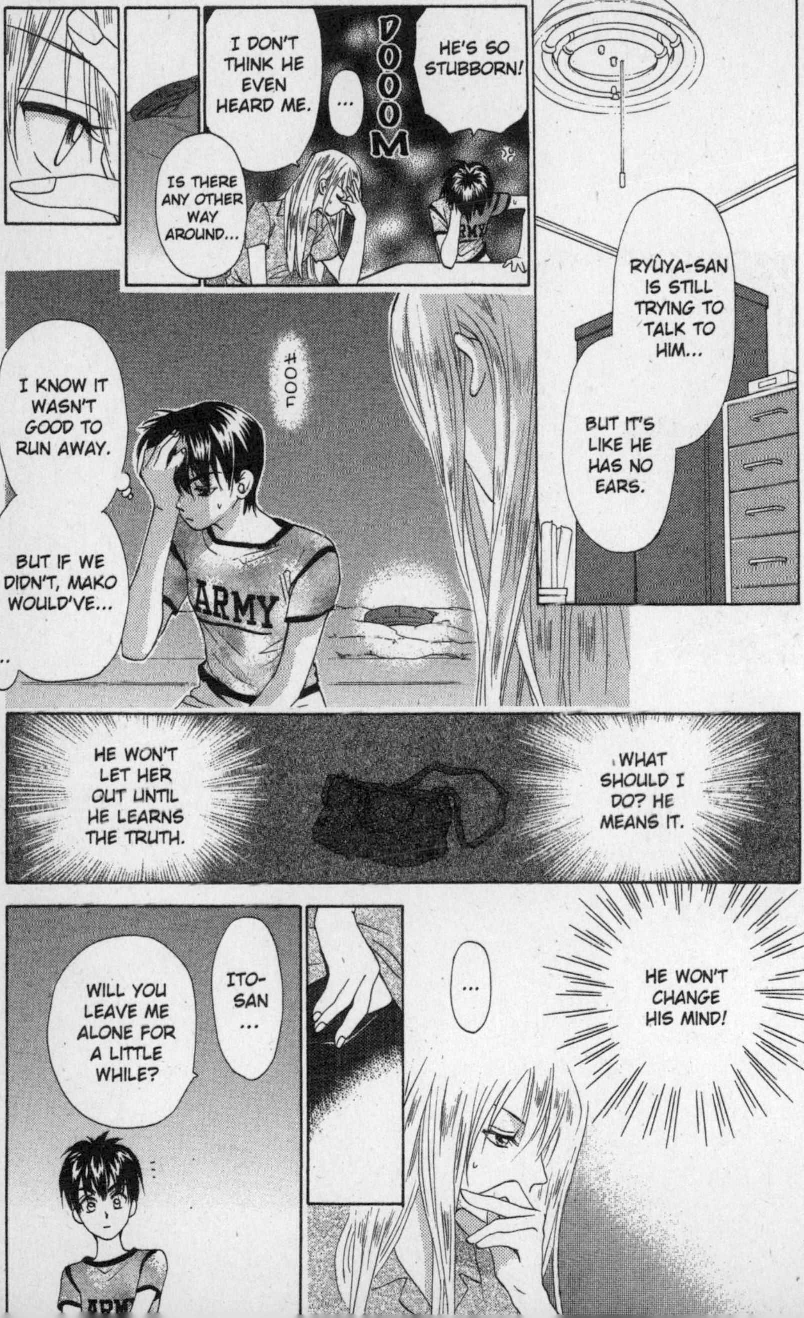
RYÛYA-SAN IS STILL TRYING TO TALK TO HIM...
BUT IT'S LIKE HE HAS NO EARS.
HE'S SO STUBBORN!
DOOOM
...
I DON'T THINK HE EVEN HEARD ME.
IS THERE ANY OTHER WAY AROUND...
I KNOW IT WASN'T GOOD TO RUN AWAY.
BUT IF WE DIDN'T, MAKO WOULD'VE...
...
WHAT SHOULD I DO? HE MEANS IT.
HE WON'T LET HER OUT UNTIL HE LEARNS THE TRUTH.
HE WON'T CHANGE HIS MIND!
...
ITO-SAN...
WILL YOU LEAVE ME ALONE FOR A LITTLE WHILE?

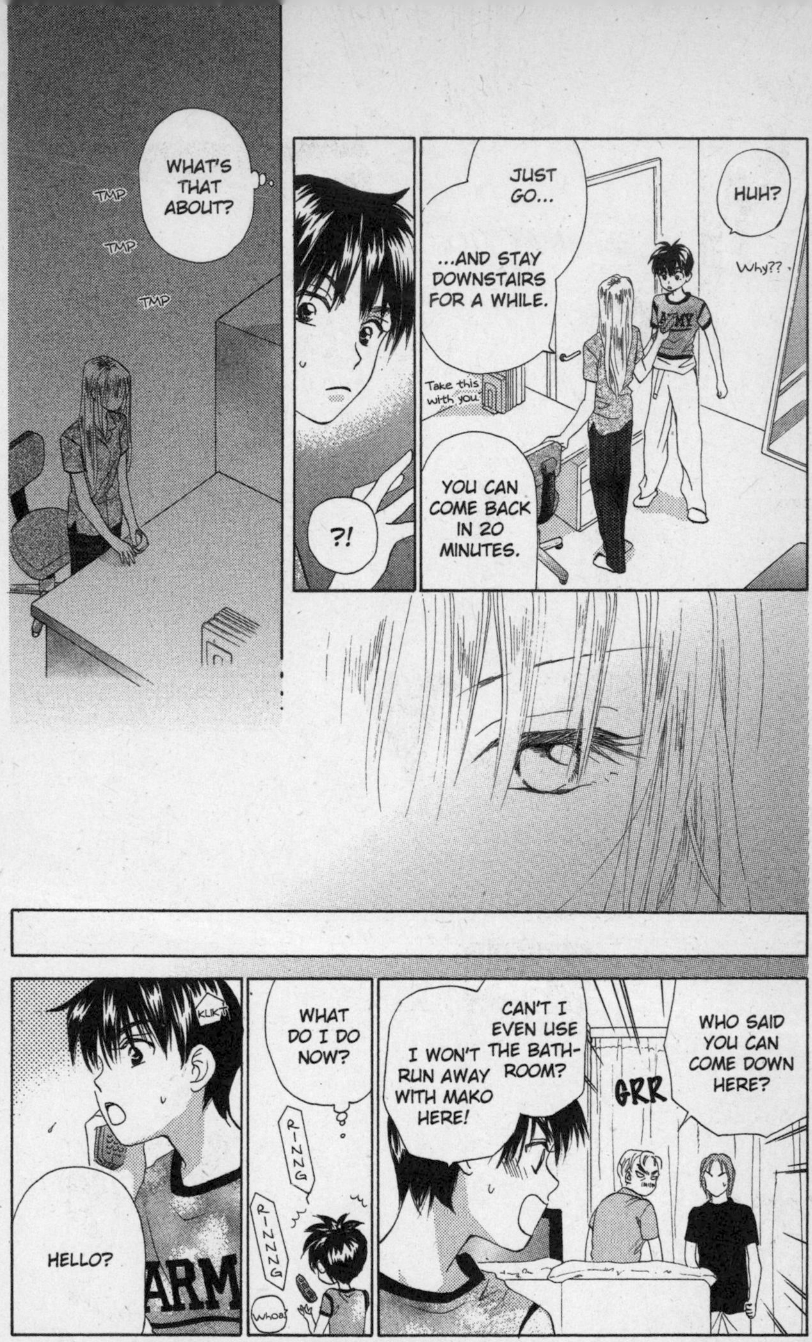
JUST GO...
HUH?
Why??
...AND STAY DOWNSTAIRS FOR A WHILE.
Take this with you
YOU CAN COME BACK IN 20 MINUTES.
?!
WHAT'S THAT ABOUT?
TMP
TMP
TMP
WHO SAID YOU CAN COME DOWN HERE?
GRR
CAN'T I EVEN USE THE BATH-ROOM?
I WON'T RUN AWAY WITH MAKO HERE!
WHAT DO I DO NOW?
RINNG
RINNNG
WHOA!
KLIK
HELLO?

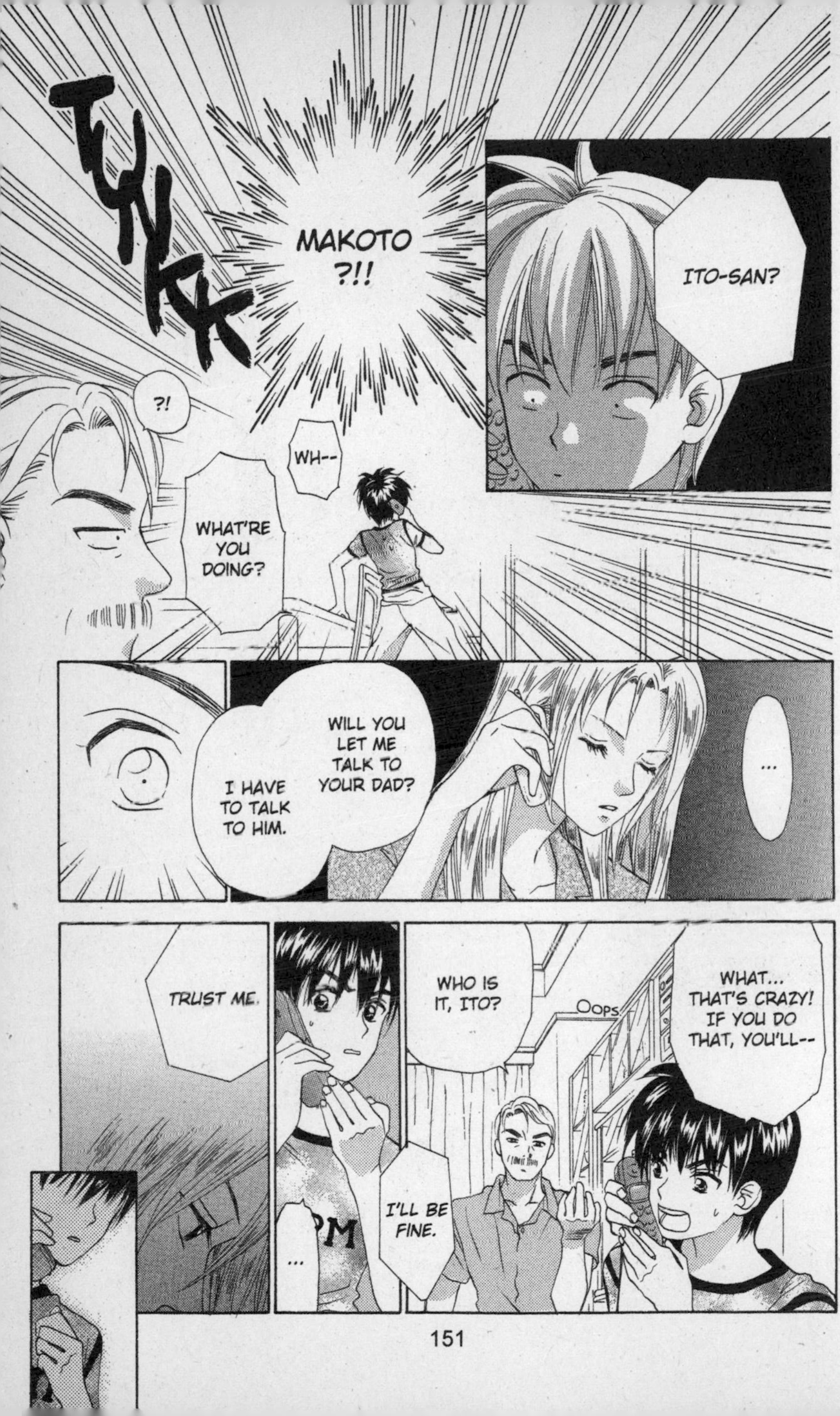

ITO-SAN?
MAKOTO ?!!
TUKK
?!
WH--
WHAT'RE YOU DOING?
...
WILL YOU LET ME TALK TO YOUR DAD?
I HAVE TO TALK TO HIM.
WHAT... THAT'S CRAZY! IF YOU DO THAT, YOU'LL--
WHO IS IT, ITO?
OOPS
I'LL BE FINE.
...
TRUST ME.

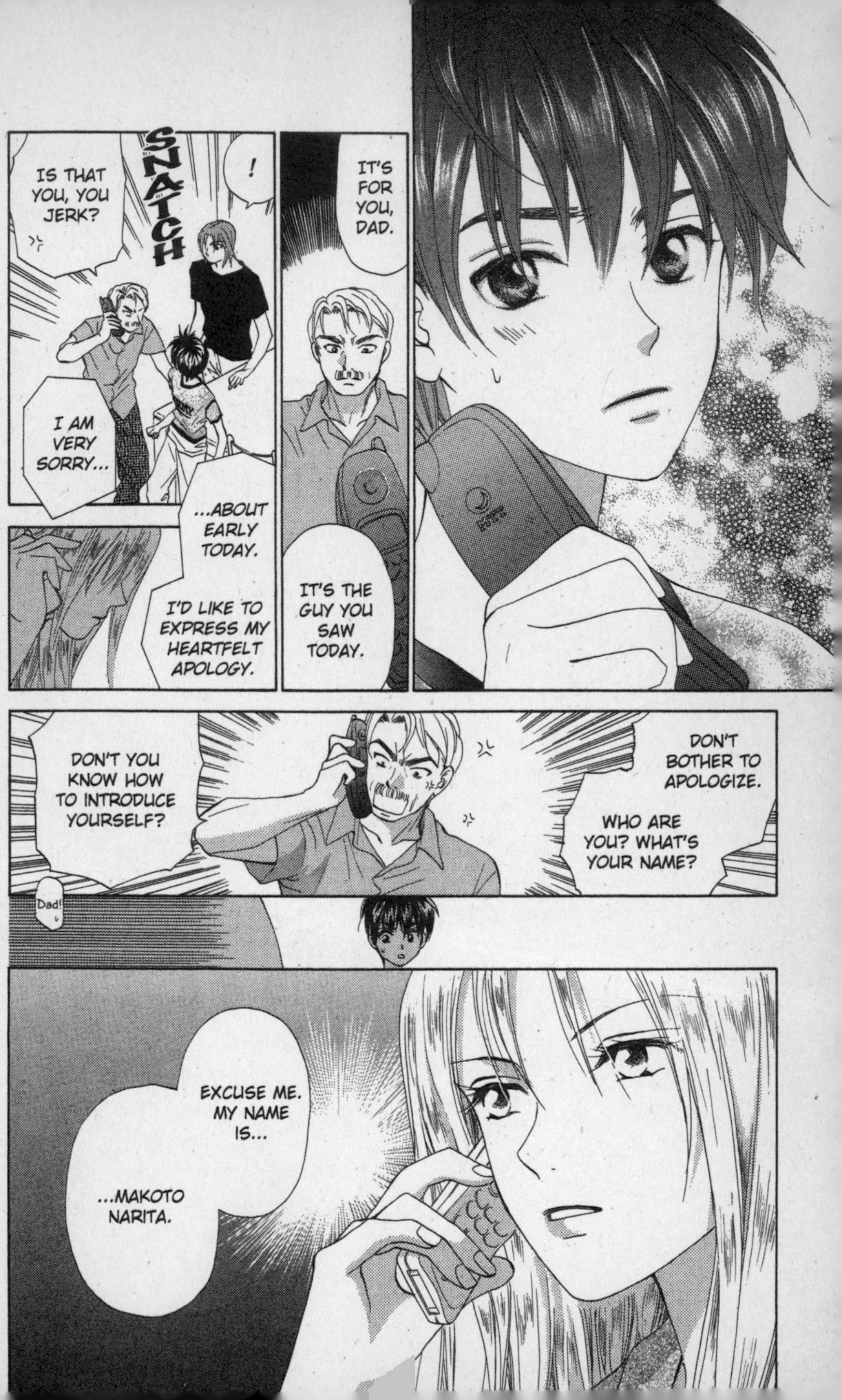
IT'S FOR YOU, DAD.
IT'S THE GUY YOU SAW TODAY.
!
SNATCH
IS THAT YOU, YOU JERK?
I AM VERY SORRY...
...ABOUT EARLY TODAY.
I'D LIKE TO EXPRESS MY HEARTFELT APOLOGY.
DON'T BOTHER TO APOLOGIZE.
WHO ARE YOU? WHAT'S YOUR NAME?
DON'T YOU KNOW HOW TO INTRODUCE YOURSELF?
Dad!
EXCUSE ME. MY NAME IS...
...MAKOTO NARITA.

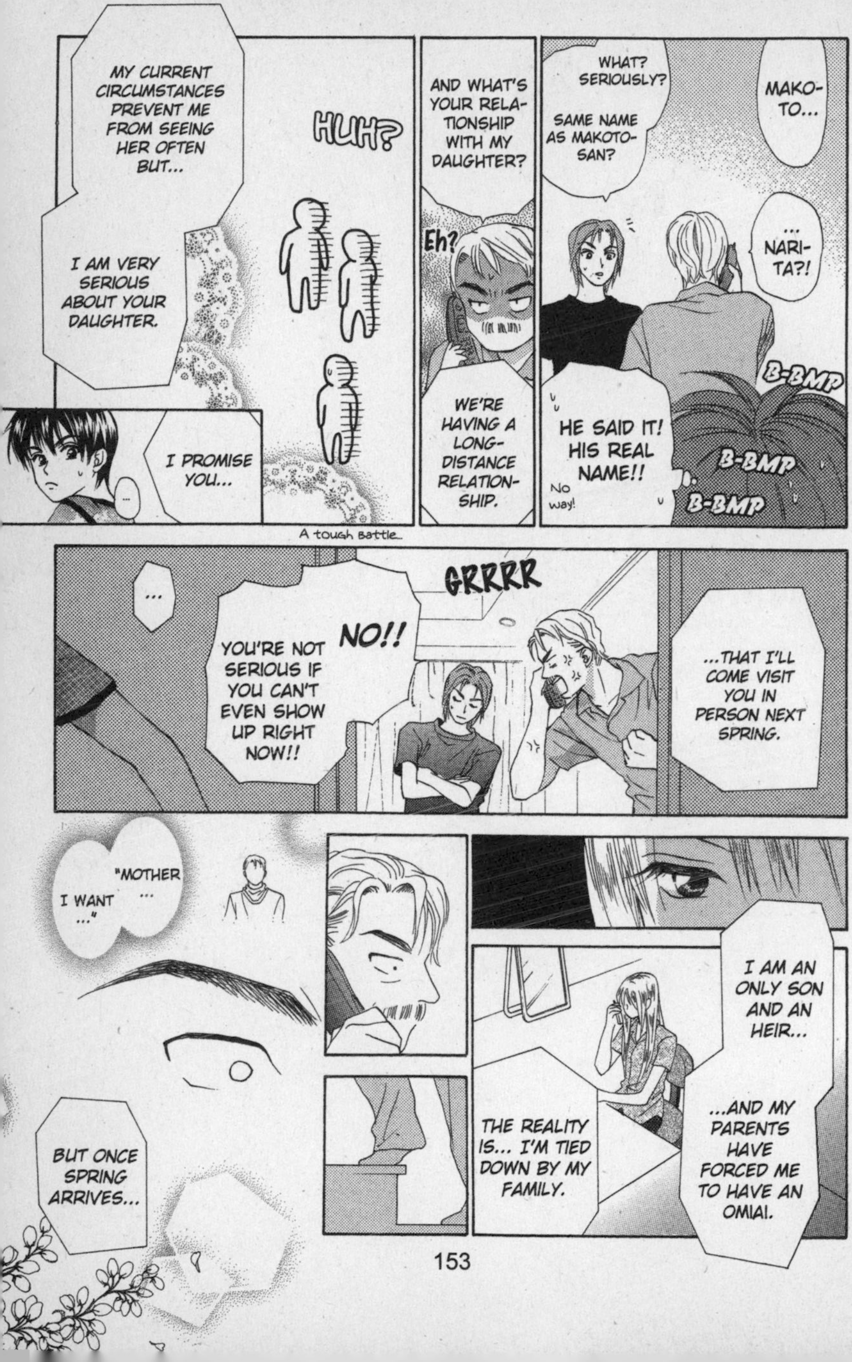
MAKO-TO...
...NARITA?!
B-BMP
B-BMP
B-BMP
WHAT? SERIOUSLY?
SAME NAME AS MAKOTO-SAN?
HE SAID IT! HIS REAL NAME!!
No way!
AND WHAT'S YOUR RELA-TIONSHIP WITH MY DAUGHTER?
Eh?
WE'RE HAVING A LONG-DISTANCE RELATION-SHIP.
MY CURRENT CIRCUMSTANCES PREVENT ME FROM SEEING HER OFTEN BUT...
HUH?
I AM VERY SERIOUS ABOUT YOUR DAUGHTER.
I PROMISE YOU...
...
A tough battle.
...THAT I'LL COME VISIT YOU IN PERSON NEXT SPRING.
GRRRR
NO!!
YOU'RE NOT SERIOUS IF YOU CAN'T EVEN SHOW UP RIGHT NOW!!
...
I AM AN ONLY SON AND AN HEIR...
...AND MY PARENTS HAVE FORCED ME TO HAVE AN OMIAI.
THE REALITY IS... I'M TIED DOWN BY MY FAMILY.
"MOTHER... I WANT..."
BUT ONCE SPRING ARRIVES...

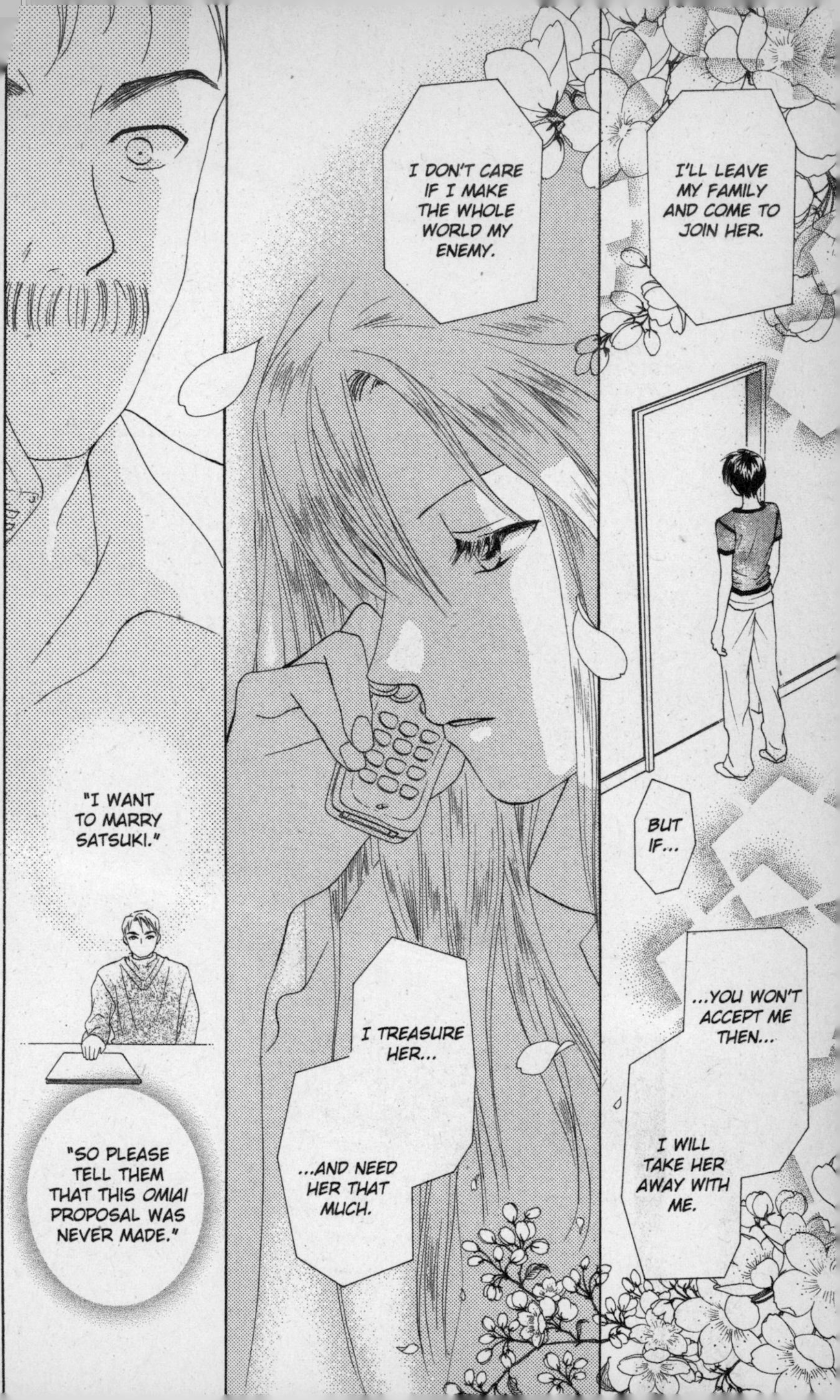
I'LL LEAVE MY FAMILY AND COME TO JOIN HER.
BUT IF...
...YOU WON'T ACCEPT ME THEN...
I WILL TAKE HER AWAY WITH ME.
I DON'T CARE IF I MAKE THE WHOLE WORLD MY ENEMY.
I TREASURE HER...
...AND NEED HER THAT MUCH.
"I WANT TO MARRY SATSUKI."
"SO PLEASE TELL THEM THAT THIS *OMIAI* PROPOSAL WAS NEVER MADE."

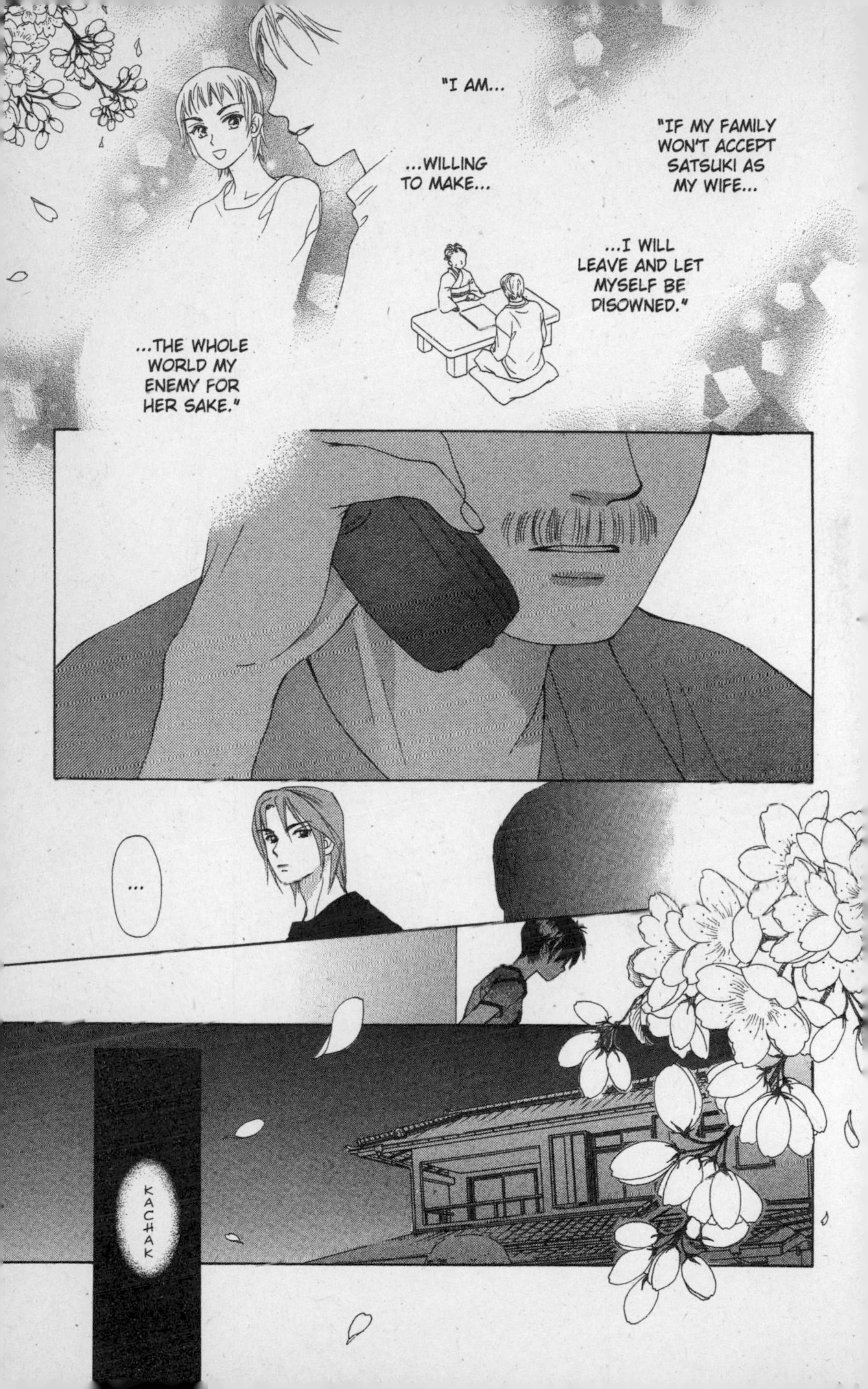
"IF MY FAMILY WON'T ACCEPT SATSUKI AS MY WIFE...
...I WILL LEAVE AND LET MYSELF BE DISOWNED."
"I AM...
...WILLING TO MAKE...
...THE WHOLE WORLD MY ENEMY FOR HER SAKE."
...
KACHAK

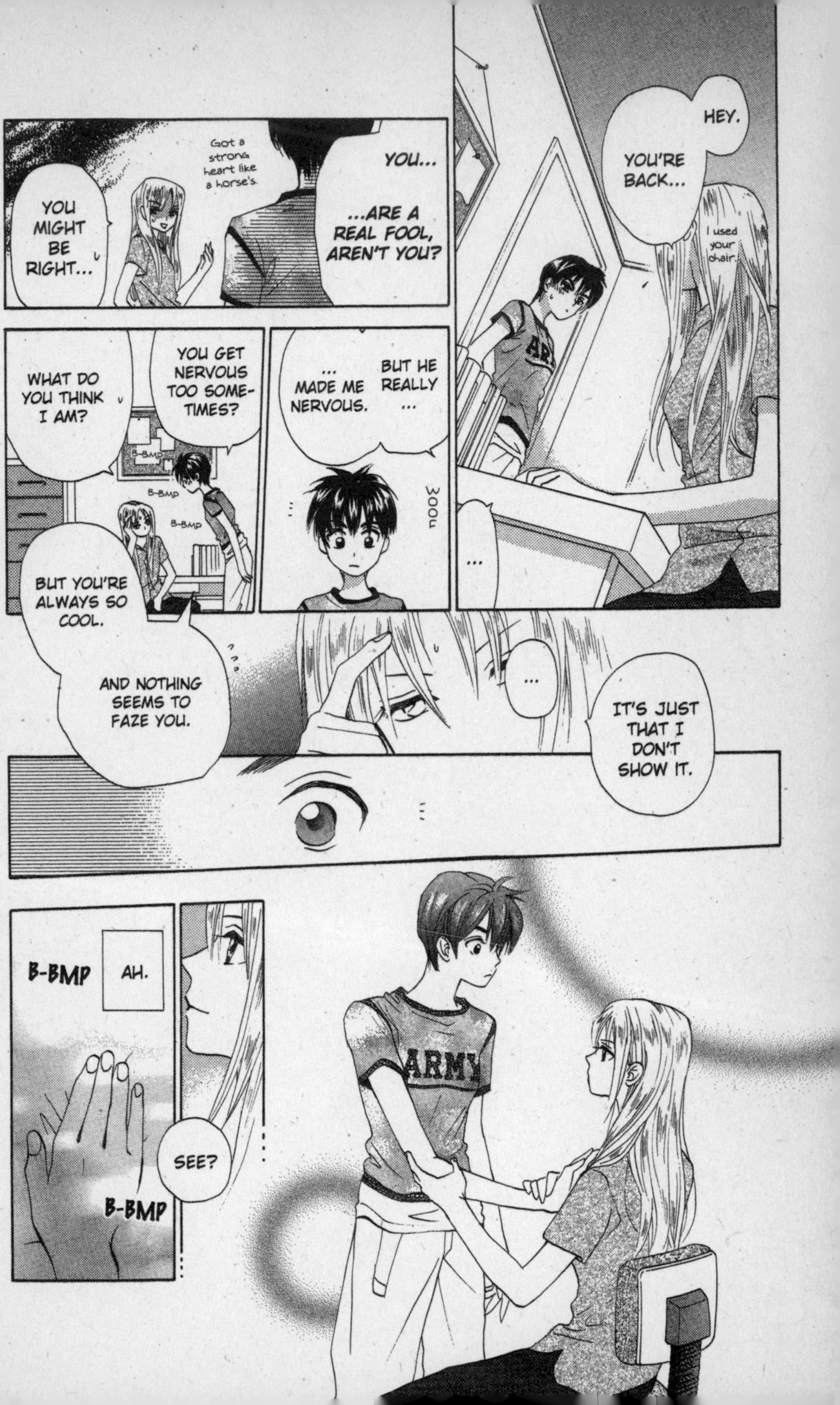
HEY.
YOU'RE BACK...
I used your chair.
...
YOU...
...ARE A REAL FOOL, AREN'T YOU?
Got a strong heart like a horse's.
YOU MIGHT BE RIGHT...
BUT HE REALLY ...
... MADE ME NERVOUS.
WOOF
YOU GET NERVOUS TOO SOME-TIMES?
WHAT DO YOU THINK I AM?
B-BMP
B-BMP
B-BMP
BUT YOU'RE ALWAYS SO COOL.
AND NOTHING SEEMS TO FAZE YOU.
...
IT'S JUST THAT I DON'T SHOW IT.
AH.
B-BMP
SEE?
B-BMP

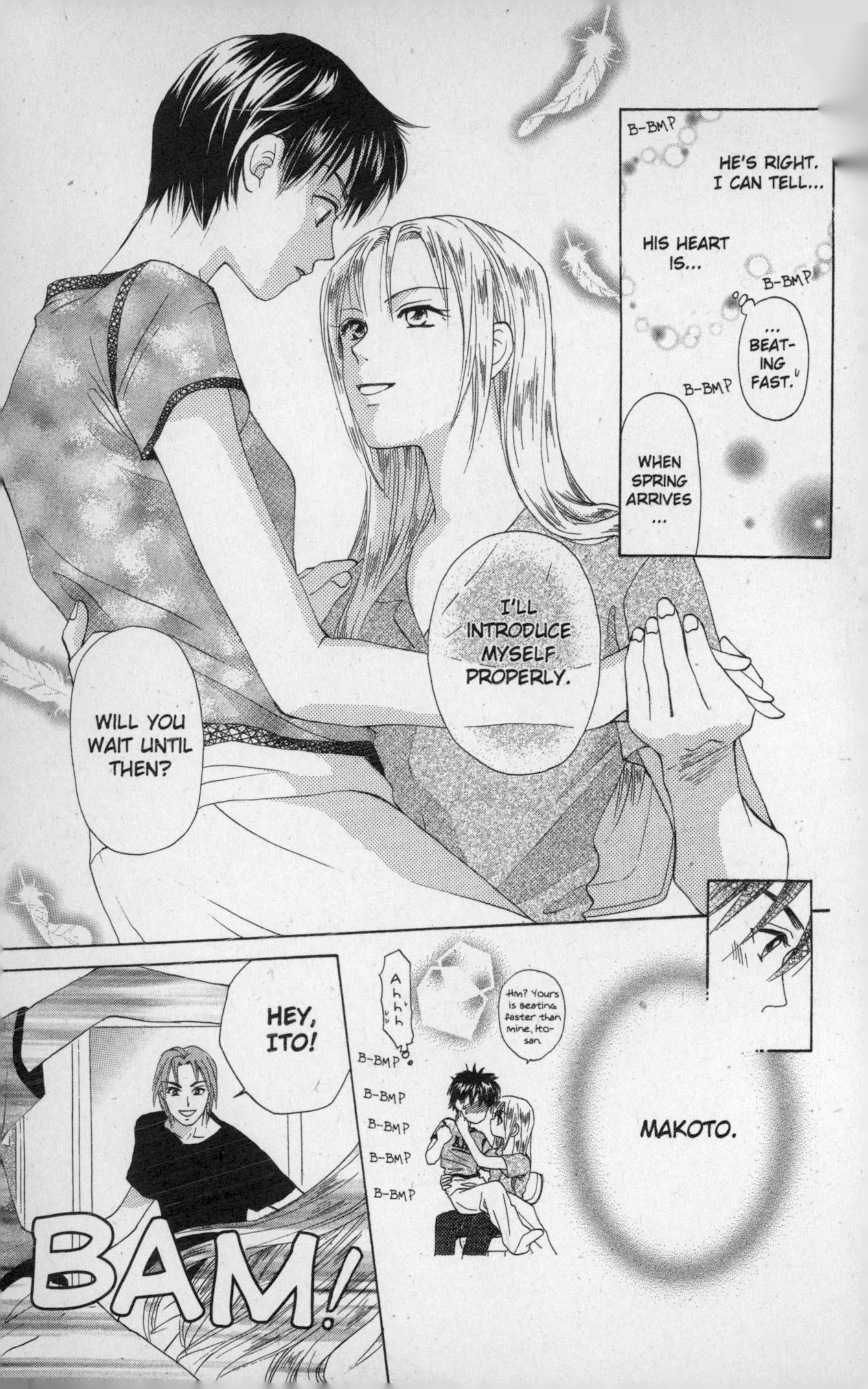
B-BMP
HE'S RIGHT. I CAN TELL...
HIS HEART IS...
B-BMP
...BEATING FAST.
B-BMP
WHEN SPRING ARRIVES...
I'LL INTRODUCE MYSELF PROPERLY.
WILL YOU WAIT UNTIL THEN?
MAKOTO.
Hm? Yours is beating faster than mine, Ito-san.
Ahhh
B-BMP
B-BMP
B-BMP
B-BMP
B-BMP
HEY, ITO!
BAM!

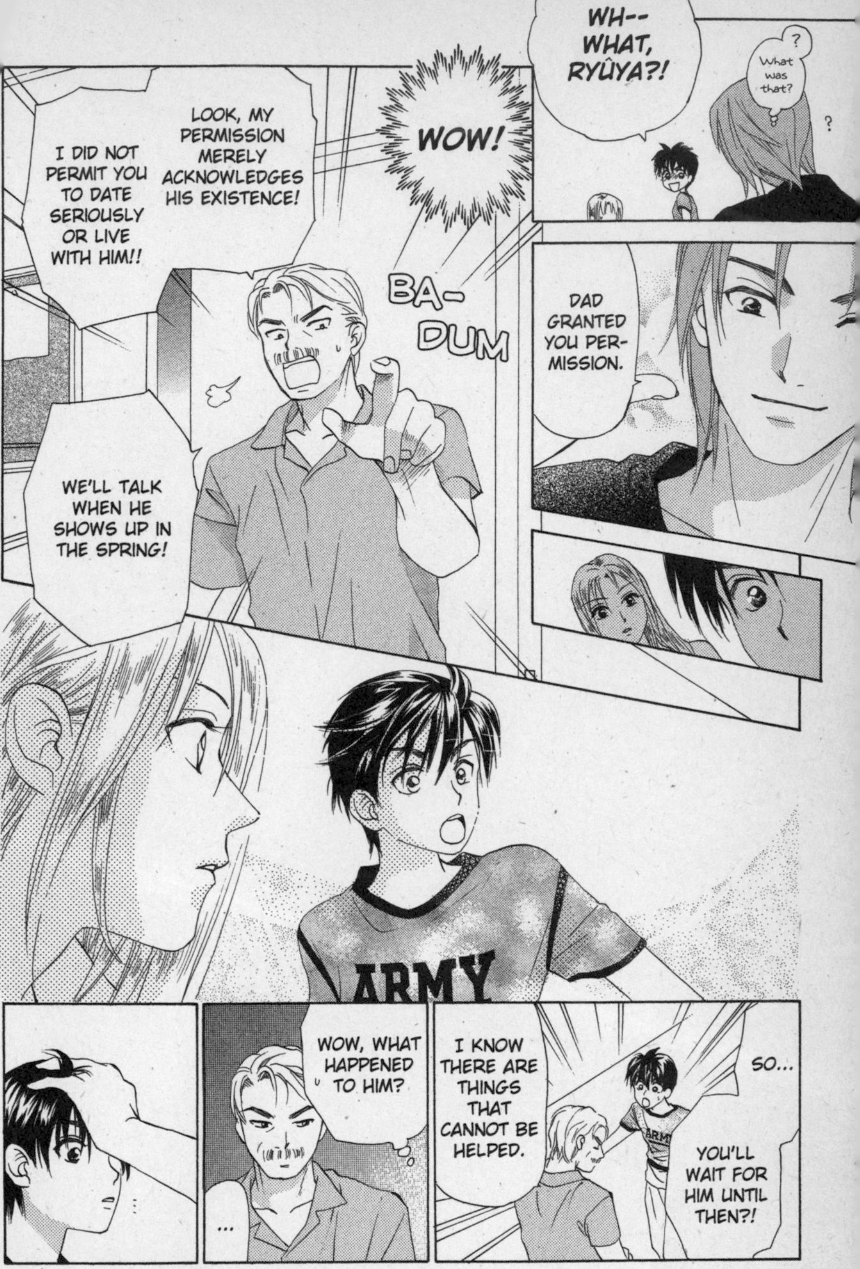
WH-- WHAT, RYÛYA?!
?
What was that?
?
DAD GRANTED YOU PERMISSION.
WOW!
LOOK, MY PERMISSION MERELY ACKNOWLEDGES HIS EXISTENCE!
I DID NOT PERMIT YOU TO DATE SERIOUSLY OR LIVE WITH HIM!!
BA-DUM
WE'LL TALK WHEN HE SHOWS UP IN THE SPRING!
ARMY
SO...
YOU'LL WAIT FOR HIM UNTIL THEN?!
ARMY
I KNOW THERE ARE THINGS THAT CANNOT BE HELPED.
WOW, WHAT HAPPENED TO HIM?
...
...

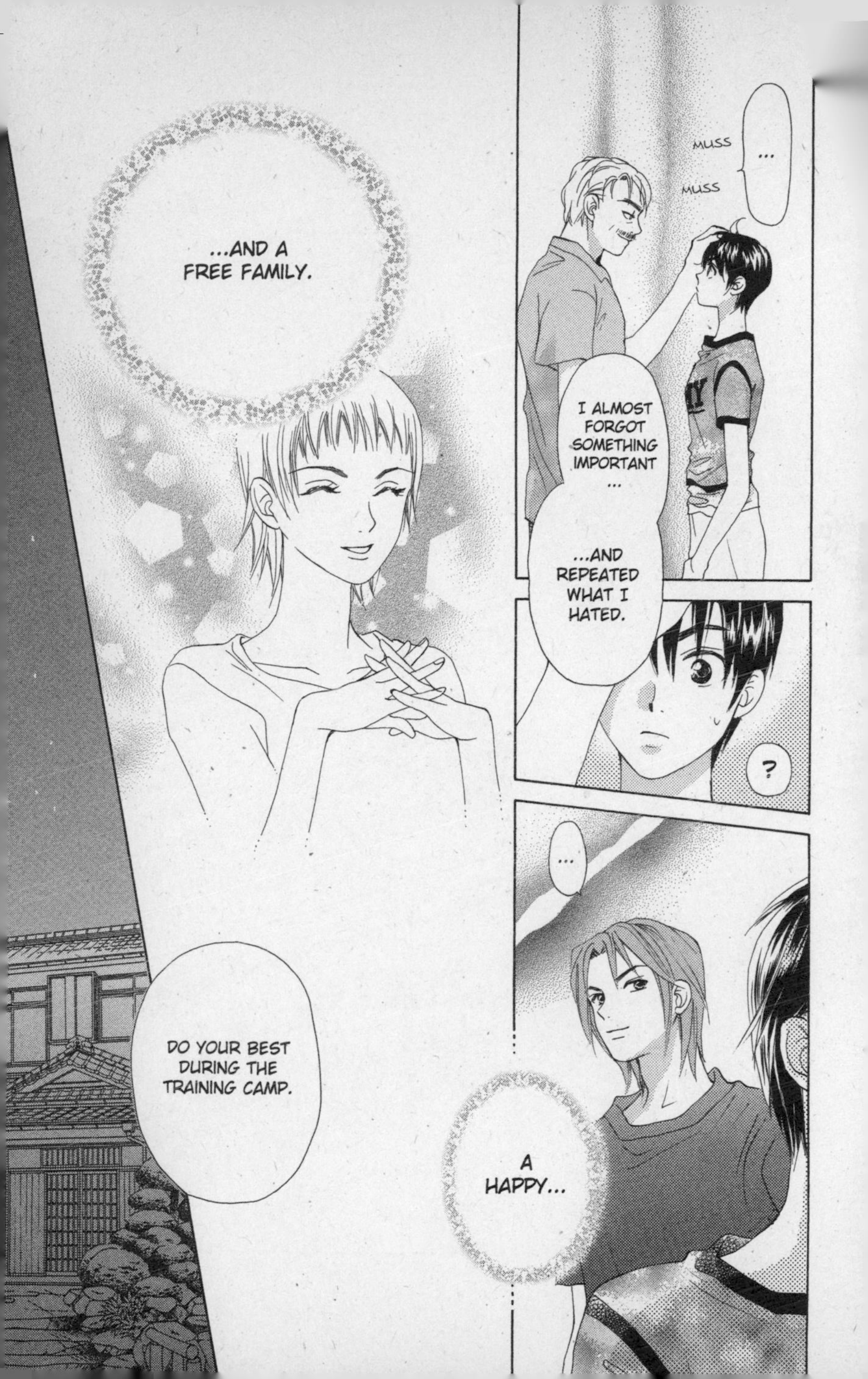
MUSS
MUSS
...
I ALMOST FORGOT SOMETHING IMPORTANT ...
...AND REPEATED WHAT I HATED.
?
...
A HAPPY...
...AND A FREE FAMILY.
DO YOUR BEST DURING THE TRAINING CAMP.

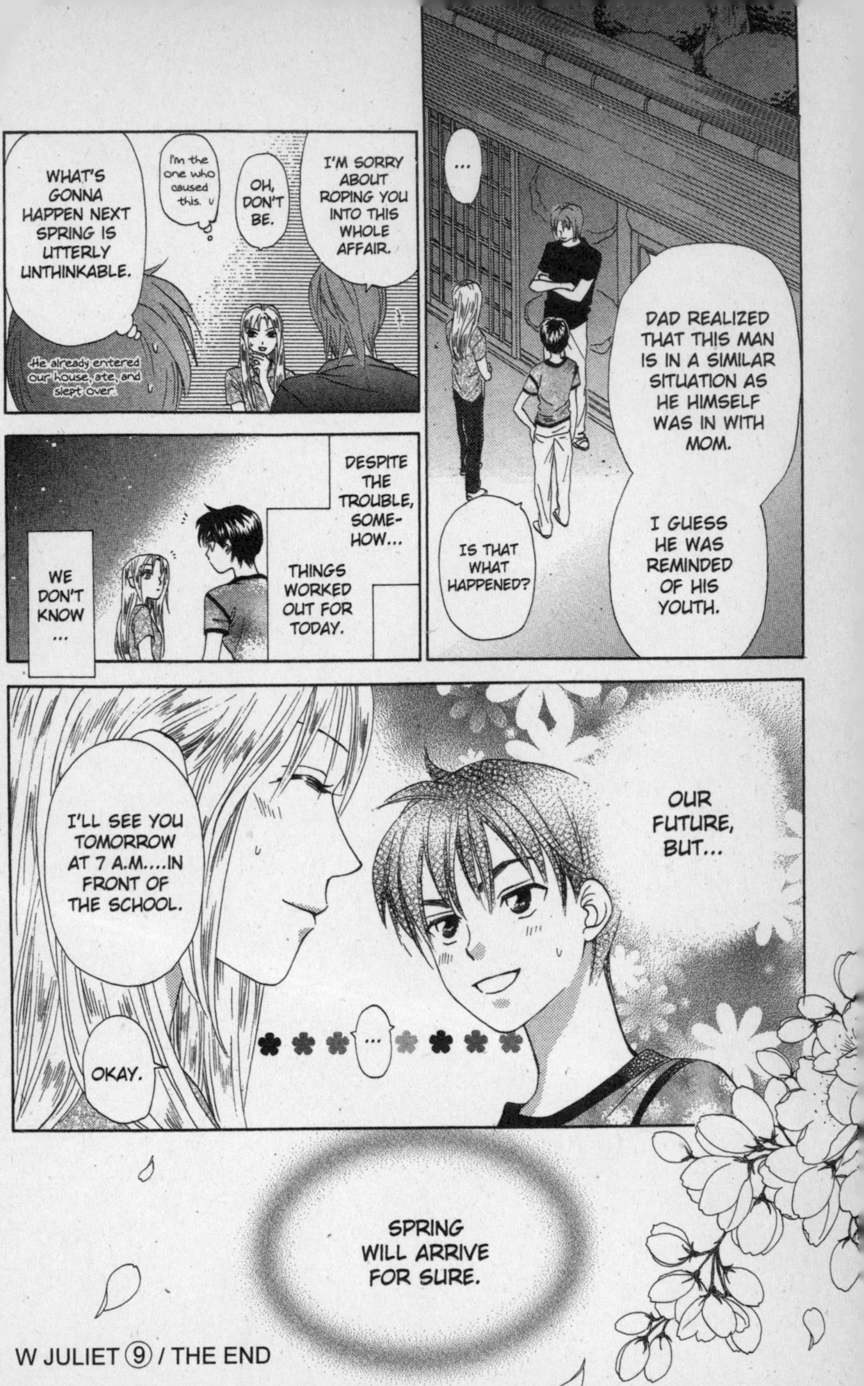
...
DAD REALIZED THAT THIS MAN IS IN A SIMILAR SITUATION AS HE HIMSELF WAS IN WITH MOM.
I GUESS HE WAS REMINDED OF HIS YOUTH.
IS THAT WHAT HAPPENED?
I'M SORRY ABOUT ROPING YOU INTO THIS WHOLE AFFAIR.
OH, DON'T BE.
I'm the one who caused this.
WHAT'S GONNA HAPPEN NEXT SPRING IS UTTERLY UNTHINKABLE.
He already entered our house, ate, and slept over.
DESPITE THE TROUBLE, SOME-HOW...
THINGS WORKED OUT FOR TODAY.
WE DON'T KNOW ...
OUR FUTURE, BUT...
I'LL SEE YOU TOMORROW AT 7 A.M.....IN FRONT OF THE SCHOOL.
...
OKAY.
SPRING WILL ARRIVE FOR SURE.

W JULIET ⑨ / THE END

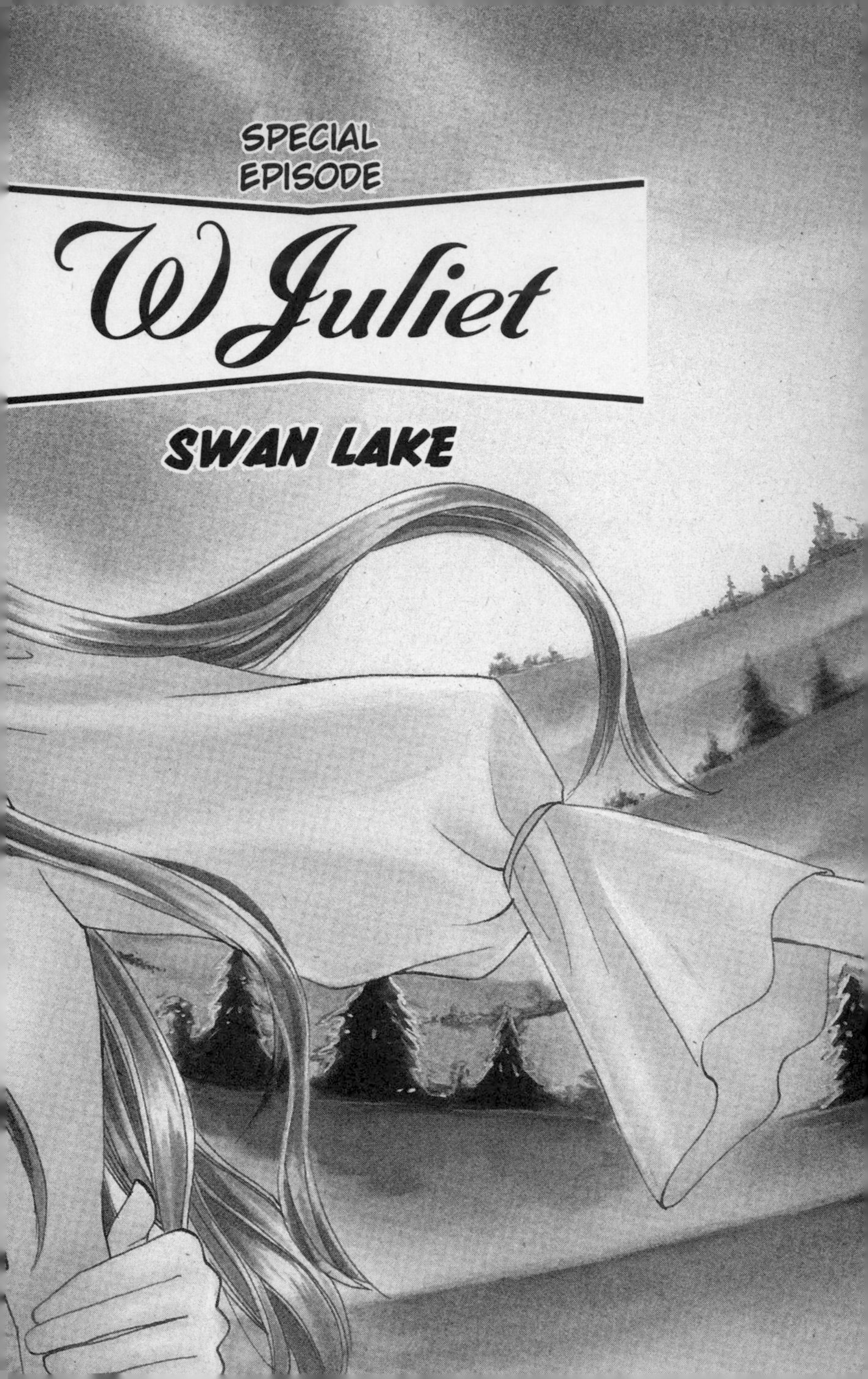
SPECIAL EPISODE
W Juliet
SWAN LAKE

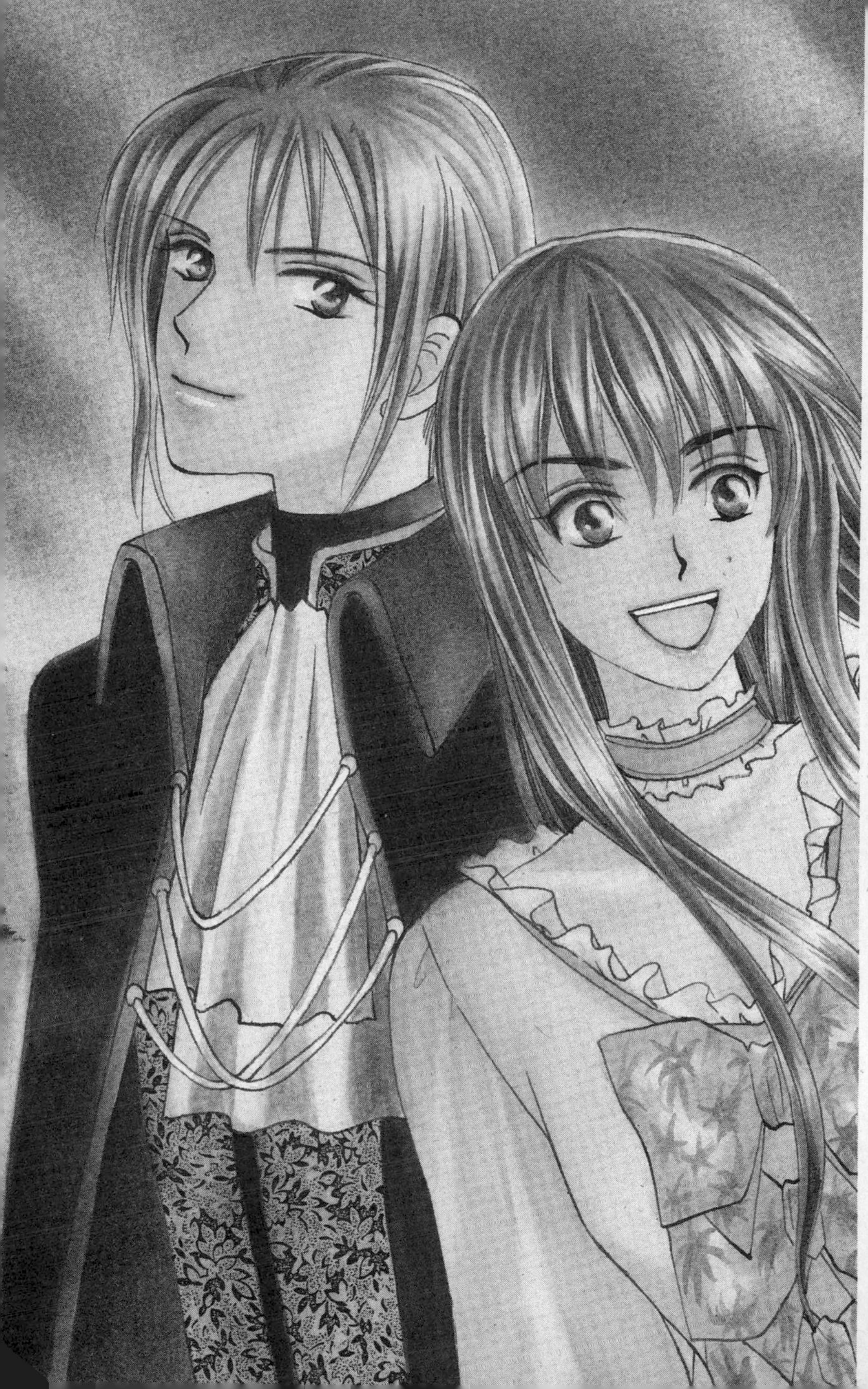

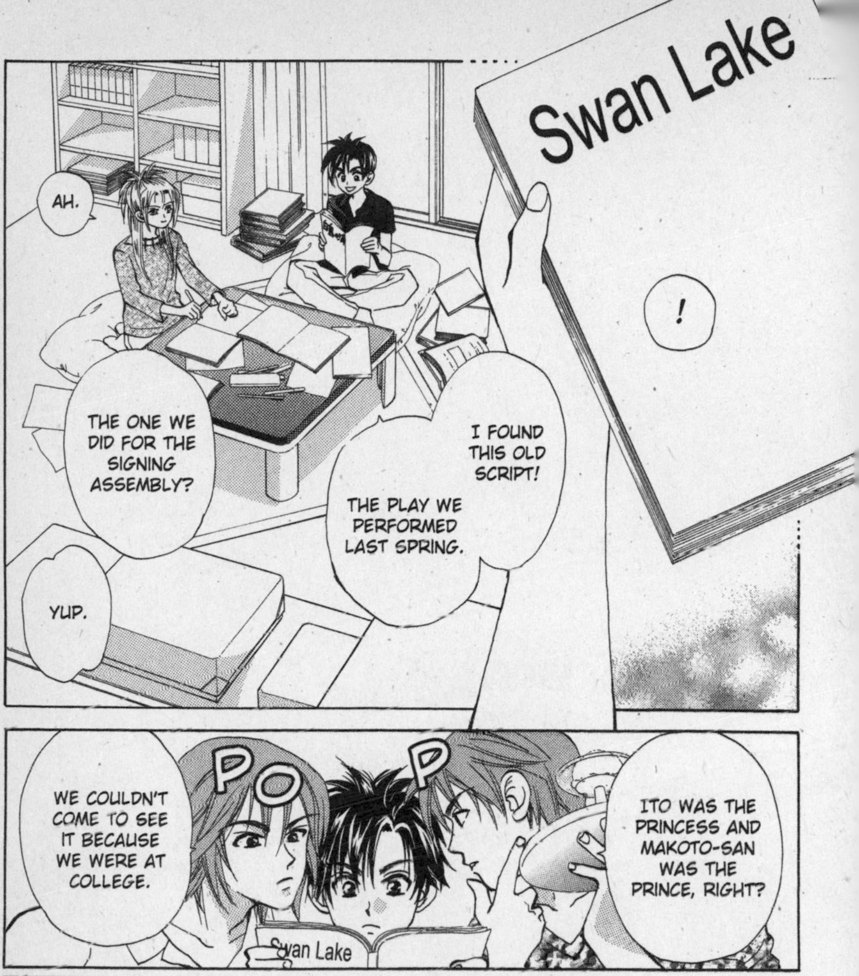
Swan Lake
!
I FOUND THIS OLD SCRIPT!
THE PLAY WE PERFORMED LAST SPRING.
AH.
THE ONE WE DID FOR THE SIGNING ASSEMBLY?
YUP.
ITO WAS THE PRINCESS AND MAKOTO-SAN WAS THE PRINCE, RIGHT?
POP
WE COULDN'T COME TO SEE IT BECAUSE WE WERE AT COLLEGE.
Swan Lake

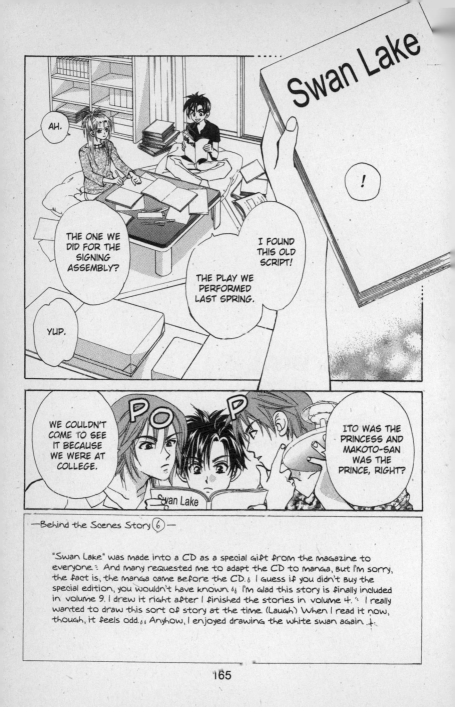

—Behind the Scenes Story ⑥—

"Swan Lake" was made into a CD as a special gift from the magazine to everyone. And many requested me to adapt the CD to manga, but I'm sorry, the fact is, the manga came before the CD. I guess if you didn't buy the special edition, you wouldn't have known. I'm glad this story is finally included in volume 9. I drew it right after I finished the stories in volume 4. I really wanted to draw this sort of story at the time. (Laugh) When I read it now, though, it feels odd. Anyhow, I enjoyed drawing the white swan again.

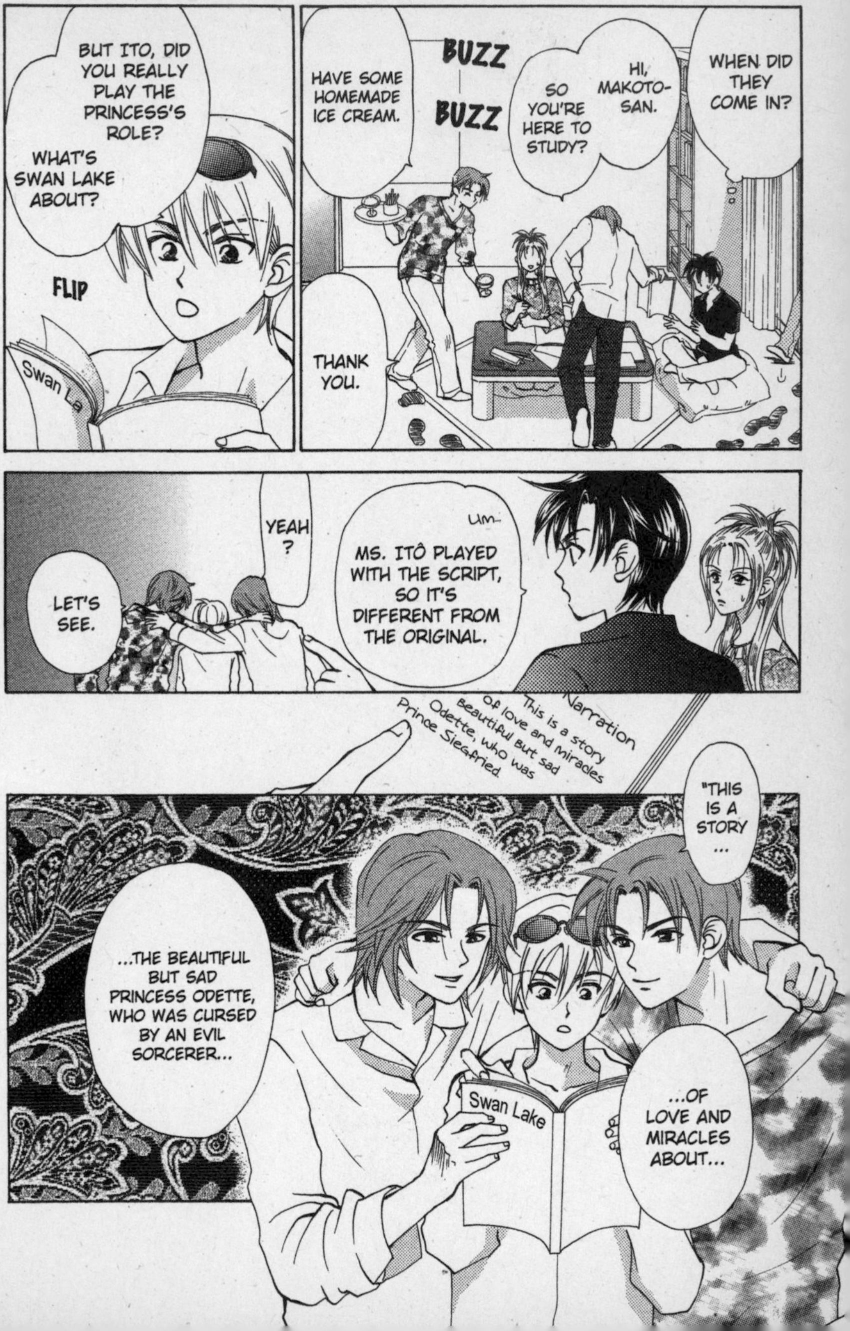
WHEN DID THEY COME IN?
HI, MAKOTO-SAN.
SO YOU'RE HERE TO STUDY?
BUZZ
BUZZ
HAVE SOME HOMEMADE ICE CREAM.
THANK YOU.
BUT ITO, DID YOU REALLY PLAY THE PRINCESS'S ROLE?
WHAT'S SWAN LAKE ABOUT?
FLIP
Swan La
Um...
MS. ITÔ PLAYED WITH THE SCRIPT, SO IT'S DIFFERENT FROM THE ORIGINAL.
YEAH ?
LET'S SEE.
Narration
This is a story of love and miracles
Beautiful but sad Odette, who was
Prince Siegfried.
"THIS IS A STORY ...
...OF LOVE AND MIRACLES ABOUT...
...THE BEAUTIFUL BUT SAD PRINCESS ODETTE, WHO WAS CURSED BY AN EVIL SORCERER...
Swan Lake

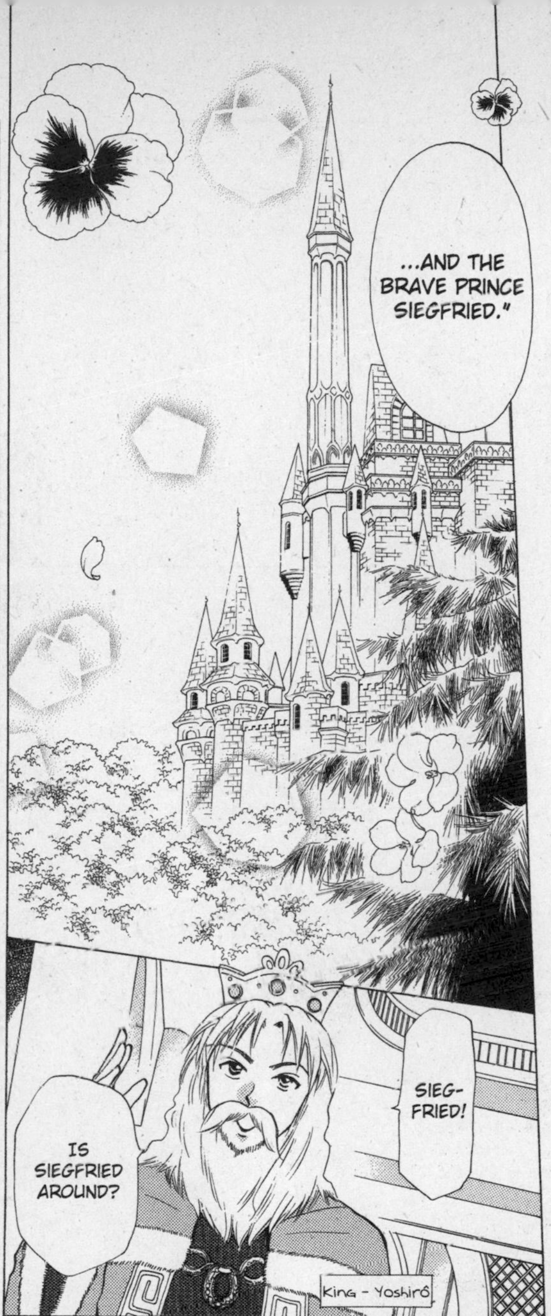

...AND THE BRAVE PRINCE SIEGFRIED."
SIEG-FRIED!
IS SIEGFRIED AROUND?
King - Yoshirô

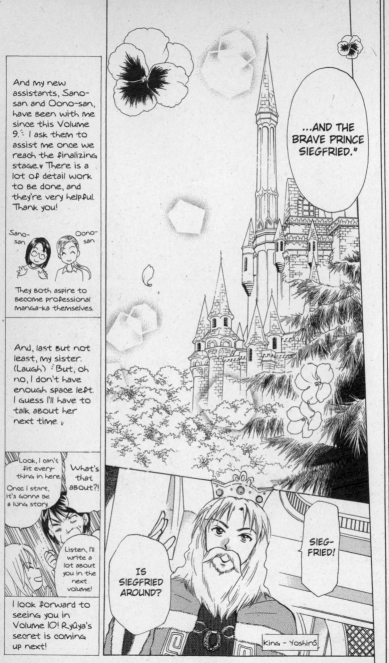

And my new assistants, Sano-san and Oono-san, have been with me since this Volume 9. I ask them to assist me once we reach the finalizing stage. There is a lot of detail work to be done, and they're very helpful. Thank you!

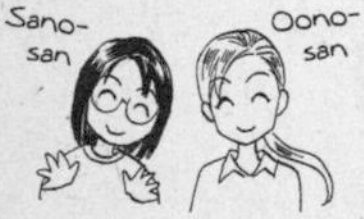

Sano-san
Oono-san

They both aspire to become professional manga-ka themselves.

And, last but not least, my sister. (Laugh) But, oh no, I don't have enough space left. I guess I'll have to talk about her next time.

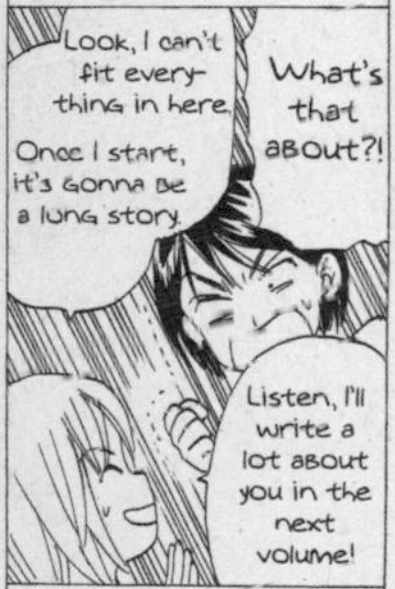

What's that about?!
Look, I can't fit everything in here. Once I start, it's gonna be a long story.
Listen, I'll write a lot about you in the next volume!

I look forward to seeing you in Volume 10! Ryûya's secret is coming up next!

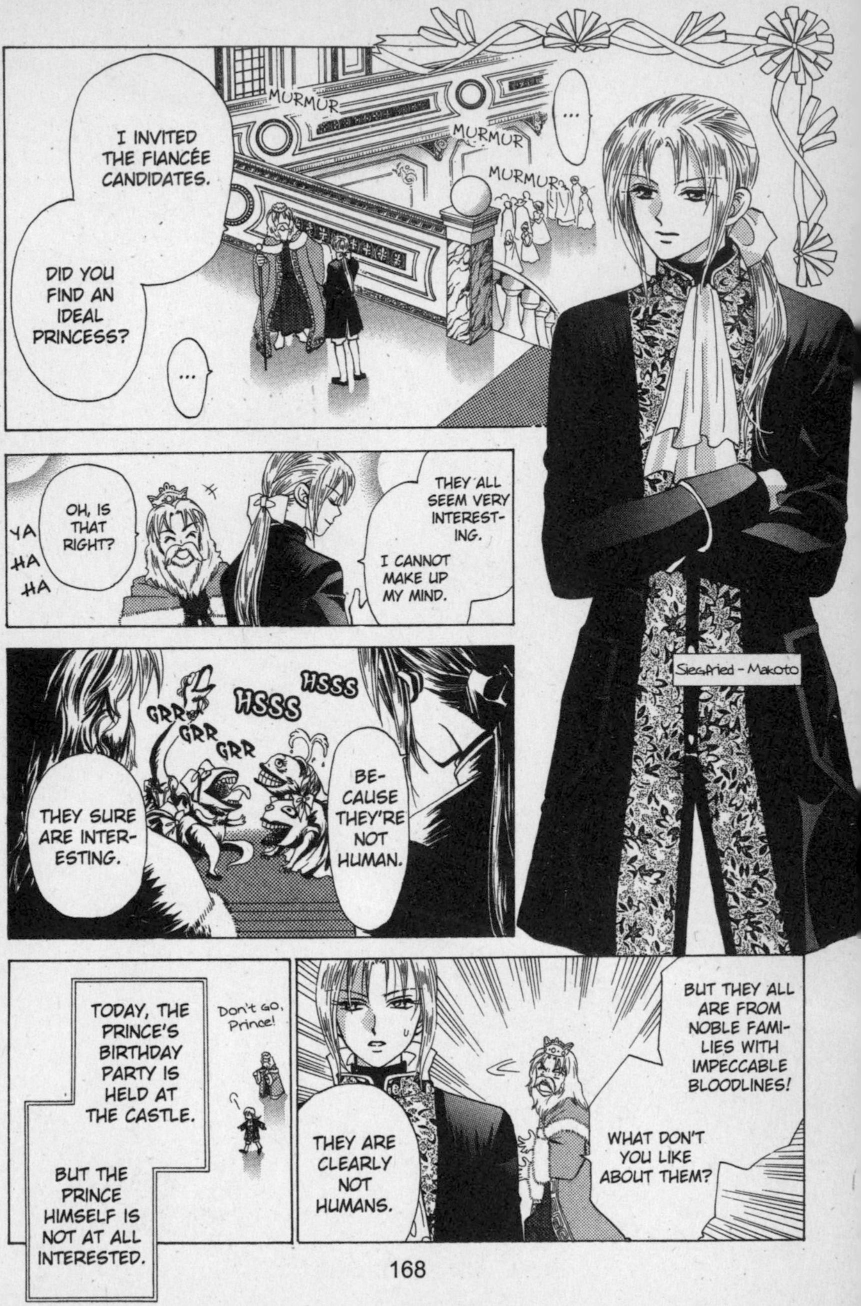
...
Siegfried - Makoto
MURMUR
MURMUR
MURMUR
I INVITED THE FIANCÉE CANDIDATES.
DID YOU FIND AN IDEAL PRINCESS?
...
THEY ALL SEEM VERY INTEREST-ING.
I CANNOT MAKE UP MY MIND.
OH, IS THAT RIGHT?
YA HA HA
HSSS
HSSS
GRR GRR GRR
BE-CAUSE THEY'RE NOT HUMAN.
THEY SURE ARE INTER-ESTING.
BUT THEY ALL ARE FROM NOBLE FAMI-LIES WITH IMPECCABLE BLOODLINES!
WHAT DON'T YOU LIKE ABOUT THEM?
THEY ARE CLEARLY NOT HUMANS.
TODAY, THE PRINCE'S BIRTHDAY PARTY IS HELD AT THE CASTLE.
Don't GO, Prince!
BUT THE PRINCE HIMSELF IS NOT AT ALL INTERESTED.

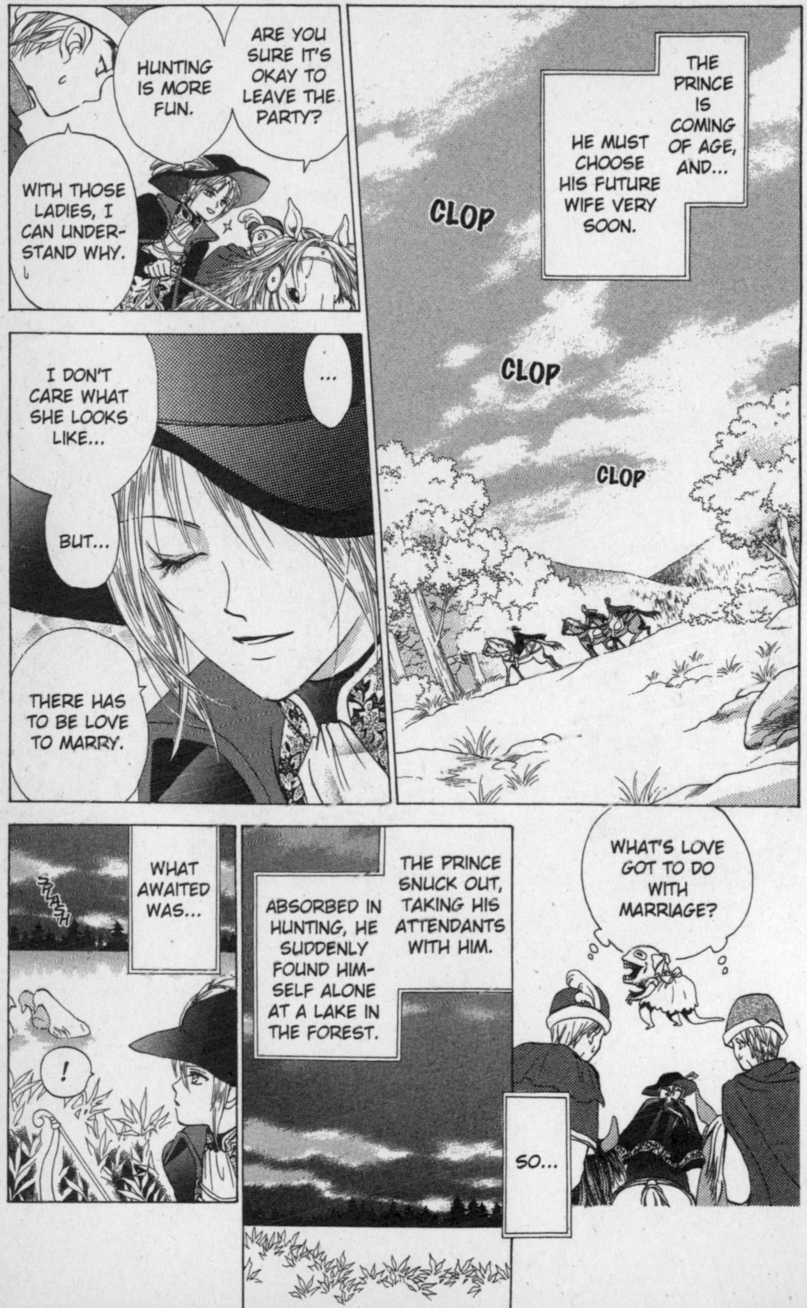
THE PRINCE IS COMING OF AGE, AND...
HE MUST CHOOSE HIS FUTURE WIFE VERY SOON.
CLOP
CLOP
CLOP
ARE YOU SURE IT'S OKAY TO LEAVE THE PARTY?
HUNTING IS MORE FUN.
WITH THOSE LADIES, I CAN UNDERSTAND WHY.
...
I DON'T CARE WHAT SHE LOOKS LIKE...
BUT...
THERE HAS TO BE LOVE TO MARRY.
WHAT'S LOVE GOT TO DO WITH MARRIAGE?
SO...
THE PRINCE SNUCK OUT, TAKING HIS ATTENDANTS WITH HIM.
ABSORBED IN HUNTING, HE SUDDENLY FOUND HIMSELF ALONE AT A LAKE IN THE FOREST.
WHAT AWAITED WAS...
SPLASH
!

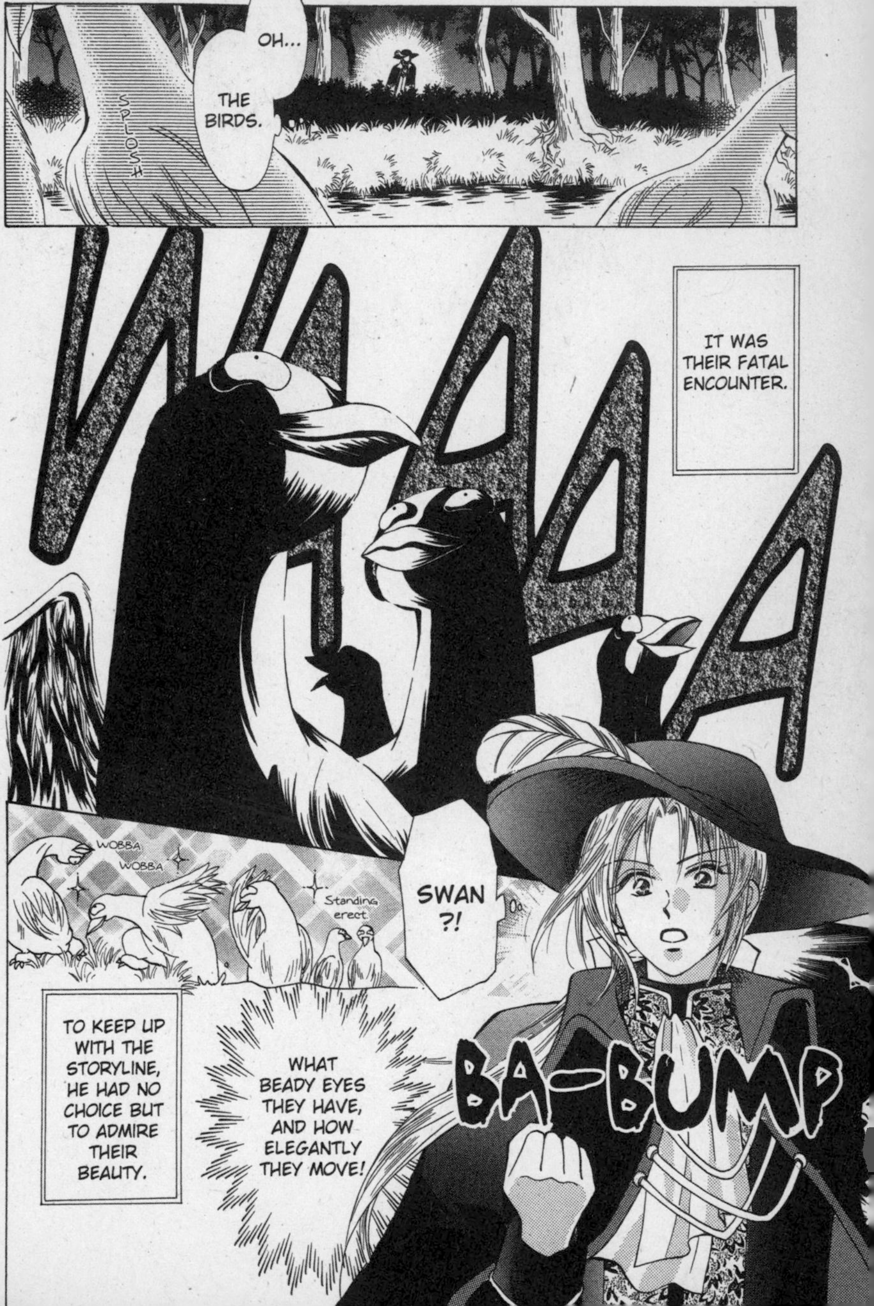
OH...
THE BIRDS.
SPLOSH
IT WAS THEIR FATAL ENCOUNTER.
WAAAA
SWAN ?!
BA-BUMP
WHAT BEADY EYES THEY HAVE, AND HOW ELEGANTLY THEY MOVE!
TO KEEP UP WITH THE STORYLINE, HE HAD NO CHOICE BUT TO ADMIRE THEIR BEAUTY.
Standing erect.
WOBBA WOBBA

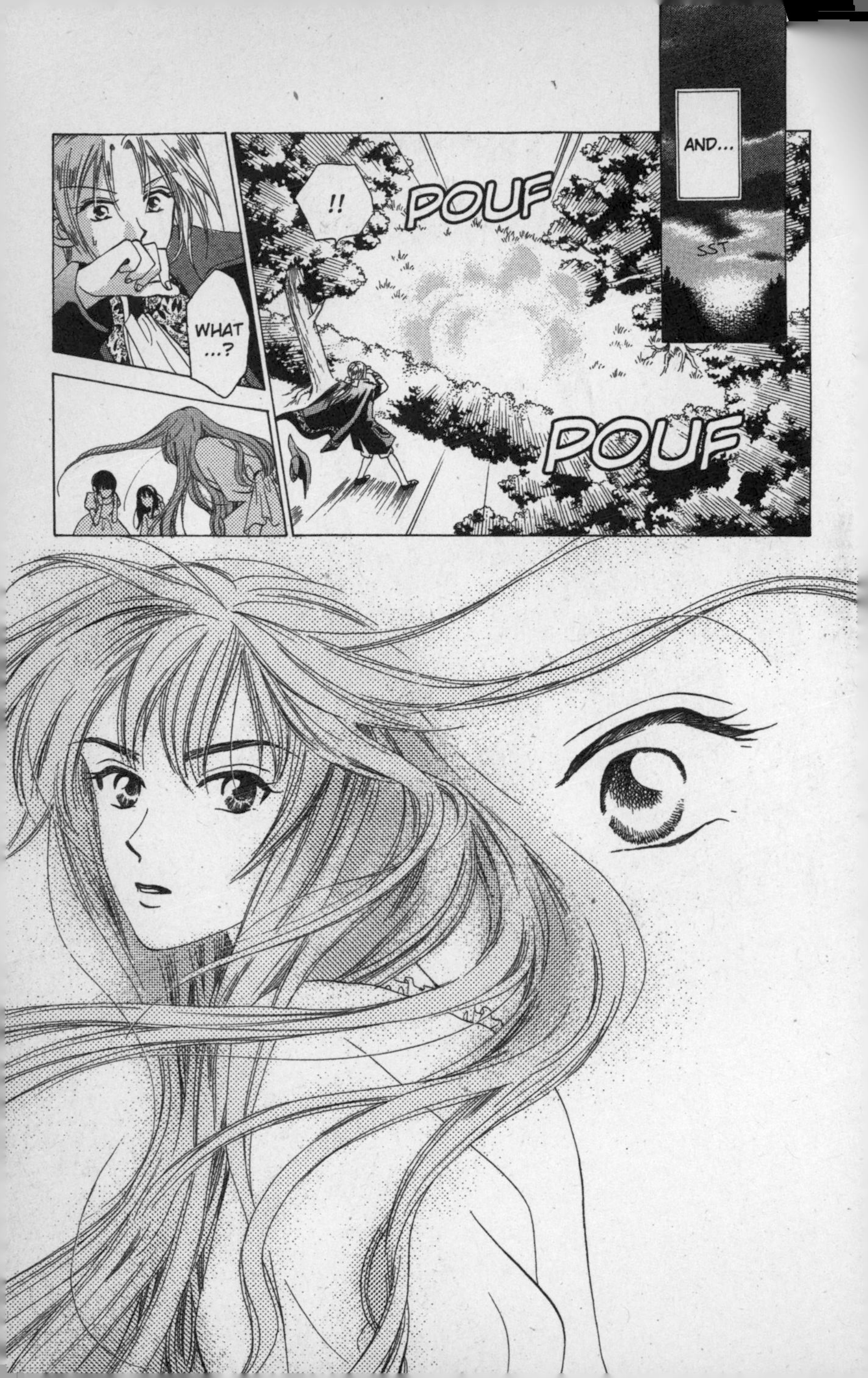
AND...
SST
!!
POUF
POUF
WHAT ...?

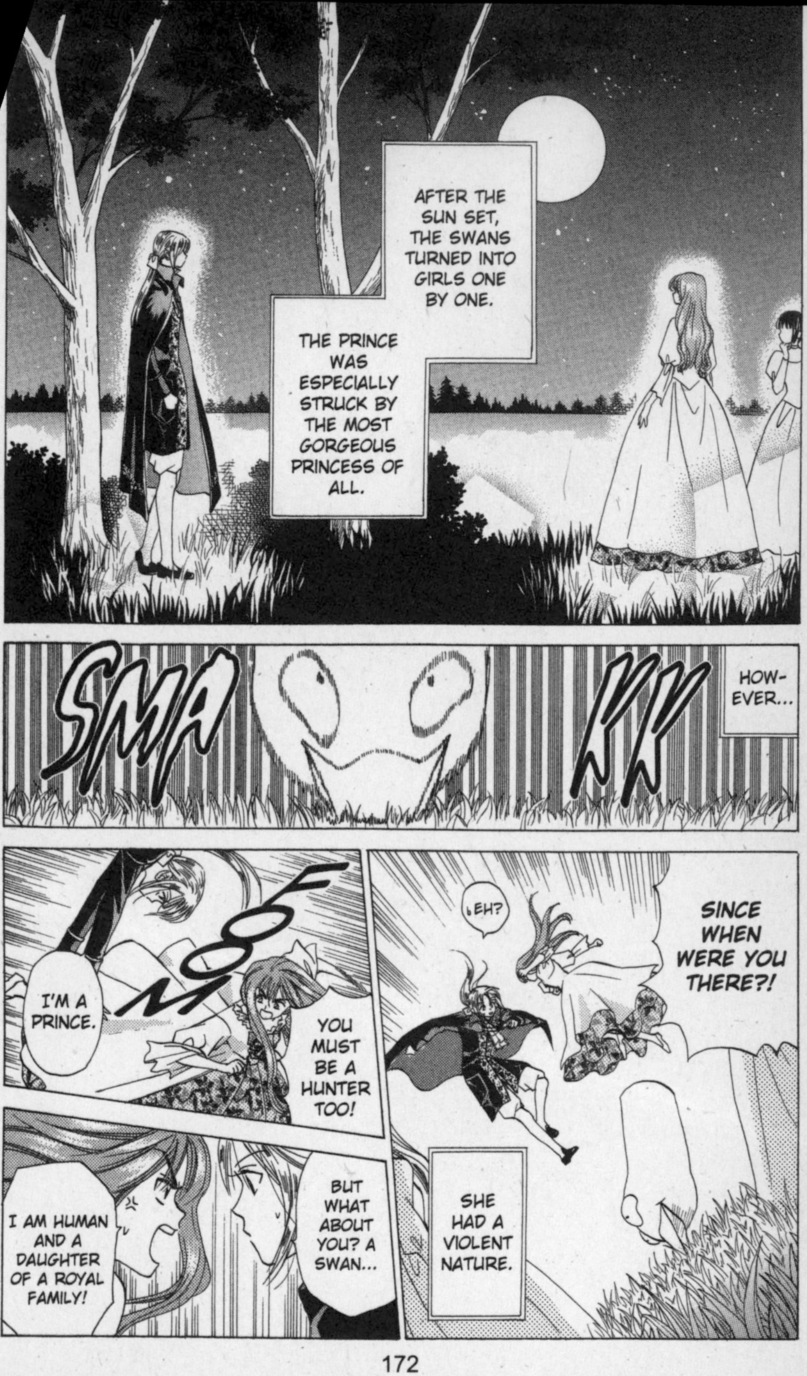
AFTER THE SUN SET, THE SWANS TURNED INTO GIRLS ONE BY ONE.
THE PRINCE WAS ESPECIALLY STRUCK BY THE MOST GORGEOUS PRINCESS OF ALL.
HOW-EVER...
SMAKK
SINCE WHEN WERE YOU THERE?!
EH?
SHE HAD A VIOLENT NATURE.
FOOM
YOU MUST BE A HUNTER TOO!
I'M A PRINCE.
BUT WHAT ABOUT YOU? A SWAN...
I AM HUMAN AND A DAUGHTER OF A ROYAL FAMILY!

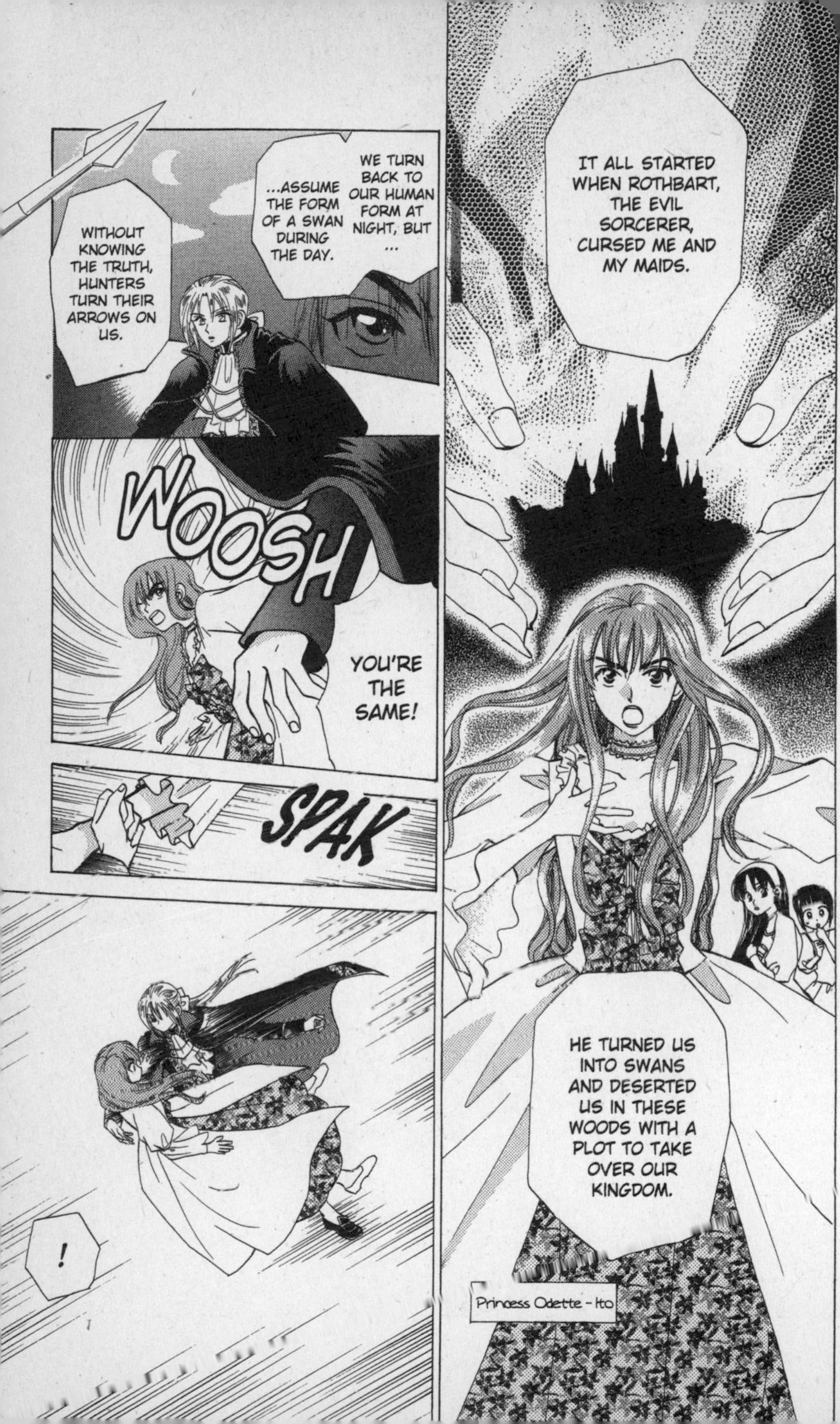
IT ALL STARTED WHEN ROTHBART, THE EVIL SORCERER, CURSED ME AND MY MAIDS.
HE TURNED US INTO SWANS AND DESERTED US IN THESE WOODS WITH A PLOT TO TAKE OVER OUR KINGDOM.
Princess Odette - Ito
WE TURN BACK TO OUR HUMAN FORM AT NIGHT, BUT ...
...ASSUME THE FORM OF A SWAN DURING THE DAY.
WITHOUT KNOWING THE TRUTH, HUNTERS TURN THEIR ARROWS ON US.
WOOSH
YOU'RE THE SAME!
SPAK
!

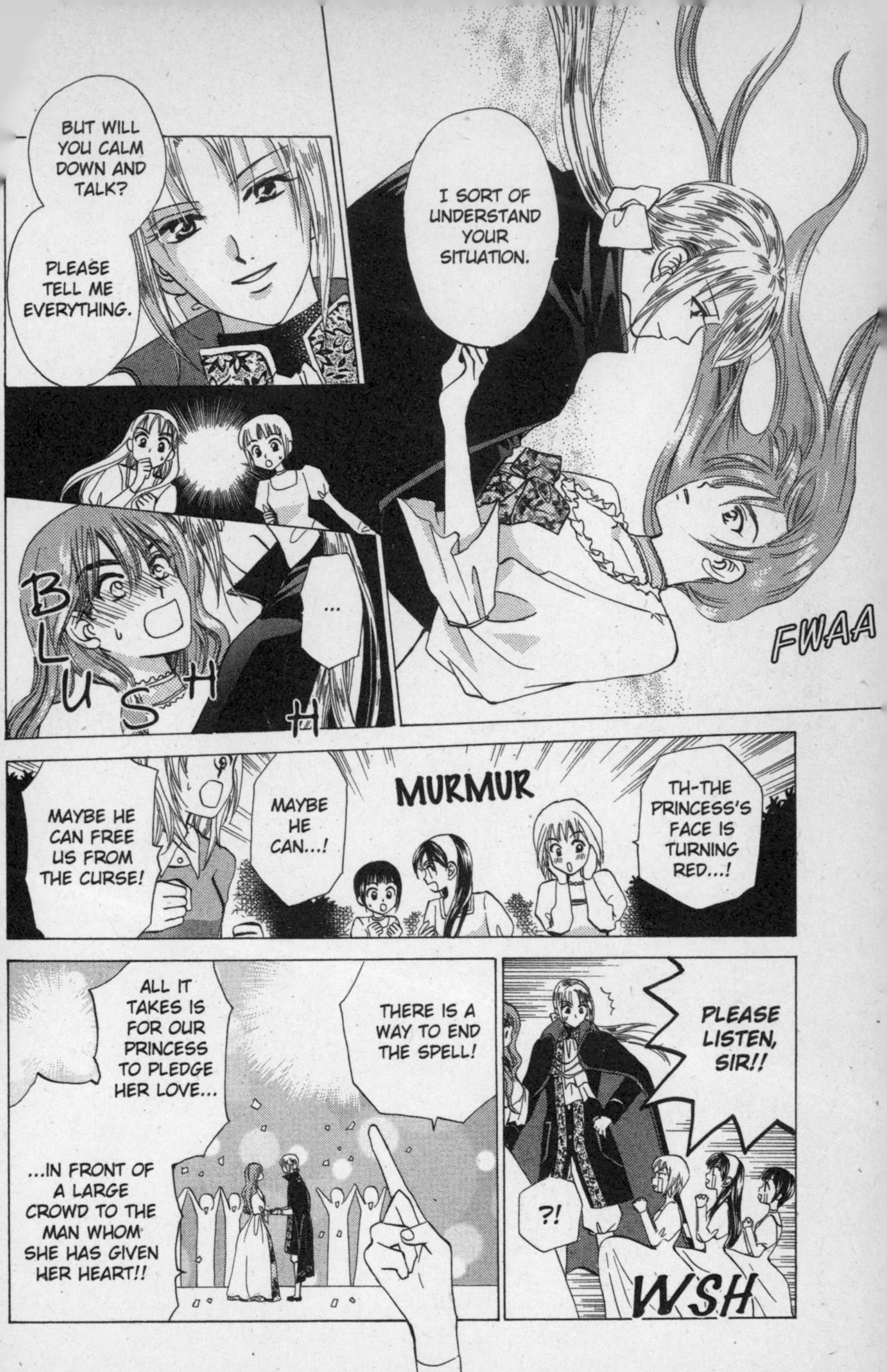
I SORT OF UNDERSTAND YOUR SITUATION.
FWAA
BUT WILL YOU CALM DOWN AND TALK?
PLEASE TELL ME EVERYTHING.
...
BLUSH
H
TH-THE PRINCESS'S FACE IS TURNING RED...!
MURMUR
MAYBE HE CAN...!
MAYBE HE CAN FREE US FROM THE CURSE!
PLEASE LISTEN, SIR!!
?!
WSH
THERE IS A WAY TO END THE SPELL!
ALL IT TAKES IS FOR OUR PRINCESS TO PLEDGE HER LOVE...
...IN FRONT OF A LARGE CROWD TO THE MAN WHOM SHE HAS GIVEN HER HEART!!

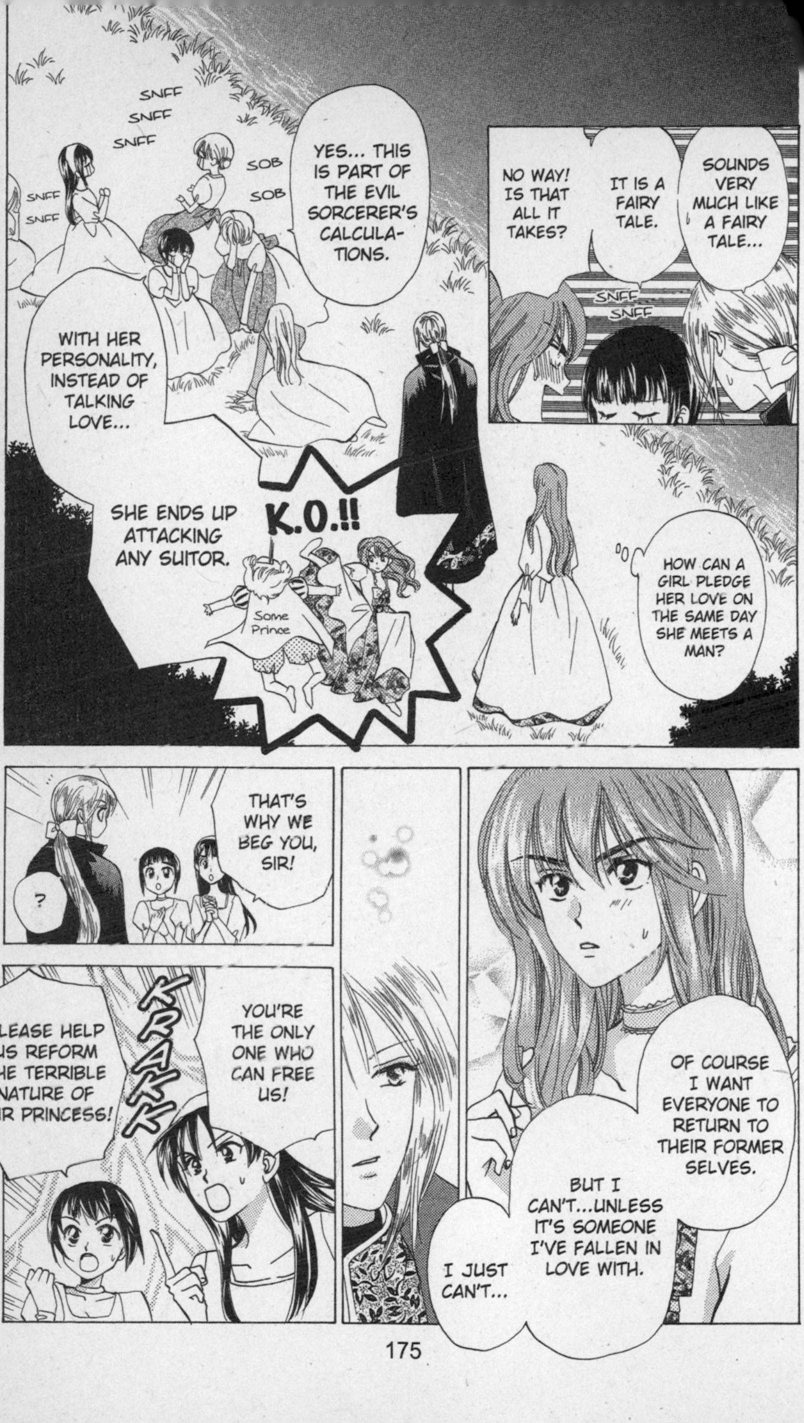
SOUNDS VERY MUCH LIKE A FAIRY TALE...
IT IS A FAIRY TALE.
NO WAY! IS THAT ALL IT TAKES?
SNFF SNFF
YES... THIS IS PART OF THE EVIL SORCERER'S CALCULATIONS.
SOB SOB
SNFF SNFF SNFF
SNFF SNFF
WITH HER PERSONALITY, INSTEAD OF TALKING LOVE...
HOW CAN A GIRL PLEDGE HER LOVE ON THE SAME DAY SHE MEETS A MAN?
K.O.!!
SHE ENDS UP ATTACKING ANY SUITOR.
Some Prince
OF COURSE I WANT EVERYONE TO RETURN TO THEIR FORMER SELVES.
BUT I CAN'T...UNLESS IT'S SOMEONE I'VE FALLEN IN LOVE WITH.
I JUST CAN'T...
THAT'S WHY WE BEG YOU, SIR!
?
YOU'RE THE ONLY ONE WHO CAN FREE US!
KRAKK
PLEASE HELP US REFORM THE TERRIBLE NATURE OF OUR PRINCESS!

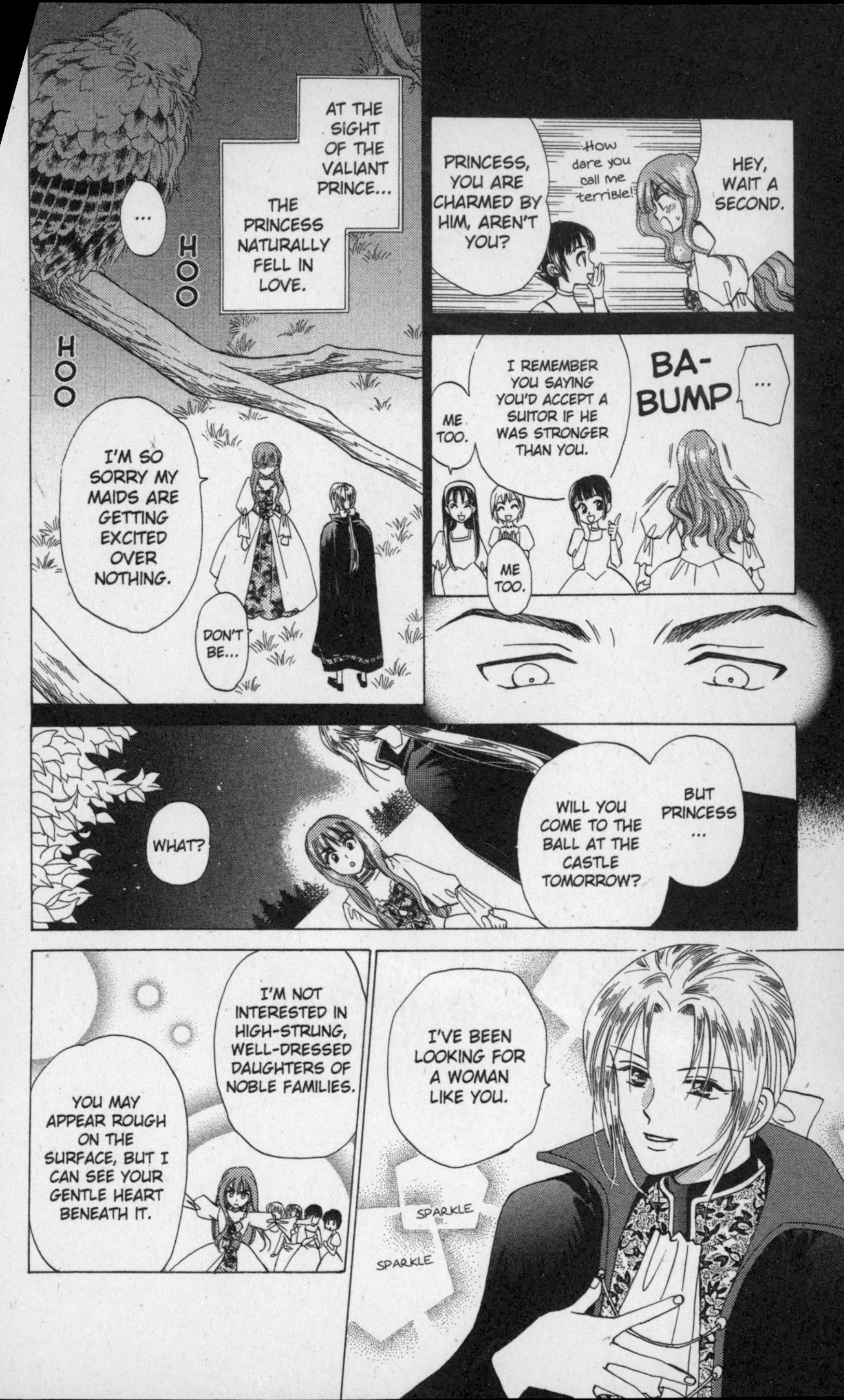

HEY, WAIT A SECOND.
How dare you call me terrible!
PRINCESS, YOU ARE CHARMED BY HIM, AREN'T YOU?
...
BA-BUMP
I REMEMBER YOU SAYING YOU'D ACCEPT A SUITOR IF HE WAS STRONGER THAN YOU.
ME TOO.
ME TOO.
AT THE SIGHT OF THE VALIANT PRINCE...
THE PRINCESS NATURALLY FELL IN LOVE.
...
HOO
HOO
I'M SO SORRY MY MAIDS ARE GETTING EXCITED OVER NOTHING.
DON'T BE...
BUT PRINCESS...
WILL YOU COME TO THE BALL AT THE CASTLE TOMORROW?
WHAT?
I'VE BEEN LOOKING FOR A WOMAN LIKE YOU.
SPARKLE
SPARKLE
I'M NOT INTERESTED IN HIGH-STRUNG, WELL-DRESSED DAUGHTERS OF NOBLE FAMILIES.
YOU MAY APPEAR ROUGH ON THE SURFACE, BUT I CAN SEE YOUR GENTLE HEART BENEATH IT.

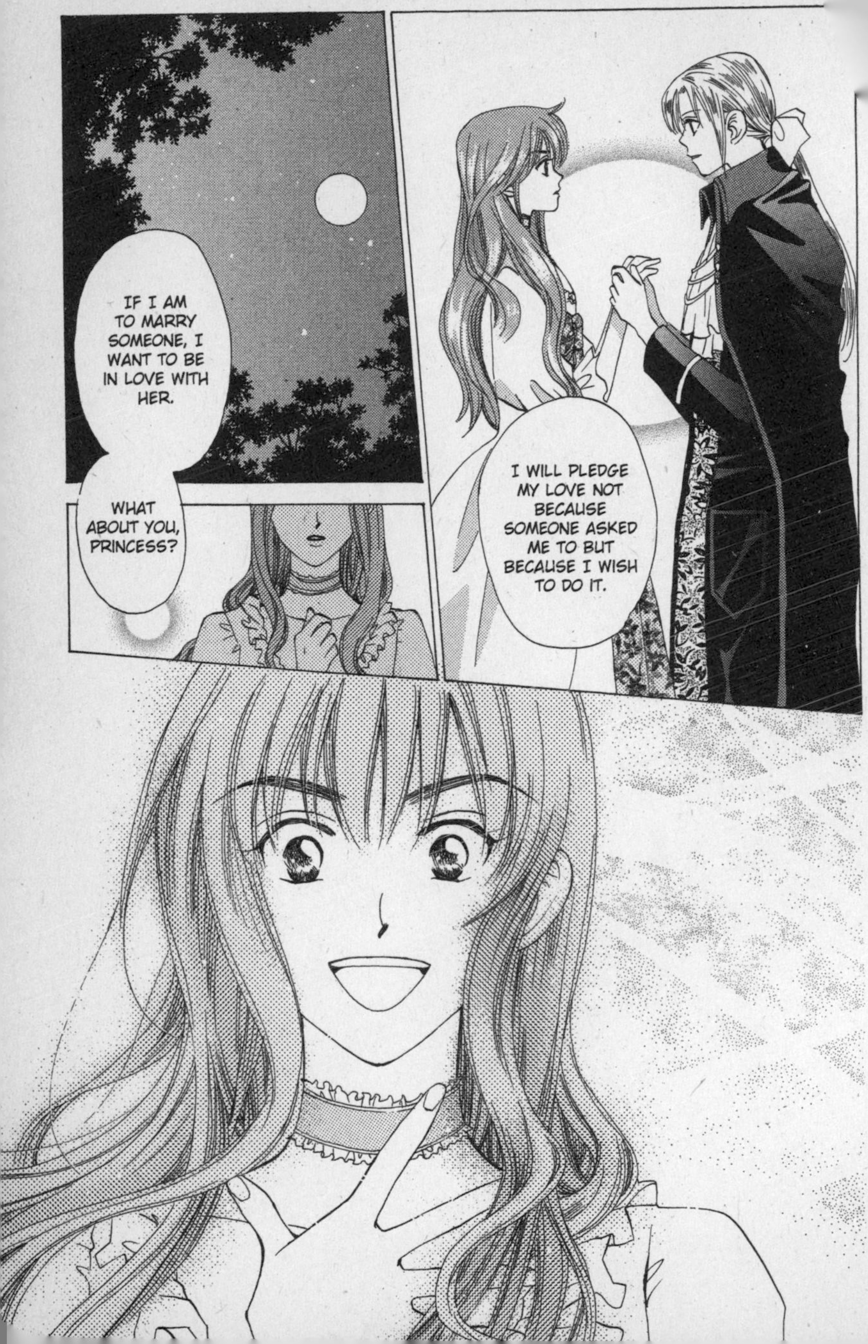
I WILL PLEDGE MY LOVE NOT BECAUSE SOMEONE ASKED ME TO BUT BECAUSE I WISH TO DO IT.
IF I AM TO MARRY SOMEONE, I WANT TO BE IN LOVE WITH HER.
WHAT ABOUT YOU, PRINCESS?

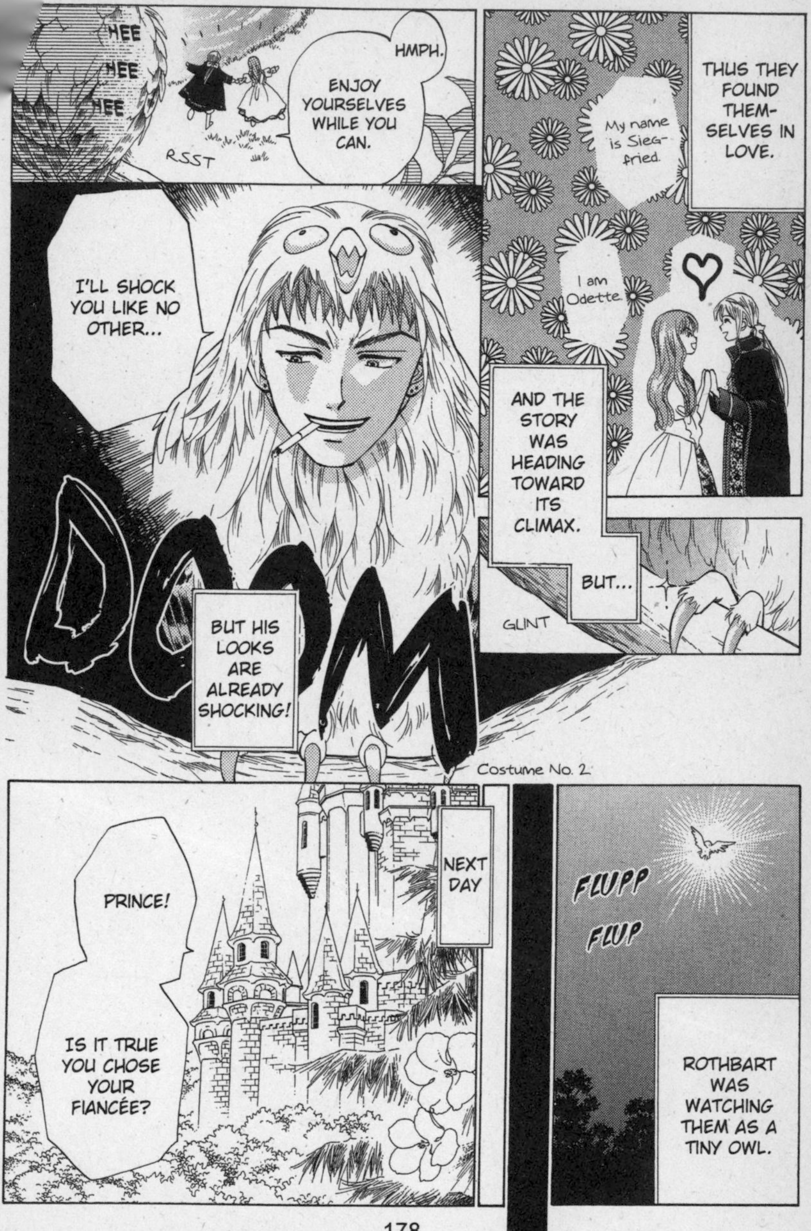
THUS THEY FOUND THEMSELVES IN LOVE.
My name is Siegfried.
I am Odette.
AND THE STORY WAS HEADING TOWARD ITS CLIMAX.
BUT...
GLINT
HMPH.
ENJOY YOURSELVES WHILE YOU CAN.
HEE HEE HEE
RSST
I'LL SHOCK YOU LIKE NO OTHER...
DOOM
BUT HIS LOOKS ARE ALREADY SHOCKING!
Costume No. 2
FLUPP
FLUP
ROTHBART WAS WATCHING THEM AS A TINY OWL.
NEXT DAY
PRINCE!
IS IT TRUE YOU CHOSE YOUR FIANCÉE?

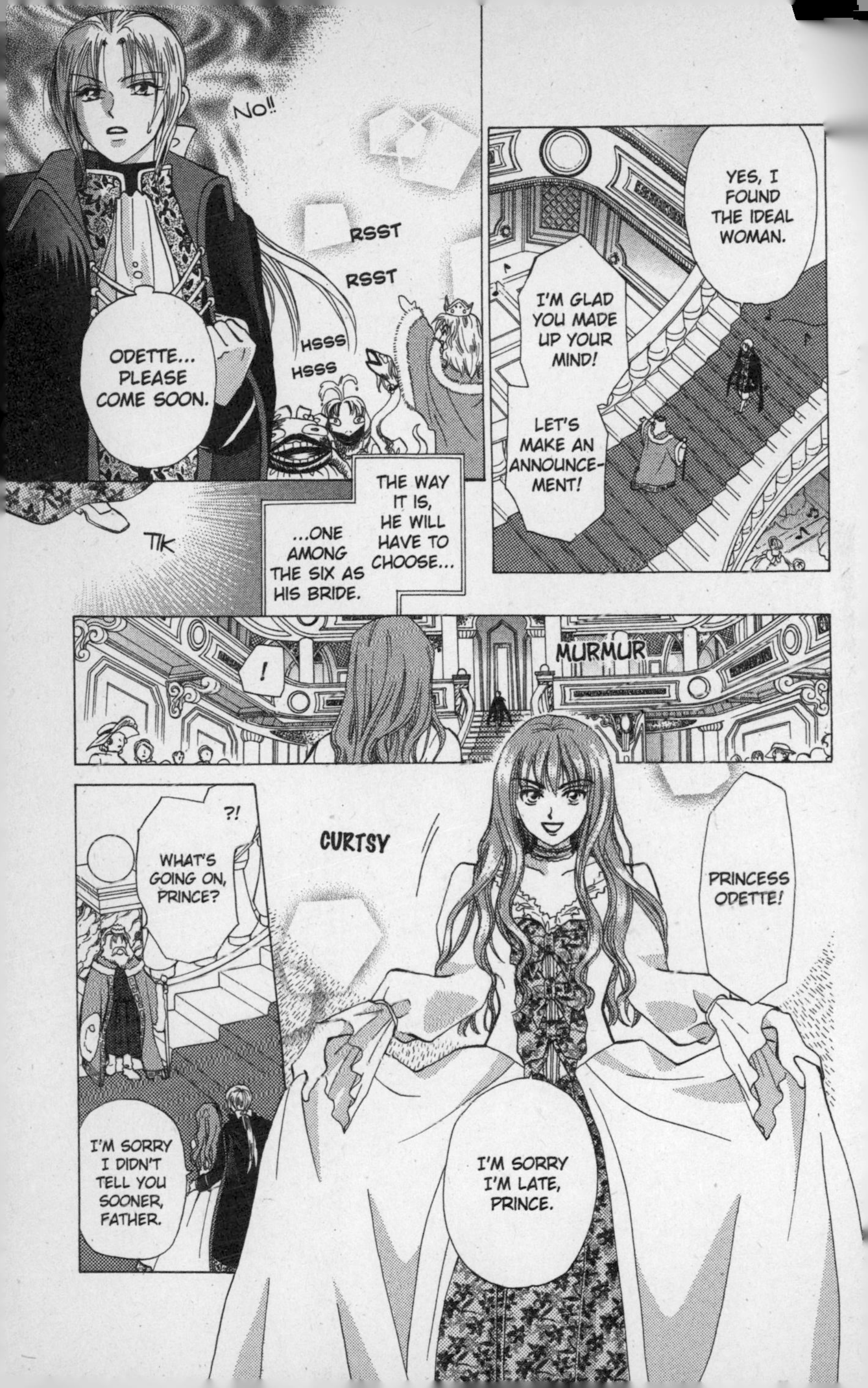
YES, I FOUND THE IDEAL WOMAN.
I'M GLAD YOU MADE UP YOUR MIND!
LET'S MAKE AN ANNOUNCEMENT!
No!!
RSST
RSST
HSSS
HSSS
ODETTE... PLEASE COME SOON.
THE WAY IT IS, HE WILL HAVE TO CHOOSE...
...ONE AMONG THE SIX AS HIS BRIDE.
TIK
MURMUR
!
PRINCESS ODETTE!
CURTSY
I'M SORRY I'M LATE, PRINCE.
?!
WHAT'S GOING ON, PRINCE?
I'M SORRY I DIDN'T TELL YOU SOONER, FATHER.

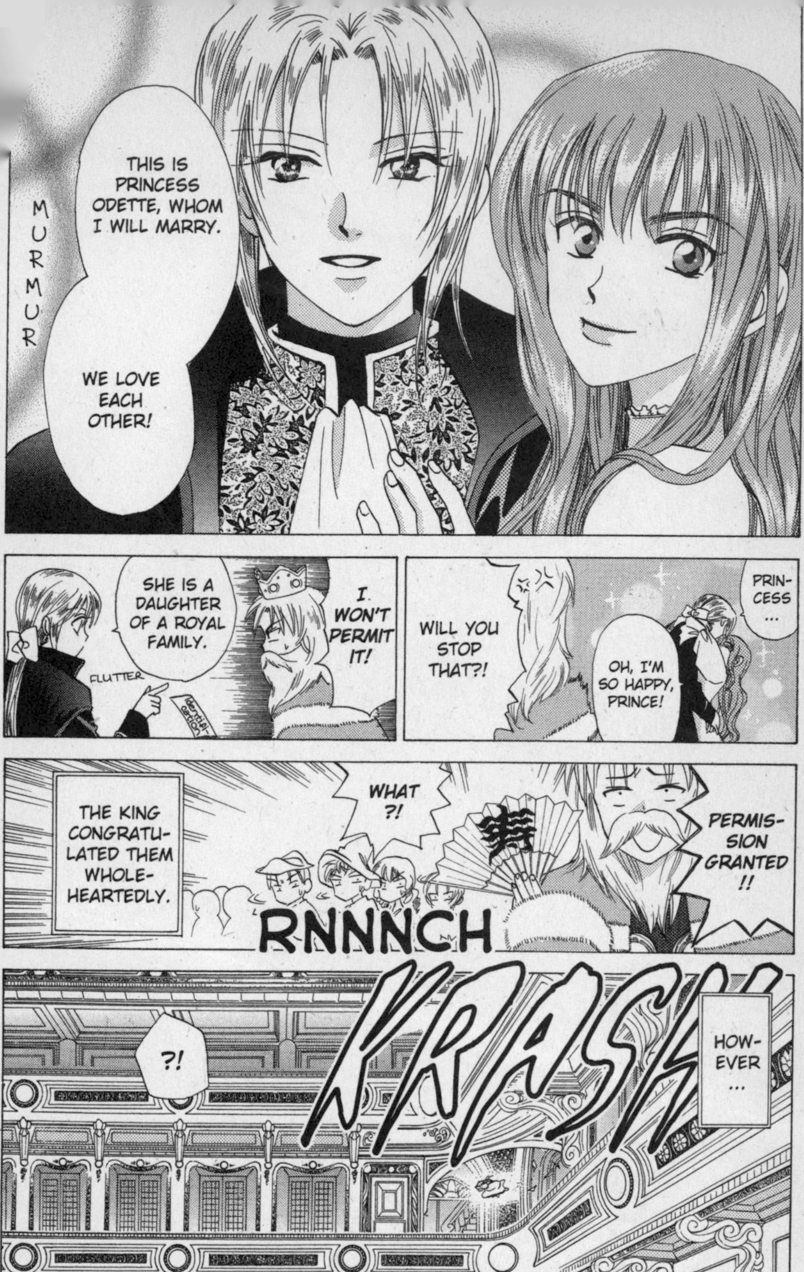
THIS IS PRINCESS ODETTE, WHOM I WILL MARRY.
MURMUR
WE LOVE EACH OTHER!
PRIN-CESS ...
OH, I'M SO HAPPY, PRINCE!
WILL YOU STOP THAT?!
I WON'T PERMIT IT!
SHE IS A DAUGHTER OF A ROYAL FAMILY.
FLUTTER
PERMIS-SION GRANTED !!
WHAT ?!
THE KING CONGRATU-LATED THEM WHOLE-HEARTEDLY.
RNNNCH
HOW-EVER ...
KRASH
?!

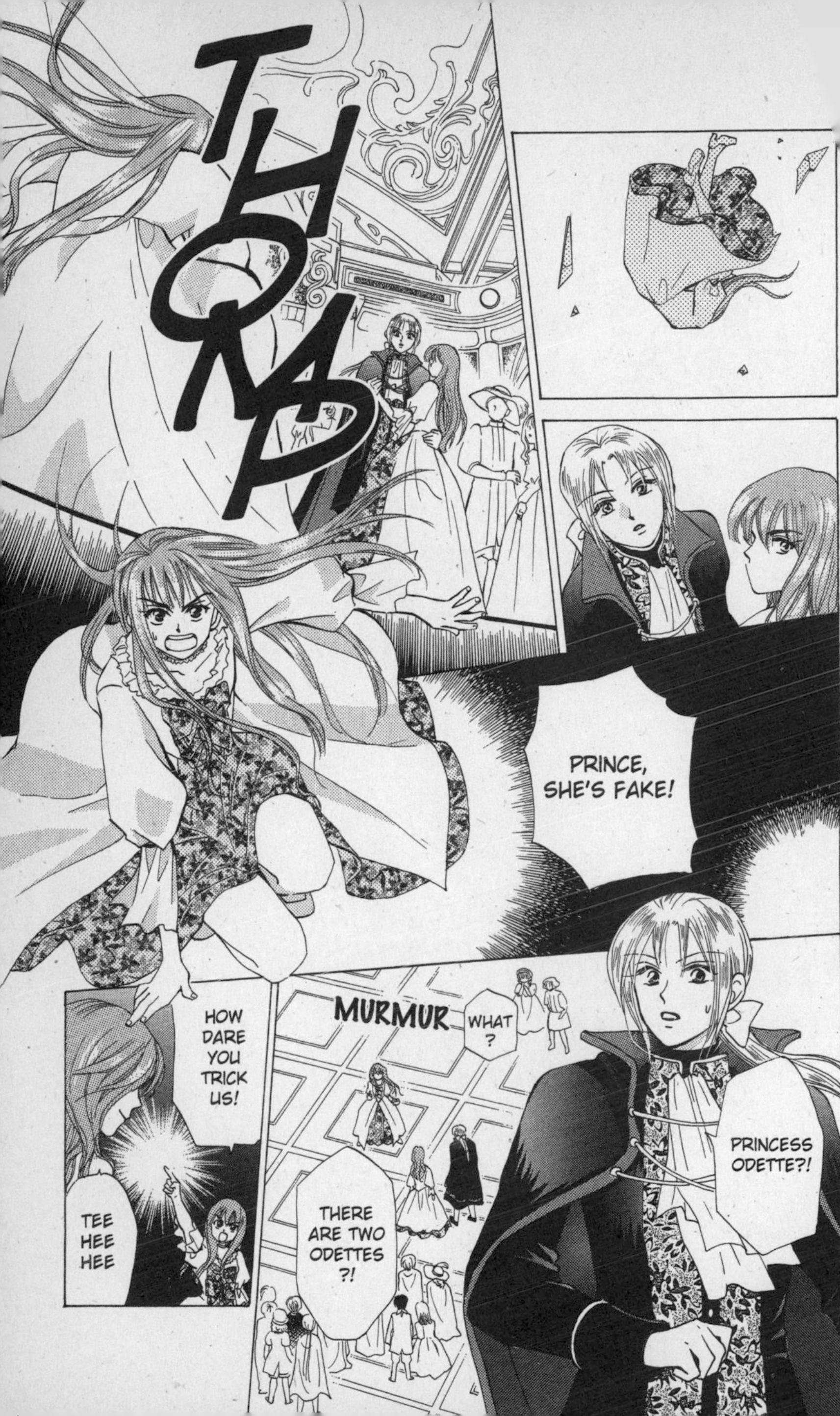
THOMP
PRINCE, SHE'S FAKE!
PRINCESS ODETTE?!
MURMUR
WHAT?
THERE ARE TWO ODETTES?!
HOW DARE YOU TRICK US!
TEE HEE HEE

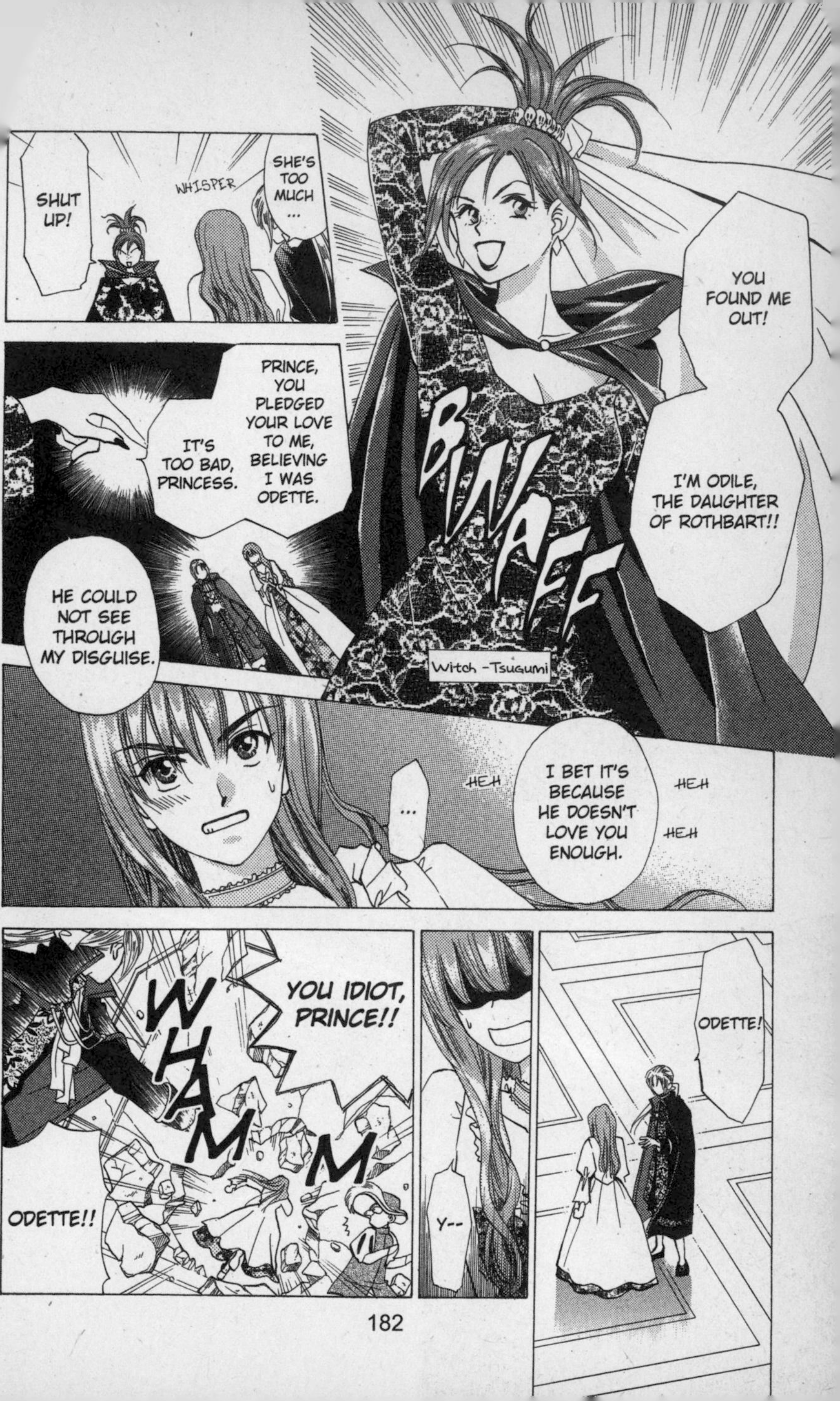
YOU FOUND ME OUT!
I'M ODILE, THE DAUGHTER OF ROTHBART!!
BWAFF
Witch -Tsugumi
SHE'S TOO MUCH ...
WHISPER
SHUT UP!
PRINCE, YOU PLEDGED YOUR LOVE TO ME, BELIEVING I WAS ODETTE.
IT'S TOO BAD, PRINCESS.
HE COULD NOT SEE THROUGH MY DISGUISE.
HEH
I BET IT'S BECAUSE HE DOESN'T LOVE YOU ENOUGH.
HEH
HEH
...
ODETTE!
Y--
YOU IDIOT, PRINCE!!
WHAMM
ODETTE!!

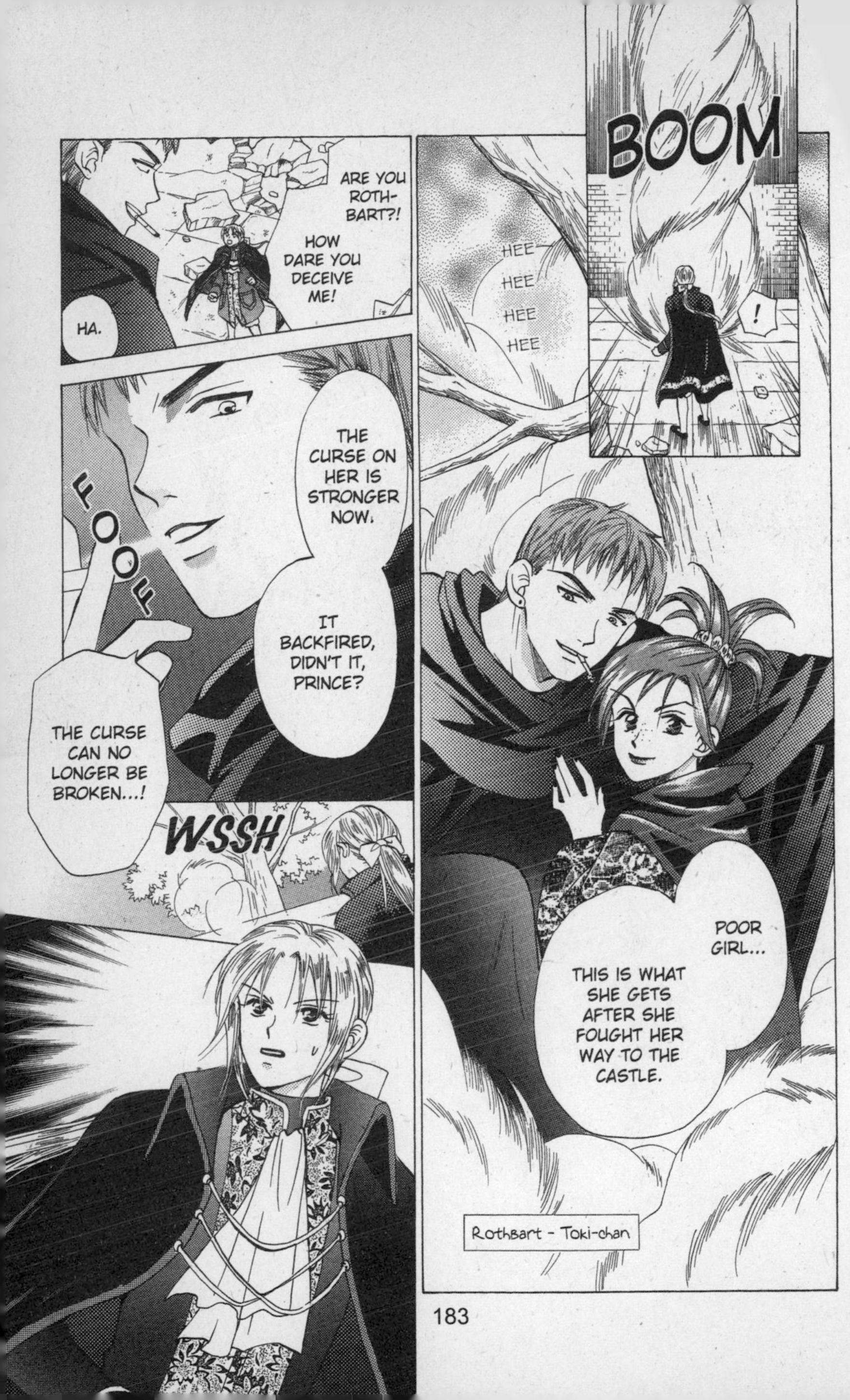
BOOM
!
HEE HEE HEE HEE
POOR GIRL...
THIS IS WHAT SHE GETS AFTER SHE FOUGHT HER WAY TO THE CASTLE.
Rothbart - Toki-chan
ARE YOU ROTH-BART?!
HOW DARE YOU DECEIVE ME!
HA.
THE CURSE ON HER IS STRONGER NOW.
FOOF
IT BACKFIRED, DIDN'T IT, PRINCE?
THE CURSE CAN NO LONGER BE BROKEN...!
WSSH

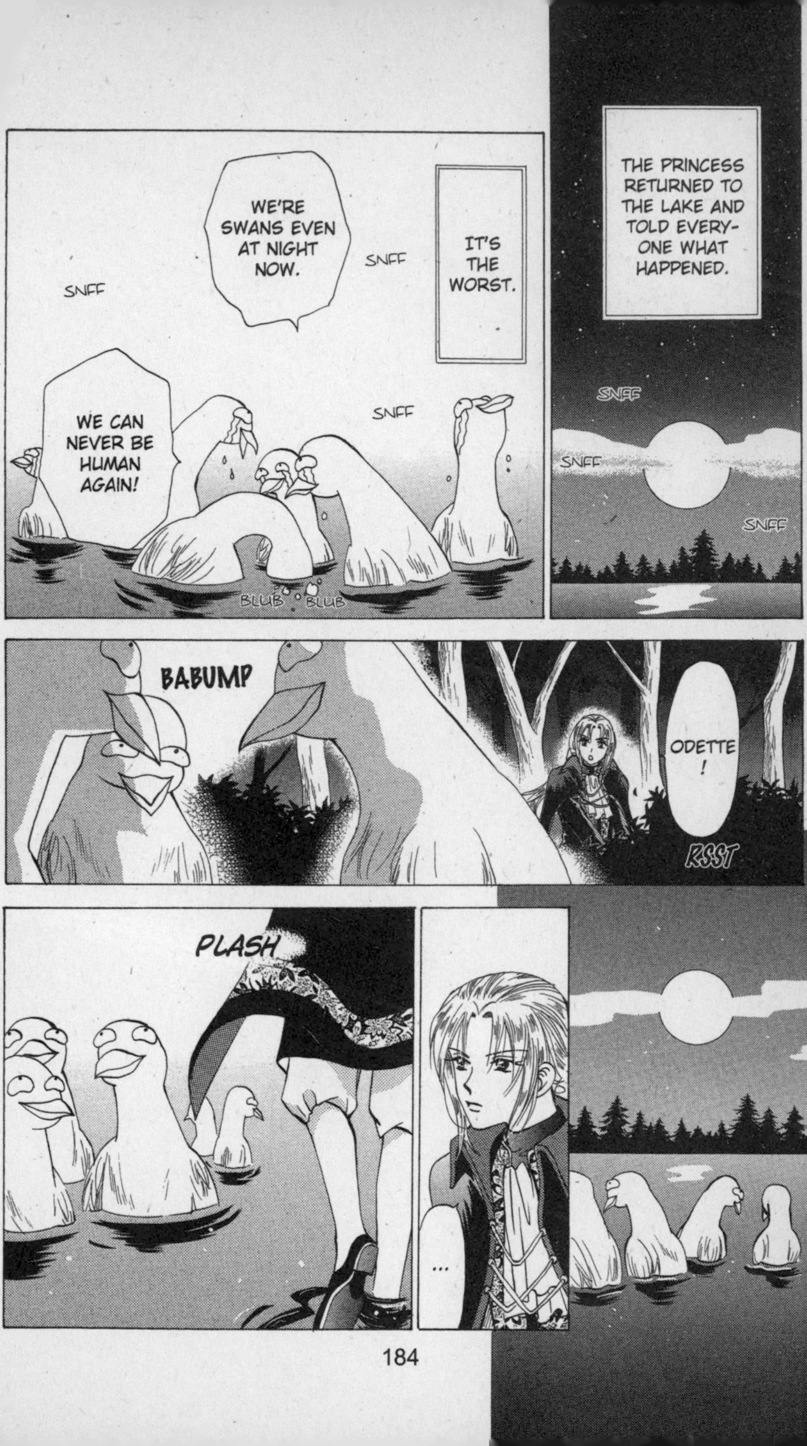

THE PRINCESS RETURNED TO THE LAKE AND TOLD EVERY-ONE WHAT HAPPENED.
SNFF
SNFF
SNFF
IT'S THE WORST.
SNFF
WE'RE SWANS EVEN AT NIGHT NOW.
SNFF
SNFF
WE CAN NEVER BE HUMAN AGAIN!
BLUB BLUB
ODETTE !
RSST
BABUMP
...
PLASH

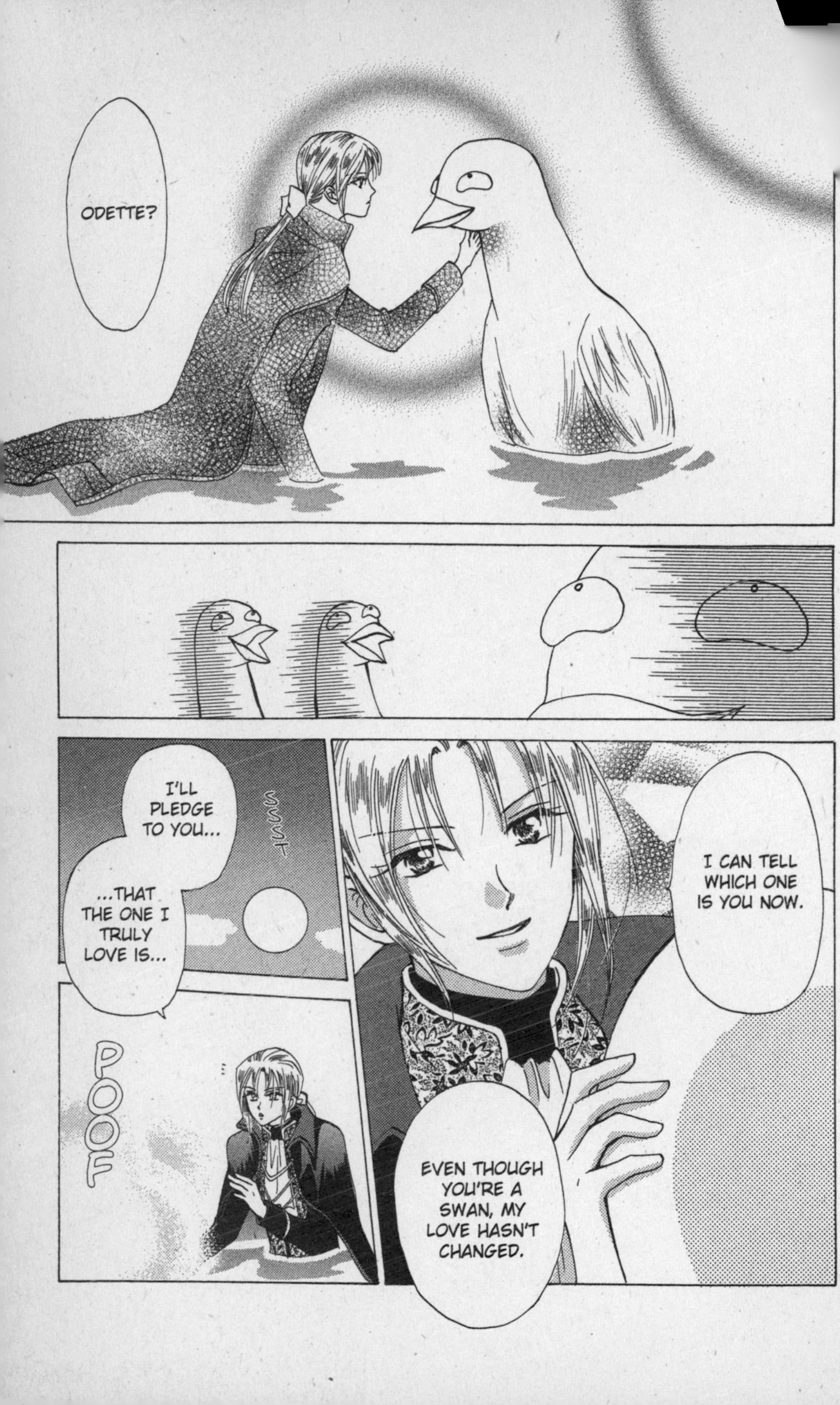
ODETTE?
I CAN TELL WHICH ONE IS YOU NOW.
EVEN THOUGH YOU'RE A SWAN, MY LOVE HASN'T CHANGED.
I'LL PLEDGE TO YOU...
...THAT THE ONE I TRULY LOVE IS...
POOF

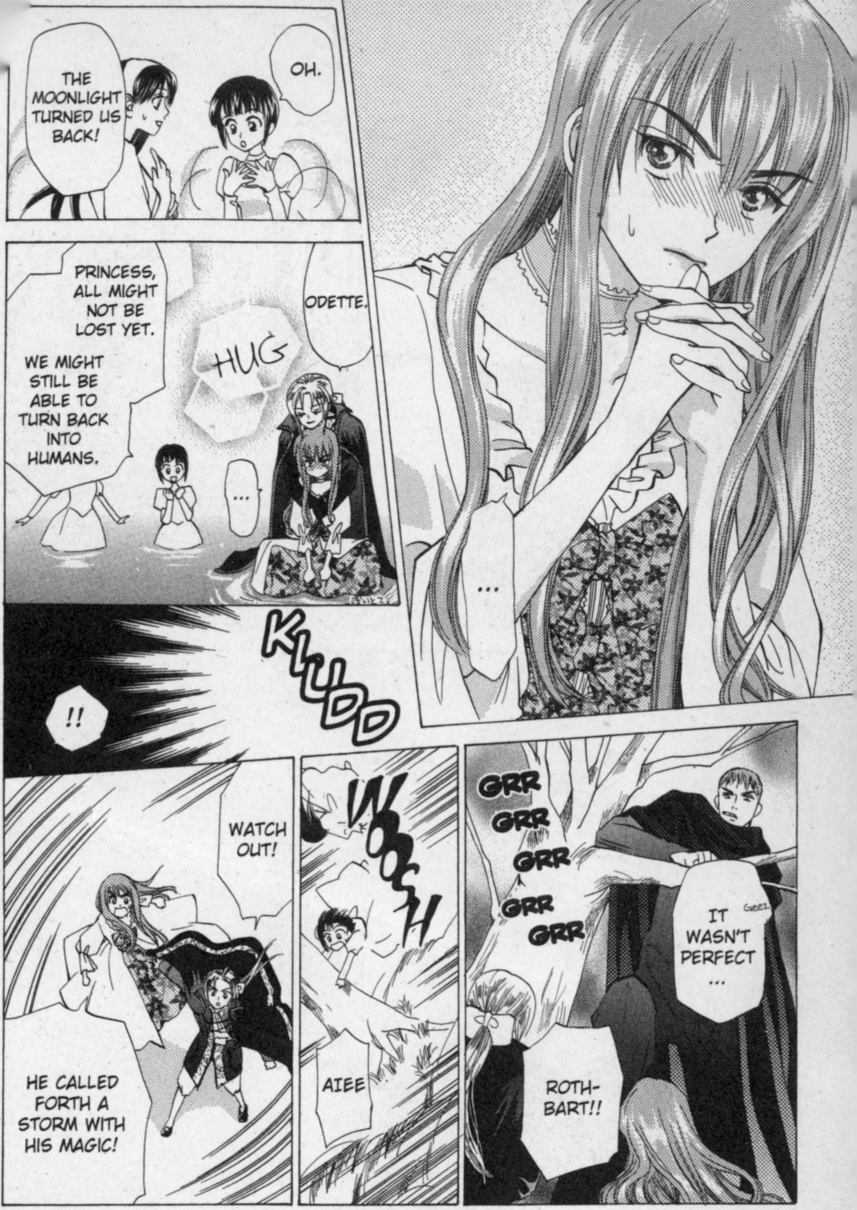
...
OH.
THE MOONLIGHT TURNED US BACK!
ODETTE.
HUG
...
PRINCESS, ALL MIGHT NOT BE LOST YET.
WE MIGHT STILL BE ABLE TO TURN BACK INTO HUMANS.
KLUDD
!!
GRR GRR GRR GRR GRR
IT WASN'T PERFECT ...
Geez
ROTH-BART!!
WOOSH
AIEE
WATCH OUT!
HE CALLED FORTH A STORM WITH HIS MAGIC!

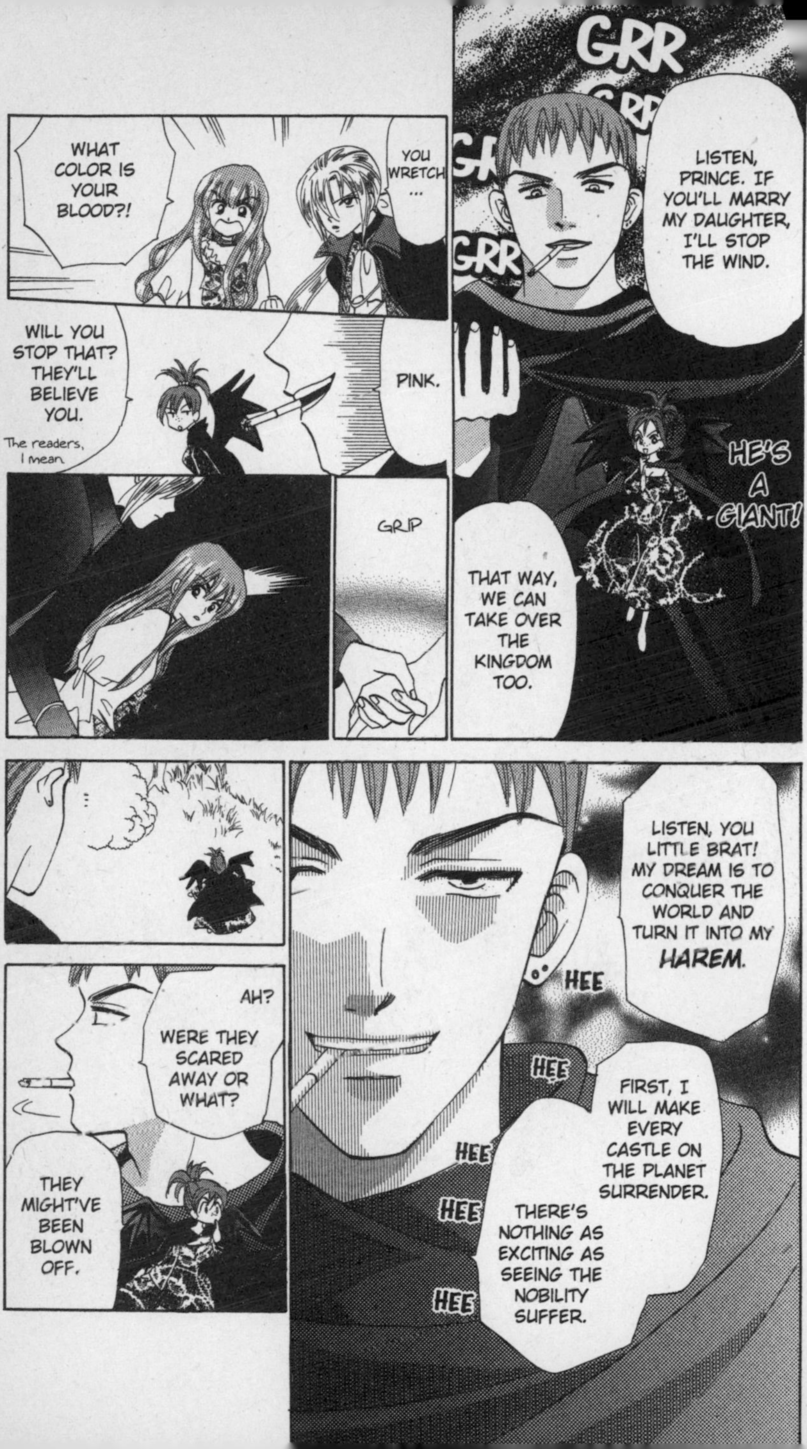
GRR
GRR
GRR
GRR
LISTEN, PRINCE. IF YOU'LL MARRY MY DAUGHTER, I'LL STOP THE WIND.
THAT WAY, WE CAN TAKE OVER THE KINGDOM TOO.
HE'S A GIANT!
YOU WRETCH ...
WHAT COLOR IS YOUR BLOOD?!
PINK.
WILL YOU STOP THAT? THEY'LL BELIEVE YOU.
The readers, I mean.
GRIP
LISTEN, YOU LITTLE BRAT! MY DREAM IS TO CONQUER THE WORLD AND TURN IT INTO MY HAREM.
HEE
HEE
FIRST, I WILL MAKE EVERY CASTLE ON THE PLANET SURRENDER.
HEE
HEE
THERE'S NOTHING AS EXCITING AS SEEING THE NOBILITY SUFFER.
HEE
...
AH?
WERE THEY SCARED AWAY OR WHAT?
THEY MIGHT'VE BEEN BLOWN OFF.

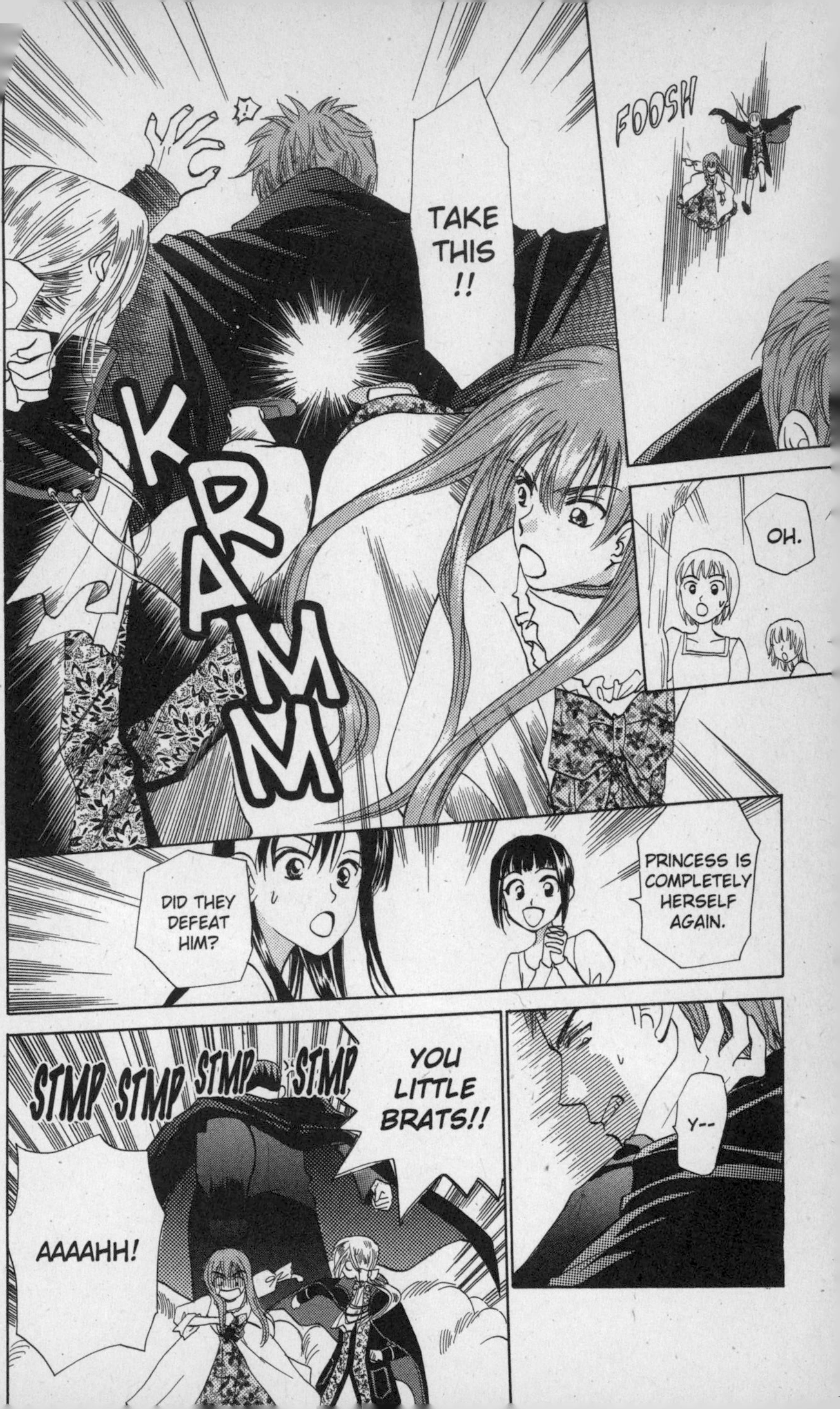
FOOSH
OH.
TAKE THIS!!
KRAMM
PRINCESS IS COMPLETELY HERSELF AGAIN.
DID THEY DEFEAT HIM?
Y--
YOU LITTLE BRATS!!
STMP STMP STMP STMP
AAAAHH!

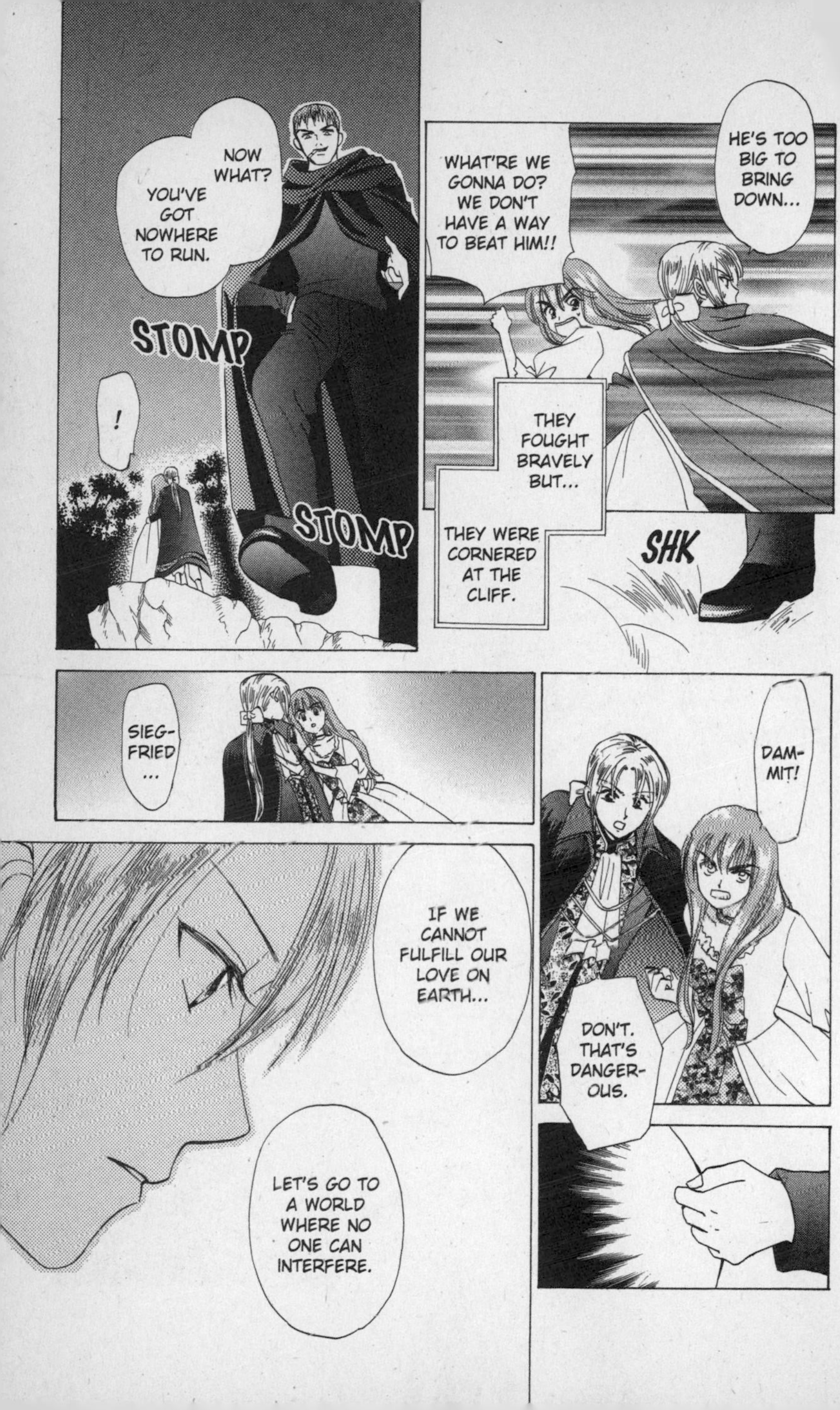
HE'S TOO BIG TO BRING DOWN...
WHAT'RE WE GONNA DO? WE DON'T HAVE A WAY TO BEAT HIM!!
THEY FOUGHT BRAVELY BUT...
THEY WERE CORNERED AT THE CLIFF.
SHK
NOW WHAT? YOU'VE GOT NOWHERE TO RUN.
STOMP
!
STOMP
DAM-MIT!
DON'T. THAT'S DANGER-OUS.
SIEG-FRIED ...
IF WE CANNOT FULFILL OUR LOVE ON EARTH...
LET'S GO TO A WORLD WHERE NO ONE CAN INTERFERE.

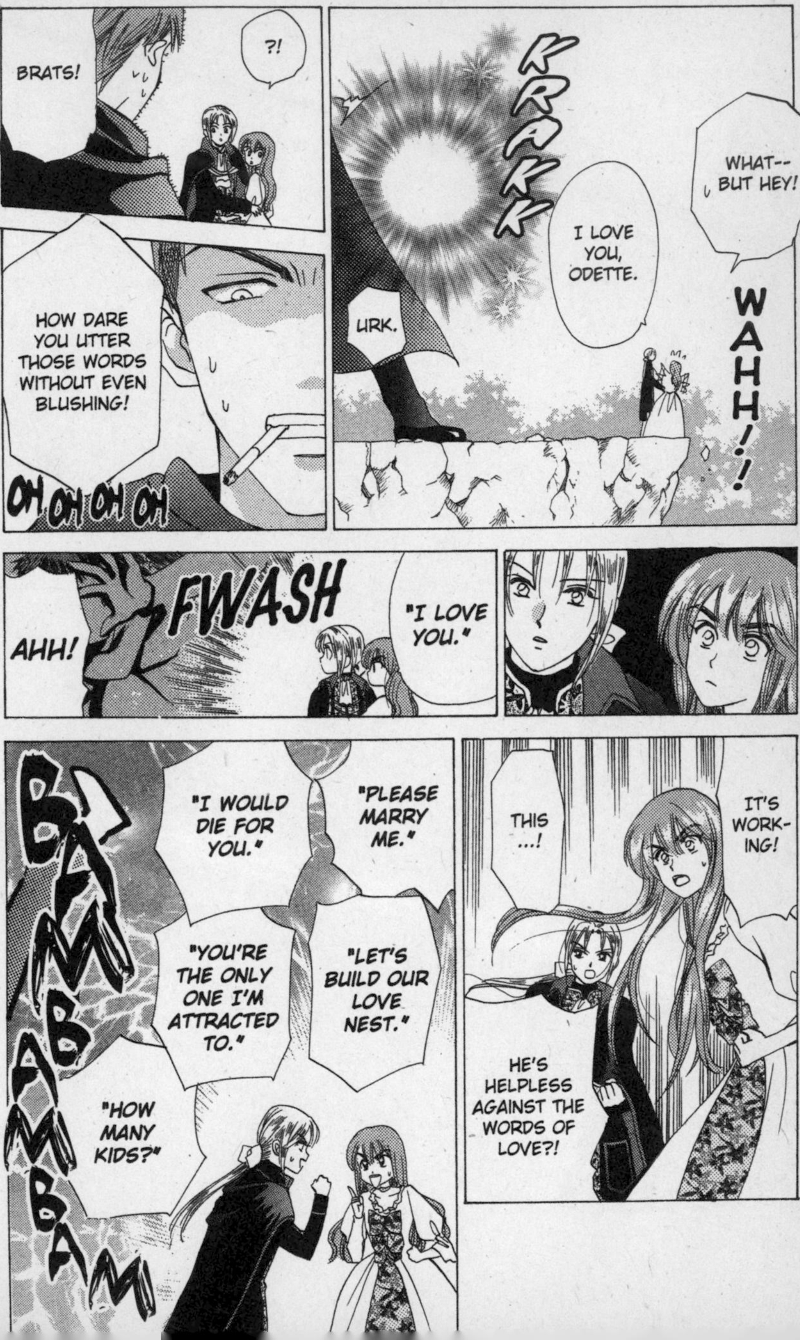
WHAT-- BUT HEY!
KRAKK
I LOVE YOU, ODETTE.
WAHH!!
URK.
?!
BRATS!
HOW DARE YOU UTTER THOSE WORDS WITHOUT EVEN BLUSHING!
OH OH OH OH
"I LOVE YOU."
FWASH
AHH!
IT'S WORK-ING!
THIS ...!
HE'S HELPLESS AGAINST THE WORDS OF LOVE?!
"PLEASE MARRY ME."
"I WOULD DIE FOR YOU."
"LET'S BUILD OUR LOVE NEST."
"YOU'RE THE ONLY ONE I'M ATTRACTED TO."
BAM BAM BAM
"HOW MANY KIDS?"

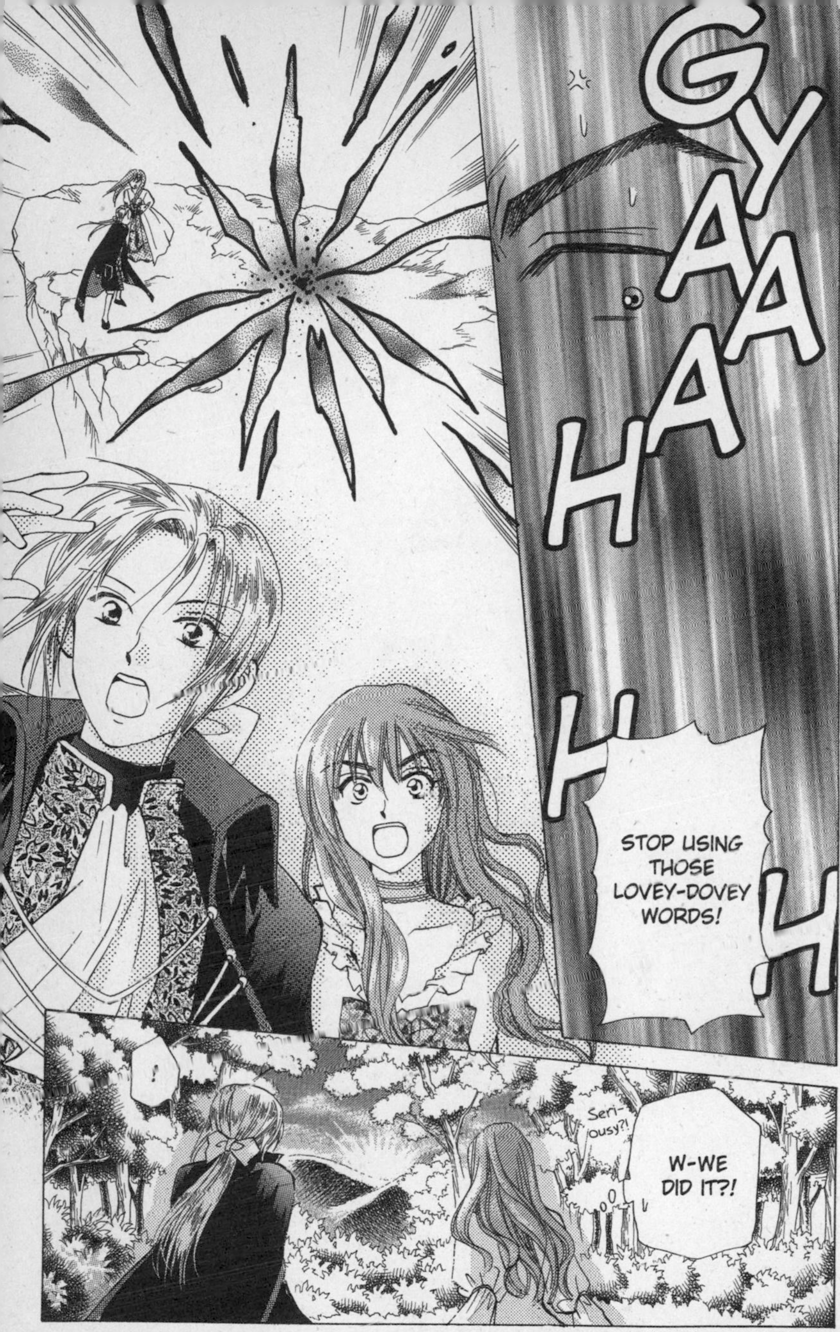
GYAAAHAAHHH
STOP USING THOSE LOVEY-DOVEY WORDS!
W-WE DID IT?!
Seri-ousy?!

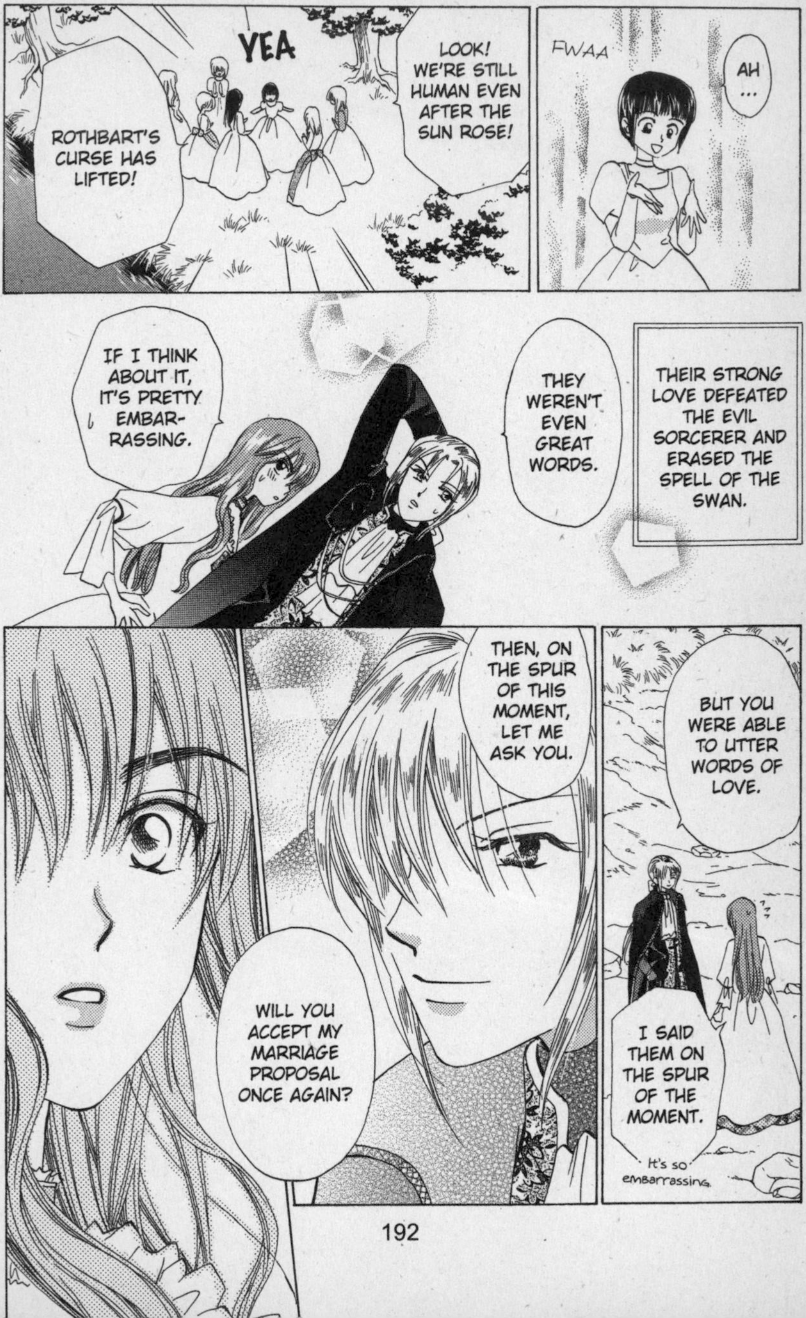
FWAA
AH ...
LOOK! WE'RE STILL HUMAN EVEN AFTER THE SUN ROSE!
YEA
ROTHBART'S CURSE HAS LIFTED!
THEIR STRONG LOVE DEFEATED THE EVIL SORCERER AND ERASED THE SPELL OF THE SWAN.
THEY WEREN'T EVEN GREAT WORDS.
IF I THINK ABOUT IT, IT'S PRETTY EMBAR-RASSING.
BUT YOU WERE ABLE TO UTTER WORDS OF LOVE.
I SAID THEM ON THE SPUR OF THE MOMENT.
It's so embarrassing.
THEN, ON THE SPUR OF THIS MOMENT, LET ME ASK YOU.
WILL YOU ACCEPT MY MARRIAGE PROPOSAL ONCE AGAIN?

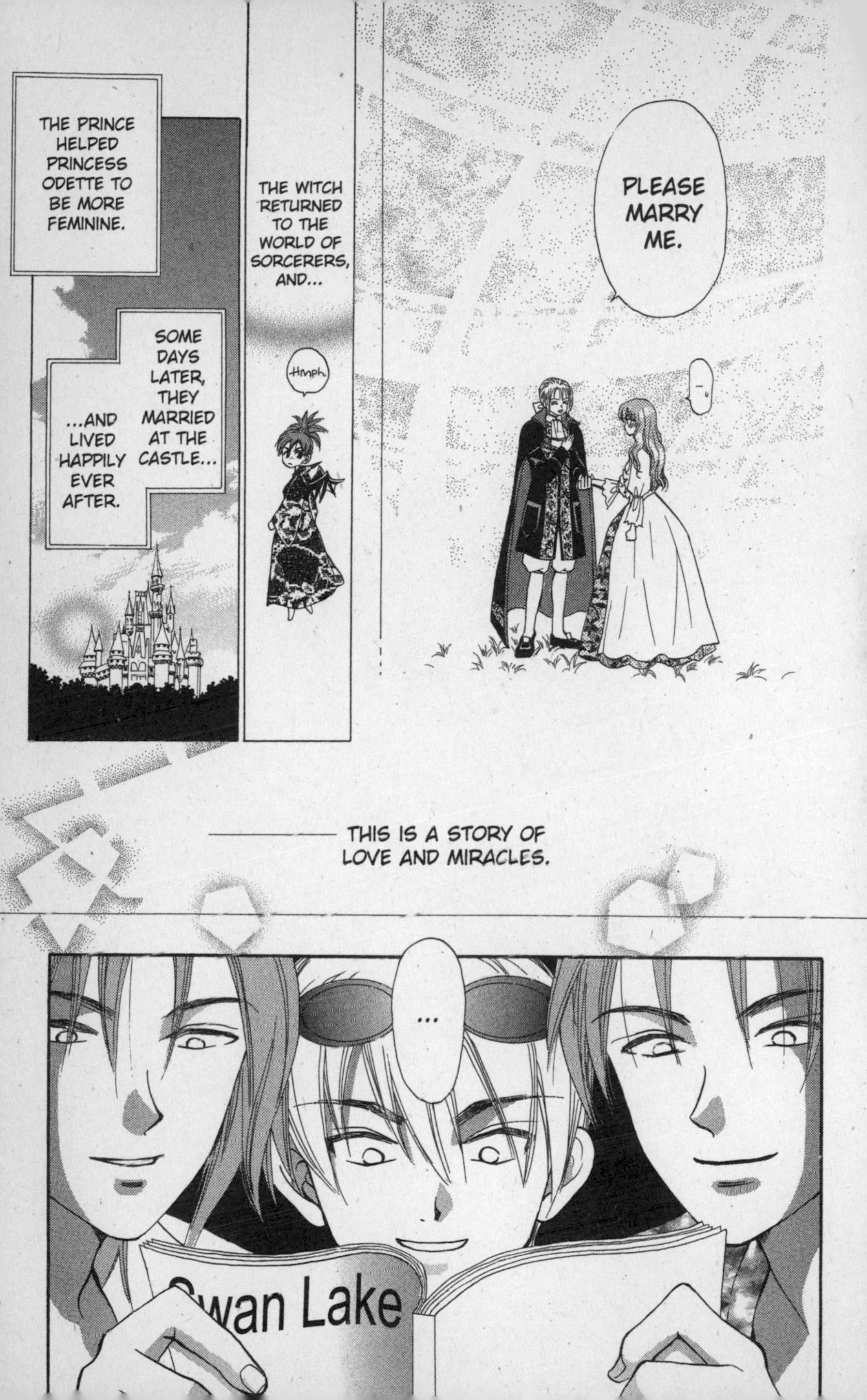
PLEASE MARRY ME.
...
THE WITCH RETURNED TO THE WORLD OF SORCERERS, AND...
Hmph.
THE PRINCE HELPED PRINCESS ODETTE TO BE MORE FEMININE.
SOME DAYS LATER, THEY MARRIED AT THE CASTLE...
...AND LIVED HAPPILY EVER AFTER.
THIS IS A STORY OF LOVE AND MIRACLES.
...
Swan Lake

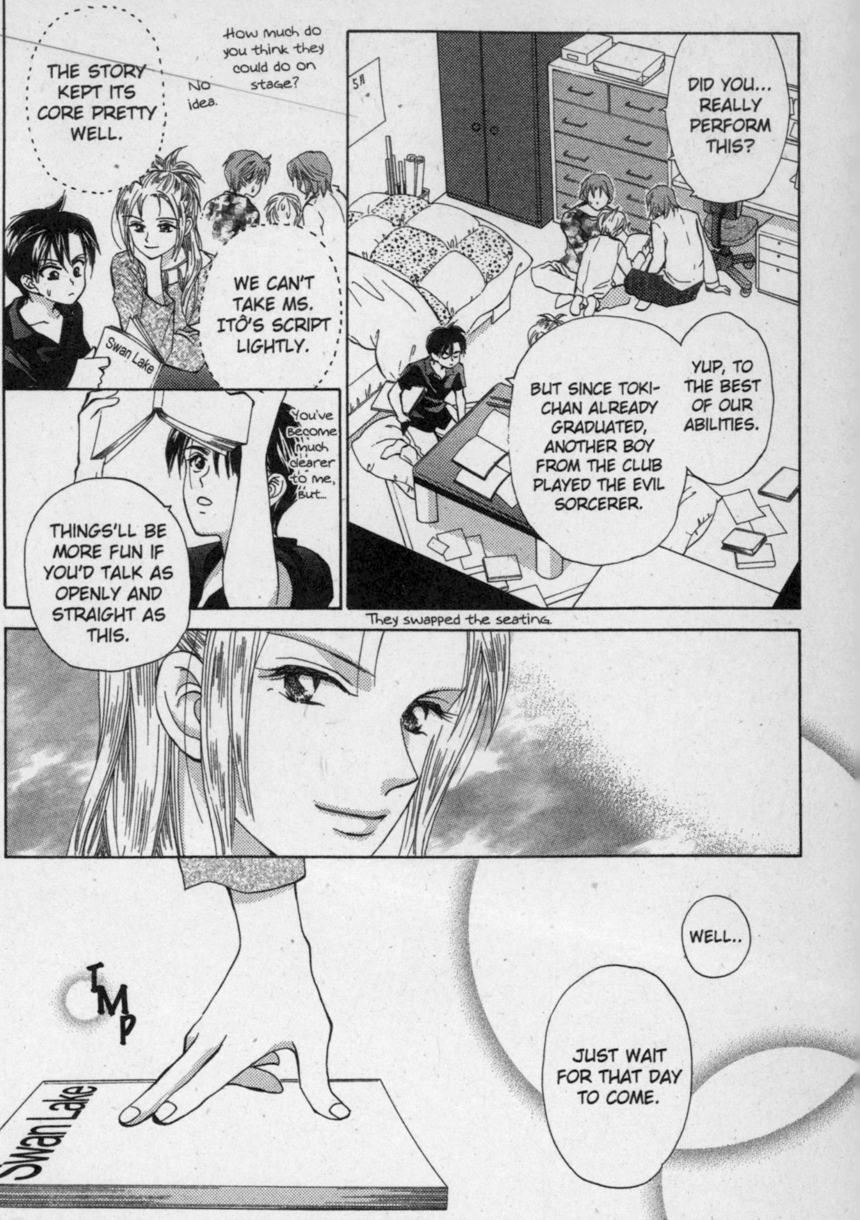
DID YOU... REALLY PERFORM THIS?
YUP, TO THE BEST OF OUR ABILITIES.
BUT SINCE TOKI-CHAN ALREADY GRADUATED, ANOTHER BOY FROM THE CLUB PLAYED THE EVIL SORCERER.
They swapped the seating.
How much do you think they could do on stage?
No idea.
THE STORY KEPT ITS CORE PRETTY WELL.
WE CAN'T TAKE MS. ITÔ'S SCRIPT LIGHTLY.
Swan Lake
You've become much clearer to me, but...
THINGS'LL BE MORE FUN IF YOU'D TALK AS OPENLY AND STRAIGHT AS THIS.
WELL..
JUST WAIT FOR THAT DAY TO COME.
TMP
Swan Lake

W JULIET SPECIAL EPISODE / THE END

THE VOLUME-ENDING AFTERWORD MANGA

BEHIND THE SCENES STORY

~ Autograph Session Report ~

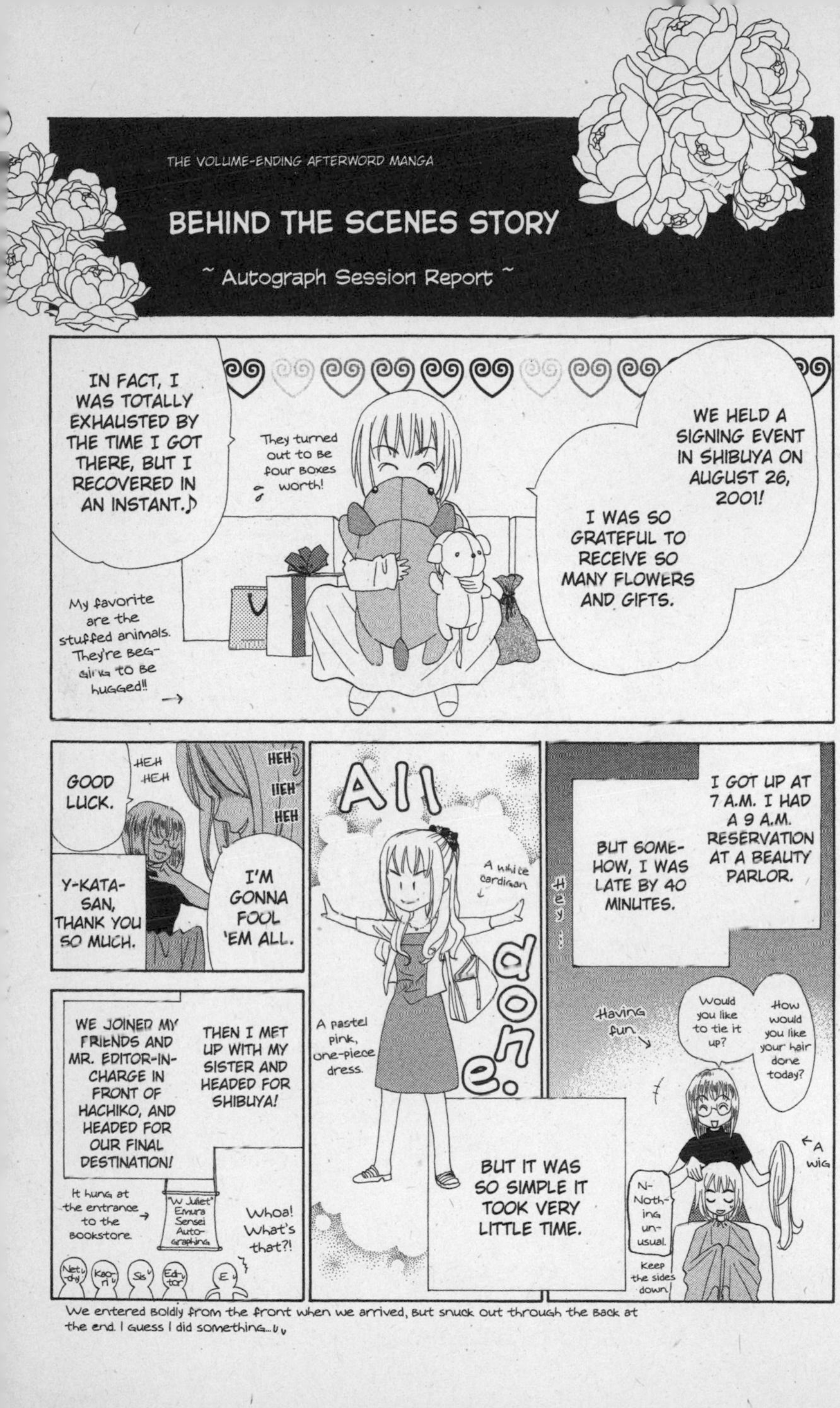

WE HELD A SIGNING EVENT IN SHIBUYA ON AUGUST 26, 2001!
I WAS SO GRATEFUL TO RECEIVE SO MANY FLOWERS AND GIFTS.
They turned out to be four boxes worth!
IN FACT, I WAS TOTALLY EXHAUSTED BY THE TIME I GOT THERE, BUT I RECOVERED IN AN INSTANT.♪
My favorite are the stuffed animals. They're beg-ging to be hugged!!
I GOT UP AT 7 A.M. I HAD A 9 A.M. RESERVATION AT A BEAUTY PARLOR.
BUT SOME-HOW, I WAS LATE BY 40 MINUTES.
Hey...
How would you like your hair done today?
Would you like to tie it up?
Having fun
A wig
N-Nothing unusual.
Keep the sides down.
All done.
A white cardigan
A pastel pink, one-piece dress.
BUT IT WAS SO SIMPLE IT TOOK VERY LITTLE TIME.
HEH HEH HEH
I'M GONNA FOOL 'EM ALL.
HEH HEH
GOOD LUCK.
Y-KATA-SAN, THANK YOU SO MUCH.
THEN I MET UP WITH MY SISTER AND HEADED FOR SHIBUYA!
WE JOINED MY FRIENDS AND MR. EDITOR-IN-CHARGE IN FRONT OF HACHIKO, AND HEADED FOR OUR FINAL DESTINATION!
"W Juliet" Emura Sensei Auto-graphing
It hung at the entrance to the bookstore.
Whoa! What's that?!
Netchy
Kaori
Sis
Editor
E

We entered boldly from the front when we arrived, but snuck out through the back at the end. I guess I did something...

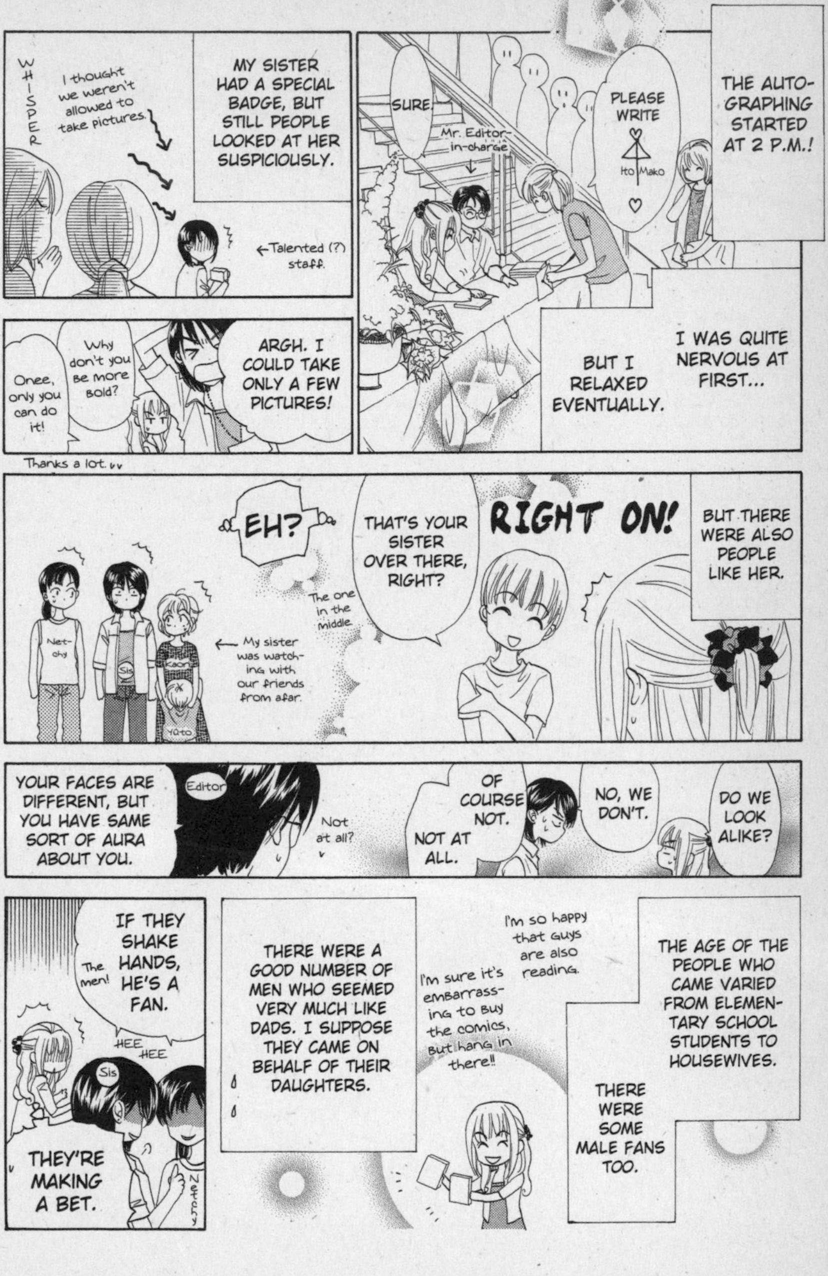
THE AUTO-GRAPHING STARTED AT 2 P.M.!
PLEASE WRITE ♡ Ito Mako ♡
SURE.
Mr. Editor-in-charge
I WAS QUITE NERVOUS AT FIRST...
BUT I RELAXED EVENTUALLY.
MY SISTER HAD A SPECIAL BADGE, BUT STILL PEOPLE LOOKED AT HER SUSPICIOUSLY.
WHISPER
I thought we weren't allowed to take pictures.
←Talented (?) staff.
ARGH. I COULD TAKE ONLY A FEW PICTURES!
Why don't you be more bold?
Onee, only you can do it!
Thanks a lot.
BUT THERE WERE ALSO PEOPLE LIKE HER.
RIGHT ON!
THAT'S YOUR SISTER OVER THERE, RIGHT?
The one in the middle
EH?
← My sister was watching with our friends from afar.
Net-chy
Sis
Kaori
Yuto
DO WE LOOK ALIKE?
NO, WE DON'T.
OF COURSE NOT.
NOT AT ALL.
Not at all?
Editor
YOUR FACES ARE DIFFERENT, BUT YOU HAVE SAME SORT OF AURA ABOUT YOU.
THE AGE OF THE PEOPLE WHO CAME VARIED FROM ELEMENTARY SCHOOL STUDENTS TO HOUSEWIVES.
THERE WERE SOME MALE FANS TOO.
I'm so happy that guys are also reading.
I'm sure it's embarrassing to buy the comics, but hang in there!!
THERE WERE A GOOD NUMBER OF MEN WHO SEEMED VERY MUCH LIKE DADS. I SUPPOSE THEY CAME ON BEHALF OF THEIR DAUGHTERS.
IF THEY SHAKE HANDS, HE'S A FAN.
The men!
HEE HEE
Sis
THEY'RE MAKING A BET.
Netchy

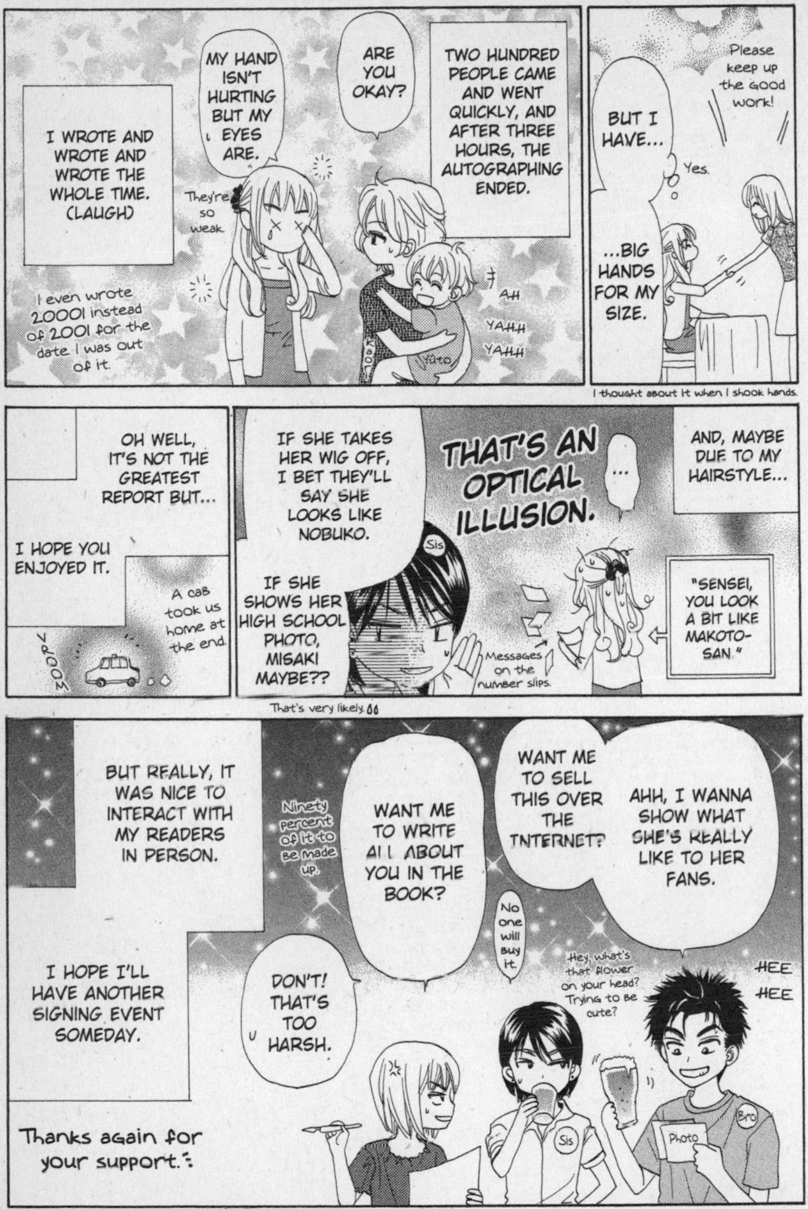

Please keep up the good work!
BUT I HAVE...
Yes.
...BIG HANDS FOR MY SIZE.
I thought about it when I shook hands.
TWO HUNDRED PEOPLE CAME AND WENT QUICKLY, AND AFTER THREE HOURS, THE AUTOGRAPHING ENDED.
ARE YOU OKAY?
MY HAND ISN'T HURTING BUT MY EYES ARE.
They're so weak.
I WROTE AND WROTE AND WROTE THE WHOLE TIME. (LAUGH)
Kaori
Yuto
AH
YAHH
YAHH
I even wrote 20001 instead of 2001 for the date. I was out of it.
AND, MAYBE DUE TO MY HAIRSTYLE...
"SENSEI, YOU LOOK A BIT LIKE MAKOTO-SAN."
Messages on the number slips.
THAT'S AN OPTICAL ILLUSION.
...
IF SHE TAKES HER WIG OFF, I BET THEY'LL SAY SHE LOOKS LIKE NOBUKO.
Sis
IF SHE SHOWS HER HIGH SCHOOL PHOTO, MISAKI MAYBE??
That's very likely.
OH WELL, IT'S NOT THE GREATEST REPORT BUT...
I HOPE YOU ENJOYED IT.
A cab took us home at the end.
VROOM
AHH, I WANNA SHOW WHAT SHE'S REALLY LIKE TO HER FANS.
WANT ME TO SELL THIS OVER THE INTERNET?
No one will buy it.
HEE
HEE
Hey, what's that flower on your head? Trying to be cute?
WANT ME TO WRITE ALL ABOUT YOU IN THE BOOK?
Ninety percent of it to be made up.
DON'T! THAT'S TOO HARSH.
Bro
Photo
Sis
BUT REALLY, IT WAS NICE TO INTERACT WITH MY READERS IN PERSON.
I HOPE I'LL HAVE ANOTHER SIGNING EVENT SOMEDAY.
Thanks again for your support.

Cultural Notes

Takoyaki (Octopus Balls)

[reference page 19] Takoyaki is a popular Japanese dumpling made of batter, octopus, pickled ginger, green onions, and other ingredients. Although it can be made at home using special cast-iron molds, it's usually served on the street as fast food—and is perfectly suited for Japanese festivals where food stands crowd the street.

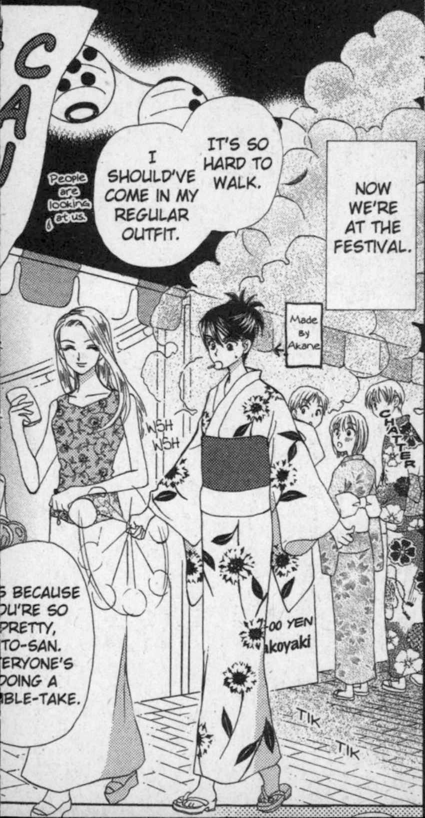
NOW WE'RE AT THE FESTIVAL.
IT'S SO HARD TO WALK.
I SHOULD'VE COME IN MY REGULAR OUTFIT.
People are looking at us.
Made By Akane
CHATTER
WSH WSH
TIK
TIK

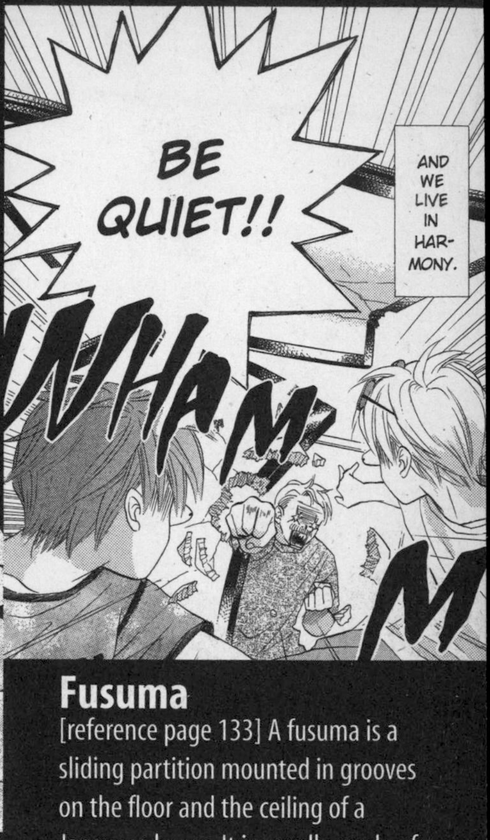
AND WE LIVE IN HARMONY.
BE QUIET!!
WHAM

Fusuma

[reference page 133] A fusuma is a sliding partition mounted in grooves on the floor and the ceiling of a Japanese house. It is usually made of thick paper that covers a wood frame. While shoji, with its translucent, thin sheet of paper, is easy to poke a hole through with a finger, a fusuma requires some effort to damage. Thus, its paper covering does not need to be replaced frequently. It makes a perfect medium for paintings and designs that provide part of the interior decoration of a Japanese house.

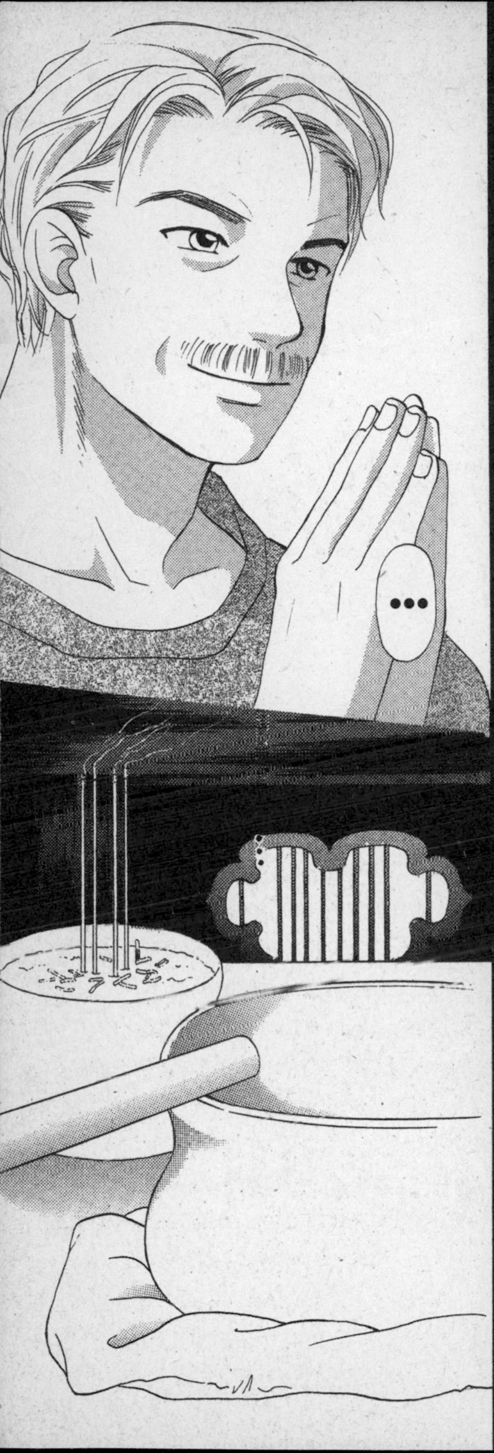
...

Obon

[reference page 132]

A Japanese Buddhist holiday to honor and commemorate ancestors, Obon has long become a family reunion holiday and is acknowledged and practiced by many Japanese regardless of their religious beliefs. During the Obon week, people who live and work in the cities return to their hometowns and visit and clean the graves of their ancestors. In some parts of Japan, Obon is celebrated in mid-July, but the main Obon week is in mid-August. It has become one of Japan's major holidays, and is accompanied by intensive domestic and international travel activities in much the same way as many major U.S. holidays are.

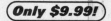

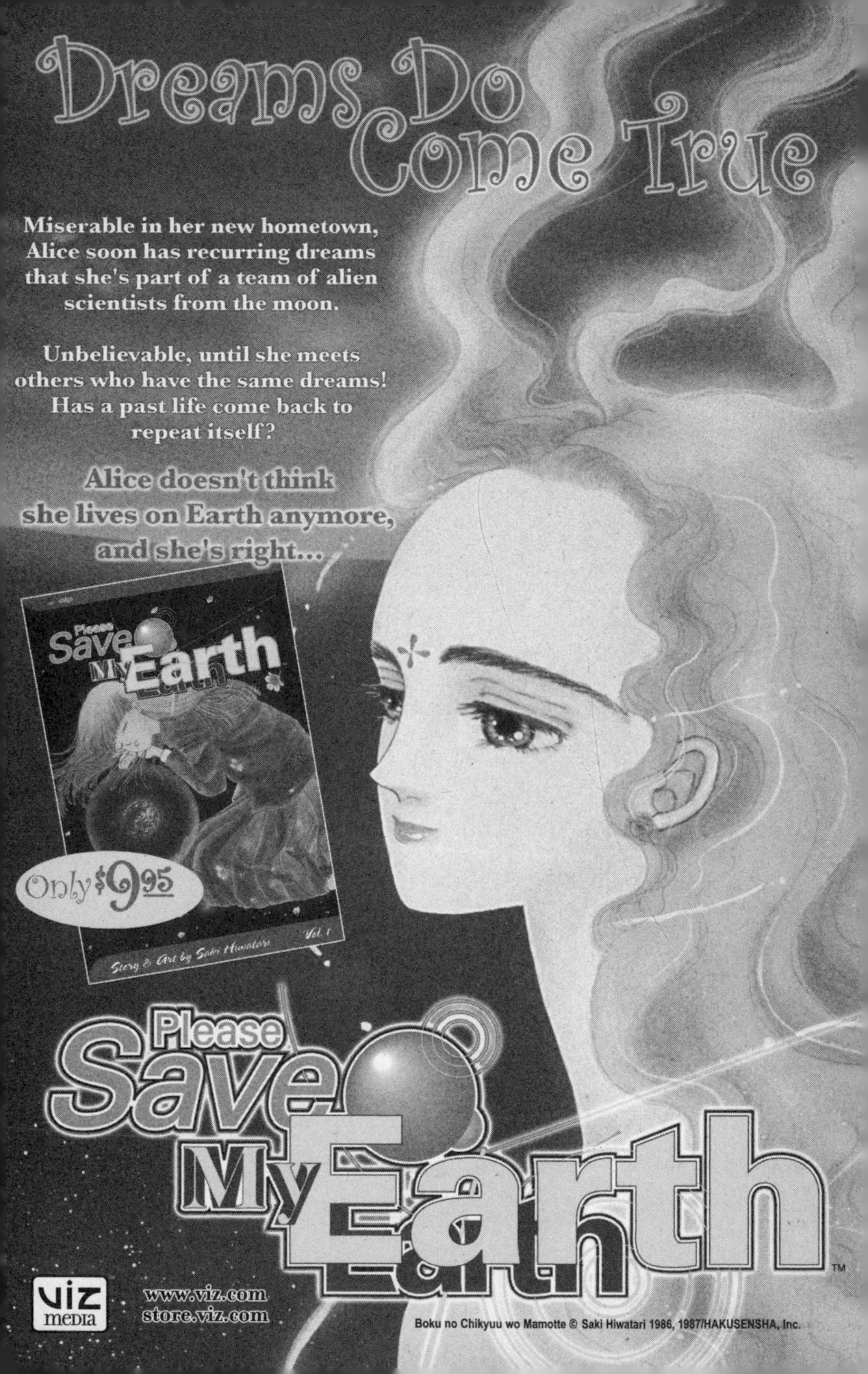
Dreams Do Come True
Miserable in her new hometown, Alice soon has recurring dreams that she's part of a team of alien scientists from the moon.
Unbelievable, until she meets others who have the same dreams! Has a past life come back to repeat itself?
Alice doesn't think she lives on Earth anymore, and she's right...
Please Save My Earth
Vol. 1
Story & Art by Saki Hiwatari
Only $9.95
Please Save My Earth™
viz media
www.viz.com
store.viz.com
Boku no Chikyuu wo Mamotte © Saki Hiwatari 1986, 1987/HAKUSENSHA, Inc.

LOVE SHOJO? LET US KNOW!

☐ Please do NOT send me information about VIZ Media products, news and events, special offers, or other information.

☐ Please do NOT send me information from VIZ' trusted business partners.

Name: _____

Address: _____

City: _____ **State:** _____ **Zip:** _____

E-mail: _____

☐ **Male** ☐ **Female** **Date of Birth** (mm/dd/yyyy): ___ / ___ / ___ (Under 13? Parental consent required)

What race/ethnicity do you consider yourself? (check all that apply)

☐ White/Caucasian   ☐ Black/African American   ☐ Hispanic/Latino

☐ Asian/Pacific Islander   ☐ Native American/Alaskan Native ☐ Other: _____

What VIZ shojo title(s) did you purchase? (indicate title(s) purchased)

_____

What other shojo titles from other publishers do you own? _____

_____

Reason for purchase: (check all that apply)

☐ Special offer   ☐ Favorite title / author / artist / genre

☐ Gift   ☐ Recommendation   ☐ Collection

☐ Read excerpt in VIZ manga sampler ☐ Other _____

Where did you make your purchase? (please check one)

☐ Comic store   ☐ Bookstore   ☐ Mass/Grocery Store

☐ Newsstand   ☐ Video/Video Game Store

☐ Online (site:_____)   ☐ Other _____

How many shojo titles have you purchased in the last year? How many were VIZ shojo titles?
(please check one from each column)

SHOJO MANGA	VIZ SHOJO MANGA
☐ None	☐ None
☐ 1 – 4	☐ 1 – 4
☐ 5 – 10	☐ 5 – 10
☐ 11+	☐ 11+

What do you like most about shojo graphic novels? **(check all that apply)**

☐ Romance
☐ Drama / conflict
☐ Fantasy
☐ Comedy
☐ Real-life storylines
☐ Relatable characters
☐ Other ______________________________

Do you purchase every volume of your favorite shojo series?

☐ Yes! Gotta have 'em as my own
☐ No. Please explain: ______________________________

Who are your favorite shojo authors / artists? ______________________________

____

What shojo titles would like you translated and sold in English? ______________________________

____

THANK YOU! Please send the completed form to:

NJW Research
ATTN: VIZ Media Shojo Survey
42 Catharine Street
Poughkeepsie, NY 12601

Your privacy is very important to us. All information provided will be used for internal purposes only and will not be sold or otherwise divulged.